THE NEW ENCYCLOPEDIA OF DAYLILIES

THE NEW ENCYCLOPEDIA OF

Daylilies

MORE THAN 1700 OUTSTANDING SELECTIONS

TED L. PETIT *and* JOHN P. PEAT

TIMBER PRESS

Portland | London

Frontispiece and title page photos: 'Black Eyed Bully', photograph by Keith Miner; Unnamed Seedling, photograph by Ted L. Petit; 'Velvet Red', photograph by John P. Peat; 'Forever Knights', photograph by John P. Peat.

This revised, expanded work incorporates portions of *The Color Encyclopedia of Daylilies*, published in 2000, and *The Daylily: A Guide for Gardeners*, published in 2004.

Published in 2008 by

Timber Press, Inc.
The Haseltine Building
133 S.W. Second Avenue, Suite 450
Portland, Oregon 97204-3527, U.S.A.

www.timberpress.com

Timber Press, Inc.
2 The Quadrant
135 Salusbury Road
London NW6 6RJ

www.timberpress.co.uk

For contact information regarding editorial, marketing, sales, and distribution in the United Kingdom, see www.timberpress.co.uk.

Printed in China

Library of Congress Cataloging-in-Publication Data

Petit, Ted L.
  The new encyclopedia of daylilies / Ted L. Petit and John P. Peat.
      p. cm.
  "This revised, expanded work incorporates portions of the Color encyclopedia of daylilies, published in 2000, and The daylily: a guide for gardners, published in 2004."
  Includes bibliographical references and index.
  ISBN-13: 978-0-88192-858-7
  1. Daylilies--Encyclopedias. 2. Daylilies--Pictorial works. I. Peat, John P. II. Petit, Ted L. Color encyclopedia of daylilies. III. Peat, John P. Daylily. IV. Title.
  SB413.D3P483 2008
  635.9'3432--dc22   2008002936

A catalog record for this book is also available from the British Library.

Contents

Preface and Acknowledgments

This book was written to update the first edition of *The Color Encyclopedia of Daylilies*. We have expanded and revised the information in the first edition, and have updated and increased the number of images throughout the book. Some chapters, such as those on the species and the history of the daylily, are similar to the corresponding chapters in the original book, because little has changed regarding these aspects of daylilies. Other chapters have changed markedly. We have added a chapter on patterned daylilies, as their impact has increased dramatically since the first edition.

When we wrote the first edition of this book, there were approximately 40,000 registered daylilies. In the interim, that number has increased to approximately 60,000. With so many plants available, it was a difficult task to decide which daylilies to include in this book. We based our decisions on a number of factors. First, we endeavored to present those plants that we felt were the most worthy and worthwhile cultivars available, based on our own personal experience. We also relied on a number of other sources, including the American Hemerocallis Society (AHS) popularity polls and the winners of the various AHS awards. Finally, in an attempt to determine which plants are the most widely grown and sold, we consulted the *Eureka Daylily Reference Guide*. We would like to express our grateful appreciation to *Guide* author Ken Gregory for his cooperation and information used in the selection of daylily cultivars featured in this book. This guide and other gardening sources are listed in Additional Resources at the back of the book.

In this revised edition, we have included older, classic flowers, whose beauty has stood the test of time. We have also included some of the newest cutting-edge daylilies, with an entire chapter devoted to some hybrids that are not yet registered and not yet available for purchase. We tried to cover as many types of daylilies as possible, in terms of ploidy, form, color, dormancy, and so on. We hope to have reached a balance among these many dimensions. We have made every effort to ensure that the pictures and information in our final manuscript are accurate, but it is not possible for us to personally know every cultivar in this book. We ask for your understanding if any error has occurred.

Also, please understand that daylily cultivars are named by the hybridizers who create them. These names are not necessarily proper English names, and at times they may appear grammatically incorrect. Once registered with the AHS, however, these names become the official identification of the plants and cannot be changed. Some names in this book may appear to be misspelled, but we have endeavored to accurately represent the official AHS names for all cultivars. Further, hybridizers do not always provide complete details regarding their cultivars when registering them with the AHS. As a result, some cultivars in this book, particularly those registered in the early days of the Society, have incomplete information.

We would like to thank those photographers who allowed us to use their daylily photographs. Without their help, this undertaking would not have been possible. Finally, we would like to thank those friends and family members who gave their support during this lengthy and often exhausting effort. After the book is completed and sent to press, they are what really matter.

Chapter One

THE DAYLILY PLANT

Those of us who love daylilies may wonder why it is important to know about the plant under the flower. Knowledge of the overall plant will help gardeners in hybridizing, cultivating, and acquiring daylilies and will deepen their appreciation of the flowers. Understanding the total plant, therefore—flowers, foliage, and roots—can greatly increase our overall enjoyment of daylilies.

The captions describing each of the daylilies pictured in this book contain detailed descriptions about the plant and the flower. The figure captions also indicate if a cultivar has won an award from the American Hemerocallis Society (AHS), including the awards described here. The order of the awards within each caption are by the prestige of the award, highest listed first. The Honorable Mention is the first official stamp of approval by the AHS, and must be won before an Award of Merit may be given. An Award of Merit is the second step to the Stout Medal, and indicates that a cultivar is not only distinctive and beautiful but also has performed well over a wide geographic area. The Stout Silver Medal (often referred to as the Stout Medal) is the highest honor bestowed upon a cultivar by the AHS. The Lennington All-American Award is awarded for outstanding performance over a wide geographic area. The Extra Large Diameter Award recognizes outstanding extra large flower diameters of 7 in. (18 cm) or larger. The Early Season Bloom award recognizes outstanding early season blooming daylilies. The Donn Fischer Memorial Cup is awarded to the most outstanding miniature cultivar less than 3 in. (7.6 cm). The Annie T. Giles Award is awarded to the best small-flowered daylily of 3 in. (7.6 cm) or greater, but less than 4.5 in. (11.5 cm). The Ida Munson Award recognizes the most outstanding double-flowered daylily. The Don C. Stevens Award is given annually to the best eyed or banded daylily. The Eugene S. Foster Award is given for the best late-blooming cultivar. The Harris Olson Spider Award recognizes the most outstanding cultivar that meets the definition of spider or spider-variant. The Lambert/Webster Award is for the most outstanding unusual form daylily. The R. W. Munson Jr. Award recognizes the most outstanding distinctly patterned daylily.

In addition to those awards currently given by the AHS, some cultivars have been given awards that are no longer awarded by the Society. These include the L. Ernest Plouf Award, which was awarded to the best consistently fragrant dormant daylily. The Robert P. Miller Memorial Award was given for the best near-white daylily. The Richard C. Peck Memorial Award was given for the best tetraploid daylily. The James E. Marsh Award was given for the best purple or lavender daylily.

The captions throughout the book also contain information about specific aspects of the plant, including plant parts, flower characteristics, flowering season, ploidy, and dormancy. To better understand these figure captions, therefore, the reader will also need to understand the terminology used, which we will describe next.

PLANT PARTS

The primary parts of the daylily, like most other plants, are the root system and foliage. Prior to the bloom season, flower stalks, or scapes, emerge from the base of the plant. Usually flower buds visibly begin forming immediately after the scapes begin to emerge. Plants send up a single scape at a time, although they can send up a second, third, or even more scapes during a season. These extra scapes are referred to as recurrent scapes, and plants that send up more than one scape during a season are referred to as recurrent. Recurrent scapes extend the plant's bloom time, and are more common in warm climates with an extended bloom season, and less common in cold climates, where the bloom season is shorter. The number of flowers on a scape varies anywhere from under 10 to over 60 blooms. On some, there may be only a few buds at the top of the scape; these are referred to as top-budded. Other daylilies have scapes that branch. Obviously, more branches can carry more buds, which, like recurrent scapes, increase the bloom time and enjoyment of the plant.

Sometimes small plants, known as proliferations, form on the flower scape as it matures. Proliferations form from tiny buds just above small leaflets (known as bracts) on the side of the scape.

The roots of the daylily are typically fibrous, or fleshy, which allows the plant to store food and water. Thus, bare-rooted daylilies are more easily transported

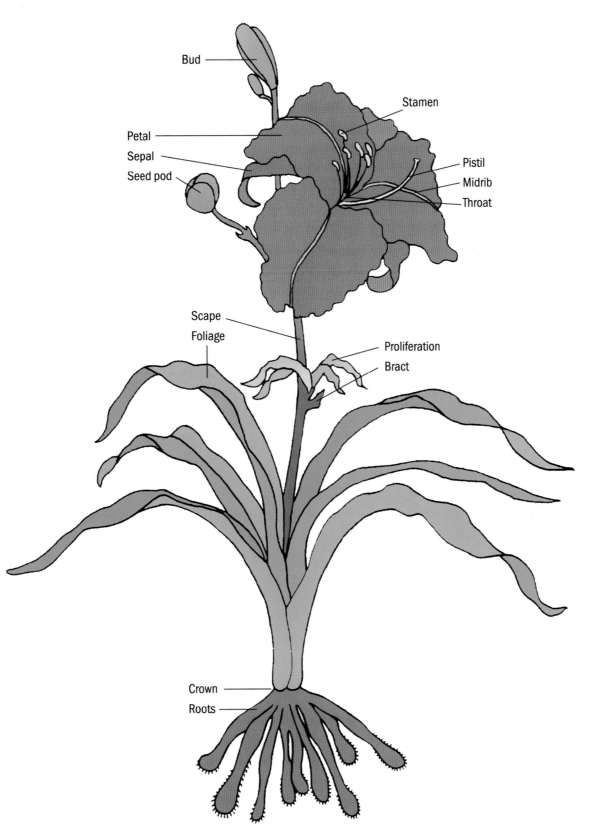

Parts of a daylily plant. *Watercolor by Richard Haynes.*

than most other perennials because the plant is capable of sustaining itself with stored nutrients. The point at which the roots meet the foliage is known as the crown and contains the growing point of the plant. This primary growing point is also known as the apical meristem.

Between each of the leaves at the crown is a bud, and therefore a potential growing point. When a scape emerges, the bud closest to the scape usually breaks dormancy and begins to grow, causing the plant to divide into two plants. Sometimes, additional buds break dormancy, causing the plant to burst into many plants. Like the buds of most other plants, daylily buds do or do not break dormancy and begin to grow depending on one or more plant hormones. Thus, daylily plant division and multiplication can be induced by the application of hormones, the most commonly used being indole-3-acetic acid (IAA) and 6-benzylaminopurine (BAP). These hormones can be used to increase plant division, which may be important for new, expensive plants. Application of these hormones can increase plant production by inducing active growth and division of the buds at the crown as well as the buds that form proliferations on the scapes.

The swordlike leaves emerge from the crown in an alternating fashion that creates a fan shape. Because of this, a single daylily plant is often referred to as a fan. A daylily plant consists of a single plant or a clump if the individual plant has divided. Therefore, daylily catalogs often indicate if they are selling a single fan, double division (two plants), or clump. A named daylily plant is often referred to as a cultivar.

The typical daylily flower is composed of three sepals, three petals, six stamens, and one pistil. The stamens are the male part of the flower and the pistil is the female part. Each stamen contains an anther, or pollen sac, at the tip. The anthers are closed in the early morning when the flowers first open, but as the temperature warms they burst open to reveal the fluffy, yellow-to-orange pollen. Some plants have very pale, almost white pollen, which is generally sterile. The pollen on some cultivars will form hard clumps, another indication of sterile pollen.

At the end of the pistil is the stigma. As the anthers open, the stigma becomes sticky to receive the pollen. The pistil connects to the ovary at the base of the flower and provides the passageway for the pollen to reach the ovary. If successfully pollinated, the ovary will form a seed pod.

FLOWER CHARACTERISTICS

To describe the different possible flower colors and patterns, daylily growers and hybridizers have divided the flower into several parts, which include the throat, the eye or watermark, the petal self, and the petal edge. The different qualities of these parts are then used to describe and categorize the many daylily hybrids.

The "throat," also sometimes called the "center" or the "heart," is the very center of the flower where the petals form a narrow funnel meeting at the base of the pistil. Some individuals use the term "heart" to describe a smaller area in the very center of the throat. The throat color is usually green, orange, or yellow. Most new hybrids have a green throat because gardeners generally find that green gives a cool focal point to the flower.

Daylilies are categorized by two primary characteristics: their self color and the presence of an eye or watermark. The "self" refers to the flattest, widest part of the petal, which carries the primary color of the bloom. The "eye" or "eyezone" is a darker area surrounding the throat of the flower (see those pictured in chapter 5). The eye can be a small dark band or it can take up most of the petal area. If this area surrounding the throat is lighter, rather than darker, than the self color, it is referred to as a "watermark" or a "halo." 'Orchid Electra' (see photo on page 146) shows an excellent example of a watermark. In addition, the petal edges can be darker or lighter than the petal self. Darker petal edges are referred to as a "picotee." Picotees and light edges can be very narrow to very wide, taking up to one-third or more of the petal width. Many new tetraploid hybrids have very dramatic gold edges. When a contrasting edge such as a picotee or gold edge is very narrow, it is referred to as a "wire edge," as if the flower has an edge made of gold wire. More recently, we have seen the emergence of orange edges, green edges, shark's teeth, and tendrils. It is difficult to predict what new characteristics will appear on the petal edges.

Flower color can be more complex in many cultivars. For example, the petals may contain a blend of more than one color; these are known as polychrome flowers. A bitone flower has petals that are a darker shade than the sepals. In a reverse bitone, the sepals are a darker shade than the petals. Bicolor flowers have petals and sepals of two entirely different colors. Describing color is very subjective, and the color of flowers, photographs, and images is dependent on a wide variety of influences, such as growing conditions, temperature, amount of sunlight, film type or digital camera used in photography. The descriptions used in this book are taken from those provided by the hybridizers. Therefore, some of the photographs of daylilies in this book may not appear to exactly match the descriptions, because hybridizers describe the color as seen in their own gardens.

The terms "form" and "substance" are often used to describe daylily flowers. Form refers to the shape of the flower, most commonly characterizing petal width (from narrow to wide). Substance is more difficult to define, referring to the heaviness or thickness of the petal. While some petals may be thin and flexible, flowers with heavy substance have thick, hard, plastic-like petals. Flowers can also vary from heavily ruffled to little or no ruffling, with non-ruffled flowers being referred to as "tailored." In some modern cultivars, the ruffling can be so extreme as to form large loops which are overlaid on the petal surface. These are often referred to as "owl ears" or "angel wings." While extensive ruffling and looping can create a dramatic visual effect, it has also introduced a new problem into the daylily, because some of these ruffles can interlock and prevent the flower from opening.

'Emperor's Toy' (Elizabeth H. Hudson, 1975). Evergreen. Scape 18 in. (46 cm); flower 3.75 in. (9.5 cm). Midseason. An example of a lavender and cream bicolor. Diploid. 'Blue Vision' x 'Pixie Prince'. *Photograph by Patrick Stamile.*

'Moonlight Orchid' (David L. Talbott, 1986). Semi-evergreen. Scape 28 in. (71 cm); flower 6.5 in. (16.5 cm). Early midseason. An example of a lavender and lighter lavender bitone. Diploid. *Photograph by Patrick Stamile.*

FLOWERING SEASON

Peak daylily bloom in North America varies from May in the Deep South of the United States to mid-July in the northern part of the United States and in southern Canada. Of course, in countries south of the equator the bloom season ranges from November to mid-January. Many modern cultivars send up recurrent scapes to extend the season. The bloom season of a daylily is categorized according to the start of bloom, and generally is divided into early, midseason, and late. However, in an attempt to be more specific, some hybridizers have divided the season even further, describing the bloom time as extra early, early, early midseason, midseason, midseason late, late, and very late. Since the season can vary markedly between different years and different geographical areas, even within 200 miles (322 km), it is not possible to give exact times to define the different seasonal categories. The relative period when a daylily blooms during the bloom season remains the same across different climates; that is, early blooming cultivars will bloom before other cultivars whether in warm or cold climates.

Some new hybrids have an extended season and may begin blooming very early and continue with rebloom through the entire bloom season. Many gardeners look for "ever-blooming" hybrids, ones that bloom nearly throughout the whole season. 'Stella de Oro' is a popular reblooming daylily. Due to its simple flower form, 'Stella de Oro' (Jablonski, 1975) has been surpassed as a garden flower by newer cultivars; however, it remains a long-blooming and widely recognized cultivar, particularly in cooler climates where it performs best.

DIPLOID VS. TETRAPLOID

The majority of the older daylily cultivars are diploids, which means they contain the normal number of 22 chromosomes. However, since 1960 a large number of daylilies have been treated with colchicine, a chemical that allows the number of chromosomes in the cell to double as if the cell were about to divide, but then prevents the cell as a whole from undergoing normal cell division. This results in cells, and therefore plants, known as tetraploids, which contain 44 chromosomes, double the normal number. This doubling of the chromosome count (genetic material) in tetraploids leads to larger flowers with heavier substance and more vibrant colors. If a diploid cultivar such as 'Janice Brown' (Brown, E.C., 1986) has been successfully treated and converted, then the converted plant will be tetraploid and referred to as 'Tetra Janice Brown' or 'Tet. Janice Brown.' This, then, distinguishes it from the original diploid plant, which, of course, may still be found in many gardens. Each cultivar name is unique to one cultivar; therefore, no two cultivars will have the same name if registered with the American Hemerocallis Society.

PARENTAGE

Understanding the parental background of a cultivar is as important as understanding the parentage of a famous racehorse, in order to breed the favorable characteristics into future generations. Alternatively, if one of the parents is reported to be susceptible to disease, one can avoid breeding this undesirable trait into the next generation by not using progeny from that parent in breeding. Therefore, most serious hybridizers who are concerned about the overall plant keep careful records of the genetic background of their daylilies. This means recording both the pod (female) and pollen (male) parents of their seedlings, a simple but time-consuming task. This can result in fairly long and complex combinations of parents, similar to that of a human family tree. The parents of each generation are written within successive sets of parentheses in order to clearly track the genetic background of the plant. This results, for example, in parentage for a particular cultivar that would be recorded as: ((Paternal grandmother × paternal grandfather) × (maternal grandmother × maternal grandfather)). Unfortunately, not all hybridizers keep records on parentage, and accidents, such as losing tags, can happen to even the most dedicated hybridizer. Therefore, the parentage of some cultivars is listed as either "unknown parents" or "seedling."

DORMANCY

The winter foliage performance of daylilies is generally categorized as dormant, evergreen, or semi-evergreen. Dormant daylilies, like deciduous trees, are plants that lose or shed their leaves during the winter. This results in plants whose leaves die back to beneath ground level in the winter. In the spring, new foliage emerges from the ground as a compact growing point.

Since the plant loses its leaves in the winter, the term "deciduous" may be more scientifically correct. However, because the term "dormant" is so widely used in describing daylilies, we have used that term in this book. Evergreen daylily foliage remains green throughout the winter, although the foliage can be killed, or frozen back, in cold climates even though the plant itself is not killed. Semi-evergreens retain varying degrees of foliage on either side of the growing point, but may become dormant at the center of the plant, showing no new growth until spring. The topic of dormancy can be relatively complex. Some cultivars are referred to as hard dormants, which implies that they are at the extreme end of the dormancy scale: they go fully dormant, require a long winter chilling period in order to flourish, and may not survive in climates with warm winters. Cultivars at the other end of the extreme are often referred to as pure evergreens, which implies that the plants grow throughout the winter and require little or no chilling to flourish. However, hybridizers have been crossbreeding evergreen and dormant daylilies for many, many generations; therefore, most new hybrids contain varying degrees of dormancy. Thus, it would be more correct to indicate where a particular plant fits within a long continuum from fully dormant to fully evergreen. While the terms dormant, semi-evergreen, and

An evergreen daylily. *Photograph by Ted L. Petit.*

A semi-evergreen daylily
emerging in the spring.
Photograph by Ted L. Petit.

evergreen remain commonplace, gardeners should be aware that these terms are meant as a general guide only.

There is a great deal of misunderstanding regarding the relationship between dormancy and cold hardiness, or the ability to survive in warm climates. It is important to realize that there is no direct correlation between dormancy and cold tolerance. Most daylily plants survive from very warm climates to very cold ones. In climates with little or no winter chilling (such as USDA Zone 10), some dormant plants will not get enough winter chilling to survive. These plants will dwindle in size and eventually die. Plants with a more semi-evergreen or evergreen plant habit may grow and multiply, but not receive enough chilling to bloom. However, many dormant plants will thrive even in mild climates with only a few frosts in a typical winter. In extremely cold climates, some daylily cultivars may not survive a harsh winter or a winter with little or no snow cover to protect the plants from extreme temperature fluctuations. There are some evergreen plants, referred to as tender evergreens, that cannot survive winter freezes. Because of this, historically it was recommended that gardeners in extremely cold climates plant dormant varieties. However, we now realize that this information is not correct. During extremely cold winters, some dormant cultivars will be killed, while evergreens planted in the same bed will overwinter well. Since there is no direct relationship between dormancy and winter hardiness, some hybridizers have begun to discuss plant hardiness to a particular USDA zone, which is more helpful in predicting probable regional success. Gardeners who live in climatic extremes, either extremely cold or very tropical, should consult with gardeners in their area to see if there are some cultivars, dormants or evergreens, which will not perform well in that area.

A dormant daylily emerging in spring.
Photograph by Ted L. Petit.

Chapter Two

HISTORY OF THE DAYLILY

The history of the daylily spans thousands of years, from its ancient cultivation in Asia and its discovery and importation by avid collectors in the West, to those collectors' early struggles to hybridize and convert the plant to tetraploid, and ultimately to the creation and dramatic craze for the exquisite modern hybrids. The full story is as much about the people who dedicated their lives to acquiring and changing these plants as it is about the plants themselves.

ORIGIN OF THE GENUS

The story begins in Asia, primarily in China, where daylilies have been cultivated for thousands of years. R. W. Munson Jr. (1989) reported that the earliest known reference to daylilies is from China, dated 2697 BC, when Chi Pai wrote a materia medica for Emperor Huang Ti. The people of the region enjoyed daylilies as much for utilitarian reasons, such as medicine and food, as for the beauty of the flowers. By 1500 AD the daylily had made its way into Europe, probably via land

and sea trade routes. The herbalists Dodonaeus, Clusius, and Lobelius described and illustrated the daylily in the late 1500s. When Linneaus introduced the now standard binomial system of nomenclature in 1753, he placed daylilies in the genus *Hemerocallis* within the family Liliaceae. The term *Hemerocallis* is from the Greek *hemera*, meaning "a day," and *kallos*, meaning "beauty," therefore "beauty for a day." The nomenclature was altered by Dahlgren, Clifford, and Yeo, who in 1985 proposed a new system of classification, now widely accepted, that placed daylilies in their own family, Hemerocallidaceae. Several books describe much of the early history of daylilies in greater detail. Excellent reviews are available from Walter Erhardt, *Hemerocallis: Daylilies* (1992), R. W. Munson Jr., *Hemerocallis: The Daylily* (1989), and A. B. Stout, *Daylilies* (1934).

The period from 1700 to 1900 was the era of plant hunting, a time marked by the search for new daylily species. A theory popular among Westerners at this time was that the Garden of Eden could be re-created by gathering together all the beautiful plants that had been scattered around the globe at the fall of Adam and Eve. (Perhaps this romantic pursuit has been the quiet, subconscious dream of all gardeners through the ages.) In the eighteenth and nineteenth centuries botanists and plant collectors set out around the world to discover new plants and bring them to the West. The excitement of discovery and adventure in new lands filled this period. Individuals such as Ernest Wilson, George Forrest, Francis Kingdon-Ward, and Joseph Rock brought many new species of daylilies to Europe and America. Despite their efforts, by 1900 only half the known species of *Hemerocallis* had been introduced to the West.

Ultimately, it was the collaboration of Albert Steward and Arlow B. Stout that had the greatest impact on collecting new *Hemerocallis* species and advancing our knowledge about them. Steward lived in China and taught botany at the University of Nanking, regularly gathering daylilies from their native habitat. He sent these specimens to Stout, then the director of The New York Botanical Garden. As Sydney Eddison describes him in *A Passion for Daylilies*, "By all accounts, Dr. Stout was a dedicated scientist but not a gregarious man." After the death of his only son, Stout sought solace and refuge in his garden where "this starchy old gentleman" fell in love with daylilies. Stout received more than 50 shipments of seed and plants from China during his time at The New York Botanical Garden. He became the foremost authority on daylilies, undertaking the first comprehensive description and classification of the species. He also began a rigorous breeding program which opened the doors to future hybridizing efforts by others. As a tribute to his contributions, the Stout Medal is the highest award bestowed on a daylily by the American Hemerocallis Society.

The daylilies now found in gardens and in commerce around the world are hybrids many, many generations from the species. Indeed, the species have become primarily of historical interest. It takes some effort now to locate *Hemerocallis* species, for they have been surpassed by modern hybrids and are rarely seen for sale in commercial gardens. The most likely place to find them is in older home sites in North America and Europe, still forming lovely color accents where they have been growing wild for generations.

Hemerocallis fulva var. *rosea*. *Photograph by Carl Sigel.*

H. aurantiaca. *Photograph by Carl Sigel.*

SPECIES OF *HEMEROCALLIS*

Arlow B. Stout's 1934 book *Daylilies* remains the historically definitive work on the species, but other botanists have published reports describing additional species. The end result is that authorities do not agree upon the number of species in existence. However, most classification schemes suggest approximately 20 different *Hemerocallis* species. Writers also divide the species into groups differently. For example, Erhardt (1992) and Barnes (2004) suggest that the species be broken into five main groups, while Munson (1989) suggests the classification described later in this chapter. More recent attempts to categorize daylilies based on biochemical or genetic examinations have made definitive statements on the number of species even more difficult.

A detailed description of the species is of more than purely academic interest, for within these plants lies the key to all the many facets of modern daylilies. The variety of colors, scape heights, branching, forms, doubling, and so on, are all held within this small gene pool. Perhaps even more interesting are the phenomenal changes that have occurred in daylilies in the mere 60 to 70 years since hybridizing seriously began in the 1940s. A quick glance at the species at that time shows the petals narrow and without ruffling, and the colors restricted to yellow, orange, and rust. This limited gene pool has given forth immense diversity. Hybridizers have created flowers varying in size from 2 in. (5 cm) to more than 12 in. (30.5 cm) in diameter, from round and ruffled to the narrow spiders, and in virtually every color of the rainbow–all in little over half a century. Given the phenomenal diversity in the flower form and color, as well as many other aspects of the modern daylily now at our disposal, what will the next half-century bring?

Another important factor about the species is that we may not have taken complete advantage of all the characteristics offered from the very beginning. The race to improve the daylily may have left behind some very important species traits. For example, *Hemerocallis fulva* var. *kwanso* has rust-colored double flowers. Although few people are likely to suggest that it is as beautiful as the newer cultivars, it has many extra layers of true petals, more than have yet been achieved in modern hybrids. Or, consider *H. multiflora*, which can carry 75 to 100 blooms–what happened to this heavy-blooming characteristic? Perhaps most interesting is *H. graminea*, whose flowers stay open for two to three days: imagine how this would change the way we think about our "beauty for a day." The species offer dwarf plants as well as plants with 6 ft. (1.8 m) scapes. Some plants bloom very early, some in midseason, and some very late in the season. Some are fully dormant and some are fully evergreen. And finally, some flowers are pure selfs of one color and some have a distinctly darker eye. Though interest in the species may be primarily historical, the species have supplied all the building blocks on which to create entire hybridizing programs. Hybrids have not fully highlighted the features of the species, a fact that should prompt daylily hybridizers to reconsider the possibilities these remarkable plants offer.

A detailed description of *Hemerocallis* species is beyond the scope of this book. The following is a brief overview derived from the published sources by Stout, Erhardt, Munson, and Barnes.

George Forrest documented a group of compact dwarf plants with very short scapes in southwest China, sometimes referred to as the Nana Group. This group includes *Hemerocallis nana*, *H. plicata*, and *H. forrestii*. *Hemerocallis nana* has slender scapes generally bearing only one flower, *H. plicata* bears eight flowers with a faint rust halo, and *H. forrestii* has five to ten orange blooms.

Several species of daylilies have yellow flowers, and are often referred to as the Citrina Group. *Hemerocallis flava*, mentioned in botanical literature as early as 1570, has been popular in European gardens for centuries, and is commonly called the lemon lily. It has bright lemon-yellow flowers that begin blooming early and re-bloom into the season. More recently, it has been suggested that the correct botanical name for this species is *H. lilioasphodelus*. *Hemerocallis minor* has low-growing, lemon-yellow flowers with brownish red-tinged sepals. It has fully dormant foliage and also begins blooming early in the season. *Hemerocallis thunbergii* bears yellow flowers on well-branched scapes that can reach 3 to

H. 'Flore Pleno'. *Photograph by Carl Sigel.*

H. hakuunensis. Photograph by Carl Sigel.

H. fulva var. *cypriani*. *Photograph by Curtis and Linda Sue Barnes.*

4 ft. (.9 to 1.2 m) in midsummer. *Hemerocallis citrina* is also dormant and bears yellow flowers in midsummer on very tall, well-branched scapes that hold more than 60 buds; the blooms are nocturnal.

Hemerocallis fulva, referred to as the fulva group, is distinct for its brownish to rusty red flower color. The plants are semi-evergreen, with scapes reaching 50 in. (1.3 m) carrying day-blooming flowers that peak during midseason. The fulva species has a number of single-flowered varieties, including the rosy red-flowered *H. fulva* var. *rosea*. *Hemerocallis fulva* var. *kwanso* and *H. fulva* 'Flore Pleno' are double flowered. *Hemerocallis* 'Kwanso Variegata' often has white-striped, variegated foliage, although the variegation is not consistent. Unfortunately, these double-flowered species are triploids (having 33 chromosomes), making them virtually, if not completely, sterile.

Several species have orange to gold flowers. *Hemerocallis aurantiaca*, an evergreen believed to have come from Japan, has 3 ft. (.9 m), top-branched scapes. There is some question as to whether *H. aurantiaca* is a true species or a hybrid, and whether it is related to the other orange-flowered species or is a member of the fulva group. *Hemerocallis exaltata* carries light orange flowers on 4 to 5 ft. (1.2 to 1.5 m) scapes that bloom in midseason. *Hemerocallis multiflora* is a dormant plant with 3 ft. (.9 m), highly branched scapes carrying numerous flowers that bloom from mid- to late season until frost. Some have suggested that multiflora forms a separate group, along with *H. plicata* described above. *Hemerocallis dumortierii* blooms very early in the spring on scapes that can be shorter than the foliage. The early blooming *H. middendorffii* has 3 in. (7.6 cm) flowers of a uniform orange on unbranched scapes. Some have suggested that the latter two species form a separate group, the Middendorffi Group, which also includes *H. hakuuensis* (pictured on page 21).

Shiu-Ying Hu described the following species in 1968. *Hemerocallis altissima* has 4 to 6.5 ft. (1.2 to 2 m) scapes with pale yellow, nocturnal, 3 in. (7.6 cm) flowers. *Hemerocallis coreana* has yellow flowers on 20 to 32 in. (50 to 81 cm) scapes, and *H. esculenta* has 25 to 35 in. (63 to 89 cm) scapes carrying five to six orange flowers. There is some question about which group these plants belong in; some suggest that their yellow flowers make them members of the citrina group, while others question whether they are a true species or a hybrid. *Hemerocallis graminea* is a dwarf plant with 30 in. (75 cm) scapes with unique orange flowers that remain open for two to three days. *Hemerocallis hakuunensis* has 34 to 40 in. (86 to 102 cm) scapes carrying six to eleven orange flowers. *Hemerocallis littorea* bears orange flowers with a dark brown eyezone.

The lack of consensus about the number of species and their relationship to each other will remain until we have further information from ecological, morphological, biochemical, and genetic studies.

H. minor (Miller, 1768). Dormant. Scape 24 in. (61 cm); flower 3.5 in. (9 cm). Early midseason. A bright cadmium-yellow with brownish red on the back of the sepals. Originating from eastern Siberia, northern China, Mongolia, and Korea. Diploid. *Photograph by Curtis and Linda Sue Barnes.*

H. middendorffii (E. R. Trautvetter & C. A. Meyer, 1856). Dormant. Scape 14 in. (35.5 cm); flower 3 in. (7.6 cm). Extra early. An intense light orange self. Originating from Siberia, Japan, and Sakhalin Island. Diploid. *Photograph by Curtis and Linda Sue Barnes.*

H. thunbergii (Barr Baker, 1890). Dormant. Scape 45 in. (114 cm); flower 4 in. (10 cm). Midseason late. A bright lemon-yellow with a green throat. Originating from China and Japan. Diploid. *Photograph by Curtis and Linda Sue Barnes.*

H. citrina (E. Baroni, 1897). Dormant. Scape 45 in. (114 cm); flower 5.5 in. (14 cm). Midseason late. A pale lemon-yellow flower above a green throat with blue-green foliage carrying 30 to 50 flowers on a stem. Originating from Shensi, China. Diploid. *Photograph by Carl Sigel.*

H. multiflora (Arlow B. Stout, 1929). Dormant. Scape 40 in. (101 cm); flower 3 in. (7.6 cm). Late. A medium orange to cadmium-yellow self. Originating from Hunan, China. Diploid. *Photograph by Curtis and Linda Sue Barnes.*

H. fulva (C. Linnaeus, 1931). Dormant. Scape 40 in. (101 cm); flower 5 in. (12.7 cm). Early midseason. A rusty orange to red and rosy pink flower with many flowers on a stem. Originating from China. Diploid. *Photograph by Carl Sigel.*

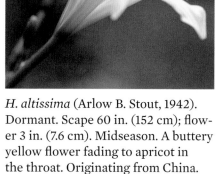

H. dumortierii (C. Morren, 1934). Dormant. Scape 24 in. (61 cm); flower 4 in. (10 cm). Early. A deep orange trumpet formed flower carrying 2 to 4 flowers on a stem. Originating from Japan, Korea, Manchuria, and eastern Siberia. Diploid. *Photograph by Carl Sigel.*

H. altissima (Arlow B. Stout, 1942). Dormant. Scape 60 in. (152 cm); flower 3 in. (7.6 cm). Midseason. A buttery yellow flower fading to apricot in the throat. Originating from China. Diploid. *Photograph by Carl Sigel.*

H. fulva var. *kwanso* 'Variegata' (Arlow B. Stout, 1947). Dormant. Scape 36 in. (91 cm);. Midseason late. A fulvous red double with a darker eyezone with lighter veining and variegated green and white foliage. Originating from Japan. Triploid. 'Green Kwanso' × 'Flore Pleno'.

Chapter Three

HISTORY OF DAYLILY HYBRIDIZING

The flowers of newer hybrid daylilies are different from those of the species shown in chapter 2. The progressive change from the species flowers to the daylilies of today is a tribute to the hard work of amateur and professional hybridizers around the world. Hybridizing can take the daylily flower in literally any direction, depending on the vision of the breeder. Each bloom pictured in this book started as an inspiration in the mind of a hybridizer. Because the hybrid story is as much about people, their personalities, and their dreams as it is about flowers, the road from the species plants to today's hybrids has been fraught with clashes of ego and personality. Sydney Eddison's *A Passion for Daylilies* (1992) tells the full tale of the people behind the plants.

Daylily hybridizing began with the early collectors who had access to the original species plants. Little plant material was available and progress was slow. Gradually, new hybrids were introduced, more material became available, and the daylily flower became more diverse in form, color, and other characteristics. Gradually the rate of advancement increased. Many breeders have contributed to these advancements, some through their backyard gardens, and others through major hybridizing programs. It is impossible to discuss everyone who has played a role in the progress of the daylily, but following are introductions to those whose energy and vision have left an indelible stamp on the plant.

EARLY EFFORTS

Arlow B. Stout was unquestionably the father of daylily hybridizing in North America. While director at The New York Botanical Garden he received plants of *Hemerocallis* species from Asia, which he classified, and with which he began to hybridize. In his classic book *Daylilies* (1934), he describes in detail his efforts to cross the different species plants to produce new daylily varieties with novel features. For example, his book contains a full-color plate tracing of 'Theron', "the first truly red daylily" back to four species (*H. flava*, *H. europa*, *H. aurantiaca*, and *H. thunbergii*). He produced his first cultivar, 'Mikado', in 1929, and continued to work with daylilies until his retirement from the Botanical Garden in 1948. During the 1930s and 1940s, Stout was a dominant figure in the daylily world in the United States.

These early years did not belong to Stout alone, however. Even before the turn of the century, George Yeld and Amos Perry had begun their hybridizing programs in England. Their breeding was also necessarily based on work with species plants. Some of their hybrids became very important in the more extensive breeding programs in the United States, but the impact of their efforts was greatly reduced because of difficulties in transporting plants across the ocean. Despite Yeld and Perry's very important contributions, the vast majority of daylily hybridizing was, and continues to be, conducted in the United States. A number of serious hybridizers now operate in other parts of the world, however, especially Europe, Australia, and Canada.

As more hybridizers began to work with daylilies in the 1940s and 1950s, the look of the flower began to change. The progressive winners of the American Hemerocallis Society's Stout Medal illustrate the history of these changes. The photographs in this chapter show representative flowers from the Stout Medal collection as well as other widely grown and award-winning cultivars, pictured in chronological order.

Early hybridizing efforts had a number of hurdles to overcome. The most important first goals included clarifying the color of the flower, particularly the rusty color of *Hemerocallis fulva*. The colors found in the species were limited to yellow, orange, and rusty red; therefore, the early hybridizers worked toward increasing the color range. Some of the initial efforts, even by Stout, produced true reds and clear pinks. The first hybrids also had narrow petals with no ruffling, prompting efforts to widen and ruffle the petals.

Some major hybridizers involved in these efforts during the 1940s and 1950s included Elizabeth "Betty" Nesmith, Bright "Ophelia" Taylor, and Ralph W. Wheeler. All accounts of Betty Nesmith, proprietor of Fairmount Gardens in Lowell, Massachusetts, indicate that she was a strong, determined, extraordinarily focused person. She turned this energy toward producing flowers of clear color, particularly pinks, purples, and reds. Her 'Potentate' and Wheeler's 'Amherst' became two foundation plants for breeding purples. Ophelia Taylor of Ocala, Florida concentrated her efforts on flower form and style. Her 'Prima Donna' was one of the first clear pastel daylilies, large and wide-petaled. It was used heavily in hybridizing and went on to win the Stout Medal in 1955. Ralph Wheeler, born in New York, fell in love with *Amaryllis* and then daylilies after he moved to Florida. He concentrated on flowers that he considered unique and special. The work of these three hybridizers carried the daylily forward from the early "post-species" plants of the Stout era toward larger, clearer flowers in a variety of colors.

The period from 1950 to 1975 saw dramatic changes in the look of the daylily, due primarily to the increasing number of people interested in the flower. During this time, enthusiasm for the daylily grew dramatically. As the flower became more attractive, more people were drawn to it, which in turn increased the interest in breeding. The registration of new hybrids increased to over 15,000, and new breeders surfaced. A group of hybridizers emerged in the Chicago area led by Ezra Kraus, David Hall, and Elmer Claar, turning their region into the center of daylily hybridizing. Kraus, then chairman of the department of botany at the University of Chicago, had assembled the most extensive daylily collection in the Midwest. A bachelor and serious scientist, Kraus dedicated himself to a carefully planned, structured breeding program, focusing primarily on reds, pinks, and melons. Hall, an attorney and friend of Kraus, bred daylilies as a hobby and created reds, very clear pinks, and roses. Claar, who constructed and managed real estate and hotel projects, was an avid collector of many things, including daylilies. His hybridizing hobby led to broad-petaled, ruffled yellows, and a line of reds that had a major impact on red breeding.

Outside the Chicago area, several other breeders were working diligently during this period. W. B. MacMillan of Abbeville, Louisiana, managed to produce seedlings that bloomed in one year instead of the usual two to three, thus racing ahead in the hybridizing field. His greatest successes in color were cream-pinks, pastels, and yellows, but he is best known for the flower form he developed. His daylilies were very round and ruffled for their time, so much so that "the MacMillan form" came to define round and ruffled flowers. Edna Spalding was another Louisiana breeder of that era. Although she bred daylilies merely for pleasure and forced them to compete with her vegetable garden, she had a keen eye and a strong sense for quality and made great advances with pinks and purples. Two other southerners, Frank and Peggy Childs of Georgia, worked for 30 years with daylilies of every conceivable color in both single and double forms. Their 'Catherine Woodbery' (1967), a clear lavender-pink, was eventually converted to a tetraploid and formed the basis of much future work at the tetraploid level.

After 1975, the tetraploid revolution dominated daylily hybridizing, but a number of breeders continued to work with diploid daylilies. Ra Hansen carried out an extensive program in Florida, producing bold and dramatic flowers that reflected the dynamic persona of this former Miss Texas finalist. Pauline Henry was another prominent diploid hybridizer who continued to work on her Siloam series. She produced a large number of prize-winning cultivars in a range of colors that vary in form from miniatures to large flowers and doubles.

THE TETRAPLOID REVOLUTION

While breeders were hard at work hybridizing new diploid daylilies, a behind-the-scenes revolution quietly and forever changed *Hemerocallis*. The 1940s saw the first attempts to treat daylilies with colchicine and convert them from diploid to tetraploid, but the efforts were difficult to confirm and caused little notice in daylily circles. Hamilton Traub, Quinn Buck, and Robert Schreiner each reported successfully converting a daylily in 1947, 1948, and 1949, respectively. They introduced tetraploid plants in the following years, but the plants were primitive compared to the diploids of the day and garnered little attention. It was not until the now-famous 1961 American Hemerocallis Society convention in Chicago that the tetraploid daylily made known its true impact.

Two years prior to the convention, Orville Fay and Bob Griesbach self-pollinated their induced tetraploid 'Crestwood Ann' (1961), producing a pod with four viable seeds. These seedlings established a line of seed-grown tetraploids that bloomed in time for the 1961 convention. To say the least, this created a stir among the attendees. Adding to the excitement, Fay proclaimed that within 10 years diploid daylilies would be obsolete. His statement raised a furor among diploid breeders who were being told that the efforts of their hard work would soon disappear. Only a handful of the more visionary hybridizers clearly saw the importance of this break. Most diploid hybridizers were offended and saw the breakthrough as a challenge to be defeated at every possible turn.

R. W. Munson Jr., a quiet, reserved architect who began hybridizing daylilies when he was still a teenager, was a major player in this new tetraploid revolution. He was a bachelor living with his mother and sister, dedicated to working with diploids to create a line of clear pastels. After 27 years of hybridizing diploids, Munson attended the 1961 Chicago convention. There he realized the potential importance of tetraploid daylilies and decided to change his program to a tetraploid line. He made a pact with fellow breeders Steve Moldovan and Virginia Peck to pursue tetraploids, despite the obstacles. The early converted daylilies were almost sterile, so that a season of hard work that would have produced tens of thousands of new diploid daylilies produced only a handful of tetraploid seedlings. The undertaking was arduous, and the work was frustrating. Against a background of great pessimism and what initially seemed insurmountable odds, Munson, Peck, and Moldovan, along with Charles Reckamp, pioneered the tetraploid daylily and brought it to its present position at the forefront of daylily growing.

But daylily lovers remained divided into two hostile camps, diploid supporters and tetraploid supporters. While the diploid hybridizing programs raced ahead, creating round, ruffled flowers, the tetraploid breeding was painfully slow, and, as a consequence, hybridizing efforts lagged behind. The vast majority of society members refused to accept the new tetraploids, seeing them as coarse and unrefined. As a result, despite their revolutionizing effect on the daylily, Munson, Reckamp, Peck, and Moldovan all died without receiving the Stout Medal. Since the 1980s and 90s, the hostility has begun to subside, as the tetraploids have become increasingly beautiful and more hybridizers have switched over. Today, tetraploids are the mainstream in most large, prominent hybridizing efforts.

Virginia Peck made remarkable advances in breeding full and ruffled forms into a variety of colors. Her cultivar 'Dance Ballerina Dance' (1976) was widely used in hybridizing because of its excellent ruffling. Charles Reckamp at Mission Gardens, in Techny, Illinois, created a line of dormant tetraploid pastel flowers with ruffled petals and gold edges.

Munson worked with his mother, Ida, and together they produced daylilies in every available color. Their plants 'Betty Warren Woods' (1987) and 'Ida's Magic' (1988) became the standards for refinement and were among the most important and widely used hybrids in the late 1990s. Despite Munson's many extraordinary accomplishments, his passion was always for purples and pastels. While many hybridizers focused merely on improving the flower, Munson's primary focus was always on improving the overall plant habit. He was ever-mindful of the pitfalls of short-sighted hybridizing and was painfully aware of the problems that hybridizers had ignored in their breeding of other flowers. He was determined to keep the daylily safe from shortcomings such as susceptibility to black spot fungus that had come to plague the modern hybrid tea rose, or sensitivity to the rot that had been bred into the newer irises. His primary goal was to make the daylily a carefree, ever-blooming perennial that would grow across a broad climatic range with no dependence on chemicals or special treatment.

Steve Moldovan began working with diploids before becoming interested in tetraploids. Moldovan bred northern hardy cultivars with tender cultivars in an effort to produce hybrids that were more widely adaptable. He is best known for his purples and pinks that were hardy in his Ohio garden.

HYBRIDIZERS OF TODAY

There are hundreds of people, if not thousands, hybridizing daylilies today. Prominent hybridizers whose programs are currently on the cutting edge include Jeff and Elizabeth Salter, a team of hybridizers in Gainesville, Florida. Jeff, a quiet, reserved man by nature and an attorney by training, took the daylily to new levels in terms of full-formed, wide-petaled, ruffled, heavily substanced flowers. Some of Jeff's most significant achievements have been 'Ed Brown' (1994), 'Moonlit Masquerade' (1992), and 'Elizabeth Salter' (1990), all of which won the Stout Medal. Elizabeth, the granddaughter of Ida Munson and niece of R. W. Munson Jr., grew up among daylilies. She has concentrated on small and miniature flowers and has created a line with unique, complex, blue, and patterned eyes. Elizabeth has won the Donn Fischer Memorial Cup nine times, more than any other hybridizer in the history of the AHS. Some of her most celebrated creations include 'Crystal Blue Persuasion' (1996), 'Mary Ethel Anderson' (1995), and 'Patchwork Puzzle' (1990), to mention a few.

Patrick and Grace Stamile, retired teachers, are another team in Florida. Patrick has worked on medium to large-flowered tetraploids, and is best known for his eyed and pink cultivars. He has produced a number of small to medium flowers, which he has included in his award-winning Candy series. Pat has also made major contributions to the overall plant, including arching foliage and tall, well-branched scapes. Pat has won the Stout Medal three times, for his 'Wedding Band' (1987), 'Strawberry Candy' (1989), and 'Custard Candy' (1989), along with many other AHS awards. Grace has focused on small and miniature flowers that are on short, well-proportioned scapes. She is best known for her miniature patterned and blue-eyed singles as well as her miniature "popcorn" doubles. She has won the Donn Fischer Memorial Cup twice, for her 'Baby Blues' (1990) and 'You Angel You' (1993).

Dan Trimmer, another Florida hybridizer, continues to focus on bringing converted diploids into the tetraploid lines. Dan has worked with bold eyes, pure color, and beautiful form in both narrow and wide-petaled flowers. Some of his most popular introductions have included 'Jane Trimmer' (2002), 'Across the Universe' (2004), 'Cherry Valentine' (1999), and 'Carol Todd' (2006). His wife, Jane Trimmer, has also been hybridizing spiders such as 'String Theory' (2005), as well as small flowers, including her miniature doubles, such as 'Micro Dots' (2003).

Ted L. Petit, a professor of neuroscience and co-author of this book, has concentrated on creating large, ornate flowers of every color, which are heavily ruffled, most with gold edges. In his Florida garden, Ted has created a line of large, ornate doubles, as well as blue-eyed and patterned flowers. He has also worked to improve overall plant vigor and health, introducing plants that are increasingly resistant to daylily diseases. Some of his more significant introductions include 'Ferengi Gold' (1994), 'Mardi Gras Ball' (1996), 'John Peat' (2001), and 'April LaQuinta' (2006).

Larry Grace, near Dothan, Alabama, has made improvements in round, ruffled, gold-edged flowers; his passion has always been pastels. He sold his hybridizing program to Frank Smith, in central Florida, who has introduced many of Larry's plants, and has started a hybridizing program of his own focusing on large, ornate tetraploids. Larry Grace quickly began hybridizing again. Larry has worked hard on improving overall plant performance, and converts many diploids to add diversity to his program. Some of Larry's most popular creations include 'J. T. Davis' (1999), 'Bill Robinson' (Larry Grace and Frank Smith, 2004), 'Bridey Greeson' (Larry Grace and Frank Smith, 2003), and 'Moment in the Sun' (Larry Grace and Frank Smith, 2004).

John, Marjorie, and John Kinnebrew Jr. manage another central Florida garden. They have pushed the envelope with heavy, ornate gold edges, but also work with doubles and small flowers and patterned eyes. Some of their more significant introductions include 'Spacecoast Sea Shells' (2003), 'Alexa Kathryn' (2003), 'Darla Anita' (1999), and 'Jerry Nettles' (2002).

Many other hybridizers are also putting their own vision of a new look on the daylily. John P. Peat, a co-author of this book, has begun to impact large-flowered daylilies, particularly those with bold, dramatic eyes and edges. He has recently expanded his program and is creating a three-acre (1.21 ha) garden in North Florida. Some of John's more popular flowers include 'Adventures With Ra' (2001), 'Jammin' With Jane' (2005), 'Linda Sierra' (2006), and 'Reyna' (2002). The primary impact of E. R. Joiner has been on the double daylily, including such beauties as 'Peggy Jeffcoat' (1995). Jack B. Carpenter in Texas is working with both diploid and tetraploid lines in a variety of sizes and colors. Jack has made an impact on very large flowers and patterned eyes such as 'Texas Kaleidoscope' (2001) and 'Lavender Blue Baby' (1996). Karol Emmerich of Springwood Gardens has been developing a very cold-hardy northern line of dramatic large-flowered tetraploids that will survive in her harsh Minnesota climate. Some of her more noted introductions include 'Born to Reign' (2005) and 'Heartbeat of Heaven' (2004). Ludlow Lambertson has worked extensively with unusual form daylilies, developing a line of blue-eyed and -patterned daylilies, such as his 'Blue Hippo' (2005). In California, Stan and Bonnie Holley along with Jeff Corbett started Gold Coast Daylilies. Some of their introductions have included 'Shelter Cove' (2002) and 'Bonnie Holley' (2005). Gunda and Tony Abajian of Ledgewood Gardens in central Florida have been working on a variety of lines, but are best known for their blue-eyed and -patterned daylilies, including 'In Cahoots' (2002). George Doorakian, a retired biochemist, has been breeding in his Massachusetts garden. George has made remarkable progress in enhancing large dramatic green eyes, producing plants such as 'Malachite Prism' (1999). Dan Hansen of Ladybug Daylilies has continued his mother Ra Hansen's lines with his white-edged reds, such as 'Roses in Snow' (1999), being particularly popular. John Rice of Kentucky has produced a number of different looks in his flowers, with his lacy-edged 'Bass Gibson' (2006) gaining attention.

In Canada, Henry Lorraine has continued the lines that he and his former partner Doug Lycett started, creating a line of very cold-hardy plants that flourish in Canada. David Kirchhoff has worked primarily with reds and doubles, while his partner, Mort Morss, has focused primarily on complex eyes and patterns. Jamie Gossard of Heavenly Gardens in Ohio has made major headway working primarily with spiders and patterned eyes. He has produced very dramatic lines that thrive in his Ohio climate. Bob Schwarz of Long Island, New York, has been a major figure working on unusual form daylilies, including his popular 'Twisted Sister' (1999). Lee Pickles of Chattanooga Daylily Gardens in Tennessee has worked with a variety of lines, but his eyes and reds, such as 'Awesome Bob' (2001), have gained particular attention. Linda Agin in northern Alabama has been working with large, dramatic flowers and has just begun to introduce plants, such as her beautiful 'Linda Beck' (2005). Jeff and Jackie Pryor have continued their work in both diploid and tetraploid single and double flowers. Tim Bell has been producing beautiful large-flowered full formed tetraploids, such as 'Hebrew Maiden' (2005) in his exquisite formal gardens in Georgia.

'Green Kwanso' (Arlow B. Stout, 1917). Dormant. Scape 36 in. (91 cm). Midseason. A fulvous red with a darker eyezone triploid.

'Dauntless' (Arlow B. Stout, 1935). Semi-evergreen. Scape 36 in. (91 cm). Early midseason. A yellow to light orange with a small darker burgundy eyezone above a green throat. Diploid. Stout Silver Medal 1954. Award of Merit 1951. *Photograph by Rejean Millette.*

'Patricia' (Arlow B. Stout, 1935). Evergreen. Scape 36 in. (91 cm). Midseason. A small yellow flower with a dark green throat. Diploid. Award of Merit 1950. *Photograph by Rejean Millette.*

'Chloe' (Elizabeth Nesmith, 1938). Dormant. Scape 30 in. (76 cm). Midseason. A light polychrome with a darker halo. Diploid. Award of Merit 1952.

'Persian Princess' (Elizabeth Nesmith, 1938). Dormant. Scape 40 in. (101 cm). Early midseason. A dark red self. Diploid. Award of Merit 1951.

'Bold Courtier' (Elizabeth Nesmith, 1939). Semi-evergreen. Scape 38 in. (96 cm). Midseason. A narrow-petaled red with white midribs above a green throat. Diploid. Award of Merit 1950. *Photograph by Rejean Millette.*

'Duchess of Windsor' (Hamilton P. Traub and Mynelle Hayward, 1939). Evergreen. Scape 29 in. (74 cm). Midseason. A light yellow-orange polychrome with a halo eyezone. Diploid. Award of Merit 1950.

'Hesperus' (Jacobs M. Sass, 1940). Dormant. Scape 48 in. (122 cm). Midseason late. A yellow to light orange. Diploid. Stout Silver Medal 1950. *Photograph by Francis Gatlin.*

'Pink Charm' (Elizabeth Nesmith, 1940). Semi-evergreen. Scape 40 in. (101 cm). Midseason. A large pink with nice ruffling above a green throat. Diploid. Award of Merit 1951.

'Bertrand Farr' (Arlow B. Stout, 1941). Evergreen. Scape 30 in. (76 cm). Midseason. A narrow-petaled red with large white midribs on the sepals and petals. Diploid. 'Patricia' × 'Charmaine'. Award of Merit 1951. *Photograph by Rejean Millette.*

'Caballero' (Arlow B. Stout, 1941). Evergreen. Scape 40 in. (101 cm). Early midseason. A bicolor orange-red self with white midribs and a yellow to green throat. Diploid. Award of Merit 1951.

'Dominion' (Arlow B. Stout, 1941). Semi-evergreen. Scape 40 in. (101 cm). Early midseason. A medium orange-red self with a darker red eyezone. Diploid. Award of Merit 1952.

'Gay Troubadour' (Elizabeth Nesmith, 1941). Dormant. Scape 40 in. (101 cm). Midseason late. A medium orange-red bicolor with orange-red sepals. Diploid. Award of Merit 1951.

'Kanapaha' (John V. Watkins, 1941). Evergreen. Scape 38 in. (96 cm). Early midseason. A medium orange-red self. Diploid. Award of Merit 1950.

'Ruby Supreme' (Ralph W. Wheeler, 1941). Evergreen. Scape 36 in. (91 cm). Midseason. A dark orange-red self. Diploid. Award of Merit 1950.

'Su-Lin' (Elizabeth Nesmith, 1941). Dormant. Scape 35 in. (89 cm). Midseason. A light violet-red bicolor with light yellow sepals. Diploid. Award of Merit 1952.

'Athlone' (Hugh M. Russell, 1942). Evergreen. Scape 48 in. (122 cm). Midseason. A bicolor orange-red with lighter midribs. Diploid. Award of Merit 1952.

'Black Prince' (Hugh M. Russell, 1942). Dormant. Scape 42 in. (107 cm). Early midseason. A dark red to burgundy with a green throat. Diploid. Award of Merit 1951.

'Mrs. Hugh Johnson' (Hugh M. Russell, 1942). Dormant. Scape 42 in. (107 cm). Early midseason. A dark orange-red self. Diploid. Award of Merit 1950.

'Painted Lady' (Hugh M. Russell, 1942). Evergreen. Scape 36 in. (91 cm). Midseason. A narrow-petaled rusty orange with a darker eyezone. Diploid. Stout Silver Medal 1951. Award of Merit 1950. *Photograph by Debbie and Duane Hurlbert.*

'Royal Ruby' (Elizabeth Nesmith, 1942). Semi-evergreen. Scape 38 in. (96 cm). Early midseason. A medium orange-red self. Diploid. Award of Merit 1950.

'Bountiful' (Paul H. Cook, 1943). Dormant. Scape 32 in. (81 cm). Midseason. A light yellow self. Diploid. 'Hyperion' × unknown. Award of Merit 1952.

'Jean' (Clint McDade, 1943). Dormant. Scape 38 in. (96 cm). Very late. A medium orange-red bitone with medium orange sepals. Diploid. Award of Merit 1951.

'Potentate' (Elizabeth Nesmith, 1943). Dormant. Scape 42 in. (107 cm). Midseason. A dark violet-red self. Diploid. Stout Silver Medal 1952. Award of Merit 1950.

'Valiant' (Paul H. Cook, 1943). Dormant. Scape 42 in. (107 cm). Midseason. A medium yellow-orange self. Diploid. Award of Merit 1953. Honorable Mention 1950.

'Easter Morn' (Ralph W. Wheeler, 1944). Evergreen. Scape 42 in. (107 cm). Early midseason. A medium yellow-orange. Diploid. Award of Merit 1951.

'Revolute' (Hans P. Sass, 1944). Dormant. Scape 46 in. (117 cm). Midseason late. A medium yellow self. Diploid. Stout Silver Medal 1953. Award of Merit 1950.

'Baggette' (Hugh M. Russell, 1945). Dormant. Scape 30 in. (76 cm). Early midseason. A bicolor rose-orange with lighter midribs. Diploid. Award of Merit 1953. Honorable Mention 1950.

'Devon Cream' (Elizabeth Nesmith, 1945). Dormant. Scape 39 in. (99 cm). Midseason. A light yellow self. Diploid. Award of Merit 1952. Honorable Mention 1950.

'Mission Bells' (David F. Hall, 1945). Dormant. Scape 36 in. (91 cm). Midseason. A light yellow self. Diploid. Award of Merit 1951. Honorable Mention 1950.

'Orange Beauty' (Hans P. Sass, 1945). Dormant. Scape 40 in. (101 cm). Midseason. A medium yellow-orange self. Diploid. Award of Merit 1950.

'Amherst' (Ralph W. Wheeler, 1946). Evergreen. Scape 36 in. (91 cm). Midseason. A medium violet-red self. Diploid. Award of Merit 1952. Honorable Mention 1950.

'Blanche Hooker' (Arlow B. Stout, 1946). Evergreen. Scape 36 in. (91 cm). Early. A medium orange-red self. Diploid. Award of Merit 1954. Honorable Mention 1950.

'Georgia' (Arlow B. Stout, 1946). Evergreen. Scape 48 in. (122 cm). Midseason late. A light orange-red polychrome with a darker eyezone. Diploid. Award of Merit 1952. Honorable Mention 1950.

'Lady Fair' (Elizabeth Nesmith, 1946). Semi-evergreen. Scape 38 in. (96 cm). Midseason late. A light orange-red polychrome. Diploid. Award of Merit 1954. Honorable Mention 1951.

'Prima Donna' (Bright "Ophelia" Taylor, 1946). Evergreen. Scape 36 in. (91 cm). Midseason. A pastel reddish orange lavender. Diploid. Stout Silver Medal 1955. Award of Merit 1952. *Photograph by Francis Gatlin*

'Rose Gem' (Arlow B. Stout, 1946). Evergreen. Scape 47 in. (119 cm). Midseason late. A medium orange-red with a halo. Diploid. Award of Merit 1953. Honorable Mention 1950.

'Cellini' (Ralph W. Wheeler, 1947). Evergreen. Scape 35 in. (89 cm). Midseason. A light yellow self. Diploid. Award of Merit 1955. Honorable Mention 1952.

'Cerise' (Ralph W. Wheeler, 1947). Evergreen. Scape 40 in. (101 cm). Midseason. A dark orange-red self. Diploid. Award of Merit 1954. Honorable Mention 1950.

'Flamboyant' (Geddes Douglas, 1947). Dormant. Scape 42 in. (107 cm). Midseason. A medium orange-yellow self with an eyezone. Diploid. Award of Merit 1953. Honorable Mention 1950.

'Naranja' (Ralph W. Wheeler, 1947). Evergreen. Scape 36 in. (91 cm). Midseason. An orange flower with a lightly ruffled edge. Diploid. Stout Silver Medal 1956. Award of Merit 1953. Honorable Mention 1950. *Photograph by Rejean Millette*

'Sideshow' (Hugh M. Russell, 1947). Evergreen. Scape 30 in. (76 cm). Early. A light orange-yellow. Diploid. Award of Merit 1956. Honorable Mention 1952.

'Cathedral Towers' (Carl S. Milliken, 1948). Evergreen. Scape 36 in. (91 cm). Midseason. A light yellow with a darker eyezone. Diploid. Award of Merit 1954. Honorable Mention 1951.

'Colonial Dame' (Carl S. Milliken, 1948). Semi-evergreen. Scape 36 in. (91 cm). A light orange-yellow with a darker eyezone. Diploid. Award of Merit 1954. Honorable Mention 1951.

'Copper Colonel' (Henry E. Sass, 1948). Dormant. Scape 40 in. (101 cm). Midseason. A medium orange. Diploid. Award of Merit 1954. Honorable Mention 1951.

'Dorothea' (Mary Lester and Carl S. Milliken, 1948). Dormant. Scape 36 in. (91 cm). Midseason. A light yellow polychrome with a darker eyezone. Diploid. Award of Merit 1954. Honorable Mention 1951.

'Flanders' (Mary Lester, 1948). Dormant. Scape 36 in. (91 cm). Midseason late. A medium orange-red self. Diploid. Award of Merit 1953. Honorable Mention 1950.

'Garnet Robe' (Carl S. Milliken, 1948). Evergreen. Scape 36 in. (91 cm). Midseason. A dark red self. Diploid. Award of Merit 1953. Honorable Mention 1950.

'High Noon' (Carl S. Milliken, 1948). Evergreen. Scape 36 in. (91 cm). Midseason. A dark orange-yellow self. Diploid. Stout Silver Medal 1958. Award of Merit 1955. Honorable Mention 1952.

'Knighthood' (Ralph M. Schroeder, 1948). Dormant. Scape 43 in. (109 cm). Early midseason. A dark red self. Diploid. 'Dominion' × Kraus seedling #3. Award of Merit 1954. Honorable Mention 1951.

'Lady Bountiful' (Mary Lester, 1948). Dormant. Scape 45 in. (114 cm). Midseason. A light yellow. Diploid. Award of Merit 1955. Honorable Mention 1952.

'Maid Marian' (Mary Lester, 1948). Dormant. Scape 42 in. (107 cm). Midseason. A light red self. Diploid. Award of Merit 1955. Honorable Mention 1952.

'Midwest Star' (Hans P. Sass, 1948). Semi-evergreen. Scape 48 in. (122 cm). Midseason. A light yellow self. Diploid. Award of Merit 1954. Honorable Mention 1951.

'North Star' (David F. Hall, 1948). Dormant. Scape 38 in. (96 cm). Midseason. A pale yellow self. Diploid. Award of Merit 1955. Honorable Mention 1952.

'Pink Bowknot' (Bright "Ophelia" Taylor, 1948). Evergreen. Scape 42 in. (107 cm). Midseason. A light red-orange self. Diploid. Award of Merit 1955. Honorable Mention 1952.

'Queen Esther' (Hans P. Sass, 1948). Dormant. Scape 36 in. (91 cm). Midseason. A dark orange-red self. Diploid. Award of Merit 1953. Honorable Mention 1950.

'Ruffled Pinafore' (G. Milliken, 1948). Evergreen. Scape 30 in. (76 cm). Midseason. An orange to yellow. Diploid. Stout Silver Medal 1957. Award of Merit 1954. *Photograph by Francis Gatlin.*

'Ruth Lehman' (Ezra Jacob Kraus, 1948). Dormant. Scape 36 in. (91 cm). Midseason. An orange-tinged red-lavender polychrome. Diploid. Award of Merit 1957. Honorable Mention 1954.

'Brocade' (Bright "Ophelia" Taylor, 1949). Evergreen. Scape 42 in. (107 cm). Midseason. A light red-orange with a halo. Diploid. 'Prima Donna' × unknown. Award of Merit 1956. Honorable Mention 1953.

'Cibola' (Howard M. Hill, 1949). Dormant. Scape 36 in. (91 cm). Midseason. A light yellow-orange self. Diploid. 'Valiant' × 'Orange Beauty'. Award of Merit 1956. Honorable Mention 1953.

'Evelyn Claar' (Ezra Jacob Kraus, 1949). Dormant. Scape 30 in. (76 cm). Early midseason. A rose-lavender with a darker eyezone above a green center. Diploid. Award of Merit 1955. Honorable Mention 1952. *Photograph by Rejean Millette.*

'Golden Triangle' (Hamilton P. Traub, 1949). Scape 44 in. (112 cm). Midseason. A medium orange-yellow self. Diploid. Award of Merit 1957. Honorable Mention 1954.

'Griselle' (Stanley E. Saxton, 1949). Evergreen. Scape 32 in. (81 cm). Early midseason. A medium red self. Diploid. 'Bertrand Farr' × 'Theron'. Award of Merit 1956. Honorable Mention 1953.

'Mabel Fuller' (Ezra Jacob Kraus, 1949). Dormant. Scape 36 in. (91 cm). Midseason late. A medium orange-red self. Diploid. 'J. S. Gaynor' × (('J. S. Gaynor' × 'Gypsy') × ('Dominion' × 'Cressida')). Award of Merit 1955. Honorable Mention 1952.

'Midwest Majesty' (Jacobs M. Sass, 1949). Dormant. Scape 50 in. (127 cm). Midseason. A yellow with a strong peach overlay above a deep, dark green throat. Diploid. Award of Merit 1953. Honorable Mention 1950. *Photograph by Rejean Millette.*

'Nantahala' (Bright "Ophelia" Taylor, 1949). Evergreen. Scape 36 in. (91 cm). Early. A light orange with a small halo. Diploid. Award of Merit 1957. Honorable Mention 1954.

'Pink Prelude' (Elizabeth Nesmith, 1949). Semi-evergreen. Scape 39 in. (99 cm). Midseason. A light red self. Diploid. Award of Merit 1955. Honorable Mention 1952.

'Raven' (Ralph W. Wheeler, 1949). Evergreen. Scape 36 in. (91 cm). Early. A dark orange-red self. Diploid. Award of Merit 1956. Honorable Mention 1953.

'Ringlets' (Ezra Jacob Kraus, 1949). Dormant. Scape 30 in. (76 cm). Early midseason. A dark orange-yellow self. Diploid. ('Mrs. W. H. Wyman' × 'Rosalind') × (('Dominion' × 'J. S. Gaynor') × ('Dominion' × 'Cinnabar')). Award of Merit 1958. Honorable Mention 1955.

'Show Girl' (Ralph W. Wheeler, 1949). Scape 40 in. (101 cm). Early midseason. A light violet-red self. Diploid. Award of Merit 1956. Honorable Mention 1953.

'The Doctor' (Mrs. Elmer A. Claar, 1949). Dormant. Scape 36 in. (91 cm). Early midseason. A medium orange-red self. Diploid. Award of Merit 1955. Honorable Mention 1952.

'Crimson Glory' (Carl Carpenter, 1950). Dormant. Scape 42 in. (107 cm). Early midseason. A dark red self. Diploid. Award of Merit 1958. Honorable Mention 1955.

'Kindly Light' (LeMoine J. Bechtold, 1950). Dormant. Scape 28 in. (71 cm); flower 7.5 in. (19 cm). Midseason. A very famous and popular arching bright yellow. Diploid. Honorable Mention 1955. *Photograph by Mary Anne Leisen.*

'Marie Wood' (William T. Wood, 1950). Dormant. Scape 36 in. (91 cm). Early midseason. A light red self. Diploid. Award of Merit 1957. Honorable Mention 1954.

'Neyron Rose' (Ezra Jacob Kraus, 1950). Semi-evergreen. Scape 30 in. (76 cm). Midseason. A rich raspberry-red with striking white midribs above a tangerine throat. Diploid. 'Gypsy',

'Amaryllis', and 'Dauntless' ancestry. Award of Merit 1956. Honorable Mention 1953.

'Salmon Sheen' (Bright "Ophelia" Taylor, 1950). Evergreen. Scape 34 in. (86 cm). Early. A medium red-orange. Diploid. Stout Silver Medal 1959. Award of Merit 1956. Honorable Mention 1953.

'Atlas' (Ezra Jacob Kraus, 1951). Dormant. Scape 34 in. (86 cm). Midseason late. A narrow-petaled yellow with a bright green center. Diploid. 'Magnus' × ('Dominion' × 'J. S. Gaynor'). Award of Merit 1958. Honorable Mention 1955. *Photograph by John Benoot.*

'Bess Ross' (Elmer A. Claar, 1951). Dormant. Scape 36 in. (91 cm). Midseason. An orange-red. Diploid. Stout Silver Medal 1962. Award of Merit 1957. *Photograph by Francis Gatlin.*

'Colonel Joe' (Mary Lester, 1951). Dormant. Scape 40 in. (101 cm). Early. A light yellow self. Diploid. 'Limelight' × seedling. Award of Merit 1956. Honorable Mention 1953.

'Coral Mist' (David F. Hall, 1951). Dormant. Scape 24 in. (61 cm). Midseason. A shell-pink self. Diploid. Award of Merit 1958. Honorable Mention 1955. *Photograph by Debbie and Duane Hurlbert.*

'Gene Wild' (Mary Lester, 1951). Evergreen. Scape 30 in. (76 cm). Early. A light orange-yellow polychrome with a darker halo. Diploid. 'Peach Blush' × unknown. Award of Merit 1957. Honorable Mention 1954.

'Goldensong' (Ezra Jacob Kraus, 1951). Dormant. Scape 30 in. (76 cm). Midseason. A medium yellow-orange self. Diploid. 'Yellowstone' × 'Mrs. W. H. Wyman'. Award of Merit 1959. Honorable Mention 1956.

'Picture' (Mary Lester, 1951). Dormant. Scape 40 in. (101 cm). Midseason. A light orange-red self. Diploid. 'Maid Marian' × 'Laurel'. Award of Merit 1957. Honorable Mention 1954.

'Pink Damask' (James C. Stevens, 1951). Dormant. Scape 36 in. (91 cm). Midseason. A unique shade of pink with slightly lighter midribs and narrow petals. Diploid. Award of Merit 1957. Honorable Mention 1954.

'Pink Dream' (Frank and Peggy Childs, 1951). Dormant. Scape 40 in. (101 cm). Midseason. A light red self. Diploid. Award of Merit 1956. Honorable Mention 1953.

'Shooting Star' (David F. Hall, 1951). Dormant. Scape 38 in. (96 cm). Midseason late. A light yellow self. Diploid. Award of Merit 1959. Honorable Mention 1954.

'Capri' (Carl S. Milliken, 1952). Evergreen. Scape 36 in. (91 cm). Midseason. A rosy apricot blend. Diploid. 'Ruffled Pinafore' × 'Colonial Dame'. Award of Merit 1959. Honorable Mention 1956.

'Gay Lark' (H. P. Connell, 1952). Evergreen. Scape 36 in. (91 cm). Midseason. A light red-orange polychrome self. Diploid. Award of Merit 1958. Honorable Mention 1955.

'Nashville' (Elmer A. Claar, 1952). Dormant. Scape 38 in. (96 cm). Midseason. A yellowish melon flower with a small green center. Diploid. Award of Merit 1957. Honorable Mention 1954. *Photograph by Rejean Millette.*

'Quincy' (Bright "Ophelia" Taylor, 1952). Evergreen. Scape 36 in. (91 cm). Midseason late. A light orange-yellow with a darker eyezone. Diploid. Award of Merit 1958. Honorable Mention 1955.

'Summer Love' (G. Milliken, 1952). Evergreen. Scape 36 in. (91 cm). Midseason. A deep yellow self. Diploid. ('Golden West' × 'Wau-bun') × 'High Noon'. Award of Merit 1959. Honorable Mention 1955.

'Alan' (Elmer A. Claar, 1953). Dormant. Scape 36 in. (91 cm). Midseason late. A narrow-petaled red self with lighter midribs. Diploid. Award of Merit 1960. Honorable Mention 1957.

'Cosette' (Carl S. Milliken, 1953). Evergreen. Scape 36 in. (91 cm). Early. A yellow dusted rose. Diploid. ('Duchess of Windsor' × 'Linda') × (('Golden West' × 'Caballero') × seedling). Award of Merit 1958. Honorable Mention 1955.

'Cradle Song' (Carl S. Milliken, 1953). Evergreen. Scape 22 in. (56 cm). Midseason. A medium yellow self. Diploid. ('Golden West' × 'Wau-Bun') × 'High Noon'. Award of Merit 1959. Honorable Mention 1955.

'Delta Girl' (H. P. Connell, 1953). Evergreen. Scape 26 in. (66 cm). A light yellow self. Diploid. Award of Merit 1960. Honorable Mention 1957.

'Fairy Wings' (Mary Lester, 1953). Dormant. Scape 36 in. (91 cm). Early midseason. A light yellow. Diploid. Stout Silver Medal 1960. Award of Merit 1957. Honorable Mention 1954. *Photograph by Francis Gatlin.*

'Green Envy' (George E. Lenington, 1953). Evergreen. Scape 32 in. (81 cm). Midseason late. A light yellow to orange self with an eyezone. Diploid. 'Painted Lady' × unknown. Award of Merit 1960. Honorable Mention 1957.

'Hearts Afire' (Hooper P. Connell, 1953). Evergreen. Scape 36 in. (91 cm). Midseason. A medium red self. Diploid. 'Avernus' × unknown. Award of Merit 1959. Honorable Mention 1956.

'Jack Frost' (Mary Lester, 1953). Dormant. Scape 36 in. (91 cm). Midseason. A light green-yellow self. Diploid. Award of Merit 1957. Honorable Mention 1954.

'President Rice' (Elmer A. Claar, 1953). Dormant. Scape 33 in. (84 cm). Midseason. A medium orange-yellow self. Diploid. Award of Merit 1961. Honorable Mention 1958.

'Golden Chimes' (Huber A. Fischer, 1954). Dormant. Scape 46 in. (117 cm); flower 2.75 in. (7 cm). Early midseason. A chrome-yellow self. 'Bijou' × seedling. Donn Fischer Memorial Cup 1962. Award of Merit 1961. Honorable Mention 1956.

'Golden Galeon' (Carl S. Milliken, 1954). Evergreen. Scape 36 in. (91 cm). Midseason. A deep apricot. Diploid. 'Ruffled Pinafore' × 'High Noon'. Award of Merit 1958.

'Jade Crest' (John W. Armistead, 1954). Evergreen. Scape 36 in. (91 cm). Midseason. A chrome lemon self. Diploid. 'Golden Moth' × unknown. Award of Merit 1962. Honorable Mention 1957.

'Lime Painted Lady' (Hugh M. Russell, 1954). Semi-evergreen. Scape 36 in. (91 cm). Midseason. A light greenish yellow self. Diploid. Award of Merit 1962. Honorable Mention 1959. *Photograph by Lynn Thor.*

'Multnomah' (Ezra Jacob Kraus, 1954). Dormant. Scape 24 in. (61 cm). Midseason late. An apricot overlaid pale pink flower with a small green center. Diploid. Seedling × 'Ruth Lehman'. Stout Silver Medal 1963. Award of Merit 1960. Honorable Mention 1957. *Photograph by Rejean Millette.*

'Pink Imperial' (David F. Hall, 1954). Dormant. Scape 32 in. (81 cm). Midseason. A pink self. Diploid. Award of Merit 1961. Honorable Mention 1958.

'Playboy' (Ralph W. Wheeler, 1954). Evergreen. Scape 30 in. (76 cm). Early midseason. A deep orange self. Diploid. 'Naranja' × seedling. Stout Silver Medal 1961. Award of Merit 1958. Honorable Mention 1955.

'Thumbelina' (Huber A. Fischer, 1954). Dormant. Scape 15 in. (38 cm). Midseason. An orange self. Diploid. 'Port' × seedling. Donn Fischer Memorial Cup 1965. Honorable Mention 1956.

'Tinker Bell' (J. C. Stevens, 1954). Dormant. Scape 30 in. (76 cm). Early midseason. An orange self. Diploid. Donn Fischer Memorial Cup 1963.

'Capitol Dome' (Henry E. Sass, 1955). Dormant. Scape 46 in. (117 cm). Midseason. A dark yellow self. Diploid. Award of Merit 1960. Honorable Mention 1956.

'Clackamas' (Ezra Jacob Kraus, 1955). Dormant. Scape 24 in. (61 cm). Midseason. A tangerine-orange and coral-pink. Diploid. Seedling 5076 × 'Ruth Lehman'. Award of Merit 1962. Honorable Mention 1959.

'Golden Dewdrop' (Bright "Ophelia" Taylor, 1955). Evergreen. Scape 14 in. (35.5 cm). Early midseason. An orange-yellow self. Diploid. Award of Merit 1960. Honorable Mention 1957.

'Green Valley' (Huber A. Fischer, 1955). Dormant. Scape 30 in. (76 cm). Midseason late. A yellow self with a dark green throat. Diploid. Seedling × 'Green and Gold'. Lenington All-American Award 1973. Award of Merit 1962. Honorable Mention 1959.

'Hallcroft' (David F. Hall, 1955). Dormant. Scape 32 in. (81 cm). Midseason late. A pink self. Diploid. Award of Merit 1963. Honorable Mention 1960.

'Lyric' (Frank and Peggy Childs, 1955). Dormant. Scape 26 in. (66 cm). Midseason. A geranium-pink self. Diploid. Award of Merit 1960. Honorable Mention 1957.

'Magic Dawn' (David F. Hall, 1955). Dormant. Scape 38 in. (96 cm). Early midseason. A rose-lavender with white midribs above a large yellow to green throat. Diploid. Award of Merit 1959. Honorable Mention 1956. *Photograph by Rejean Millette.*

'Melody Lane' (David F. Hall, 1955). Dormant. Scape 36 in. (91 cm). Midseason. A cream and cinnamon blend. Diploid. Award of Merit 1963. Honorable Mention 1958.

'Pink Orchid' (David F. Hall, 1955). Dormant. Scape 36 in. (91 cm). Early midseason. A blend of salmon-peach and shell-pink. Diploid. Award of Merit 1959. Honorable Mention 1956.

'Silver Sails' (H. P. Connell, 1955). Evergreen. Scape 34 in. (86 cm). Early midseason. A pale cream self. Diploid. Award of Merit 1959. Honorable Mention 1956.

'Summer Interlude' (David F. Hall, 1955). Dormant. Scape 38 in. (96 cm). Midseason. A dark red self. Diploid. Award of Merit 1960. Honorable Mention 1957.

'War Eagle' (David F. Hall, 1955). Evergreen. Scape 34 in. (86 cm). Early midseason. A dark red self. Diploid. Award of Merit 1960. Honorable Mention 1957.

'Wind Song' (Hugh M. Russell, 1955). Semi-evergreen. Scape 28 in. (71 cm); flower 6 in. (15 cm). Midseason. A blend of cream flushed with pink above cream throat. Diploid. 'Sugar Babe' × 'Hope Diamond'. Award of Merit 1981. Honorable Mention 1978.

'Cartwheels' (Orville W. Fay and Hugh M. Russell, 1956). Dormant. Scape 30 in. (76 cm). Midseason late. A deep yellow to orange flower above a small green throat. Diploid. 'Soledad' × 'Signal Light'. Stout Silver Medal 1966. Award of Merit 1961. Honorable Mention 1958.

'Chetco' (Ezra Jacob Kraus, 1956). Dormant. Scape 34 in. (86 cm). Midseason. A Chinese-yellow self. Diploid. 'Double Value' × 'Manitou'. Award of Merit 1961. Honorable Mention 1958.

'Delectable' (Frank and Peggy Childs, 1956). Dormant. Scape 32 in. (81 cm). Midseason. A melon-pink self. Diploid. 'Gratitude' × seedling. Award of Merit 1961. Honorable Mention 1958.

'Flying Saucer' (Wilma B. Flory, 1956). Dormant. Scape 40 in. (101 cm). Midseason. A lightly ruffled light yellow self above a green throat. Diploid. 'Cellini' × 'High Noon'. Award of Merit 1960. Honorable Mention 1957.

'Garden Sprite' (Mary Lester, 1956). Dormant. Scape 28 in. (71 cm). Early midseason. An apricot self. Diploid. Award of Merit 1961. Honorable Mention 1957.

'Jake Russell' (Hugh M. Russell, 1956). Dormant. Scape 36 in. (91 cm). Early midseason. A gold self with a velvety sheen. Diploid. ('Golden Dream' × 'Calypso Dawn') × 'Dawn'. Award of Merit 1959. Honorable Mention 1956.

'Lady Inara' (David F. Hall, 1956). Dormant. Scape 26 in. (66 cm). Early midseason. A lightly ruffled pink self. Diploid. Award of Merit 1962. Honorable Mention 1959. *Photograph by Karen Newman.*

'Mentone' (H. P. Connell, 1956). Evergreen. Scape 28 in. (71 cm). Early midseason. A pale old rose self. Diploid. Award of Merit 1964. Honorable Mention 1959.

'April Breeze' (Mary Lester, 1957). Dormant. Scape 36 in. (91 cm). A Dresden-yellow self. Diploid. Award of Merit 1963. Honorable Mention 1960.

'Burning Daylight' (Huber A. Fischer, 1957). Dormant. Scape 28 in. (71 cm); flower 6 in. (15 cm). Midseason. A glowing orange self. Diploid. 'Smiling Thru' × seedling. Award of Merit 1967. Honorable Mention 1964.

'Drama Girl' (Frank and Peggy Childs, 1957). Dormant. Scape 30 in. (76 cm). Midseason. A flamingo pink. Diploid. 'Gratitude' × seedling. Award of Merit 1961. Honorable Mention 1958.

'Frances Fay' (Orville W. Fay, 1957). Dormant. Scape 24 in. (61 cm). Early midseason. A slightly ruffled clear melon self. Diploid. Stout Silver Medal 1964. Lenington All-American Award 1970. Award of Merit 1961. Honorable Mention 1958.

'Full Reward' (Franklin A. McVicker and F. C. Murphy, 1957). Dormant. Scape 34 in. (86 cm). Early midseason. A cadmium-yellow self with a deep green throat. Diploid. Stout Silver Medal 1967. Award of Merit 1963. Honorable Mention 1960. *Photograph by Rejean Millette.*

'George Cunningham' (David F. Hall, 1957). Dormant. Scape 38 in. (96 cm). Midseason. A lightly ruffled melon blend above a yellow throat. Diploid. Award of Merit 1962. Honorable Mention 1959.

'Grand Canyon' (Bertie Farris, 1957). Evergreen. Scape 24 in. (61 cm). Extra early. A buff and lavender bicolor. Diploid. Award of Merit 1964. Honorable Mention 1961.

'Lucky Strike' (George E. Lenington, 1957). Semi-evergreen. Scape 28 in. (71 cm). Early midseason. A light dawn pink blend. Diploid. Parents unknown. Award of Merit 1963. Honorable Mention 1960.

'May Hall' (David F. Hall, 1957). Dormant. Scape 35 in. (89 cm). Early midseason. A pink blend. Diploid. Stout Silver Medal 1969. Award of Merit 1965. Honorable Mention 1962. *Photograph by Curtis and Linda Sue Barnes.*

'McPick' (George E. Lenington, 1957). Semi-evergreen. Scape 24 in. (61 cm). Early midseason. A yellow with light rosy flush. Diploid. Annie T. Giles Award 1964. Award of Merit 1962. Honorable Mention 1959.

'Myra Hinson' (Eunice Whitten, 1957). Evergreen. Scape 18 in. (46 cm). Early midseason. A light lemon-yellow self. Diploid. Award of Merit 1964. Honorable Mention 1960.

'Nobility' (Frank and Peggy Childs, 1957). Semi-evergreen. Scape 32 in. (81 cm). Midseason late. A light yellow self. Diploid. 'High Noon' × 'Spungold'. Award of Merit 1962. Honorable Mention 1959.

'Soleil D'Or' (Ralph W. Wheeler, 1957). Evergreen. Scape 40 in. (101 cm). A lemon self. Diploid. Award of Merit 1961. Honorable Mention 1958.

'Curls' (Ezra Jacob Kraus, 1958). Dormant. Scape 20 in. (51 cm). Dormant. A tangerine-orange self. Diploid. 'Ringlets' × 'Rhodora'. Donn Fischer Memorial Cup 1964. Award of Merit 1965. Honorable Mention 1962.

'Dorcas' (Edna Spalding, 1958). Evergreen. Scape 36 in. (91 cm). Early. A burnt orange self. Diploid. Award of Merit 1962. Honorable Mention 1959.

'Dream Mist' (R. W. Munson Jr., 1958). Evergreen. Scape 48 in. (122 cm). Midseason. An ivory-cream and rose bicolor. Diploid. 'Show Girl' × ('Mission Bells' × 'Prima Donna'). Award of Merit 1966. Honorable Mention 1966.

'Golden Showpiece' (Clara Mae Pittard, 1958). Evergreen. Scape 40 in. (101 cm). Midseason. A dusted gold self. Diploid. Award of Merit 1964. Honorable Mention 1960. *Photograph by Karen Newman.*

'Great Scott' (Elmer A. Claar, 1958). Dormant. Scape 36 in. (91 cm). Midseason. A gold flushed polychrome. Diploid. Award of Merit 1964. Honorable Mention 1961.

'Rare China' (David F. Hall, 1958). Dormant. Scape 38 in. (96 cm). Midseason. A yellow and rose blend. Diploid. Award of Merit 1964. Honorable Mention 1961.

'Veiled Beauty' (David F. Hall, 1958). Dormant. Scape 32 in. (81 cm). Midseason. A yellow brushed with pink near the tips of petals and sepals. Diploid. Award of Merit 1964. Honorable Mention 1960. *Photograph by Pam Erikson.*

'Angel Robes' (Bright "Ophelia" Taylor, 1959). Evergreen. Scape 30 in. (76 cm). Early. A pale yellow self with a green throat. Diploid. Award of Merit 1965. Honorable Mention 1962.

'Corky' (Huber A. Fischer, 1959). Dormant. Scape 34 in. (86 cm). Midseason. A bright lemon-yellow flower. Diploid. Seedling × 'Mignon'. Donn Fischer Memorial Cup 1967. Honorable Mention 1963.

'Grecian Gift' (Edna Spalding, 1959). Evergreen. Scape 32 in. (81 cm). Early. A brick red self. Diploid. Award of Merit 1963. Honorable Mention 1960.

'June Rhapsody' (Frank and Peggy Childs, 1959). Dormant. Scape 30 in. (76 cm). Early midseason. A pink self with a green to gold throat. Diploid. Award of Merit 1963. Honorable Mention 1960.

'Lexington' (Elmer A. Claar, 1959). Dormant. Scape 34 in. (86 cm). Midseason. A light yellow self. Diploid. Award of Merit 1965. Honorable Mention 1962.

'Louise Russell' (Orville W. Fay and H. M. Russell, 1959). Dormant. Scape 22 in. (56 cm). Midseason late. A baby-ribbon pink self. Diploid. Award of Merit 1964. Honorable Mention 1961.

'Luxury Lace' (Edna Spalding, 1959). Dormant. Scape 32 in. (81 cm). Midseason. A Mars-orange self above a deep green throat. Diploid. Stout Silver Medal 1965. Annie T. Giles Award 1965. Lenington All-American Award 1970. Award of Merit 1962. Honorable Mention 1959.

'Pappy Gates' (W.R. Gates, 1959). Semi-evergreen. Scape 34 in. (86 cm). Early midseason. A gold overlaid with rose and rich gold in throat area. Diploid. 'Ruffled Pinafore' × 'Golden Galleon'. Award of Merit 1964. Honorable Mention 1961.

'Pink Reflection' (Frank and Peggy Childs, 1959). Dormant. Scape 34 in. (86 cm). Early midseason. A pink bitone. Diploid. Award of Merit 1963. Honorable Mention 1960.

'Queen of Hearts' (Mary Lester, 1959). Dormant. Scape 30 in. (76 cm). Early midseason. A bright crimson self with a green throat. Diploid. ('Picture' × seedling) × seedling. Award of Merit 1963. Honorable Mention 1960.

'Silver King' (Sally Lake, 1959). Dormant. Scape 34 in. (86 cm). Early midseason. A light yellow self with a green throat. Diploid. 'Shooting Star' × 'High Noon'. Award of Merit 1967. Honorable Mention 1962.

'Ava Michelle' (Wilma B. Flory, 1960). Semi-evergreen. Scape 18 in. (45.7 cm). Midseason late. A light yellow self with a green throat. Diploid. Seedling × 'High Noon'. Stout Silver Medal 1970. Award of Merit 1965. *Photograph by Francis Gatlin.*

'Buttered Rum' (Frances Craig, 1960). Semi-evergreen. Scape 22 in. (56 cm). Midseason. A buff pastel yellow with an India-buff eyezone. Diploid.

'Cadence' (Orville W. Fay and Julia B. Hardy, 1960). Dormant. Scape 28 in. (71 cm). Midseason. A melon self. Diploid. Award of Merit 1966. Honorable Mention 1962.

'Carey Quinn' (David F. Hall, 1960). Dormant. Scape 30 in. (76 cm). Early midseason. A red self with a gold throat. Diploid. Award of Merit 1966. Honorable Mention 1962. *Photograph by Pam Erikson.*

'Fashion Model' (Mary Lester, 1960). Dormant. Scape 36 in. (91 cm). Early midseason. A pale pink-melon blend with a pale green throat. Diploid. 'Multnomah' × seedling. Award of Merit 1967. Honorable Mention 1964.

'Fleeta' (Elmer A. Claar, 1960). Dormant. Scape 36 in. (91 cm). Midseason. A brilliant red self. Diploid. 'Alan' × seedling. Award of Merit 1968. Honorable Mention 1965.

'Grand Champion' (Mary Lester, 1960). Dormant. Scape 36 in. (91 cm). Early midseason. A canary-yellow self with a pale green throat. Diploid. 'Lady Isabel' × 'Elizabeth Payne'. Award of Merit 1967. Honorable Mention 1964.

'Hush Now' (Hugh M. Russell, 1960). Dormant. Scape 24 in. (61 cm). Early midseason. A melon self. Diploid. Award of Merit 1963. Honorable Mention 1960.

'Lona Eaton Miller' (Ezra Jacob Kraus and Robert H. Shilling, 1960). Dormant. Scape 17 in. (43 cm). Midseason. A moderate orange-yellow with very pale violet midrib. Diploid. 'Ringlets' seedling. Donn Fischer Memorial Cup 1969. Honorable Mention 1963.

'Mary Lawrence' (W. B. MacMillan, 1960). Dormant. Scape 23 in. (58 cm). Midseason. A pink self. Diploid. Seedling × 'Frances Fay'. Award of Merit 1965. Honorable Mention 1962.

'Meadowbrook Green' (W. R. Gates, 1960). Dormant. Scape 30 in. (76 cm). Early midseason. A greenish golden yellow self with an apple-green throat. Diploid. Seedling × 'Golden Galleon'. Award of Merit 1966. Honorable Mention 1962.

'Melon Balls' (Allen J. Wild, 1960). Dormant. Scape 32 in. (81 cm). Midseason. A glowing melon with orchid overtones. Diploid. Annie T. Giles Award 1966. Award of Merit 1965. Honorable Mention 1962. *Photograph by Debbie and Duane Hurlbert.*

'Puritan Maid' (Edna Spalding, 1960). Semi-evergreen. Scape 28 in. (71 cm). Early. A tangerine-orange with a faint pink halo above a green throat. Diploid. Award of Merit 1966. Honorable Mention 1962.

'Serenata' (Mary Lester, 1960). Dormant. Scape 30 in. (76 cm). Early midseason. An apricot-melon with a green throat. Diploid. Seedling × 'Ruth Lehman'. Award of Merit 1965. Honorable Mention 1962.

'Skiatook Cardinal' (Laura Pearl Hancock, 1960). Dormant. Scape 28 in. (71 cm). Midseason. A red with a darker shaded eyezone and a green center deep in the throat. Diploid. Lenington All-American Award 1972. Award of Merit 1967. Honorable Mention 1963.

'Solo' (Charles E. Branch, 1960). Dormant. Scape 32 in. (81 cm). Midseason. A light yellow self with a green throat. Diploid. 'Strutter' × seedling. Award of Merit 1966. Honorable Mention 1962.

'Sprite' (Elmer A. Claar and Scotty Parry, 1960). Dormant. Scape 28 in. (71 cm). Midseason. A clear yellow self with a green throat. Diploid. Award of Merit 1963.

'Superfine' (Orville W. Fay and Julia B. Hardy, 1960). Dormant. Scape 34 in. (86 cm). Midseason. A pink-melon self. Diploid. Seedling × 'Frances Fay'. Award of Merit 1965. Honorable Mention 1962.

'Satin Glass' (Orville W. Fay and Julia B. Hardy, 1960). Dormant. Scape 34 in. (86 cm). Midseason. A pale melon-yellow above a green throat. Diploid. Stout Silver Medal 1968. Lenington All-American Award 1971. Award of Merit 1965. Honorable Mention 1962. *Photograph by Francis Gatlin.*

'Sweet Harmony' (David F. Hall, 1960). Dormant. Scape 32 in. (81 cm). Midseason. A pinkish buff with a green throat. Diploid. Award of Merit 1970. Honorable Mention 1966. *Photograph by Pam Erikson.*

'Angel Choir' (Edna Spalding, 1961). Dormant. Scape 33 in. (84 cm). Early midseason. A poppy-red self with a medium yellow throat. Diploid. Award of Merit 1967. Honorable Mention 1964.

'Ante Bellum' (R. W. Munson Jr., 1961). Evergreen. Scape 36 in. (91 cm). Early midseason. A pale lemon-cream self. Diploid. 'Queensware' × seedling. Award of Merit 1966. Honorable Mention 1962.

'Buried Treasure' (Steve Moldovan, 1961). Dormant. Scape 32 in. (81 cm). Early. An ivory-yellow with white midribs and a large green throat. Diploid. 'Atlas' × 'Satin Glass'. Award of Merit 1966. Honorable Mention 1962.

'Chipper Cherry' (David F. Hall, 1961). Dormant. Scape 38 in. (96 cm). Early. A cherry-red self with a soft yellow throat. Diploid. Award of Merit 1969. Honorable Mention 1966.
Photograph by Rejean Millette.

'Cortis Rice' (Ezra Jacob Kraus and William Lehman, 1961). Dormant. Scape 36 in. (91 cm); flower 5 in. (12.7 cm). Midseason late. A chrome-yellow self. Diploid. Seedling × 'Ruth Lehman'. Award of Merit 1967. Honorable Mention 1964.

'Crestwood Ann' (Orville W. Fay and Robert Griesbach, 1961). Dormant. Scape 25 in. (63 cm). Early midseason. A medium melon self. Tetraploid. 'Betty Rice' × seedling. Award of Merit 1966. Honorable Mention 1963.

'Lula Mae Purnell' (Ezra Jacob Kraus and Robert H. Shilling, 1961). Dormant. Scape 21 in. (53 cm). Midseason. A moderate orange-yellow self with a brilliant yellow to green throat. Diploid. 'Ringlets' × seedling. Donn Fischer Memorial Cup 1966. Award of Merit 1967. Honorable Mention 1964.

'Tony Wille' (Elmer A. Claar, 1961). Dormant. Scape 34 in. (86 cm). Midseason. A light yellow self. Diploid. Award of Merit 1966. Honorable Mention 1962.

'Double Decker' (Benton Thomas, 1962). Evergreen. Scape 26 in. (66 cm). Early midseason. A light gold self. Diploid. Seedling × 'Cockade'. Award of Merit 1969. Honorable Mention 1966.

'Emperors Robe' (Orville W. Fay, 1962). Dormant. Scape 25 in. (63 cm); flower 6.5 in. (16.5 cm). Early midseason. An orchid rose blend with a yellow throat. Diploid. 'Spring Hill' × 'Superfine'. Award of Merit 1968. Honorable Mention 1965.

'Exalted Ruler' (David F. Hall, 1962). Dormant. Scape 32 in. (81 cm); flower 8 in. (20 cm). Early midseason. A bright pink blend with a deep rose halo. Diploid. Award of Merit 1970. Honorable Mention 1967.

'Frankly Fabulous' (Frank and Peggy Childs, 1962). Dormant. Scape 32 in. (81 cm). Early midseason. A melon-pink blend with a green to gold throat. Diploid. Award of Merit 1970. Honorable Mention 1965.

'Heavenly Promise' (James W. Terry, 1962). Evergreen. Scape 34 in. (86 cm). Early midseason. A greenish yellow self with a green throat. Diploid. 'Jade Crest' × 'Flying Saucer'. Award of Merit 1968. Honorable Mention 1965.

'Hopper Connell' (Bertie Farris, 1962). Evergreen. Scape 26 in. (66 cm). Early midseason. A greenish tint over pale yellow with a bright green throat. Diploid. Award of Merit 1968. Honorable Mention 1965.

'Jubilee Pink' (Edna Spalding, 1962). Semi-evergreen. Scape 28 in. (71 cm). Midseason late. A deep pink self with a large green throat. Diploid. Award of Merit 1967. Honorable Mention 1964.

'Love That Pink' (David F. Hall, 1962). Dormant. Scape 26 in. (66 cm). Early midseason. A pink self. Diploid. Award of Merit 1968. Honorable Mention 1965.

'Nob Hill' (David F. Hall, 1962). Dormant. Scape 36 in. (91 cm). Early midseason. A pale pink bitone. Diploid. Award of Merit 1968. Honorable Mention 1965.

'Pink Lightning' (David F. Hall, 1962). Dormant. Scape 30 in. (76 cm). Early midseason. A pink blend. Diploid. Award of Merit 1970. Honorable Mention 1967.

'Prairie Charmer' (James E. Marsh, 1962). Dormant. Scape 20 in. (51 cm). Early midseason. A pinkish melon with a deep bluish purple eyezone above a green throat. Diploid. Seedling × 'Varsity'. Award of Merit 1969. Honorable Mention 1966.

'Renee' (William J. Dill, 1962). Dormant. Scape 24 in. (61 cm). Midseason. A light yellow self with a green throat. Diploid. 'Fancywork' × seedling. Stout Silver Medal 1971. Annie T. Giles Award 1968. Award of Merit 1968. Honorable Mention 1965.

'Rocky Ford' (D. R. McKeithan, 1962). Dormant. Scape 38 in. (96 cm). Midseason. A melon with pale lavender midribs and a dark green throat. Diploid. 'Multnomah' × seedling. Award of Merit 1971. Honorable Mention 1967.

'Showman' (Frank and Peggy Childs, 1962). Dormant. Scape 26 in. (66 cm). Early midseason. An apricot blend. Diploid. Award of Merit 1968. Honorable Mention 1965.

'Suzie Wong' (Robert M. Kennedy, 1962). Dormant. Scape 24 in. (61 cm). Early midseason. A yellow self. Diploid. Annie T. Giles Award 1971. Award of Merit 1967. Honorable Mention 1964.

'Apricot Angel' (Charlotte Holman, 1963). Semi-evergreen. Scape 18 in. (46 cm); flower 8 in. (20 cm). Early midseason. A pink-melon self. Diploid. 'Garden Sprite' × 'Doctor Holman'. Donn Fischer Memorial Cup 1972.

'Bitsy' (Lucille Warner, 1963). Semi-evergreen. Scape 18 in. (46 cm); flower 1.5 in. (4 cm). Extra early. A lemon-yellow self above a green throat. Diploid. 'Pinocchio' × 'Sooner Gold'. Donn Fischer Memorial Cup 1968. Award of Merit 1969. Honorable Mention 1966.

'Buddy' (Elmer A. Claar and Scotty Parry, 1963). Dormant. Scape 32 in. (81 cm). Midseason. A rose-pink self. Diploid. Award of Merit 1968. Honorable Mention 1965.

'Cashmere' (Allen J. Wild, 1963). Dormant. Scape 36 in. (91 cm); flower 5 in. (12.7 cm). Early midseason. A cream-yellow brushed with rose blend above a green throat. Diploid. Award of Merit 1970. Honorable Mention 1966.

'Jest' (Irma W. Searles, 1963). Dormant. Scape 20 in. (51 cm); flower 3 in. (7.6 cm). Midseason late. A lemon self with a green throat. Diploid. ('Picture' × 'Ringlets') × Fancywork'. Lenington All-American Award 1975. Award of Merit 1972. Honorable Mention 1969.

'Lavaliere' (John R. Lambert Jr., 1963). Evergreen. Scape 33 in. (84 cm); flower 4.5 in. (11.5 cm). Extra early. A pale ivory becoming a salmon-pink with an apple-green throat. Diploid. Seedling × 'Dorcas'. Award of Merit 1971. Honorable Mention 1967.

'Lavender Flight' (Edna Spalding, 1963). Semi-evergreen. Scape 34 in. (86 cm); flower 6.25 in. (16 cm). Early midseason. A deep lavender self with green-yellow throat. Diploid. Stout Silver Medal 1973. Award of Merit 1968. *Photograph by Francis Gatlin.*

'Little Rainbow' (Charles Reckamp, 1963). Dormant. Scape 24 in. (61 cm); flower 2 in. (5 cm). Early midseason. A melon-pink, cream-yellow, and orchid polychrome with an orange throat. Diploid. Annie T. Giles Award 1967. Award of Merit 1973. Honorable Mention 1970. *Photograph by Andrea Weaver.*

'Pink Fluff' (Edna Spalding, 1963). Semi-evergreen. Scape 28 in. (71 cm); flower 5 in. (12.7 cm). Early. A dainty pink with a darker halo and a yellow to green throat. Diploid. Award of Merit 1969. Honorable Mention 1966.

'Prairie Chief' (James E. Marsh, 1963). Dormant. Scape 27 in. (69 cm). Midseason. A red self with a yellow throat. Diploid. Award of Merit 1972. Honorable Mention 1968.

'Sea Gold' (David F. Hall, 1963). Dormant. Scape 22 in. (56 cm); flower 5 in. (12.7 cm). Midseason late. An amber-peach blend with an orange throat. Diploid. Award of Merit 1969. Honorable Mention 1966. *Photograph by Karen Newman.*

'Step Forward' (David F. Hall, 1963). Dormant. Scape 30 in. (76 cm). Early midseason. A pink blend with a small soft yellow throat. Diploid. Award of Merit 1970. Honorable Mention 1967.

'Winning Ways' (Allen J. Wild, 1963). Dormant. Scape 32 in. (81 cm); flower 6 in. (15 cm). Early midseason. A greenish yellow self with a small green throat. Diploid. Stout Silver Medal 1974. Award of Merit 1971. Honorable Mention 1968. *Photograph by Pam Erikson.*

'Annie Welch' (Elmer A. Claar and Scotty Parry, 1964). Dormant. Scape 24 in. (61 cm); flower 6 in. (15 cm). Midseason. A soft pink self. Diploid. Award of Merit 1969. Honorable Mention 1966. *Photograph by Karen Newman.*

'Green Flutter' (Lucille Williamson, 1964). Semi-evergreen. Scape 20 in. (51 cm); flower 3 in. (7.6 cm). Late. A canary-yellow self with a green throat. Diploid. Stout Silver Medal 1976. Annie T. Giles Award 1970. Lenington All-American Award 1980. Award of Merit 1973. Honorable Mention 1970. *Photograph by Mary Anne Leisen.*

'Carita' (Mary Lester, 1964). Dormant. Scape 20 in. (51 cm); flower 6 in. (15 cm). Midseason late. A very pale pink self with a green throat. Diploid. 'Dolly Madison' × 'Dresden Dream'. Award of Merit 1970. Honorable Mention 1967.

'Green Glitter' (Mattie C. Harrison, 1964). Evergreen. Scape 32 in. (81 cm); flower 7 in. (18 cm). Early midseason. A pale yellow with a chartreuse throat. Diploid. 'Nobility' × seedling. Stout Silver Medal 1977. Award of Merit 1973. *Photograph by Curtis and Linda Sue Barnes.*

'Guardian Angel' (R. Sherman Gore and Helene Murphy, 1964). Semi-evergreen. Scape 26 in. (66 cm); flower 4 in. (10 cm). Early midseason. A near-white self with a light green throat. Diploid. Annie T. Giles Award 1972. Honorable Mention 1970.

'Hortensia' (Charles E. Branch, 1964). Dormant. Scape 34 in. (86 cm); flower 5 in. (12.7 cm). Midseason. A nicely ruffled yellow self with a green throat. Diploid. Stout Silver Medal 1972. Award of Merit 1969. Honorable Mention 1966. *Photograph by Rejean Millette.*

'Jimmie Kilpatrick' (R. W. Munson Jr., 1964). Evergreen. Scape 28 in. (71 cm); flower 5 in. (12.7 cm). Early midseason. A rose-pink blend with a chartreuse throat. Diploid. 'Sleeping Beauty' × seedling. Award of Merit 1971. Honorable Mention 1968.

'Kings Grant' (Frank and Peggy Childs, 1964). Dormant. Scape 30 in. (76 cm); flower 6 in. (15 cm). Early midseason. An apricot-peach self. Diploid. Award of Merit 1970. Honorable Mention 1967.

'Little Wart' (Edna Spalding, 1964). Dormant. Scape 24 in. (61 cm); flower 8 in. (20 cm). Midseason. A lavender self with a green throat. Diploid. Annie T. Giles Award 1969. Award of Merit 1975. Honorable Mention 1972.

'Master Touch' (David F. Hall, 1964). Dormant. Scape 30 in. (76 cm); flower 6.5 in. (16.5 cm). Early midseason. A pink self with a tangerine throat. Diploid. Award of Merit 1974. Honorable Mention 1970.

'Red Ribbons' (George E. Lenington, 1964). Evergreen. Scape 42 in. (107 cm); flower 8 in. (20 cm). A red self with a greenish to yellow throat. Diploid. 'Wanda' × 'Mabel Fuller'. *Photograph by Chris Petersen.*

'Red Siren' (Elmer A. Claar and Scotty Parry, 1964). Dormant. Scape 34 in. (86 cm); flower 5.5 in. (14 cm). Midseason. A red self. Diploid. Award of Merit 1971. Honorable Mention 1968.

'Sail On' (Elmer A. Claar and Scotty Parry, 1964). Dormant. Scape 34 in. (86 cm); flower 5.5 in. (14 cm). Midseason. A red self. Diploid. Award of Merit 1970. Honorable Mention 1967.

'William Munson' (W. B. MacMillan, 1964). Evergreen. Scape 22 in. (56 cm); flower 6 in. (15 cm). Midseason late. A martius-yellow self. Diploid. Seedling × 'Satin Glass'. Award of Merit 1970. Honorable Mention 1967.

'Pink Superior' (Orville W. Fay and Julia B. Hardy, 1964). Dormant. Scape 24 in. (61 cm). Midseason. A pink self with a green throat. Diploid. Award of Merit 1969. Honorable Mention 1966.

'Winsome Lady' (William R. Gates, 1964). Dormant. Scape 24 in. (61 cm); flower 5.5 in. (14 cm). Early. A blush-pink self with a deep green throat. Diploid. 'Satin Glass' × 'Superfine'. Lenington All-American Award 1974. Award of Merit 1971. Honorable Mention 1968.

'Arkansas Post' (Lee Parker, 1965). Semi-evergreen. Scape 36 in. (91 cm); flower 6 in. (15 cm). Midseason. A pink-beige with a deep orchid eyezone and a green throat. Diploid. Award of Merit 1974. Honorable Mention 1970.

'Bambi Doll' (Allen J. Wild, 1965). Dormant. Scape 28 in. (71 cm); flower 4 in. (10 cm). Early midseason. A pale pink self with a green throat. Diploid. Annie T. Giles Award 1973. Award of Merit 1971. Honorable Mention 1968. *Photograph by Karen Newman.*

'Irene Felix' (Elmer A. Claar and Scotty Parry, 1965). Dormant. Scape 34 in. (86 cm); flower 6.5 in. (16.5 cm). Midseason. A yellow self. Diploid. Award of Merit 1969. Honorable Mention 1965.

'Kathleen Elsie Randall' (Orville W. Fay, 1965). Dormant. Scape 27 in. (69 cm); flower 5 in. (12.7 cm). Early. A creamy melon with orchid midribs and a greenish to yellow throat. Tetraploid. ('Frances Fay' × 'First Formal') × 'Crestwood Ann'. Award of Merit 1971. Honorable Mention 1968.

'Prairie Moonlight' (James E. Marsh, 1965). Semi-evergreen. Scape 34 in. (86 cm); flower 8 in. (20 cm). Midseason. A cream-yellow self with a green throat. Diploid. Award of Merit 1971. Honorable Mention 1968.

'Rozavel' (John R. Lambert Jr., 1965). Semi-evergreen. Scape 33 in. (84 cm); flower 7 in. (18 cm). Early. A raspberry-red self with an apricot throat. Diploid. Award of Merit 1973. Honorable Mention 1970.

'Tovarich' (R. W. Munson Jr., 1965). Evergreen. Scape 28 in. (71 cm). Early midseason. A dark red with a green throat. Diploid. 'Hyde Park' × 'War Eagle'. Award of Merit 1971. Honorable Mention 1968.

'Toyland' (Charles Reckamp, 1965). Dormant. Scape 24 in. (61 cm); flower 2 in. (5 cm) . Midseason. A tangerine-pink blend with a red eyezone above a green throat. Diploid. (('Skeeter × 'Betty Rice') × ('Ringlets' × 'Lady of Northbrook')) × 'Satin Glass'. Donn Fischer Memorial Cup 1971. Honorable Mention 1970.

'Twenty Third Psalm' (W. B. MacMillan, 1965). Evergreen. Scape 26 in. (66 cm); flower 6 in. (15 cm). Early. A very pale pink with a strong pink halo and a chartreuse throat. Diploid. Award of Merit 1972. Honorable Mention 1969.

'White Formal' (George E. Lenington, 1965). Semi-evergreen. Scape 30 in. (76 cm); flower 5.5 in. (14 cm). Midseason. A near-white self with a green throat. Diploid. Lenington All-American Award 1977. Award of Merit 1972. Honorable Mention 1969.

'Celestial Light' (W. B. MacMillan, 1966). Dormant. Scape 28 in. (71 cm); flower 5 in. (12.7 cm). Early. A light cream self with a green throat. Diploid. Seedling × 'Epilogue'. Award of Merit 1974. Honorable Mention 1970.

'Clarence Simon' (W. B. MacMillan, 1966). Evergreen. Scape 28 in. (71 cm); flower 6 in. (15 cm). Midseason. A pink-melon self above a green throat. Diploid. Seedling × 'Satin Glass'. Stout Silver Medal 1975. Lenington All-American Award 1976. Award of Merit 1972. Honorable Mention 1969.

'Dorothy Lambert' (John R. Lambert Jr., 1966). Dormant. Scape 32 in. (81 cm); flower 6 in. (15 cm). A pink with a bluish mauve eyezone above a pale yellow throat. Diploid. 'Temptress' × seedling. Award of Merit 1972. Honorable Mention 1969. *Photograph by Judy Haysley.*

'Red Mittens' (Virginia Heinemann, 1966). Dormant. Scape 24 in. (61 cm); flower 2.5 in. (6 cm). Midseason late. A red self. Diploid. 'Ringlets' × 'Lilliput'. Donn Fischer Memorial Cup 1970. Honorable Mention 1972.

'Smoky Mountain' (Mattie C. Harrison, 1966). Semi-evergreen. Scape 32 in. (81 cm); flower 7.5 in. (19 cm). Midseason. A lemon-yellow with a smoky pink overlay above a chartreuse throat. Diploid. Lenington All-American Award 1997. Honorable Mention 1971.

'Viola Parker' (W. B. MacMillan, 1966). Evergreen. Scape 32 in. (81 cm); flower 6 in. (15 cm). Early. A pink self with a bright yellow-green throat. Diploid. Seedling × 'President Giles'. Award of Merit 1973. Honorable Mention 1970. *Photograph by Karen Newman.*

'Bonnie Barbara Allen' (Virginia L. Peck, 1967). Dormant. Scape 28 in. (71 cm); flower 6 in. (15 cm). Midseason. A rose-pink self with a green to yellow throat and lighter midribs. Tetraploid. Seedling × 'Crestwood Ann'. Award of Merit 1972. Honorable Mention 1969.

'Bonnie John Seton' (Virginia L. Peck, 1967). Dormant. Scape 26 in. (66 cm); flower 7 in. (18 cm). Early midseason. A light yellow self with a green throat. Tetraploid. Award of Merit 1976. Honorable Mention 1971.

'Catherine Woodbery' (Frank Childs, 1967). Dormant. Scape 30 in. (76 cm); flower 6 in. (15 cm). Midseason late. A classic triangular orchid self with a green throat. Diploid. Award of Merit 1973. Honorable Mention 1970. *Photograph by Ted L. Petit and John P. Peat.*

'Damascus Road' (Clara Mae Pittard, 1967). Semi-evergreen. Scape 20 in. (51 cm); flower 4.5 in. (11.5 cm). Midseason. A burgundy self with a soft yellow throat. Diploid. 'Hawaiian Punch' × 'Red Aristocrat'. Award of Merit 1974. Honorable Mention 1971.

'Ethel Baker' (W. B. MacMillan, 1967). Evergreen. Scape 22 in. (56 cm); flower 5.5 in. (14 cm). Early. A deep rose-pink self. Diploid. Parents unknown. Award of Merit 1973. Honorable Mention 1970. *Photograph by Karen Newman.*

'Ice Carnival' (Frank and Peggy Childs, 1967). Dormant. Scape 28 in. (71 cm); flower 6 in. (15 cm). Midseason. A time-honored near-white triangular tailored self with a green throat. Diploid. Award of Merit 1974. Honorable Mention 1970. *Photograph by Tom Rood.*

'Lady Fingers' (Virginia L. Peck, 1967). Dormant. Scape 32 in. (81 cm); flower 6 in. (15 cm). Midseason. A light yellow-green spider with a strong green throat. Diploid. *Photograph by Patrick Stamile.*

'Lolabelle' (George E. Lenington, 1967). Semi-evergreen. Scape 18 in. (46 cm); flower 5 in. (12.7 cm). Early midseason. A chrome self with a chartreuse throat. Diploid. 'Midnight Glamour' seedling. Award of Merit 1972. Honorable Mention 1969.

'Mary Todd' (Orville W. Fay, 1967). Semi-evergreen. Scape 26 in. (66 cm); flower 6 in. (15 cm). Early. A buff self. Tetraploid. Seedling × 'Crestwood Ann'. Stout Silver Medal 1978. Richard C. Peck Memorial Award 1974. Award of Merit 1973. Honorable Mention 1970. *Photograph by John Eiseman.*

'Queen Eleanor' (Virginia L. Peck, 1967). Dormant. Scape 34 in. (86 cm); flower 5.5 in. (14 cm). Midseason. A shell-pink self with a green throat. Tetraploid. Seedling × 'Crestwood Ann'. Award of Merit 1972. Honorable Mention 1969.

'Robert Way Schlumpf' (W. B. MacMillan, 1967). Evergreen. Scape 38 in. (96 cm); flower 6 in. (15 cm). Early midseason. A near-white self. Diploid. Seedling × 'Snow White'. Award of Merit 1973. Honorable Mention 1970.

'Sir Patrick Spens' (Virginia L. Peck, 1967). Dormant. Scape 22 in. (56 cm); flower 5.5 in. (14 cm). Midseason. A red self with a greenish yellow throat. Tetraploid. Seedling × ('Alan' × seedling). Award of Merit 1972. Honorable Mention 1969. *Photograph by Pam Erikson.*

'White Cloud' (Hamilton P. Traub and Julia B. Hardy, 1967). Semi-evergreen. Scape 30 in. (76 cm). Early midseason. A near-white self. Tetraploid. Robert P. Miller Memorial Award 1975.

'Amazing Grace' (W. B. MacMillan, 1968). Evergreen. Scape 22 in. (56 cm); flower 5 in. (12.7 cm). Early midseason. A cream self with a green throat. Diploid. Award of Merit 1975. Honorable Mention 1972.

'Bright Copper' (Orville W. Fay, 1968). Semi-evergreen. Scape 25 in. (63 cm); flower 6 in. (15 cm). Midseason. A bright copper self. Tetraploid. 'Gertrude Smith' × seedling. Stout Silver Medal 1973. Honorable Mention 1973.

'Cherry Cheeks' (Virginia L. Peck, 1968). Dormant. Scape 28 in. (71 cm); flower 6 in. (15 cm). Midseason late. A rose-pink blend above a green to yellow throat. Tetraploid. Award of Merit 1975. Honorable Mention 1971.

'Chosen One' (W. B. MacMillan, 1968). Dormant. Scape 26 in. (66 cm); flower 6 in. (15 cm). Early midseason. A near-white self above a green throat. Diploid. Award of Merit 1974. Honorable Mention 1970.

'Commandment' (Charles Reckamp, 1968). Dormant. Scape 30 in. (76 cm); flower 6.5 in. (16.5 cm). A lightly ruffled orange self above an orange throat. Tetraploid. 'Minted Gold' × ('Summer Splendor' × 'Paris Gown'). Award of Merit 1977. Honorable Mention 1972. *Photograph by Debbie and Duane Hurlbert.*

'Double Bourbon' (Currier McEwen, 1968). Dormant. Scape 28 in. (71 cm); flower 4.5 in. (11.5 cm). Early midseason. An orange-brown double flower with yellow midribs and a darker eyezone. Diploid. Ida Munson Award 1981. Honorable Mention 1974. *Photograph by Debbie and Duane Hurlbert.*

'Douglas Dale' (Virginia L. Peck, 1968). Dormant. Scape 24 in. (61 cm); flower 6 in. (15 cm). Midseason. A red blend with a green throat. Tetraploid. Seedling × 'Sir Patrick Spens'. Richard C. Peck Memorial Award 1976. Award of Merit 1974. Honorable Mention 1971.

'Fabulous Favorite' (Miss Edna Lankart, 1968). Semi-evergreen. Scape 26 in. (66 cm); flower 7 in. (18 cm). Early midseason. A raspberry-red self with a chartreuse throat. Diploid. Award of Merit 1975. Honorable Mention 1972.

'Golden Prize' (Virginia L. Peck, 1968). Dormant. Scape 26 in. (66 cm); flower 7 in. (18 cm). Late. A triangular bright yellow-gold flower of classic form and long standing popularity. Tetraploid. Lenington All-American Award 1987. Award of Merit 1975. Honorable Mention 1972. *Photograph by Patrick Stamile.*

'Heather Green' (Virginia L. Peck, 1968). Dormant. Scape 30 in. (76 cm); flower 5 in. (12.7 cm). Early midseason. A pink blend with a green throat. Tetraploid. 'Bonnie Barbara Allen' × seedling. Award of Merit 1974. Honorable Mention 1971. *Photograph by Karen Newman.*

'Hope Diamond' (W. B. MacMillan, 1968). Dormant. Scape 14 in. (35.5 cm); flower 4 in. (10 cm). Early midseason. A near-white self. Diploid. 'President Giles' × seedling. Lenington All-American Award 1978. Award of Merit 1975. Honorable Mention 1972.

'Jim Cooper' (John R. Lambert Jr., 1968). Dormant. Scape 30 in. (76 cm); flower 7 in. (18 cm). Early midseason. A English vermilion blend with a green throat. Diploid. Seedling × 'Mabel Herndon'. Award of Merit 1977. Honorable Mention 1972.

'Jomico' (Oscie B. Whatley, 1968). Dormant. Scape 30 in. (76 cm); flower 5.5 in. (14 cm). Early. A light yellow self with a green throat. Diploid. Seedling × ('Solo' × 'Winning Ways'). Award of Merit 1974. Honorable Mention 1971. *Photograph by Karen Newman.*

'King of Kings' (W. B. MacMillan, 1968). Evergreen. Scape 15 in. (38 cm); flower 6 in. (15 cm). Early midseason. A lemon-yellow with a deep purple-red halo. Diploid. 'Heavenly Haviland' × 'Twenty Third Psalm'. Award of Merit 1978. Honorable Mention 1973.

'Oriental Ruby' (Huber A. Fischer, 1968). Dormant. Scape 34 in. (86 cm); flower 6 in. (15 cm). Midseason late. A carmine-red self above a green throat. Diploid. (('Atlas' × 'Limonera') × ('Multnomah' × 'High Noon')) × seedling. Lenington All-American Award 1979. Award of Merit 1975. Honorable Mention 1972.

'Perennial Pleasure' (Julia B. Hardy, 1968). Dormant. Scape 26 in. (66 cm); flower 5.5 in. (14 cm). Midseason. A light yellow self with a green throat. Diploid. ('Hortensia' × seedling) × ('Hortensia' × seedling). Award of Merit 1973. Honorable Mention 1970.

'Silver Fan' (Virginia L. Peck, 1968). Dormant. Scape 28 in. (71 cm); flower 7 in. (18 cm). Early midseason. A cream-yellow blend with a green throat. Tetraploid. Robert P. Miller Memorial Award 1974. Honorable Mention 1971. *Photograph by Karen Newman.*

'Bertie Ferris' (Elna Winniford, 1969). Dormant. Scape 20 in. (51 cm); flower 2.5 in. (6 cm). Early. A persimmon-orange self. Diploid. 'Corkey' × seedling. Stout Silver Medal 1980. Donn Fischer Memorial Cup 1973. Award of Merit 1975. *Photograph by Francis Gatlin.*

'Buddha' (Oscie B. Whatley, 1969). Dormant. Scape 30 in. (76 cm); flower 5 in. (12.7 cm). Early midseason. A black-red self with a green throat. Diploid. Award of Merit 1975. Honorable Mention 1972. *Photograph by Debi Kral.*

'Buffys Doll' (W. G. Williamson, 1969). Dormant. Scape 12 in. (30.5 cm); flower 3 in. (7.6 cm). A pink with a rose eyezone. Diploid. 'Miniature' × 'Miniature'. Annie T. Giles Award 1974.

'Call to Remembrance' (Edna Spalding, 1969). Semi-evergreen. Scape 22 in. (56 cm); flower 5 in. (12.7 cm). Early midseason. A near-white self with a green throat. Diploid. Award of Merit 1976. Honorable Mention 1972.

'Edna Spalding Memorial' (W. B. MacMillan, 1969). Evergreen. Scape 14 in. (35.5 cm); flower 4 in. (10 cm). Midseason. A yellow-green throat. Diploid. Award of Merit 1980. Honorable Mention 1977.

'Elaine Strutt' (R. H. Coe, 1969). Semi-evergreen. Scape 38 in. (96 cm); flower 4 in. (10 cm). Midseason late. A pink self. Tetraploid.

'Jakarta' (Oscie B. Whatley, 1969). Dormant. Scape 30 in. (76 cm); flower 5 in. (12.7 cm). Early midseason. A light yellow self with a green throat. Diploid. 'Solo' × seedling. Award of Merit 1975. Honorable Mention 1972.

'Kings Cloak' (R. W. Munson Jr., 1969). Evergreen. Scape 25 in. (63 cm); flower 6 in. (15 cm). Early midseason. A wine-rose blend with a mauve to wine eyezone and a yellow to lime throat. Tetraploid. 'Oriana' × seedling. Richard C. Peck Memorial Award 1975. Award of Merit 1974. Honorable Mention 1971.

'Little Wine Cup' (W. C. Carter and Loleta K. Powell, 1969). Dormant. Scape 20 in. (51 cm); flower 2 in. (5 cm) . Early. A wine self with a green throat. Diploid. 'Vada Parker' × seedling. Honorable Mention 1974.

'Moment of Truth' (W. B. MacMillan, 1969). Evergreen. Scape 23 in. (58 cm); flower 6 in. (15 cm). Midseason. A near-white self. Diploid. Seedling × 'Julia Tanner'. Stout Silver Medal 1979. Award of Merit 1976. *Photograph by Patrick Stamile.*

'My Son Rob' (Lee Parker, 1969). Semi-evergreen. Scape 28 in. (71 cm); flower 6.5 in. (16.5 cm). Early midseason. A rose self with a green throat. Diploid. 'Clarence Simon' × 'Viola Parker'. Award of Merit 1977. Honorable Mention 1974.

'Willard Gardner' (John R. Lambert Jr., 1969). Dormant. Scape 30 in. (76 cm); flower 6 in. (15 cm). Midseason. A yellow self with a green throat. Diploid. Seedling × 'Dorothy Lambert'. L. Ernest Plouf Award 1979. Honorable Mention 1974.

'Yasmin' (R. W. Munson Jr., 1969). Semi-evergreen. Scape 30 in. (76 cm); flower 6 in. (15 cm). Early midseason. A yellow and flesh blend with a green throat. Tetraploid. Seedling × 'Bonnie Barbara Allen'. Award of Merit 1976. Honorable Mention 1973. *Photograph by Debbie and Duane Hurlbert.*

'Butterpat' (Robert M. Kennedy, 1970). Dormant. Scape 20 in. (51 cm); flower 2.5 in. (6 cm). Midseason. A recurved medium yellow self with a green center. Diploid. Donn Fischer Memorial Cup 1977. Award of Merit 1977. Honorable Mention 1974. *Photograph by Ted L. Petit and John P. Peat.*

'Charbonier' (Oscie B. Whatley, 1970). Dormant. Scape 32 in. (81 cm); flower 6 in. (15 cm). Midseason. A beige self with a green throat. Diploid. 'Jakarta' × seedling. Award of Merit 1976. Honorable Mention 1973.

'Chosen Love' (T. B. Maxwell, 1970). Semi-evergreen. Scape 26 in. (66 cm); flower 6 in. (15 cm). Early midseason. A lavender self with a green throat. Diploid. Seedling × 'Ora Correne'. Award of Merit 1976. Honorable Mention 1973. *Photograph by Karen Newman.*

'Little Celena' (Lucille Williamson, 1970). Evergreen. Scape 14 in. (35.5 cm); flower 2 in. (5 cm). Early. A rose-pink self with a green throat. Diploid. 'Lavender Doll' × 'Ruthie'. Donn Fischer Memorial Cup 1980. Award of Merit 1979. Honorable Mention 1975.

'Little Grapette' (Lucille Williamson, 1970). Semi-evergreen. Scape 12 in. (30.5 cm); flower 2 in. (5 cm). Early. A grape self with a darker eyezone and a dark green throat. Diploid. 'Lavender Doll' × seedling. Donn Fischer Memorial Cup 1975. Award of Merit 1977. Honorable Mention 1974.

'Pass Me Not' (W. B. MacMillan and Paul A. Kennon, 1970). Semi-evergreen. Scape 24 in. (61 cm); flower 5.5 in. (14 cm). Early midseason. A cream, orange, and yellow blend with a maroon eyezone above a green throat. Diploid. Award of Merit 1976. Honorable Mention 1973.

'Peach Souffle' (John R. Lambert Jr., 1970). Dormant. Scape 34 in. (86 cm); flower 5.5 in. (14 cm). Midseason. A peach self. Diploid. 'Double Entendre' × 'Winning Ways'. Ida Munson Award 1979. Honorable Mention 1976. *Photograph by Rejean Millette.*

'Prairie Blue Eyes' (James E. Marsh, 1970). Semi-evergreen. Scape 28 in. (71 cm); flower 5 in. (12.7 cm). Midseason. Lavender with a near-blue eyezone above a green throat. Diploid. 'Prairie Hills' × 'Lavender Flight'. Award of Merit 1976. Honorable Mention 1973.

'Siloam Purple Plum' (Pauline Henry, 1970). Dormant. Scape 17 in. (43 cm); flower 3.75 in. (9.5 cm). Early midseason. A dark red-purple self with a green throat. Diploid. 'Cherry Chimes' × 'Little Wart'. Annie T. Giles Award 1980. Award of Merit 1979. Honorable Mention 1974.

'Jock Randall' (Virginia L. Peck, 1970). Evergreen. Scape 29 in. (74 cm); flower 6 in. (15 cm). Midseason. A large rose self with a green-yellow throat. Tetraploid. Seedling × 'Tetra Sanders Walker'. Award of Merit 1976. *Photograph by Curtis and Linda Sue Barnes.*

'Squeaky' (Ury G. Winniford, 1970). Semi-evergreen. Scape 16 in. (41 cm); flower 1.5 in. (4 cm). Early. A dark yellow self. Diploid. 'Bitsy' × 'Bertie Ferris'. Donn Fischer Memorial Cup 1974. Honorable Mention 1973.

'Tender Love' (Clarke M. Yancey and Mattie C. Harrison, 1970). Dormant. Scape 22 in. (56 cm); flower 6.5 in. (16.5 cm). Very late. A salmon-pink blend with a green throat. Diploid. L. Ernest Plouf Award 1980. Award of Merit 1979. Honorable Mention 1976.

'Ben Arthur Davis' (Allen J. Wild, 1971). Dormant. Scape 34 in. (86 cm); flower 8 in. (20 cm). Midseason. A pink-cream blend with an orchid blush and a green throat. Diploid. Award of Merit 1978. Honorable Mention 1975. *Photograph by Rejean Millette.*

'Buttered Popcorn' (Frederick M. Benzinger, 1971). Dormant. Scape 32 in. (81 cm); flower 6 in. (15 cm). Midseason late. A butter-yellow self. Tetraploid. 'Mary Todd' × [('Ann Russell' × 'Elfin') × ('Ann Russell' × 'Elfin')] × seedling. Award of Merit 2004. Honorable Mention 2001. *Photograph by Debbie and Duane Hurlbert.*

'By Myself' (Virginia L. Peck, 1971). Dormant. Scape 32 in. (81 cm); flower 6.5 in. (16.5 cm). Midseason. A light gold self. Tetraploid. Award of Merit 1978. Honorable Mention 1975. *Photograph by Karen Newman.*

'Colonel Simon' (Louise A. Simon, 1971). Evergreen. Scape 24 in. (61 cm); flower 7 in. (18 cm). Early midseason. A jonquil-yellow with a green throat. Diploid. 'Clarence Simon' × 'Tim Tanner'. Award of Merit 1977. Honorable Mention 1974.

'Ed Murray' (Edward F. Grovatt, 1971). Dormant. Scape 30 in. (76 cm); flower 4 in. (10 cm). Midseason. A black-red self with a green throat. Diploid. 'Tis Midnight' × seedling. Stout Silver Medal 1981. Annie T. Giles Award 1976. Lenington All-American Award 1983. Award of Merit 1978. Honorable Mention 1975. *Photograph by Francis Gatlin.*

'Evening Bell' (Virginia L. Peck, 1971). Dormant. Scape 23 in. (58 cm); flower 7 in. (18 cm). Early midseason. A light yellow self with a large yellow to green throat. Tetraploid. Seedling × 'Bonnie John Seton'. L. Ernest Plouf Award 1987. Award of Merit 1976. Honorable Mention 1973. *Photograph by Rejean Millette.*

'Hudson Valley' (Virginia L. Peck, 1971). Dormant. Scape 32 in. (81 cm); flower 8.5 in. (22 cm). Midseason. A greenish yellow self with a green throat. Classic triangular form. Tetraploid. 'Bonnie John Seton' × seedling. Award of Merit 1977. *Photograph by John Eiseman.*

'Ida Miles' (Julia B. Hardy, 1971). Dormant. Scape 30 in. (76 cm); flower 6.5 in. (16.5 cm). Midseason. A pale ivory to yellow self. Diploid. L. Ernest Plouf Award 1983. Honorable Mention 1973.

'Little Business' (T. B. Maxwell, 1971). Semi-evergreen. Scape 15 in. (38 cm); flower 3 in. (7.6 cm). Early midseason. A dark red velvety self with a green throat. Diploid. Seedling × 'Little Wart'. Annie T. Giles Award 1975. Award of Merit 1977. Honorable Mention 1974. *Photograph by Rejean Millette.*

'Olive Langdon' (Julia B. Hardy, 1971). Dormant. Scape 18 in. (46 cm); flower 4 in. (10 cm). Midseason. A pale yellow flower with a pink suffusion. Tetraploid. Robert P. Miller Memorial Award 1976. Honorable Mention 1975.

'Prester John' (John Mason Allgood, 1971). Dormant. Scape 26 in. (66 cm); flower 5 in. (12.7 cm). Early midseason. An orange-gold self with a green throat. Diploid. 'Court Herald' × seedling. Ida Munson Award 1976. Lenington All-American Award 1981. Award of Merit 1977. Honorable Mention 1974.

'Iron Gate Glacier' (Van M. Sellers, 1971). Dormant. Scape 28 in. (71 cm); flower 5.5 in. (14 cm). Midseason. A lemon-yellow to white self with a green throat. Diploid. Award of Merit 1978. Honorable Mention 1975.

'Double Cutie' (Betty Brown, 1972). Evergreen. Scape 13 in. (33 cm); flower 4 in. (10 cm). Early midseason. A cream-yellow small-flowered double with a green throat. Diploid. (Seedling × 'Roly Poly') × (((seedling × 'Double Challenge') × (seedling × 'Double Eagle')) × 'Double Decker'). Ida Munson Award 1975. Award of Merit 1977. *Photograph by Ted L. Petit and John P. Peat.*

'Iron Gate Iceberg' (Van M. Sellers, 1972). Evergreen. Scape 26 in. (66 cm); flower 6 in. (15 cm). Midseason. A near-white self with a green throat. Diploid. 'Robert Way Schlumpf' × 'Call to Remembrance'. Award of Merit 1979. Honorable Mention 1976.

'Little Greenie' (Ury G. Winniford, 1972). Evergreen. Scape 18 in. (46 cm); flower 4 in. (10 cm). Midseason. A yellow-green self with a green throat. Diploid. 'Gay Party' × 'Green Flutter'. Annie T. Giles Award 1978. Award of Merit 1980. Honorable Mention 1977.

'My Peggy' (W. B. MacMillan, 1972). Semi-evergreen. Scape 29 in. (74 cm); flower 7 in. (18 cm). Early. A cream blend with a green throat. Diploid. Award of Merit 1980. Honorable Mention 1977.

'Pojo' (Elna Winniford, 1972). Semi-evergreen. Scape 19 in. (48 cm); flower 3 in. (7.6 cm). Early. A small dark yellow self. Diploid. Ida Munson Award 1977. Award of Merit 1980. *Photograph by Patrick Stamile.*

'Puddin' (Robert M. Kennedy, 1972). Dormant. Scape 20 in. (51 cm); flower 2.5 in. (6 cm). Midseason. A yellow self with a green throat. Diploid. Donn Fischer Memorial Cup 1976. Award of Merit 1978. Honorable Mention 1975. *Photograph by Pam Erikson.*

'Raindrop' (Robert M. Kennedy, 1972). Semi-evergreen. Scape 12 in. (30.5 cm); flower 2 in. (5 cm). Midseason. A light yellow self. Diploid. Donn Fischer Memorial Cup 1978. Lenington All-American Award 1982. Award of Merit 1977. Honorable Mention 1974.

'Ruffled Apricot' (S. Houston Baker, 1972). Dormant. Scape 28 in. (71 cm); flower 7 in. (18 cm). Early midseason. An apricot with light lavender-pink midribs and gold-apricot throat. Tetraploid. Seedling × 'Northbrook Star'. Stout Silver Medal 1982. Award of Merit 1979. *Photograph by Debbie and Duane Hurlbert.*

'Strawberry Velvet' (Robert M. Kennedy, 1972). Semi-evergreen. Scape 26 in. (66 cm); flower 5 in. (12.7 cm). Midseason. A rose-red bitone with a light yellow throat. Diploid. Award of Merit 1979. Honorable Mention 1975.

'Cherry Festival' (Clarke M. Yancey and Mattie C. Harrison, 1973). Dormant. Scape 28 in. (71 cm); flower 6.5 in. (16.5 cm). Midseason. A cherry-red self with a green throat. Diploid. Award of Merit 1982. Honorable Mention 1978.

'Elizabeth Yancey' (Clarke M. Yancey and Mattie C. Harrison, 1973). Semi-evergreen. Scape 28 in. (71 cm); flower 5.5 in. (14 cm). Early. A light pink self with a deep green throat. Diploid. 'Tender Love' × seedling. Award of Merit 1981. Honorable Mention 1978. *Photograph by Ted L. Petit and John P. Peat.*

'Fox Grape' (John Mason Allgood, 1973). Dormant. Scape 14 in. (35.5 cm); flower 3 in. (7.6 cm). Midseason. A crush-grape with a light grape bluish eyezone above a gold to green throat. Diploid. 'Heavenly Scripture' × 'Iron Gate Glow'. Donn Fischer Memorial Cup 1981. Honorable Mention 1980.

'Gleeman Song' (Virginia L. Peck, 1973). Dormant. Scape 20 in. (51 cm); flower 6.25 in. (16 cm). Midseason. A light yellow self with a green throat. Tetraploid. Seedling × 'Evening Bell'. Award of Merit 1981. Honorable Mention 1976.

'Hazel Monette' (Olivier Monette, 1973). Evergreen. Scape 22 in. (56 cm); flower 6 in. (15 cm). Early midseason. A pink self with a green throat. Diploid. Award of Merit 1978. Honorable Mention 1975.

'John Carlo' (Elsie Spalding, 1973). Evergreen. Scape 16 in. (41 cm); flower 5.5 in. (14 cm). Early. A yellow-green self with a green throat. Diploid. Award of Merit 1981. Honorable Mention 1978.

'Little Infant' (Olivier Monette, 1973). Evergreen. Scape 20 in. (51 cm); flower 4 in. (10 cm). Midseason. A white-cream self with a green throat. Diploid. Annie T. Giles Award 1977. Award of Merit 1978. Honorable Mention 1975.

'Loving Memories' (Elsie Spalding, 1973). Evergreen. Scape 17 in. (43 cm); flower 5.5 in. (14 cm). Early. A near-white self with a green throat. Diploid. 'Eternal Blessing' × seedling. Award of Merit 1981. Honorable Mention 1978.

'Mountain Violet' (R. W. Munson Jr., 1973). Evergreen. Scape 28 in. (71 cm); flower 5 in. (12.7 cm). Midseason. A violet-purple with a purple band above a pale yellow to green throat. Tetraploid. 'Kings Cloak' × 'Chicago Regal'. Award of Merit 1981. Honorable Mention 1976. *Photograph by Chris Petersen.*

'My Belle' (Kenneth G. Durio, 1973). Evergreen. Scape 26 in. (66 cm); flower 6.5 in. (16.5 cm). Early. A salmon-pink self with a green throat. Diploid. 'Sug' × seedling. Stout Silver Medal 1984. Award of Merit 1980. *Photograph by Patrick Stamile.*

'Olivier Monette' (Olivier Monette, 1973). Evergreen. Scape 22 in. (56 cm); flower 6 in. (15 cm). Early midseason. A purple self with a yellow to green throat. Diploid. Award of Merit 1978. Honorable Mention 1975.

'Russian Rhapsody' (R. W. Munson Jr., 1973). Semi-evergreen. Scape 30 in. (76 cm); flower 6 in. (15 cm). Midseason. A violet-purple self with a dark eye and a yellow throat. Tetraploid. 'Knave' × 'Chicago Royal'. Lenington All-American Award 1989. Award of Merit 1979. Honorable Mention 1976. *Photograph by R. W. Munson Jr.*

'Sari' (R. W. Munson Jr., 1973). Semi-evergreen. Scape 26 in. (66 cm); flower 6 in. (15 cm). Midseason. An orchid self with a cream throat. Diploid. 'Persian Palace' × 'Prairie Horizon'. Award of Merit 1978. Honorable Mention 1975. *Photograph by Debbie and Duane Hurlbert.*

'Sombrero Way' (Charles Reckamp, 1973). Dormant. Scape 24 in. (61 cm); flower 5.5 in. (14 cm). Midseason late. An orange-apricot blend with a deeper throat. Tetraploid. 'Commandment' × 'Crystal Ball'. Richard C. Peck Memorial Award 1978. Award of Merit 1983. Honorable Mention 1980. *Photograph by Debbie and Duane Hurlbert.*

'Sophisticated Miss' (Elsie Spalding, 1973). Semi-evergreen. Scape 21 in. (53 cm); flower 6.25 in. (16 cm). Early. Pink with a rose halo above a green throat. Diploid. Award of Merit 1982. Honorable Mention 1979.

'Zaidee Williams' (W. B. MacMillan, 1973). Evergreen. Scape 23 in. (58 cm); flower 5.5 in. (14 cm). Early midseason. A cream and pink blend with a green throat. Diploid. 'Moment of Truth' × seedling. Award of Merit 1979. Honorable Mention 1976.

'Amy Stewart' (W. B. MacMillan, 1974). Evergreen. Scape 26 in. (66 cm); flower 6.5 in. (16.5 cm). Early. A pink self with a green throat. Diploid. Award of Merit 1980. Honorable Mention 1977.

'Apple Tart' (Tom J. Hughes, 1974). Dormant. Scape 28 in. (71 cm); flower 6 in. (15 cm). Early midseason. A dark red self with a green throat. Tetraploid. Seedling × 'Arriba'. Richard C. Peck Memorial Award 1981. Award of Merit 1980. Honorable Mention 1977. *Photograph by Karen Newman.*

'Astolat' (Virginia L. Peck, 1974). Dormant. Scape 28 in. (71 cm); flower 6.5 in. (16.5 cm). Midseason. A near-white self with a green throat. Tetraploid. Seedling × 'Tetra Catherine Woodbery'. Robert P. Miller Memorial Award 1977. Honorable Mention 1978. *Photograph by Karen Newman.*

'Baja' (Kenneth G. Durio, 1974). Semi-evergreen. Scape 26 in. (66 cm); flower 6 in. (15 cm). Early midseason. A red self with a green throat. Tetraploid. 'Sir Patrick Spens' × 'Tetra Jumbo Red'. Award of Merit 1980. Honorable Mention 1977.

'Chateau Blanc' (R. W. Munson, Jr., 1974). Evergreen. Scape 28 in. (71 cm); flower 5 in. (12.7 cm). Midseason. An ivory-white self with a yellow throat. Tetraploid. Robert P. Miller Memorial Award 1978. Honorable Mention 1980.

'Chicago Knobby' (James E. Marsh, 1974). Semi-evergreen. Scape 22 in. (56 cm); flower 6 in. (15 cm). Early midseason. A purple bitone with a deeper center and a green throat. Tetraploid. Seedling × 'Chicago Two Bits'. Richard C. Peck Memorial Award 1979. Award of Merit 1980. Honorable Mention 1977. *Photograph by Andrea Weaver.*

'Dancing Shiva' (Steve Moldovan, 1974). Dormant. Scape 22 in. (56 cm); flower 5 in. (12.7 cm). Early. A medium pink blend with a yellow to green throat. Tetraploid. Richard C. Peck Memorial Award 1980. Award of Merit 1979. Honorable Mention 1976. *Photograph by Rejean Millette.*

'Double Razzle Dazzle' (Betty B. Brown, 1974). Evergreen. Scape 25 in. (63 cm); flower 4 in. (10 cm). Early. A red self with a gold throat. Diploid. Ida Munson Award 1980. Honorable Mention 1979.

'Harry Barras' (Olivier Monette, 1974). Evergreen. Scape 26 in. (66 cm); flower 7 in. (18 cm). Early midseason. A cream-yellow self with a green throat. Diploid. Award of Merit 1981. Honorable Mention 1978.

'Lord Camden' (Robert M. Kennedy, 1974). Dormant. Scape 24 in. (61 cm); flower 4.5 in. (11.5 cm). Midseason. A bright crimson-red to raspberry self with a green throat. Diploid. Annie T. Giles Award 1981. Award of Merit 1981. Honorable Mention 1978.

'Mavis Smith' (George E. Lenington, 1974). Semi-evergreen. Scape 33 in. (84 cm); flower 5 in. (12.7 cm). Midseason. A pale cream-flushed pink with a green throat. Diploid. 'Mary Mae Simon' × seedling. Award of Merit 1981. Honorable Mention 1971.

'Olive Bailey Langdon' (R. W. Munson Jr., 1974). Semi-evergreen. Scape 28 in. (71 cm); flower 5 in. (12.7 cm). Early midseason. A lightly ruffled purple self with a yellow to green throat. Tetraploid. 'Embassy' × 'Chicago Regal'. Lenington All-American Award 1985. Award of Merit 1980. Honorable Mention 1977. *Photograph by John Benoot.*

'Peach Fairy' (Andre Viette, 1974). Dormant. Scape 26 in. (66 cm); flower 2.5 in. (6 cm). Midseason. A pink-melon self. Diploid. Donn Fischer Memorial Cup 1984. Honorable Mention 1982. *Photograph by Chris Petersen.*

'Pony Ride' (Elsie Spalding, 1974). Evergreen. Scape 15 in. (38 cm); flower 4.5 in. (11.5 cm). Midseason. A light golden yellow self with a green throat. Diploid. Award of Merit 1984. Honorable Mention 1979.

'Red Rum' (Clara May Pittard, 1974). Semi-evergreen. Scape 15 in. (38 cm); flower 4 in. (10 cm). Midseason. A rust-red self with a yellow throat. Diploid. Annie T. Giles Award 1979. Lenington All-American Award 1984. Award of Merit 1982. Honorable Mention 1979.

'Sabie' (W. B. MacMillan, 1974). Evergreen. Scape 24 in. (61 cm); flower 6 in. (15 cm). Early. A golden yellow self with a green throat. Diploid. Stout Silver Medal 1983. Award of Merit 1979. *Photograph by Ted L. Petit and John P. Peat.*

'Shibui Splendor' (R. W. Munson Jr., 1974). Evergreen. Scape 20 in. (51 cm); flower 6 in. (15 cm). Early mid-season. A large creped triangular pink self with a chartreuse throat. Diploid. 'Sari' × 'Moment of Truth'. Award of Merit 1982. *Photograph by Tom Rood.*

'Blue Happiness' (Elsie Spalding, 1975). Semi-evergreen. Scape 21 in. (53 cm); flower 7 in. (18 cm). Early. A rose flower with blue edging and a green throat. Diploid. Seedling × 'Jolly Pink Giant'. Award of Merit 1980. Honorable Mention 1977. *Photograph by Pam Erikson.*

'Chicago Candy Cane' (James E. Marsh, 1975). Semi-evergreen. Scape 23 in. (58 cm); flower 5.5 in. (14 cm). Midseason. A deep pink and cream flower with a cream to green throat. Tetraploid. 'Chicago Silky' × 'Chicago Flapper'. Award of Merit 1983. Honorable Mention 1978. *Photograph by Debbie and Duane Hurlbert.*

'Frozen Jade' (Van M. Sellers, 1975). Dormant. Scape 28 in. (71 cm); flower 5.5 in. (14 cm). Midseason. A lemon-yellow self with a green throat. Tetraploid. L. Ernest Plouf Award 1981. Richard C. Peck Memorial Award 1982. Award of Merit 1982. Honorable Mention 1979. *Photograph by Katie Cook.*

'Elizabeth Anne Hudson' (R. W. Munson Jr., 1975). Evergreen. Scape 26 in. (66 cm); flower 5.5 in. (14 cm). Early midseason. A peach-rose with a purple edge and a peach-rose eyezone above a gold throat. Tetraploid. 'Bishops Crest' × 'Tetra Sari'. Award of Merit 1982. Honorable Mention 1979.

'King Alfred' (Charles Reckamp, 1975). Dormant. Scape 26 in. (66 cm); flower 5.5 in. (14 cm). Midseason. A popular older form double in light yellow. Tetraploid. 'Crown' × 'Divine Word'. Ida Munson Award 1978. *Photograph by John Eiseman.*

'Lullaby Baby' (Elsie Spalding, 1975). Semi-evergreen. Scape 19 in. (48 cm); flower 3.5 in. (9 cm). Early midseason. A very pale cream to light pink self with a strong green heart. Diploid. Annie T. Giles Award 1982. Lenington All-American Award 1988. Award of Merit 1983. Honorable Mention 1980. *Photograph by Ted L. Petit and John P. Peat.*

'Mister Lucky' (Van M. Sellers, 1975). Dormant. Scape 28 in. (71 cm); flower 5 in. (12.7 cm). Midseason. An orange-red self with a fiery red eyezone above a yellow throat. Tetraploid. Don C. Stevens Award 2006. Award of Merit 2003. Honorable Mention 1999. *Photograph by Francois Verhaert.*

'Siloam Red Toy' (Pauline Henry, 1975). Dormant. Scape 20 in. (51 cm); flower 2.75 in. (7 cm). Early midseason. A red self with a green throat. Diploid. Donn Fischer Memorial Cup 1983. Honorable Mention 1980. *Photograph by Debbie and Duane Hurlbert.*

'Soft Caress' (Harold H. Kirk, 1975). Semi-evergreen. Scape 32 in. (81 cm); flower 5.5 in. (14 cm). Early midseason. A light yellow self with a green throat. Tetraploid. 'Lemon Majesty' × 'Elfin Knight'. Robert P. Miller Memorial Award 1981.

'Stella De Oro' (Walter Jablonski, 1975). Dormant. Scape 11 in. (28 cm); flower 2.75 in. (7 cm). Early midseason. A gold self with a very small green throat. Diploid. Stout Silver Medal 1985. Donn Fischer Memorial Cup 1979. Award of Merit 1982. Honorable Mention 1979. *Photograph by Patrick Stamile.*

'Too Marvelous' (Van M. Sellers, 1975). Dormant. Scape 24 in. (61 cm); flower 5 in. (12.7 cm). Midseason. A melon-pink blend with a green throat. Diploid. 'Anne Mcnutt' × 'Pink Charmer'. Award of Merit 1989. Honorable Mention 1984.

'Agape Love' (Elsie Spalding, 1976). Semi-evergreen. Scape 15 in. (38 cm); flower 7 in. (18 cm). Midseason. Ivory with pink midribs and a green throat. Diploid. Award of Merit 1981. Honorable Mention 1978.

'Attribution' (Elsie Spalding, 1976). Evergreen. Scape 24 in. (61 cm); flower 7.25 in. (18 cm). Early midseason. A rose-pink with white midribs and a deeper rose eyezone above a green throat. Diploid. 'Thomas Lee' × seedling. Award of Merit 1982. Honorable Mention 1979. *Photograph by Karen Newman.*

'Crown Royal' (Steve Moldovan, 1976). Dormant. Scape 28 in. (71 cm); flower 6 in. (15 cm). Early. A royal-purple with white edging and a dark purple eyezone above a yellow to green throat. Tetraploid. 'Grape Harvest' × 'Magic Robe'. James E. Marsh Award 1982. Honorable Mention 1978.

'Dance Ballerina Dance' (Virginia L. Peck, 1976). Dormant. Scape 24 in. (61 cm); flower 6 in. (15 cm). Midseason. A ruffled apricot-pink self. One of the most heavily used plants in breeding. Tetraploid. Seedling × 'Round Table'. Award of Merit 1983. *Photograph by Ted L. Petit and John P. Peat.*

'Dorethe Louise' (Virginia L. Peck, 1976). Dormant. Scape 18 in. (46 cm); flower 6.75 in. (17 cm). Midseason. A yellow-green self with a green throat. Tetraploid. 'Full Welcome' × 'Evening Bell'. Award of Merit 1984. Honorable Mention 1981. *Photograph by Karen Newman.*

'Homeward Bound' (Elsie Spalding, 1976). Evergreen. Scape 17 in. (43 cm); flower 8 in. (20 cm). Midseason. A peach with a pink overcast above a green throat. Diploid. Award of Merit 1985. Honorable Mention 1982.

'Janet Gayle' (Lucille S. Guidry, 1976). Evergreen. Scape 26 in. (66 cm); flower 6.5 in. (16.5 cm). Early. A pink-cream blend with a green throat. Diploid. Stout Silver Medal 1986. Award of Merit 1982. *Photograph by John Eiseman.*

'Jean Wooten' (David Kirchhoff, 1976). Evergreen. Scape 28 in. (71 cm); flower 5 in. (12.7 cm). Early midseason. A saffron-yellow self with a green throat. Diploid. 'Crepe Wintergreen' × 'Dynasty Gold'. Award of Merit 1984. Honorable Mention 1979.

'Joyful Occasion' (Elsie Spalding, 1976). Evergreen. Scape 20 in. (51 cm); flower 5.75 in. (14.6 cm). Midseason. A deep pink self with a green throat. Diploid. Award of Merit 1985. Honorable Mention 1982.

'Ming Snow' (Steve Moldovan, 1976). Dormant. Scape 26 in. (66 cm); flower 5 in. (12.7 cm). Early midseason. A lightly ruffled cream-pink blend with a small green center. Tetraploid. 'Commandment' × 'Concubine'. Robert P. Miller Memorial Award 1979. *Photograph by Debbie and Duane Hurlbert.*

'Molokai' (Oscie B. Whatley, 1976). Dormant. Scape 27 in. (69 cm); flower 6.5 in. (16.5 cm). Midseason. A yellow self with a green throat. Tetraploid. Seedling × 'Etzkorn'. Award of Merit 1984. Honorable Mention 1981.

'Quinn Buck' (Virginia L. Peck, 1976). Dormant. Scape 26 in. (66 cm); flower 7 in. (18 cm). Midseason. A lavender self with a green throat. Tetraploid. Seedling × 'Chicago Two Bits'. Award of Merit 1983. Honorable Mention 1980. *Photograph by Karen Newman.*

'Rosella Sheridan' (Elsie Spalding, 1976). Evergreen. Scape 21 in. (53 cm); flower 6.75 in. (17 cm). Midseason. A pink self with a green throat. Diploid. ('Pink Superior' × 'Exalted Ruler') × ('Tom Boy' × 'Big Moe'). Award of Merit 1983. Honorable Mention 1980. *Photograph by Elliot Turkiew.*

'Top Honors' (Frank Childs, 1976). Semi-evergreen. Scape 24 in. (61 cm); flower 7.5 in. (19 cm). Midseason. A tailored pale yellow self with a green throat. Diploid. Award of Merit 1984. *Photograph by Ted White.*

'Yesterday Memories' (Elsie Spalding, 1976). Evergreen. Scape 19 in. (48 cm); flower 6.5 in. (16.5 cm). Midseason. A deep pink self with a green throat. Diploid. Lenington All-American Award 1986. Award of Merit 1985. Honorable Mention 1982.

'Carolyn Criswell' (Harold L. Harris and Trudy Petree, 1977). Dormant. Scape 22 in. (56 cm); flower 4.5 in. (11.5 cm). Early. A buff-yellow self with a green throat. Diploid. 'Hope Diamond' × 'Charbonier'. Award of Merit 1982. Honorable Mention 1979. *Photograph by Rejean Millette.*

'Siloam Button Box' (Pauline Henry, 1976). Dormant. Scape 20 in. (51 cm); flower 4.5 in. (11.5 cm). Early midseason. A pale cream self with maroon eyezone, and a green throat. Diploid. Award of Merit 1983. Honorable Mention 1980. *Photograph by Ted L. Petit and John P. Peat.*

'Becky Lynn' (Lucille S. Guidry, 1977). Semi-evergreen. Scape 20 in. (51 cm); flower 6.75 in. (17 cm). Extra early. A rose blend with a green throat. Diploid. Stout Silver Medal 1987. Award of Merit 1983. *Photograph by Ted L. Petit and John P. Peat.*

'Condilla' (Albert O. Grooms, 1977). Dormant. Scape 20 in. (51 cm); flower 4.5 in. (11.5 cm). Early midseason. A classic, popular double of a deep gold color. Diploid. 'Whirling Skirt' × 'Chum'. Ida Munson Award 1984. Lenington All-American Award 1991. Award of Merit 1985. Honorable Mention 1982. *Photograph by Ted L. Petit and John P. Peat.*

'Cosmic Hummingbird' (David Kirchhoff, 1977). Semi-evergreen. Scape 26 in. (66 cm); flower 3.5 in. (9 cm). Extra early. A honey-peach with a ruby-red eyezone above a citron-green throat. Diploid. ('Little Lad' × 'Call to Remembrance') × 'Honey Doll'. Award of Merit 1984. Honorable Mention 1981.
Photograph by Karen Newman.

'Mae Graham' (Elsie Spalding, 1977). Evergreen. Scape 18 in. (46 cm); flower 6.5 in. (16.5 cm). Midseason. A rich pink blend with lighter white to pink midribs above a green throat. Diploid. Award of Merit 1983. Honorable Mention 1980. *Photograph by Debbie and Duane Hurlbert.*

'Green Puff' (Elsie Spalding, 1977). Semi-evergreen. Scape 15 in. (38 cm); flower 5 in. (12.7 cm). Midseason. A canary-yellow with a green throat. Diploid. Award of Merit 1985. Honorable Mention 1982.

'Joan Senior' (Kenneth G. Durio, 1977). Evergreen. Scape 25 in. (63 cm); flower 6 in. (15 cm). Early midseason. One of the most popular near-whites of all time, recurved, creped flower with a lime-green throat. Diploid. 'Loving Memories' × 'Little Infant'. Lenington All-American Award 1990. Award of Merit 1984. Honorable Mention 1981. *Photograph by Patrick Stamile.*

'Pa Pa Gulino' (Kenneth G. Durio, 1977). Semi-evergreen. Scape 26 in. (66 cm); flower 6 in. (15 cm). Early. A silvery salmon-pink with rose-rouge above a citron-green throat. Tetraploid. (Tetra seedling × 'Chicago Two Bits') × 'Tetra My Bell'. Ida Munson Award 1982. Honorable Mention 1982.

'Wynnson' (Olin Criswell, 1977). Dormant. Scape 24 in. (61 cm); flower 4.5 in. (11.5 cm). Early midseason. A light yellow self with a green throat. Diploid. 'Wynn' × seedling. Award of Merit 1984. Honorable Mention 1981. *Photograph by Patrick Stamile.*

'Beauty to Behold' (Van M. Sellers, 1978). Semi-evergreen. Scape 24 in. (61 cm); flower 5.5 in. (14 cm). Midseason. A wide-petaled lemon self with a green center. Diploid. ('Wynn' × 'Springtime Sonata'). Award of Merit 1985. *Photograph by Ted L. Petit and John P. Peat.*

'Blanco Real' (Harold L. Harris, 1978). Semi-evergreen. Scape 28 in. (71 cm); flower 6 in. (15 cm). Early midseason. An ivory-white self with a green throat. Tetraploid. Seedling × 'Tetra Snowfall'. Robert P. Miller Memorial Award 1981.

'Joel' (Harold L. Harris, 1978). Dormant. Scape 24 in. (61 cm); flower 5.5 in. (14 cm). Early midseason. A yellow self with a green throat. Tetraploid. (('Mary Todd' × 'Jared') × 'Proselyte') × 'Tetra Carondelet'. Award of Merit 1988. Honorable Mention 1984. *Photograph by John Eiseman.*

'Rose Swan' (Elsie Spalding, 1978). Evergreen. Scape 22 in. (56 cm); flower 6.5 in. (16.5 cm). Midseason. A rose self with a green throat. Diploid. Award of Merit 1986. Honorable Mention 1982.

'Royal Heritage' (R. W. Munson Jr., 1978). Semi-evergreen. Scape 32 in. (81 cm); flower 6 in. (15 cm). Midseason. A violet-plum with a chalky violet eyezone above a lemon to green throat. Tetraploid. ('Stasbourg' × 'Chicago Regal') × 'Empress Seal'. James E. Marsh Award 1985. Honorable Mention 1982. *Photograph by R. W. Munson Jr.*

'Sebastian' (June Williams, 1978). Evergreen. Scape 20 in. (51 cm); flower 5.5 in. (14 cm). Early midseason. A purple self with a lime-green throat. Diploid. Award of Merit 1987. *Photograph by Patrick Stamile.*

'Siloam Bo Peep' (Pauline Henry, 1978). Dormant. Scape 18 in. (46 cm); flower 4.5 in. (11.5 cm). Early midseason. A striking orchid pink blend with deep purple eyezone, and a green throat. Diploid. Annie T. Giles Award 1983. Award of Merit 1984. Honorable Mention 1981. *Photograph by Ted L. Petit and John P. Peat.*

'Snow Ballerina' (R. W. Munson Jr., 1978). Semi-evergreen. Scape 26 in. (66 cm); flower 5 in. (12.7 cm). Early midseason. A cream-white self with a yellow to green throat. Tetraploid. Robert P. Miller Memorial Award 1983. *Photograph by R. W. Munson Jr.*

'Siloam June Bug' (Pauline Henry, 1978). Dormant. Scape 23 in. (58 cm); flower 2.75 in. (7 cm). Early midseason. A gold self with a dark maroon eyezone above a green throat. Diploid. Donn Fischer Memorial Cup 1982. Award of Merit 1984. Honorable Mention 1981. *Photograph by Karen Newman.*

'Simply Pretty' (Van M. Sellers, 1978). Dormant. Scape 32 in. (81 cm); flower 6 in. (15 cm). Midseason. A deep persimmon self with a green throat. Tetraploid. Award of Merit 1986. Honorable Mention 1982. *Photograph by Karen Newman.*

'Swirling Water' (Kate A. Carpenter, 1978). Semi-evergreen. Scape 22 in. (56 cm); flower 6.5 in. (16.5 cm). Early midseason. A purple with a cream-white splash above a green throat. Diploid. 'Talent Show' × 'Impresario'. James E. Marsh Award 1981. Honorable Mention 1983. *Photograph by Ted L. Petit and John P. Peat.*

'Violet Hour' (Virginia L. Peck, 1978). Dormant. Scape 25 in. (63 cm); flower 6.5 in. (16.5 cm). Midseason. A purple self with a green throat. Tetraploid. James E. Marsh Award 1987. Honorable Mention 1982.

'White Temptation' (Van M. Sellers, 1978). Semi-evergreen. Scape 32 in. (81 cm); flower 5 in. (12.7 cm). Midseason. A very close-to-white self with a green throat. Diploid. Award of Merit 1985. Honorable Mention 1982. *Photograph by Ted L. Petit and John P. Peat.*

'Brocaded Gown' (Bryant K. Millikan, 1979). Semi-evergreen. Scape 26 in. (66 cm); flower 6 in. (15 cm). Early midseason. A lemon-cream self with a chartreuse throat. Diploid. 'Buttermilk Sky' × 'Sabie'. Stout Silver Medal 1989. Award of Merit 1986. Honorable Mention 1983. *Photograph by Francis Gatlin.*

'Christmas Is' (Clarke Yancey, 1979). Dormant. Scape 26 in. (66 cm); flower 4.5 in. (11.5 cm). Early midseason. A deep Christmas-red self with a green throat. Diploid. ((Seedling × 'Prairie Warrior') × ('Battle Hymn' × 'Cherry Festival')) × 'Cherry Festival'. Award of Merit 1985. Honorable Mention 1982.

'Wind Frills' (Inez Tarrant, 1978). Evergreen. Scape 34 in. (86 cm); flower 7 in. (18 cm). Early midseason. A cream-pink lightly ruffled with a yellow-green throat. Diploid. 'Brazosport' × seedling. Award of Merit 1989. *Photograph by Ted L. Petit and John P. Peat.*

'Frank Gladney' (Kenneth G. Durio, 1979). Evergreen. Scape 26 in. (66 cm); flower 6.5 in. (16.5 cm). Early midseason. A hot coral-cerise self with a gold throat. Tetraploid. ('Papal Court' × 'Tetra Pink Hurricane') × 'Tetra Sari'. Award of Merit 1987. Honorable Mention 1984. *Photograph by Chris Petersen.*

'Gloria Blanca' (Harold L. Harris, 1979). Dormant. Scape 22 in. (56 cm); flower 6 in. (15 cm). Midseason. A near-white self with a green throat. Tetraploid. Seedling × 'Tetra Snowfall'. Robert P. Miller Memorial Award 1982. Honorable Mention 1987.

'Jerome' (Elsie Spalding, 1979). Evergreen. Scape 22 in. (56 cm); flower 6.75 in. (17 cm). Early midseason. A yellow to orange triangular flower with a deeper eye. Diploid. Award of Merit 1987. *Photograph by John Eiseman.*

'Little Zinger' (Edna Lankart, 1979). Semi-evergreen. Scape 16 in. (41 cm); flower 2.75 in. (7 cm). Early midseason. A deep clear red self with a green throat. Diploid. Donn Fischer Memorial Cup 1986. Award of Merit 1989. *Photograph by John Eiseman.*

'Lake Norman Sunset' (Kate A. Carpenter, 1979). Semi-evergreen. Scape 19 in. (48 cm); flower 6.25 in. (16 cm). Early midseason. A creped triangular classic formed pink with white midribs and a green throat. Diploid. 'Best of Friends' × seedling. Award of Merit 1986. *Photograph by Ted L. Petit and John P. Peat.*

'Martha Adams' (Elsie Spalding, 1979). Evergreen. Scape 19 in. (48 cm); flower 6.75 in. (17 cm). Early midseason. A pink self with a green throat. Diploid. Stout Silver Medal 1988. Award of Merit 1985. *Photograph by John Eiseman.*

'Midnight Magic' (John Kinnebrew, 1979). Evergreen. Scape 28 in. (71 cm); flower 5.5 in. (14 cm). Early midseason. A striking deep black-burgundy self with a green throat. One of the most popular daylilies of all time, very fertile. Tetraploid. 'Ed Murray' × 'Kilimanjaro'. Lenington All-American Award 2002. Richard C. Peck Memorial Award 1983. Award of Merit 1986. Honorable Mention 1983. *Photograph by Ted L. Petit and John P. Peat.*

'Seductress' (Lee Gates, 1979). Evergreen. Scape 18 in. (46 cm); flower 5.5 in. (14 cm). Early midseason. A burnt lavender flower edged in darker lavender with a matching eye. Tetraploid. Award of Merit 1986. *Photograph by Patricia Loveland.*

'Siloam Double Rose' (Pauline Henry, 1979). Dormant. Scape 20 in. (51 cm); flower 6 in. (15 cm). Midseason. A bright rose with a ruby-red eyezone above a green throat. Diploid. Ida Munson Award 1986. L. Ernest Plouf Award 1982. Award of Merit 1985. Honorable Mention 1982.

'Siloam Virginia Henson' (Pauline Henry, 1979). Dormant. Scape 18 in. (46 cm); flower 4 in. (10 cm). Early midseason. A pale ivory to pink with a precise ruby-red eyezone above a green throat. Very famous and popular breeder. Diploid. Annie T. Giles Award 1985. Don C. Stevens Award 1989. Award of Merit 1986. Honorable Mention 1983. *Photograph by Ted L. Petit and John P. Peat.*

'Super Purple' (Bob Dove, 1979). Semi-evergreen. Scape 27 in. (69 cm); flower 5.75 in. (14.6 cm). Midseason. A triangular deep rich purple self with a lime-green throat. Diploid. 'Sugar Time' × seedling. Award of Merit 1989. *Photograph by Ted L. Petit and John P. Peat.*

'Snowy Apparition' (Frank and Peggy Childs, 1979). Dormant. Scape 30 in. (76 cm); flower 6.5 in. (16.5 cm). Early midseason. A near-white self with a green throat. Tetraploid. Robert P. Miller Memorial Award 1980. Honorable Mention 1985. *Photograph by Karen Newman.*

'When I Dream' (Clarke M. Yancey, 1979). Semi-evergreen. Scape 28 in. (71 cm); flower 6.5 in. (16.5 cm). Early midseason. A tailored and triangular blood-red self with a very large yellow-green throat. Diploid. (Seedling × 'Prairie Warrior') × ('Stephen Fleishel' × (seedling × 'Cherry Festival')). Award of Merit 1986. *Photograph by Jay Tompkins.*

'Benchmark' (R. W. Munson Jr., 1980). Evergreen. Scape 30 in. (76 cm); flower 6 in. (15 cm). Midseason. A lightly ruffled lavender self with a cream throat. Tetraploid. Award of Merit 1987. *Photograph by Patrick Stamile.*

'Emerald Dew' (Harold L. Harris, 1980). Dormant. Scape 28 in. (71 cm); flower 6.5 in. (16.5 cm). Early midseason. A yellow self with a green throat. Tetraploid. (('Mary Todd' × 'Jared') × 'Proselyte') × 'Tetra Carondelet'. Award of Merit 1986. Honorable Mention 1983. *Photograph by Rejean Millette.*

'Gentle Shepherd' (Clarke M. Yancey, 1980). Semi-evergreen. Scape 29 in. (74 cm); flower 5 in. (12.7 cm). Early midseason. One of the most popular near-white flowers. Classic shape and lightly ruffled with a green heart. Diploid. (('Call to Remembrance' × 'Robert Way Schlumpf') × seedling) × ('Light The Way' × (seedling × 'Tender Love')). Award of Merit 1987. Honorable Mention 1984. *Photograph by Ted L. Petit and John P. Peat.*

'Green Widow' (John J. Temple, 1980). Evergreen. Scape 26 in. (66 cm); flower 6.5 in. (16.5 cm). Early. A yellow-green self with a very green throat. Diploid. 'Celestial Light' × 'Green Avalanche'. Honorable Mention 1987. *Photograph by Mary Anne Leisen.*

'Betty Woods' (David Kirchhoff, 1980). Dormant. Scape 26 in. (66 cm); flower 5.5 in. (14 cm). Early. A Chinese-yellow self with a green heart. Diploid. (('Winning Ways' × seedling) × 'Keith Kennon') × 'Cosmic Treasure'. Stout Silver Medal 1991. Ida Munson Award 1983. Award of Merit 1987. Honorable Mention 1984. *Photograph by Patrick Stamile.*

'Fairy Tale Pink' (Charles F. Pierce, 1980). Semi-evergreen. Scape 24 in. (61 cm); flower 5.5 in. (14 cm). Midseason. Pink self with a green throat. Diploid. 'Quiet Melody' × 'Janet Gayle'. Stout Silver Medal 1990. Award of Merit 1987. *Photograph by Debbie and Duane Hurlbert.*

'Kate Carpenter' (R. W. Munson Jr., 1980). Evergreen. Scape 28 in. (71 cm); flower 6 in. (15 cm). Early midseason. A large pale pink self with a large green throat. Tetraploid. ('Wilbur Harling' × 'Kecia') × 'Pagoda Goddess'. Lenington All-American Award 1996. Award of Merit 1989. Honorable Mention 1986. *Photograph by Ted L. Petit and John P. Peat.*

'Most Noble' (R. W. Munson Jr., 1980). Evergreen. Scape 28 in. (71 cm); flower 6 in. (15 cm). Midseason. A deep yellow self, slightly ruffled and with a green throat. Tetraploid. Award of Merit 1987. *Photograph by Patrick Stamile.*

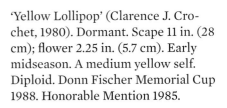

'Yellow Lollipop' (Clarence J. Crochet, 1980). Dormant. Scape 11 in. (28 cm); flower 2.25 in. (5.7 cm). Early midseason. A medium yellow self. Diploid. Donn Fischer Memorial Cup 1988. Honorable Mention 1985.

'Zinfandel' (David Kirchhoff, 1980). Evergreen. Scape 26 in. (66 cm); flower 6.5 in. (16.5 cm). Early. A wine self with a chartreuse throat. Tetraploid. 'Charles Hamil' × 'Tetra Olivier Monette'. James E. Marsh Award 1990. Honorable Mention 1984. *Photograph by Karen Newman.*

'Little Deeke' (Lucille Guidry, 1980). Evergreen. Scape 20 in. (51 cm); flower 4.5 in. (11.5 cm). Extra early. An ruffled orange-gold blend with a green throat. Diploid. Annie T. Giles Award 1993. Award of Merit 1986. *Photograph by John Eiseman.*

'Pandora's Box' (David L. Talbott, 1980). Evergreen. Scape 19 in. (48 cm); flower 4 in. (10 cm). Early midseason. A triangular pale cream with a purple eyezone, and a green throat. Diploid. ('Prairie Blue Eyes' × 'Moment of Truth') × ('Apparition' × 'Moment of Truth'). Annie T. Giles Award 1987. Award of Merit 1987. Honorable Mention 1984. *Photograph by John Eiseman.*

'After the Fall' (David Kirchhoff, 1981). Evergreen. Scape 20 in. (51 cm); flower 2.75 in. (7 cm). Extra early. A tangerine-copper blend with a yellow halo and a rust eyezone above a copper to greenish throat. Diploid. 'Cosmic Hummingbird' × 'Munchkin Moon'. Donn Fischer Memorial Cup 1996. Honorable Mention 1987. *Photograph by Rejean Millette.*

'Catherine Neal' (Jack B. Carpenter, 1981). Dormant. Scape 30 in. (76 cm); flower 6 in. (15 cm). Very late. A near-black purple self with a dark green throat. Diploid. Eugene S. Foster Award 1991. Award of Merit 1990. Honorable Mention 1985. *Photograph by John Benoot.*

'Blake Allen' (Kate A. Carpenter, 1981). Evergreen. Scape 28 in. (71 cm); flower 7 in. (18 cm). Early midseason. A deep yellow wide-petaled lightly ruffled self with a green throat. Diploid. Seedling × 'Sabie'. Award of Merit 1989. *Photograph by Patrick Stamile.*

'Brent Gabriel' (Lucille Guidry, 1981). Evergreen. Scape 20 in. (51 cm); flower 5.5 in. (14 cm). Extra early. A dramatic dark purple double with a green throat. Diploid. Ida Munson Award 1992. *Photograph by John Eiseman.*

'Charles Johnston' (Lee E. Gates, 1981). Semi-evergreen. Scape 24 in. (61 cm); flower 6 in. (15 cm). Early midseason. A narrow-petaled large cherry-red flower with a green throat. Tetraploid. Award of Merit 1988. Honorable Mention 1985. *Photograph by Ted L. Petit and John P. Peat.*

'Chorus Line' (David Kirchhoff, 1981). Evergreen. Scape 20 in. (51 cm); flower 3.5 in. (9 cm). Early. A medium pink with a rose band above a yellow halo and a dark green throat. Diploid. ('Sweet Thing' × ('Little Lad' × 'Call to Remembrance')) × 'Lullaby Baby'. Annie T. Giles Award 1986. L. Ernest Plouf Award 1988. Lenington All-American Award 1994. Award of Merit 1988. Honorable Mention 1985.

'Creative Art' (Charles F. Pierce, 1981). Semi-evergreen. Scape 16 in. (41 cm); flower 6 in. (15 cm). Midseason. A triangular light yellow self with a green throat. Diploid. 'Jade Chalice' × 'Richly Blessed'. Award of Merit 1988. *Photograph by John Eiseman.*

'Dan Tau' (Ethel Smith, 1981). Semi-evergreen. Scape 24 in. (61 cm); flower 6 in. (15 cm). Early. A smooth textured recurved cream self with a pink-blush and lime-green center. Diploid. Award of Merit 1987. *Photograph by Ted L. Petit and John P. Peat.*

'Ed Kirchhoff' (David Kirchhoff, 1981). Semi-evergreen. Scape 23 in. (58 cm); flower 5 in. (12.7 cm). Early. A saffron-yellow self with an olive-green throat. Tetraploid. (('Double Jackpot' × 'Amber Sunset') × ('Evening Gown' × 'Yasmin')) × seedling. Eugene S. Foster Award 1995. Honorable Mention 1986. *Photograph by Patrick Stamile.*

'Graceful Eye' (W. M. Spalding, 1981). Evergreen. Scape 21 in. (53 cm); flower 6 in. (15 cm). Early. A rose-lavender bloom with a purple eye surrounding a dark green throat. Diploid. Award of Merit 1988. *Photograph by Chris Petersen.*

'Ming Porcelain' (David Kirchhoff, 1981). Evergreen. Scape 28 in. (71 cm); flower 5 in. (12.7 cm). Early. A pastel ivory touched in peach and edged in gold with a wide yellow halo above a lime-green throat. Tetraploid. 'Ring of Change' × 'Tetra Lullaby Baby'. Lenington All-American Award 2001. Award of Merit 1989. Honorable Mention 1985.

'Siloam Bertie Ferris' (Pauline Henry, 1981). Dormant. Scape 16 in. (41 cm); flower 2.75 in. (7 cm). Early mid-season. A deep rose-shrimp with a deeper rose eyezone above a green throat. Diploid. Donn Fischer Memorial Cup 1989. Don C. Stevens Award 1985. Honorable Mention 1984.

'Stroke of Midnight' (David Kirchhoff, 1981). Evergreen. Scape 25 in. (63 cm); flower 5 in. (12.7 cm). Extra early. A classic deep Bordeaux-red self with a chartreuse throat. Diploid. (((('Blond Joanie' × 'Robert Way Schlumpf') × 'Karmic Treasure') × 'Double Razzle Dazzle') × 'Mozambique'. Ida Munson Award 1987. *Photograph by John Eiseman.*

'Siloam Jim Cooper' (Pauline Henry, 1981). Dormant. Scape 16 in. (41 cm); flower 3.5 in. (9 cm). Early midseason. A bright rose-red self with darker red eyezone and a green throat. Diploid. Annie T. Giles Award 1988. Award of Merit 1989. *Photograph by John Eiseman.*

'Siloam Tee Tiny' (Pauline Henry, 1981). Dormant. Scape 20 in. (51 cm); flower 2.75 in. (7 cm). Midseason. An orchid with a purple eyezone above a green throat. Diploid. Donn Fischer Memorial Cup 1987. James E. Marsh Award 1984. Honorable Mention 1984.

'Witch's Thimble' (Elizabeth H. Hudson, 1981). Semi-evergreen. Scape 14 in. (35.5 cm); flower 2.25 in. (5.7 cm). Midseason. A white-ivory with a black-purple eyezone above a green throat. Diploid. 'Elf Witch' × 'Dragon's Eye'. Donn Fischer Memorial Cup 1992. Honorable Mention 1990. *Photograph by Patrick Stamile.*

'Alec Allen' (Kate A. Carpenter, 1982). Evergreen. Scape 26 in. (66 cm); flower 5.5 in. (14 cm). Early midseason. A wide-petaled ruffled cream-yellow self with a lime-green center. Diploid. Award of Merit 1988. Honorable Mention 1985. *Photograph by John Eiseman.*

'Camden Gold Dollar' (Clarke M. Yancey, 1982). Semi-evergreen. Scape 19 in. (48 cm); flower 3 in. (7.6 cm). Early midseason. A lightly ruffled deep yellow self with a green throat. Diploid. Seedling × 'Squeaky'. Award of Merit 1989. *Photograph by Ted L. Petit and John P. Peat.*

'Fred Ham' (R. W. Munson Jr., 1982). Evergreen. Scape 24 in. (61 cm); flower 7 in. (18 cm). Midseason. A cream-yellow self with a green heart. Tetraploid. 'Chateau Blanc' × ('Tetra Ruth Bastian' × ('Astarte' × 'Embassy')). Award of Merit 1991. *Photograph by Ted L. Petit and John P. Peat.*

'Bette Davis Eyes' (David Kirchhoff, 1982). Evergreen. Scape 23 in. (58 cm); flower 5 in. (12.7 cm). Early. A lavender with a grape-purple eyezone, and an intense lime-green throat. Diploid. 'Lhasa' × 'Agape Love'. Don C. Stevens Award 1986. Award of Merit 1991. *Photograph by David Kirchhoff.*

'Enchanter's Spell' (Elizabeth H. Hudson, 1982). Semi-evergreen. Scape 18 in. (46 cm); flower 3 in. (7.6 cm). Midseason. An ivory self with a dark burgundy-purple washed eye bleeding out into the petals and sepals, and a lime-green throat. Diploid. Annie T. Giles Award 1991. Award of Merit 1992. *Photograph by John Eiseman.*

'Matt' (Harold L. Harris, 1982). Dormant. Scape 20 in. (51 cm); flower 5.5 in. (14 cm). Midseason. A yellow flower with bronze overlay and a green throat. Still popular today. Tetraploid. 'Demetrius' × ('Matthias' × 'Tetra Frank Hunter'). Award of Merit 1988. *Photograph by John Eiseman.*

'Monica Marie' (Lee Gates, 1982). Evergreen. Scape 24 in. (61 cm); flower 5 in. (12.7 cm). Early midseason. An important heavily creped wide-petaled near-white self with a green throat. Tetraploid. Award of Merit 1991. *Photograph by John Eiseman.*

'Pardon Me' (Darrel Apps, 1982). Dormant. Scape 18 in. (46 cm); flower 2.75 in. (7 cm). Midseason. A triangular tailored bright burgundy-red self with a yellow-green throat. Diploid. Seedling × 'Little Grapette'. Donn Fischer Memorial Cup 1985. Award of Merit 1987. Honorable Mention 1984. *Photograph by Ted L. Petit and John P. Peat.*

'Rose Emily' (Charlie Pierce, 1982). Semi-evergreen. Scape 18 in. (46 cm); flower 5 in. (12.7 cm). Midseason. A softly ruffled rose self with a striking green throat. Diploid. Award of Merit 1988. *Photograph by Ted L. Petit and John P. Peat.*

'Siloam Mama' (Pauline Henry, 1982). Dormant. Scape 24 in. (61 cm); flower 5.75 in. (14.6 cm). Early midseason. A wide-petaled textured yellow flower with a green throat. Diploid. L. Ernest Plouf Award 1984. *Photograph by Ted L. Petit and John P. Peat.*

New Series' (Kate A. Carpenter, 1982). Semi-evergreen. Scape 25 in. (63 cm); flower 7.5 in. (19 cm). Midseason. A clear light pink with a rose-red band, and a bright lime-green throat. Diploid. 'Arkansas Bright Eyes' × 'Shibui Splendor'. Don C. Stevens Award 1991. Award of Merit 1991. *Photograph by John Eiseman.*

'Trahlyta' (Frank and Peggy Childs, 1982). Dormant. Scape 30 in. (76 cm); flower 6.5 in. (16.5 cm). Early midseason. A grayed violet with a dark purple eyezone above a green throat. Diploid. Award of Merit 2004. Honorable Mention 2001. *Photograph by John Benoot.*

'Enchanting Blessing' (Edna Spalding, 1983). Evergreen. Scape 19 in. (48 cm); flower 5 in. (12.7 cm). Midseason. A peach-pink blend with a green throat. Diploid. Award of Merit 1990. Honorable Mention 1987. *Photograph by John Eiseman.*

'Ever So Ruffled' (Patrick Stamile, 1983). Semi-evergreen. Scape 22 in. (56 cm); flower 5 in. (12.7 cm). Midseason. A very popular classic deep yellow self with a dark green throat. Wide-petaled and ruffled. Tetraploid. 'Lahaina' × 'Supersonic Prize'. Award of Merit 1994. *Photograph by Patrick Stamile.*

'Golden Scroll' (Lucille Guidry, 1983). Dormant. Scape 19 in. (48 cm); flower 5.5 in. (14 cm). Early. A lightly ruffled cream-tangerine self with a green throat. Diploid. L. Ernest Plouf Award 1989. Award of Merit 1988. *Photograph by Ted L. Petit and John P. Peat.*

'Designer Jeans' (Sarah Sikes, 1983). Dormant. Scape 34 in. (86 cm); flower 6.5 in. (16.5 cm). Midseason. A lavender with a dark lavender eyezone and picotee edge above a yellow to green throat. Tetraploid. ('Pink Mystique' × 'Chicago Knobby') × ('Medea' × 'Chicago Knobby'). Lenington All-American Award 1995. Award of Merit 1991. Honorable Mention 1986. *Photograph by John Eiseman.*

'Rachael My Love' (David L. Talbott, 1983). Evergreen. Scape 18 in. (46 cm); flower 5 in. (12.7 cm). Early midseason. A showy golden yellow double. Diploid. 'Janet Gayle' × 'Twin Masterpiece'. Ida Munson Award 1989. Award of Merit 1991. Honorable Mention 1988. *Photograph by Patrick Stamile.*

'Hamlet' (David L. Talbott, 1983). Dormant. Scape 18 in. (46 cm); flower 4 in. (10 cm). Early midseason. A purple with a dark blue-purple halo above a green throat. Diploid. ('Prairie Blue Eyes' × 'Moment of Truth') × 'Betty Barnes'. James E. Marsh Award 1988. Honorable Mention 1987. *Photograph by Rejean Millette.*

'Sandra Elizabeth' (Donald C. Stevens, 1983). Dormant. Scape 28 in. (71 cm); flower 6 in. (15 cm). Very late. An ever-so-lightly ruffled deep yellow self. Tetraploid. 'Bengaleer' × seedling. Eugene S. Foster Award 1993. Honorable Mention 1993. *Photograph by Debbie and Duane Hurlbert.*

'Highland Lord' (R. W. Munson Jr., 1983). Semi-evergreen. Scape 22 in. (56 cm); flower 5 in. (12.7 cm). Midseason late. A very popular and classic double of wine-red color and a wire white edge on the petals and petaloids. Tetraploid. Ida Munson Award 1991. *Photograph by R. W. Munson Jr.*

'Marble Faun' (Bryant K. Millikan, 1983). Evergreen. Scape 20 in. (51 cm); flower 5 in. (12.7 cm). Early. A very recurved round cream to lemon-yellow flower with a light green heart. Diploid. 'Wynnson' × 'Brocaded Gown'. Award of Merit 1994. *Photograph by Patrick Stamile.*

'Seductor' (Lee Gates, 1983). Evergreen. Scape 18 in. (46 cm); flower 6 in. (15 cm). Extra early. A very early blooming apple-red self with a green throat. Tetraploid. 'Passionate Prize' × seedling. Award of Merit 1990. Honorable Mention 1986. *Photograph by Ted L. Petit and John P. Peat.*

'Sugar Cookie' (Darrel Apps, 1983). Evergreen. Scape 21 in. (53 cm); flower 8 in. (20 cm). Early midseason. A very famous wide-petaled ruffled cream self with a green throat. Diploid. 'Buffys Dolls' × 'Little Infant'. Annie T. Giles Award 1989. Award of Merit 1989. Honorable Mention 1986. *Photograph by Jay Tompkins.*

'Yazoo Souffle' (W. H. Smith, 1983). Semi-evergreen. Scape 26 in. (66 cm); flower 5.5 in. (14 cm). Early midseason. A very wide-petaled light apricot-pink self. Diploid. 'Yazoo Powder Puff' × 'Yazoo Powder Puff'. Ida Munson Award 1985. Award of Merit 1988. *Photograph by John Eiseman.*

'Sue Rothbauer' (Kate A. Carpenter, 1983). Semi-evergreen. Scape 20 in. (51 cm); flower 6.5 in. (16.5 cm). Early midseason. A rose self with a striking green throat. Diploid. (Seedling × 'Rose Swan') × 'Martha Adams'. Award of Merit 1990. Honorable Mention 1987. *Photograph by Ted L. Petit and John P. Peat.*

'Will Return' (W. M. Spalding, 1983). Evergreen. Scape 18 in. (46 cm); flower 5 in. (12.7 cm). Midseason. A peachy pink with a burgundy-purple eyezone above a green throat. Diploid. Don C. Stevens Award 1988. Award of Merit 1990. Honorable Mention 1987. *Photograph by John Benoot.*

'Atlanta Full House' (Trudy Petree, 1984). Dormant. Scape 27 in. (69 cm); flower 6.5 in. (16.5 cm). Midseason. A large triangular yellow self with a green heart. Tetraploid. (('Mary Todd' × 'Jared') × 'Proselyte') × 'Tetra Carondelet'. Award of Merit 1991. *Photograph by Ted L. Petit and John P. Peat.*

'Cabbage Flower' (David Kirchhoff, 1984). Evergreen. Scape 17 in. (43 cm); flower 4.5 in. (11.5 cm). Extra early. One of the most popular pastel lemon-yellow doubles, with a green throat. Diploid. 'Twin Crown' × 'Nagasaki'. Ida Munson Award 1990. *Photograph by David Kirchhoff.*

'Cajun Gambler' (Lucille S. Guidry, 1984). Evergreen. Scape 24 in. (61 cm); flower 7 in. (18 cm). Early. A burnt orange polychrome with a darker eyezone and a yellow throat. Diploid. 'Jerome' × seedling. Award of Merit 1995. Honorable Mention 1991.

'Exotic Echo' (Van M. Sellers, 1984). Dormant. Scape 16 in. (41 cm); flower 3 in. (7.6 cm). Midseason. A cream-pink blend with a washed burgundy to charcoal eye and a green throat. Sometimes double. Diploid. Annie T. Giles Award 1993. Award of Merit 1994. *Photograph by Ted L. Petit and John P. Peat.*

'Mariska' (Steve Moldovan, 1984). Dormant. Scape 28 in. (71 cm); flower 6.5 in. (16.5 cm). Midseason. A tailored pale cream-pink blend and a lemon-green throat. Tetraploid. 'Queens Castle' × 'Lilac Snow'. Award of Merit 1992. *Photograph by Ted L. Petit and John P. Peat.*

'Jolyene Nichole' (Elsie Spalding and Mrs. Shirley Guillory, 1984). Evergreen. Scape 14 in. (35.5 cm); flower 6 in. (15 cm). Midseason. A wide-petaled looping ruffled rose blend with a green throat. Diploid. Award of Merit 1993. Honorable Mention 1990. *Photograph by John Eiseman.*

'Mary's Gold' (Harold McDonell, 1984). Dormant. Scape 34 in. (86 cm); flower 6.5 in. (16.5 cm). Midseason. A large very popular brilliant golden orange self with a green throat. Real carrying power in the garden. Tetraploid. 'Creepy Crawler' × 'Spellbinder'. Award of Merit 1991. *Photograph by Ted L. Petit and John P. Peat.*

'Pearl Lewis' (Virginia L. Peck, 1984). Dormant. Scape 24 in. (61 cm); flower 6 in. (15 cm). Midseason late. A deep cream-gold self with an olive-green throat and light ruffling. Tetraploid. 'Eighteen Karat' × 'Sheer Class'. Award of Merit 1994. *Photograph by John Eiseman.*

'Scarlet Orbit' (Lee Gates, 1984). Evergreen. Scape 22 in. (56 cm); flower 6 in. (15 cm). Early. A very popular red daylily with a chartreuse throat. Tetraploid. Seedling × 'Charles Johnston'. Award of Merit 1991. *Photograph by Ted L. Petit and John P. Peat.*

'Siloam Grace Stamile' (Pauline Henry, 1984). Dormant. Scape 14 in. (35.5 cm); flower 2 in. (5 cm). Early midseason. A red with a deeper red halo and a green throat. Diploid. Donn Fischer Memorial Cup 1991. Honorable Mention 1987.

'Red Volunteer' (William Oakes, 1984). Dormant. Scape 30 in. (76 cm); flower 7 in. (18 cm). Midseason. A clear candle-red self with a gold-yellow throat. Tetraploid. Lenington All-American Award 2004. Award of Merit 1994. Honorable Mention 1989. *Photograph by Debbie and Duane Hurlbert.*

'Siloam Merle Kent' (Pauline Henry, 1984). Dormant. Scape 22 in. (56 cm); flower 5.5 in. (14 cm). Midseason. A bright orchid with deep burgundy-purple eyezone and a green throat. Diploid. Annie T. Giles Award 1992. Award of Merit 1990. *Photograph by Ted L. Petit and John P. Peat.*

'Strutter's Ball' (Steve Moldovan, 1984). Dormant. Scape 28 in. (71 cm); flower 6 in. (15 cm). Midseason. A black-purple with a very small silvery white watermark and a silky halo above a small lemon to green throat. Tetraploid. 'Houdini' × 'Damascan Velvet'. Award of Merit 1992. Honorable Mention 1989. *Photograph by Debbie and Duane Hurlbert.*

'Arctic Snow' (Patrick Stamile, 1985). Dormant. Scape 23 in. (58 cm); flower 5.5 in. (14 cm). Midseason. An ivory self with a green throat. Tetraploid. 'Porcelain Pleasure' × ('French Frosting' × 'Nuka'). Award of Merit 1992. Honorable Mention 1989. *Photograph by Patrick Stamile.*

'Barbara Mitchell' (Charles F. Pierce, 1985). Semi-evergreen. Scape 20 in. (51 cm); flower 6 in. (15 cm). Midseason. A pink self with a green throat. Diploid. 'Fairy Tale Pink' × 'Beverly Ann'. Stout Silver Medal 1992. Award of Merit 1990. Honorable Mention 1987. *Photograph by Ted L. Petit and John P. Peat.*

'Vera Biaglow' (Steve Moldovan, 1984). Dormant. Scape 28 in. (71 cm); flower 6 in. (15 cm). Midseason late. A bright rose-pink self edged in silver with a lemon-green throat. Tetraploid. 'Houdini' × 'Sinbad Sailor'. Award of Merit 1993. *Photograph by Jay Tompkins.*

'Cat's Cradle' (Ben Hager, 1985). Evergreen. Scape 38 in. (96 cm); flower 8 in. (20 cm). Early midseason. A yellow with a bronze overtone and a green heart. A true spider measuring 5.8:1. Diploid. 'Carolicolossal' × 'Kindly Light'. Award of Merit 1993. *Photograph by Jay Tompkins.*

'Elsie Spalding' (Elsie Spalding, 1985). Evergreen. Scape 14 in. (35.5 cm); flower 6 in. (15 cm). Midseason. A large ivory bloom, blushed pink with a light pink halo above a strong lime-green throat. Diploid. Award of Merit 1990. *Photograph by John Eiseman.*

'Lemon Lollypop' (Doris Simpson, 1985). Dormant. Scape 24 in. (61 cm); flower 3 in. (7.6 cm). Early. A light lemon-yellow self with a green throat. Diploid. 'Ruth Ann' × 'Stella De Oro'. L. Ernest Plouf Award 1994. Honorable Mention 1990.

'Pastel Classic' (Bryant K. Millikan and Clarence Soules, 1985). Semi-evergreen. Scape 23 in. (58 cm); flower 6 in. (15 cm). Midseason. A triangular clear pink and buff blend with a yellow-green throat. Diploid. 'Mysterious Veil' × 'Becky Lynn'. Award of Merit 1993. *Photograph by Jay Tompkins.*

'Siloam Double Classic' (Pauline Henry, 1985). Dormant. Scape 16 in. (41 cm); flower 5 in. (12.7 cm). Early midseason. A bright pink self with a green throat. Diploid. Stout Silver Medal 1993. Ida Munson Award 1988. L. Ernest Plouf Award 1985. Award of Merit 1991. Honorable Mention 1988. *Photograph by Patrick Stamile.*

'Neal Berrey' (Sarah L. Sikes, 1985). Semi-evergreen. Scape 18 in. (46 cm); flower 5 in. (12.7 cm). Midseason. A rose-pink blend with a green to yellow throat. Diploid. 'Ronda' × (('Sophisticated Miss' × 'My Belle') × 'Blue Happiness'). Stout Silver Medal 1995. Award of Merit 1992. *Photograph by Ted L. Petit and John P. Peat.*

'Priscilla's Rainbow' (Mrs. Elsie Spalding and Mrs. Shirley Guillory, 1985). Evergreen. Scape 22 in. (56 cm); flower 6.25 in. (16 cm). Midseason. A pink-lavender with rainbow halo edged in burgundy-rose above a green throat. Diploid. Award of Merit 1991. *Photograph by John Eiseman.*

'Wings of Chance' (Elsie Spalding, 1985). Evergreen. Scape 16 in. (41 cm); flower 5.5 in. (14 cm). Midseason. A deep yellow with wide rose-red band and a green throat. Diploid. Award of Merit 1993. *Photograph by John Eiseman.*

Chapter Four

SINGLES

Single daylilies in their many colors are by far the most popular flower form. The flower has a pleasing simplicity that many gardeners and enthusiasts find serene and peaceful. While many people love the doubles, minis, or spiders, the self-colored singles have retained their devoted following. As R. W. Munson Jr. once said, "There is a beauty in the simplicity of the flower, like a serene Japanese garden where less is often more."

However, hybridizers have not been happy to simply leave these flowers alone. The years have seen many hybridizing achievements, and new features have enhanced the beauty of these flowers. What began as narrow-petaled, triangular flowers have been gradually widened by hybridizers so the petals form increasingly more round flowers. As the petals increased in width, ruffling began to emerge, so that most modern daylilies are both round and ruffled. From this initial ruffling different types of ruffles have emerged, from soft looping ruffles to tightly crimped edges. Some of the newest hybrids are so ruffled that much of the petal is consumed in ruffling that extends all the way to the midrib, and into the throat area. Ruffling has also led to several types of ornate edging, such as hooks and horns, shark's teeth, and heavy gold or, more recently, green edging.

From the original color palette of yellow, orange, and rusty red, hybridizers have developed flowers of virtually every color. Reds have been clarified and intensified, and pinks have been purified into an ever-increasing range from baby-ribbon pink to deep rose. Purples and lavenders have been created in a broad color range, from a deep royal-purple to light bluish lavender. Many of them have a contrasting lighter watermark and ornate gold edging. A true blue daylily has not yet been developed, but hybrids do have eyezones of powder-blue to dark navy-blue, as shown in chapters 5 and 6. White daylilies have emerged from light pink and pale yellows to form hybrids of pure white. The black daylily has emerged from the dark red and purple lines, often with dramatic contrasting gold or shark's teeth edging. Along with color range, flower substance has increased, allowing greater weather resistance and sun tolerance.

The daylilies pictured in this chapter have been grouped into general color categories: white (cream to white), yellow (yellow to gold), orange (apricot, melon to orange), pink (peach to rose-pink), red (red to black-red), black, and lavender (lavender to purple).

WHITE (CREAM TO WHITE)

'Wedding Band' (Patrick Stamile, 1987). Semi-evergreen. Scape 26 in. (66 cm); flower 5.5 in. (14 cm). Midseason. A cream-white edged in yellow with a green throat. Tetraploid. 'French Frosting' × 'Porcelain Pleasure'. Stout Silver Medal 1996. Award of Merit 1993. *Photograph by Patrick Stamile.*

'True Gertrude Demarest' (Gertrude Demarest and Elsie Spalding, 1986). Semi-evergreen. Scape 20 in. (51 cm); flower 7.5 in. (19 cm). Early midseason. A wide-petaled tailored to lightly ruffled ivory with a pink overcast and a green throat. Diploid. Award of Merit 1994. *Photograph by John Eiseman.*

'Siloam Ralph Henry' (Pauline Henry, 1988). Dormant. Scape 18 in. (46 cm); flower 5.5 in. (14 cm). Midseason. A very popular pale ruffled ivory-blushed-pink self with a green throat. Diploid. Award of Merit 1997. *Photograph by Patrick Stamile.*

'Admiral's Braid' (Patrick Stamile, 1990). Semi-evergreen. Scape 21 in. (53 cm); flower 5.5 in. (14 cm). Midseason. A white and pink bicolor with a gold edge above a green throat. Tetraploid. 'Wedding Band' × ('Pink Scintillation' × seedling). Award of Merit 1999. Honorable Mention 1996. *Photograph by Patrick Stamile.*

'Blizzard Bay' (Jeff Salter, 1995). Semi-evergreen. Scape 28 in. (71 cm); flower 6 in. (15 cm). Late. A near-white self with a green throat. Tetraploid. 'Arctic Snow' × 'Eloquent Silence'. Eugene S. Foster Award 2002. *Photograph by Debbie and Duane Hurlbert.*

'Great White' (Patrick Stamile, 1996). Evergreen. Scape 28 in. (71 cm); flower 6.25 in. (16 cm). Early midseason. A large, wide, full and flat near-white with edges deeply ruffled and surrounded in gold. Tetraploid. 'Glacier Bay' × 'Whisper White'. Honorable Mention 2003. *Photograph by Patrick Stamile.*

'Moonlit Caress' (Jeff Salter, 1996). Semi-evergreen. Scape 26 in. (66 cm); flower 5.5 in. (14 cm). Midseason late. A near-white self with a green throat. Tetraploid. Honorable Mention 2007.

'Lime Frost' (Patrick Stamile, 1990). Dormant. Scape 27 in. (69 cm); flower 5.75 in. (14.6 cm). Very late. A green and white blend with a green throat. Tetraploid. ('Arctic Snow' × 'White Tie Affair') × 'Tetra Gentle Shepherd'. Eugene S. Foster Award 1997. *Photograph by Patrick Stamile.*

'Early Snow' (Patrick Stamile, 1996). Dormant. Scape 29 in. (74 cm); flower 7 in. (18 cm). Early. A near-white self with a green throat. Tetraploid. 'White Hot' × 'Alpine Snow'. *Photograph by Patrick Stamile.*

'Ballerina on Ice' (Victor Santa Lucia, 1997). Evergreen. Scape 24 in. (61 cm); flower 5 in. (12.7 cm). Early midseason. A cream self with a ruffled gold edge above a green throat. Tetraploid. Honorable Mention 2000. *Photograph by Sandi Jacques.*

'Pearl Harbor' (Robert Carr, 1997). Evergreen. Scape 27 in. (69 cm); flower 5.75 in. (14.6 cm). Midseason. A cream and yellow blend with a gold edge above a green throat. Tetraploid. 'Wedding Band' × 'Ida's Magic'. Award of Merit 2004. Honorable Mention 2000. *Photograph by Robert Carr.*

'Key Lime Ice' (Patrick Stamile, 1998). Evergreen. Scape 21 in. (53 cm); flower 6 in. (15 cm). Early midseason. A cream blend with a heavy braided gold edge and a grass-green throat. Tetraploid. 'Mal' × 'Great White'. Honorable Mention 2004. *Photograph by Patrick Stamile.*

'Mal' (Patrick Stamile, 1998). Evergreen. Scape 30 in. (76 cm); flower 7.25 in. (18 cm). Midseason. A cream-white blend with a green throat and a ruffled wire gold edge. Tetraploid. ('White Zone' × ('White Hot' × 'Admiral's Braid')) × ('Papillon' × 'Tetra Barbara Mitchell'). *Photograph by Patrick Stamile.*

'Dripping With Gold' (Ted L. Petit, 1998). Semi-evergreen. Scape 25 in. (63 cm); flower 5.5 in. (14 cm). Midseason. An ivory with a gold edge and a green throat. Tetraploid. ('Wedding Band' × 'Wrapped in Gold') × 'Deana's Gift'. *Photograph by Ted L. Petit.*

'Knights in White Satin' (Patrick Stamile, 1998). Semi-evergreen. Scape 32 in. (81 cm); flower 6.5 in. (16.5 cm). Midseason. A cream-white with deep heavy gold ruffling above a green throat. Tetraploid. 'Druids Chant' × 'Big Blue'. Honorable Mention 2002. *Photograph by Patrick Stamile.*

'Moon Over Monteray' (Jeff Salter, 1998). Semi-evergreen. Scape 26 in. (66 cm); flower 6 in. (15 cm). Early midseason. A cream-white with a tightly ruffled gold edge above a green throat. Tetraploid. (Seedling × 'Alexandra') × (('Tetra Cody Wedgeworth' × 'Kathleen Salter') × 'Pure and Simple'). *Photograph by Debbie and Duane Hurlbert.*

'Presumed Innocent' (Robert Carr, 1998). Evergreen. Scape 28 in. (71 cm); flower 5.5 in. (14 cm). Early midseason. An ivory-cream with a heavily ruffled gold edge above a green throat. Tetraploid. 'Quality of Mercy' × 'America's Most Wanted'. Honorable Mention 2003. *Photograph by Robert Carr.*

'Michael Miller' (Patrick Stamile, 2000). Evergreen. Scape 30 in. (76 cm); flower 6 in. (15 cm). Early midseason. A large white wide-petaled flower with a ruffled and looped gold edge above a contrasting green throat. Tetraploid. 'Great White' × 'Platinum and Gold'. *Photograph by Patrick Stamile.*

'Spacecoast Cream Supreme' (John Kinnebrew, 2001). Semi-evergreen. Scape 26 in. (66 cm); flower 6 in. (15 cm). Early midseason. A heavily ruffled light cream self above a green throat. Tetraploid. Seedling × seedling. Honorable Mention 2004. *Photograph by Francois Verhaert.*

'Make Believe Magic' (Elizabeth H. Salter, 2000). Semi-evergreen. Scape 29 in. (74 cm); flower 4.5 in. (11.5 cm). Midseason late. A cream-pink and melon blend above a lime throat. Tetraploid. 'Totally Tropical' × 'Out in Style'. Honorable Mention 2003. *Photograph by Francois Verhaert.*

'Cortina' (Patrick Stamile, 2001). Evergreen. Scape 23 in. (58 cm); flower 6 in. (15 cm). Early midseason. A smooth heavy white glistening with overtones of green and pale yellow, carrying a distinct gold edge with green highlights. Tetraploid. 'Victorian Lace' × 'Key Lime Ice'. *Photograph by Patrick Stamile.*

'Green Mystique' (Patrick Stamile, 2002). Evergreen. Scape 27 in. (69 cm); flower 5.75 in. (14.6 cm). Early midseason. A pastel cream with hints of pink. The heavily ruffled golden edges glow with a green tint accenting a deep dark green throat. Tetraploid. 'Platinum and Gold' × ('Great White' × 'Key Lime Ice'). Honorable Mention 2007. *Photograph by Patrick Stamile.*

'Isle of Man' (Dan Trimmer, 2004). Evergreen. Scape 28 in. (71 cm); flower 5 in. (12.7 cm). Evergreen. An ivory self above a green throat. Tetraploid. 'Ballerina on Ice' × 'Tetra Ruffled Masterpiece'.

'Tacia Marie' (John P. Peat, 2005). Semi-evergreen. Scape 30 in. (76 cm); flower 6.5 in. (16.5 cm). Early midseason. A white with a wire gold edge above a green throat. Tetraploid. 'Tetra Champagne Elegance' × 'Winter Palace'. *Photograph by John P. Peat.*

'President Ronald Reagan' (Frank Smith, 2006). Semi-evergreen. Scape 38 in. (96 cm); flower 6 in. (15 cm). Midseason. A wide-petaled nicely ruffled near-white with a lime-green throat. Tetraploid. 'Michael Miller' × ('Tetra Siloam Ralph Henry' × seedling). *Photograph by Frank Smith.*

'Fantastic Fringe' (Jeff Salter, 2006). Semi-evergreen. Scape 30 in. (76 cm); flower 5.5 in. (14 cm). Midseason. A pale creamy white flower with petal edges that are heavily fringed with tiny tendrils and teeth of cream and gold. Tetraploid. 'Winter Memories' × 'Lace Cookies'. *Photograph by Jeff Salter.*

'Ice Cream Emperor' (Dan Trimmer, 2006). Evergreen. Scape 25 in. (63 cm); flower 5.5 in. (14 cm). Early midseason. A beautifully ruffled pale ivory self with a striking bright green throat. Tetraploid. 'Isle of Man' × 'Tetra Evelyn Gates'. *Photograph by Dan Trimmer.*

YELLOW (YELLOW TO GOLD)

'Shockwave' (Edgar Brown, 1978). Semi-evergreen. Scape 30 in. (76 cm); flower 6 in. (15 cm). Early. A yellow-gold self with a gold throat. Tetraploid. 'Fabulous Prize' × 'Grand Prize'. Award of Merit 1983. Honorable Mention 1980. *Photograph by Debbie and Duane Hurlbert.*

'Siloam Spizz' (Pauline Henry, 1986). Dormant. Scape 18 in. (46 cm); flower 4.5 in. (11.5 cm). Midseason. A yellow self with a green throat. Diploid. L. Ernest Plouf Award 1991. Honorable Mention 1990.

'Betty Warren Woods' (R. W. Munson Jr., 1987). Evergreen. Scape 24 in. (61 cm); flower 4.5 in. (11.5 cm). Early midseason. A highly ruffled cream-yellow self with a green center. Very important vigorous fertile breeder. Tetraploid. ('Capella Light' × 'India House') × 'Ruffled Dude'. Award of Merit 2000. Honorable Mention 1997. *Photograph by Patrick Stamile.*

'Victorian Collar' (Patrick Stamile, 1988). Semi-evergreen. Scape 24 in. (61 cm); flower 6.25 in. (16 cm). Early midseason. A large round gold self with a green throat. Tetraploid. 'Ever So Ruffled' × 'Tetra Homeward Bound'. Award of Merit 1996. *Photograph by Patrick Stamile.*

'My Darling Clementine' (Jeff Salter, 1988). Evergreen. Scape 21 in. (53 cm); flower 4.5 in. (11.5 cm). Early. A very early blooming wide-petaled yellow self with a green throat. Tetraploid. Award of Merit 1997. Honorable Mention 1994. *Photograph by Patrick Stamile.*

'Ruffled Perfection' (Jack B. Carpenter, 1989). Semi-evergreen. Scape 24 in. (61 cm); flower 7 in. (18 cm). Early. A lemon-yellow self with a green throat. Diploid. Award of Merit 2000. Honorable Mention 1997. *Photograph by John Eiseman.*

'Siloam Amazing Grace' (Pauline Henry, 1989). Dormant. Scape 24 in. (61 cm); flower 5.5 in. (14 cm). Early midseason. A ruffled yellow self with a strong green throat. Diploid. Award of Merit 1996. *Photograph by Ted L. Petit and John P. Peat.*

'Smuggler's Gold' (Charles E. Branch, 1991). Dormant. Scape 24 in. (61 cm); flower 6 in. (15 cm). Midseason. A gold with a bronze overlay and a huge lemon-yellow throat. Tetraploid. 'Gentleman Lou' × 'Matt'. Award of Merit 2002. Honorable Mention 1997.

'Bill Norris' (David Kirchhoff, 1993). Semi-evergreen. Scape 29 in. (74 cm); flower 5 in. (12.7 cm). Midseason. A brilliant sunny gold self. Tetraploid. Seedling × 'Bit More Class'. Stout Silver Medal 2002. Award of Merit 2000. Honorable Mention 1997. *Photograph by David Kirchhoff.*

'Coyote Moon' (David Kirchhoff, 1994). Evergreen. Scape 28 in. (71 cm); flower 3.5 in. (9 cm). Extra early. A medium yellow with a gray-cinnamon halo. Tetraploid. ((Seedling × 'Tetra Tiny Tiki') × 'Bit More Class') × ((seedling × 'Tetra Moonlight Mist') × 'Tetra Sugar Cookie'). Honorable Mention 1998. *Photograph by Debbie and Duane Hurlbert.*

'Good Morning America' (Jeff Salter, 1992). Semi-evergreen. Scape 26 in. (66 cm); flower 6 in. (15 cm). Midseason. An ivory cream-gold blend with a green throat. Tetraploid. 'Lady Arabella' × seedling. Honorable Mention 2005. *Photograph by Ted L. Petit and John P. Peat.*

'Sherry Lane Carr' (Robert Carr, 1993). Evergreen. Scape 23 in. (58 cm); flower 6.5 in. (16.5 cm). Early midseason. A well-branched creamy butter-yellow self with a very high bud count, and a heavily ruffled gold edge. Tetraploid. Award of Merit 2002. Honorable Mention 1999. *Photograph by Ted L. Petit and John P. Peat.*

'Ferengi Gold' (Ted L. Petit, 1994). Dormant. Scape 19 in. (48 cm); flower 5.5 in. (14 cm). Early midseason. A cream-yellow with a pink-blush, green throat and tightly crimped ruffled edges. Very vigorous grower. Tetraploid. 'Betty Warren Woods' × ('Emerald Dawn' × 'Betty Warren Woods'). Award of Merit 2002. Honorable Mention 1998. *Photograph by Ted L. Petit.*

'Larry Grace' (Jeff Salter, 1994). Semi-evergreen. Scape 24 in. (61 cm); flower 6 in. (15 cm). Early midseason. A yellow self with a pink overlay, a heavily ruffled gold edge above a green throat. Tetraploid. 'Ben Adams' × ('Untamed Glory' × 'Kathleen Salter'). Award of Merit 2003. Honorable Mention 2000. *Photograph by Ted L. Petit and John P. Peat.*

'Ram' (Oscie B. Whatley, 1994). Semi-evergreen. Scape 25 in. (63 cm); flower 7 in. (18 cm). Midseason. A yellow self with a white edge above a green throat. Tetraploid. 'Fred Ham' × seedling. Award of Merit 2005. Honorable Mention 2002. *Photograph by Debbie and Duane Hurlbert.*

'All the Magic' (Jeff Salter, 1996). Semi-evergreen. Scape 26 in. (66 cm); flower 5.5 in. (14 cm). Early midseason. A cream-yellow blend with a green throat. Tetraploid. *Photograph by Ted L. Petit and John P. Peat.*

'Ever Delightful' (Jeff Salter, 1996). Evergreen. Scape 26 in. (66 cm); flower 5 in. (12.7 cm). Midseason. A lightly ruffled pale cream blend with a cinnamon edge above a green throat. Tetraploid. 'Untamed Glory' × seedling.

'America's Most Wanted' (Robert Carr, 1997). Evergreen. Scape 27 in. (69 cm); flower 6 in. (15 cm). Early. A highly ruffled well-branched golden creamy melon-yellow self with a green throat. Tetraploid. 'Sherry Lane Carr' × seedling. Award of Merit 2003. Honorable Mention 2000. *Photograph by Robert Carr.*

'Heaven's Glory' (Larry Grace, 1997). Evergreen. Scape 24 in. (61 cm); flower 6 in. (15 cm). Midseason. A yellow blend with a large yellow band above a yellow throat. Tetraploid. 'Wedding Band' × 'Ida's Magic'. Honorable Mention 2001. *Photograph by Sandi Jacques.*

'Hot Cakes' (Matthew Kaskel, 1997). Evergreen. Scape 26 in. (66 cm); flower 6 in. (15 cm). Midseason. A very ruffled golden yellow self with thick substance. Tetraploid. ('Walking on Sunshine' × ('Ever So Ruffled' × 'Glad All Over')) × 'Senegal'. *Photograph by Debbie and Duane Hurlbert.*

'Lace Cookies' (Matthew Kaskel, 1998). Evergreen. Scape 30 in. (76 cm); flower 5 in. (12.7 cm). Early. A cream-yellow ruffled self with a gold to chartreuse edge above a small green throat. Tetraploid. Seedling × seedling. Honorable Mention 2002. *Photograph by Francois Verhaert.*

'Bas Relief' (Patrick Stamile, 1999). Evergreen. Scape 26 in. (66 cm); flower 7 in. (18 cm). Early. A gold and yellow blend with a green throat. Tetraploid. 'Apricot Jade' × ('Olympic Showcase' × 'Betty Warren Woods'). *Photograph by Patrick Stamile.*

'Spacecoast Krinkles' (John Kinnebrew, 1999). Dormant. Scape 26 in. (66 cm); flower 5.75 in. (14.6 cm). Early. A heavily ruffled bright tangerine-peach self with a darker peach throat. Tetraploid. 'Betty Warren Woods' × seedling. *Photograph by Tracy Heldt.*

'Squash Dolly' (Tim Bell, 1999). Evergreen. Scape 24 in. (61 cm); flower 6 in. (15 cm). Midseason. A cream-yellow self with a green throat. Tetraploid. 'Betty Warren Woods' × 'Admiral's Braid'.

'Macho Macho Man' (Jeff Salter, 1998). Semi-evergreen. Scape 26 in. (66 cm); flower 7 in. (18 cm). Early midseason. A cream with a gold edge above a green throat. Tetraploid. Honorable Mention 2003. *Photograph by Jeff Saiter.*

'Spacecoast Discovery' (John Kinnebrew, 1998). Semi-evergreen. Scape 30 in. (76 cm); flower 6 in. (15 cm). Midseason. A cream-yellow with a gold edge and a yellow throat. Tetraploid. 'Ida's Magic' × 'Wedding Band'.

'J. T. Davis' (Larry Grace, 1999). Evergreen. Scape 24 in. (61 cm); flower 5 in. (12.7 cm). Midseason. A light yellowish pink-blush blend with gold ruffled edges and a green throat. Tetraploid. 'Surprises Inside' × seedling. Award of Merit 2007. Honorable Mention 2004. *Photograph by Larry Grace.*

'Fun in the Sunshine' (Jeff Salter, 2000). Evergreen. Scape 28 in. (71 cm); flower 6 in. (15 cm). Midseason. A lightly ruffled yellow-cream self with a bright green throat. Tetraploid. 'Summertime Splendor' × 'Larry Grace'. *Photograph by Sandi Jacques.*

'Deflector Dish' (John P. Peat, 2001). Semi-evergreen. Scape 24 in. (61 cm); flower 5.5 in. (14 cm). Midseason. A very round ruffled creamy gold flower with a deep green throat and a darker gold edge. Tetraploid. 'Capella Nova' × 'Diamonds in the Sky'. *Photograph by John P. Peat.*

'Spacecoast Cotton Candy' (John Kinnebrew, 2001). Semi-evergreen. Scape 25 in. (63 cm); flower 5 in. (12.7 cm). Early. Large, heavy, looping ruffles completely surround each peach-pink blossom continuing down into a green throat. Tetraploid. 'Spacecoast Sweetness' × 'Desert Dreams'. Honorable Mention 2004. *Photograph by Debbie and Duane Hurlbert.*

'Tough Cookie' (John P. Peat, 2001). Semi-evergreen. Scape 24 in. (61 cm); flower 6 in. (15 cm). Midseason. A narrow-petaled ruffled gold with plastic-like substance above a green throat. Tetraploid. 'Ferengi Gold' × 'Sherry Lane Carr'. *Photograph by John P. Peat.*

'Empire Returns' (Jeff Salter, 2001). Semi-evergreen. Scape 28 in. (71 cm); flower 6 in. (15 cm). Midseason. A bright golden yellow with deep sculpting and heavy substance. Tetraploid. 'Empire Strikes Back' × 'Childhood Treasure'. *Photograph by Susan Okrasinski.*

'Russell Henry Taft' (Jack B. Carpenter, 2002). Dormant. Scape 24 in. (61 cm); flower 6.5 in. (16.5 cm). Midseason. A lime-yellow blend above a green throat. Diploid. *Photograph by Jack B. Carpenter.*

'Shelter Cove' (Jeff Corbett, 2002). Evergreen. Scape 30 in. (76 cm); flower 5 in. (12.7 cm). Early midseason. A deeply sculpted, heavily ruffled, wide-petaled, cream-yellow blend above a green throat. Tetraploid. 'Ed Brown' × 'America's Most Wanted'. *Photograph by Jeff Corbett.*

'Spacecoast Gold Bonanza' (John Kinnebrew, 2002). Semi-evergreen. Scape 24 in. (61 cm); flower 6.75 in. (17 cm). Early midseason. A golden round flat form with plump wide petals and sepals. A terrific ruffled golden edge, and very heavy substance. Tetraploid. 'Spacecoast Krinkles' × 'Sherry Lane Carr'. Honorable Mention 2005. *Photograph by Francois Verhaert.*

'Spacecoast Passion Released' (John Kinnebrew, 2002). Evergreen. Scape 30 in. (76 cm); flower 6 in. (15 cm). Early midseason. A pink-yellow blend with a gold edge above a green throat. Tetraploid. 'Spacecoast Starburst' × 'Childhood Treasure'. *Photograph by Francois Verhaert.*

'Candied Popcorn Perfection' (Robert Carr, 2003). Evergreen. Scape 25 in. (63 cm); flower 5.75 in. (14.6 cm). Midseason. A cream-yellow with a heavily ruffled yellow to gold edge above small dark green center. Tetraploid. 'Pearl Harbor' × 'Presumed Innocent'. Honorable Mention 2007. *Photograph by John Benoot.*

'Florida's Garden Light' (Frank Smith and Larry Grace, 2003). Semi-evergreen. Scape 28 in. (71 cm); flower 5.5 in. (14 cm). Midseason. A very ruffled, cream flower with a gold edge and a chartreuse overlay above a bright green throat. Tetraploid. Seedling × seedling. *Photograph by Francois Verhaert.*

'Power of Silence' (Ted L. Petit, 2003). Semi-evergreen. Scape 24 in. (61 cm); flower 5.5 in. (14 cm). Midseason. A gold and yellow self above a green throat. Tetraploid. 'Karl Petersen' × 'Joint Venture'. *Photograph by Ted L. Petit.*

'Doppler Effect' (John P. Peat, 2003). Semi-evergreen. Scape 25 in. (63 cm); flower 6.25 in. (16 cm). Early midseason. A cream with wire orange edge above a dark green throat. Tetraploid. ('Something Wonderful' × ('Deanna's Gift' × 'Betty Warren Woods')) × 'Joint Venture'. *Photograph by John P. Peat.*

'Patsy Carpenter' (Jack B. Carpenter, 2003). Evergreen. Scape 26 in. (66 cm); flower 7 in. (18 cm). Early. A nicely ruffled yellow polychrome above a bright green throat. Tetraploid. 'Bill Norris' × 'Tetra Rainbow Radiance'. *Photograph by Francois Verhaert.*

'Sarasota' (Ted L. Petit, 2003). Semi-evergreen. Scape 27 in. (69 cm); flower 5.5 in. (14 cm). Midseason. A gold self above a green throat. Tetraploid. 'Bernice Pappas' × 'New Ways to Dream'. *Photograph by Ted L. Petit.*

'Wonders Never Cease' (Robert Carr, 2003). Evergreen. Scape 28 in. (71 cm); flower 5.75 in. (14.6 cm). Early midseason. A pale yellow to cream-gold flower with thick substance and a heavily ruffled gold edge above a deep green throat. Tetraploid. 'Ballerina on Ice' × 'Sherry Lane Carr'. *Photograph by Sue Brown.*

'Creator's Song' (Tim Bell, 2004). Evergreen. Scape 28 in. (71 cm); flower 6.5 in. (16.5 cm). Early midseason. A sunny yellow blend with a pink tint above a green throat. Tetraploid. 'Summertime Splendor' × seedling. *Photograph by Tim Bell.*

'Evelyn Kloeris' (Jack B. Carpenter, 2004). Evergreen. Scape 23 in. (58 cm); flower 6.5 in. (16.5 cm). Early midseason. A cream-yellow polychrome with yellow-gold edge above yellow throat. Tetraploid. 'Never Say Goodbye' × ('Sea Swept Dreams' × 'Tetra Magical Melody'). Honorable Mention 2007. *Photograph by Jack B. Carpenter.*

'Expensive Taste' (Ted L. Petit, 2004). Semi-evergreen. Scape 20 in. (51 cm); flower 6 in. (15 cm). Midseason. A cream with a gold edge above a green throat. Tetraploid. 'Dreams of Heroes' × 'J. T. Davis'. *Photograph by Ted L. Petit.*

'Golden Tentacles' (Ludlow Lambertson, 2004). Semi-evergreen. Scape 26 in. (66 cm); flower 5.5 in. (14 cm). Early midseason. A medium gold with dark gold tentacle edge above a green throat. Tetraploid. Seedling × 'Way Cool'. *Photograph by Ludlow Lambertson.*

'Moment in the Sun' (Larry Grace and Frank Smith, 2004). Semi-evergreen. Scape 28 in. (71 cm); flower 6.5 in. (16.5 cm). Midseason. A cream self with a heavily ruffled gold edge above a small green center. Tetraploid. 'Tetra Siloam Ralph Henry' × 'J. T. Davis'. Honorable Mention 2007. *Photograph by Frank Smith.*

'Piranha Smiles' (Eddy Scott, 2004). Evergreen. Scape 25 in. (63 cm); flower 5 in. (12.7 cm). Early. A yellow blend with pink highlights and a thick gold hooked edge above a green throat. Tetraploid. 'Golden Baubles' × 'Macho Macho Man'.

'Song of the Empire' (Jack B. Carpenter, 2004). Semi-evergreen. Scape 28 in. (71 cm); flower 5.75 in. (14.6 cm). Midseason. A gold self above a green throat. Tetraploid. 'Supreme Empire' × 'America's Most Wanted'.

<0295; JC2:002> 'Bonnie Holley' (Jeff Corbett, 2005). Evergreen. Scape 30 in. (76 cm); flower 6 in. (15 cm). Midseason. A peach-melon blend above a green throat, with grooving extending out from the throat. Tetraploid. 'Ed Brown' × 'America's Most Wanted'. *Photograph by Jeff Corbett.*

'Aunt Leona' (Frank Smith, 2006). Semi-evergreen. Scape 28 in. (71 cm); flower 7 in. (18 cm). Midseason. A clear-colored, soft pastel coral with large broad ruffled petals complementing the large blunt sepals. Tetraploid. 'Spanish Wedding Gown' × 'Porto Fino'. *Photograph by Frank Smith.*

'Helen Bessinger' (Herbert Phelps, 2006). Semi-evergreen. Scape 26 in. (66 cm); flower 6 in. (15 cm). Early midseason. A wide-petaled peach with heavy substance and a gold edge above a deep bright green throat. Tetraploid. ('J. T. Davis' × 'Great White') × ('Glacier Bay' × 'Tetra Siloam Ralph Henry'). *Photograph by Herbert Phelps.*

'Holy Guacamole' (Jeff Salter, 2006). Semi-evergreen. Scape 26 in. (66 cm); flower 5 in. (12.7 cm). Early midseason. A deep gold with a peach overlay carrying a heavily ruffled dark green edge above a deep dark green throat. Tetraploid. *Photograph by Francois Verhaert.*

'Move Over Dolly' (John P. Peat, 2006). Semi-evergreen. Scape 28 in. (71 cm); flower 6.5 in. (16.5 cm). Early midseason. A wonderful, ruffled golden yellow with a green throat. When the humidity increases, the petal edges form salmon-pink mountainous protruberances. Very unique. Tetraploid. 'Nature's Showman' × 'Darla Anita'. *Photograph by John P. Peat.*

'Pansy Yellow' (Patrick Stamile, 2006). Evergreen. Scape 34 in. (86 cm); flower 7 in. (18 cm). Midseason. A beautifully ruffled cream-yellow flower above a green throat. Tetraploid. (('Ballerina on Ice' × ('Key Lime Ice' × 'Great White')) × 'Dream Runner'). *Photograph by Patrick Stamile.*

'Plastic Surgeon' (John P. Peat, 2006). Semi-evergreen. Scape 15 in. (38 cm); flower 6.5 in. (16.5 cm). Early mid-season. A very heavy, waxy substance flower with wide heavily ruffled petals above a dark green throat. Tetraploid. 'Macho Macho Man' × 'Felecia Grace'. *Photograph by John P. Peat.*

'Pretty Bird' (John P. Peat, 2006). Semi-evergreen. Scape 23 in. (58 cm); flower 6.5 in. (16.5 cm). Early midseason. A golden cream with a pink-blush flower, carrying heavily ruffled chartreuse-gold edges above a very dark green throat. Tetraploid. 'Moment in the Sun' × 'Angels and Ecstacy'. *Photograph by John P. Peat.*

'Ten Gallon Hat' (Dan Trimmer, 2006). Evergreen. Scape 25 in. (63 cm); flower 6.25 in. (16 cm). Early midseason. A nicely ruffled golden yellow self with a tiny faint green throat. Tetraploid. 'California Girl' × 'Emerald Splendor'. *Photograph by Dan Trimmer.*

ORANGE (APRICOT, MELON TO ORANGE)

'Sweet Shalimar' (Ra Hansen, 1986). Evergreen. Scape 24 in. (61 cm); flower 6 in. (15 cm). Midseason. A deep persimmon-veined-orange with an olive throat. Diploid. (('Dynasty Gold' × 'Martha Adams') × ('Orange Joy' × 'Janet Gayle')) × 'Ann Crochet'. Eugene S. Foster Award 1994. Honorable Mention 1991. *Photograph by Ra Hansen.*

'Orange Velvet' (Enman R. Joiner, 1988). Semi-evergreen. Scape 30 in. (76 cm); flower 6.5 in. (16.5 cm). Midseason. A lightly ruffled medium orange self with a green heart. Diploid. 'Copper Lantern' × 'Golden Scroll'. Lenington All-American Award 1999. Award of Merit 1995. Honorable Mention 1992. *Photograph by Ted L. Petit and John P. Peat.*

'Pure and Simple' (Jeff Salter, 1993). Semi-evergreen. Scape 28 in. (71 cm); flower 5.5 in. (14 cm). Early midseason. An orange-sherbet self with an olive-green throat. Tetraploid. 'Alexandra' × seedling. Award of Merit 2005. Honorable Mention 2002. *Photograph by John Eiseman.*

'Tangerine Horses' (Matthew Kaskel, 1996). Evergreen. Scape 28 in. (71 cm); flower 4.5 in. (11.5 cm). Early midseason. An orange-tangerine self with an olive-green throat. Tetraploid. 'Spanish Glow' × (seedling × 'My Darling Clementine'). Award of Merit 2006. Honorable Mention 2003. *Photograph by Debbie and Duane Hurlbert.*

'Spacecoast Sweetness' (John Kinnebrew, 1998). Semi-evergreen. Scape 21 in. (53 cm); flower 4 in. (10 cm). Early. A lightly ruffled tangerine-orange with a pink overlay and a yellow throat. Tetraploid. 'Little Mystic Moon' × (seedling × 'Elizabeth Salter'). Honorable Mention 2002. *Photograph by John Benoot.*

'Primal Scream' (Curt Hanson, 1994). Dormant. Scape 34 in. (86 cm); flower 7.5 in. (19 cm). Midseason late. An orange-tangerine self with a green throat. Tetraploid. 'Tangerine Parfait' × 'Mauna Loa'. Stout Silver Medal 2003. Lambert/Webster Award 2001. Award of Merit 2000. Honorable Mention 1997. *Photograph by Curt Hanson.*

'Rags to Riches' (Robert Carr, 1997). Evergreen. Scape 28 in. (71 cm); flower 5.5 in. (14 cm). Midseason. An orange blend bitone with very heavy ruffling and a wire gold edge above an olive-green throat. Tetraploid. 'Victorian Collar' × ('Sherry Lane Carr' × seedling). Honorable Mention 2001. *Photograph by Ted L. Petit and John P. Peat.*

'Beyond Riches' (Robert Carr, 1999). Evergreen. Scape 28 in. (71 cm); flower 5 in. (12.7 cm). Early midseason. An orange-coral blend with a gold edge above a yellow to green throat. Tetraploid. (((('Angelus Angel' × 'Midnight Magic') × 'Ruffled Lemon Lace') × 'America's Most Wanted'). Honorable Mention 2004. *Photograph by Debbie and Duane Hurlbert.*

'Bernice Pappas' (Ted L. Petit, 1999). Semi-evergreen. Scape 22 in. (56 cm); flower 7 in. (18 cm). Midseason. These very large flowers are a bright golden orange-sherbet with very wide, round, ruffled petals. Tetraploid. 'Stone Ponies' × 'Joint Venture'. *Photograph by Ted L. Petit.*

'Electric Marmalade Magic' (John Kinnebrew, 2001). Semi-evergreen. Scape 22 in. (56 cm); flower 5.75 in. (14.6 cm). Early midseason. A nicely ruffled orange self above a green throat. Tetraploid. Seedling × 'Spacecoast Starburst'. *Photograph by Susan Okrasinski.*

'American Freedom' (Frank Smith and Larry Grace, 2003). Semi-evergreen. Scape 28 in. (71 cm); flower 6 in. (15 cm). Early. A vibrant orange-peach blend with heavily ruffled gold edge above a dark green throat. Tetraploid. 'Tetra Ultimate Perfection' × 'J. T. Davis'. *Photograph by John Benoot.*

'New Ways to Dream' (Ted L. Petit, 2000). Semi-evergreen. Scape 24 in. (61 cm); flower 5.5 in. (14 cm). Midseason. A bright clear orange with an intense crunchy orange edge and a green throat. The heavily ruffled crimped edges extend into the throat. Tetraploid. 'Storyville Child' × 'America's Most Wanted'. *Photograph by Ted L. Petit.*

'Carved Pumpkin Pie' (Jeff Salter, 2003). Semi-evergreen. Scape 30 in. (76 cm); flower 6 in. (15 cm). Midseason. An orange self above heavily green sculpted throat. Tetraploid. *Photograph by Francois Verhaert.*

'Mark Alan Carpenter' (Jack B. Carpenter, 2003). Evergreen. Scape 22 in. (56 cm); flower 7 in. (18 cm). Midseason. A bronze-orange blend above a green throat. Tetraploid. 'August Morn' × 'Tetra Texas Whopper Stopper'.

'Bass Gibson' (John Rice, 2005). Dormant. Scape 32 in. (81 cm); flower 5.5 in. (14 cm). Early midseason. A bright yellow and orange flower with exceptionally toothy edges above a green center. Tetraploid. 'Forestlake Ragamuffin' × seedling. *Photograph by John Rice.*

'Paula Nettles' (John Kinnebrew, 2005). Evergreen. Scape 32 in. (81 cm); flower 6 in. (15 cm). Early midseason. A rich amber with a yellow edge above a green throat. Tetraploid. 'Spacecoast Passion Released' × 'Forestlake Ragamuffin'. *Photograph by John Kinnebrew.*

'Spacecoast Sunkist Splendor' (John Kinnebrew, 2005). Evergreen. Scape 24 in. (61 cm); flower 6.5 in. (16.5 cm). Early. A heavily ruffled orange self above a green throat. Tetraploid. 'Spacecoast Citrus Kiss' × 'Spacecoast Gold Bonanza'. *Photograph by John Kinnebrew.*

'Forestlake Jason Harding' (Fran Harding, 2006). Dormant. Scape 28 in. (71 cm); flower 7 in. (18 cm). Midseason. A cantaloupe self with a heavy yellow ruffled edge above a tangerine throat. Tetraploid. ('Jim McKinney' × 'Forestlake Gentle On My Mind') × 'Forestlake Lawdy How Gaudy'. *Photograph by Fran Harding.*

'Electric Orange Emperor' (Jeff Salter, 2006). Evergreen. Scape 27 in. (69 cm); flower 6 in. (15 cm). Midseason. A bright deep orange flower with carving extending out from the midrib above a small green throat. Tetraploid. 'Carved Pumpkin Pie' × 'Concrete Empire'. *Photograph by Jeff Salter.*

PINK (PEACH TO ROSE-PINK)

'Spacecoast Pumpkin Power' (John Kinnebrew, 2006). Semi-evergreen. Scape 32 in. (81 cm); flower 6.5 in. (16.5 cm). Early. Spice-orange flowers with sculpting and a tightly crimped ruffled edge. Tetraploid. 'Spacecoast Citrus Kick' × seedling. *Photograph by John Kinnebrew.*

'Codie Wedgeworth' (Tomas Wilson, 1986). Evergreen. Scape 26 in. (66 cm); flower 6 in. (15 cm). Early. A lightly ruffled deep pastel pink self with a green throat. Diploid. 'Pink Pioneer' × 'Beverly Ann'. Award of Merit 1992. *Photograph by Jay Tompkins.*

'Sweet Ole Man' (Frank Smith, 2006). Semi-evergreen. Scape 32 in. (81 cm); flower 7 in. (18 cm). Midseason. A clear, concolor orange with large, thick ruffled petals and very wide, beautifully formed sepals. Tetraploid. Seedling × 'Linda's Magic'. *Photograph by Frank Smith.*

'Gingham Maid' (Lucille Guidry, 1986). Dormant. Scape 23 in. (58 cm); flower 7.25 in. (18 cm). Early. A very large triangular pink-cream slight bitone with a lime-green throat. Diploid. L. Ernest Plouf Award 1995. *Photograph by John Eiseman.*

'Janice Brown' (Edwin C. Brown, 1986). Semi-evergreen. Scape 21 in. (53 cm); flower 4.5 in. (11.5 cm). Early midseason. A bright pink with a rose-pink eyezone and a green throat. Diploid. Stout Silver Medal 1994. Annie T. Giles Award 1990. Don C. Stevens Award 1990. Award of Merit 1992. Honorable Mention 1989. *Photograph by Ted L. Petit and John P. Peat.*

'Smoky Mountain Autumn' (Lucille Guidry, 1986). Dormant. Scape 18 in. (46 cm); flower 5.75 in. (14.6 cm). Early. A rose-pink blend with raised ruffles, rose-lavender halo and an olive-green throat. Diploid. L. Ernest Plouf Award 1990. Award of Merit 1992. Honorable Mention 1989. *Photograph by John Eiseman.*

'Ellen Christine' (Clarence J. Crochet, 1987). Semi-evergreen. Scape 23 in. (58 cm); flower 7 in. (18 cm). Midseason. A pink and gold blend with a dark green throat. Diploid. 'Ann Crochet' × 'Curly Ripples'. Ida Munson Award 1994. Award of Merit 1993. Honorable Mention 1990. *Photograph by Rejean Millette.*

'Frosted Pink Ice' (Patrick Stamile, 1987). Dormant. Scape 28 in. (71 cm); flower 5 in. (12.7 cm). Early midseason. A blue-pink self with a green throat. Diploid. 'Gun Metal' × ('Lavender Dew' × 'Rose Swan'). L. Ernest Plouf Award 1996. Honorable Mention 1990. *Photograph by Patrick Stamile.*

'Josephine Marina' (Jack B. Carpenter, 1987). Dormant. Scape 21 in. (53 cm); flower 7.5 in. (19 cm). Late. A very large lightly ruffled apricot-peach self with an olive-green throat. Diploid. Award of Merit 1993. *Photograph by John Eiseman.*

'Antique Rose' (Sarah Sikes, 1987). Semi-evergreen. Scape 25 in. (63 cm); flower 5.5 in. (14 cm). Midseason. A loosely ruffled rose-pink with a green-yellow throat. Diploid. ('Ronda × ('Sophisticated Miss' × 'My Belle')) × 'Blue Happiness'. Award of Merit 1994. *Photograph by Ted L. Petit and John P. Peat.*

'Pink Flirt' (Margaret DeKerlegand, 1987). Semi-evergreen. Scape 20 in. (51 cm); flower 6 in. (15 cm). Early. A scalloped ruffled bright pink self with a green throat. Diploid. 'Blushing Parfait' × 'Morning Cheerfulness'. Award of Merit 1995. *Photograph by Ted L. Petit and John P. Peat.*

'Xia Xiang' (Oliver Billingslea, 1988). Semi-evergreen. Scape 22 in. (56 cm); flower 6 in. (15 cm). Midseason. A wide-petaled clear deep pink self with a green throat. Diploid. 'Fairy Tale Pink' × 'While Angels Sing'. Award of Merit 1996. Honorable Mention 1993. *Photograph by John Eiseman.*

'Elizabeth Salter' (Jeff Salter, 1990). Semi-evergreen. Scape 22 in. (56 cm); flower 5.5 in. (14 cm). Midseason. A wide-petaled ruffled salmon-pink self with a green throat. Very popular. Tetraploid. Stout Silver Medal 2000. Award of Merit 1998. Honorable Mention 1995. *Photograph by Ted L. Petit and John P. Peat.*

'Magic Lace' (Tom Wilson, 1988). Dormant. Scape 23 in. (58 cm); flower 6 in. (15 cm). Early midseason. A pastel pink self with a green throat. Diploid. 'Lauren Leah' × 'Catherine Neal'. Award of Merit 1995. Honorable Mention 1992. *Photograph by Debbie and Duane Hurlbert.*

'Susan Weber' (Charles E. Branch, 1989). Semi-evergreen. Scape 26 in. (66 cm); flower 5.75 in. (14.6 cm). Late. A light rose-pink with rose edging and a yellow to green throat. Diploid. 'Great Thou Art' × 'Fairy Tale Pink'. Eugene S. Foster Award 2001. Award of Merit 1999. Honorable Mention 1996. *Photograph by Ted L. Petit and John P. Peat.*

'Autumn Wood' (Hazel Dougherty, 1991). Dormant. Scape 24 in. (61 cm); flower 5.5 in. (14 cm). Midseason. A peach and green polychrome with a peach-green throat. Diploid. Award of Merit 2001. Honorable Mention 1998. *Photograph by Tom Rood.*

'Sabra Salina' (Tom Wilson, 1991). Dormant. Scape 22 in. (56 cm); flower 6 in. (15 cm). Early midseason. A soft pale pink with a gold halo above a green throat. Diploid. ('Beverly Ann' × seedling) × 'Codie Wedgeworth'. Award of Merit 1999. Honorable Mention 1996. *Photograph by Ted L. Petit and John P. Peat.*

'Something Wonderful' (Jeff Salter, 1991). Semi-evergreen. Scape 28 in. (71 cm); flower 5 in. (12.7 cm). Early midseason. An ivory cream-pink self with a distinct ruffled gold edge and a lime-green throat. Tetraploid. Award of Merit 2002. Honorable Mention 1997.

'Tahitian Waterfall' (Oliver Billingslea, 1991). Semi-evergreen. Scape 26 in. (66 cm); flower 5.5 in. (14 cm). Early midseason. A rose and peach blend with a green throat. Diploid. 'Smoky Mountain Autumn' × ('Tahitian Pink' × 'Neal Berrey'). Honorable Mention 1996. *Photograph by Debbie and Duane Hurlbert.*

'Adrienne's Surprise' (Ra Hansen, 1992). Evergreen. Scape 26 in. (66 cm); flower 4.5 in. (11.5 cm). Late. A silver-rose-pink with a darker rose halo above a green throat. Diploid. ('Heaven Can Wait' × seedling) × 'Ruffled Beauty'. Eugene S. Foster Award 1999. Honorable Mention 1997.

'Best Kept Secret' (David Kirchhoff, 1992). Evergreen. Scape 28 in. (71 cm); flower 5.5 in. (14 cm). Midseason. A rose-pink with a coral-rose watermark. Tetraploid. ('Ming Porcelain' × 'Inner View') × 'Tetra Blue Happiness'. Award of Merit 1998. Honorable Mention 1995. *Photograph by David Kirchhoff.*

'Dena Marie' (Jack B. Carpenter, 1992). Dormant. Scape 26 in. (66 cm); flower 6.75 in. (17 cm). Midseason. A rose-pink self with a yellow to green throat. Diploid. L. Ernest Plouf Award 1999. Award of Merit 2000. Honorable Mention 1997. *Photograph by Debbie and Duane Hurlbert.*

'Forestlake Ragamuffin' (Fran Harding, 1993). Dormant. Scape 28 in. (71 cm); flower 5.5 in. (14 cm). Early midseason. A shell-pink self with gold shark's teeth crimped ruffled edge and a green throat. Very popular. Tetraploid. 'Decatur Piecrust' × (seedling × ('Lahaina' × 'Yuma')). Honorable Mention 2005. *Photograph by Fran Harding.*

'Seminole Wind' (Patrick Stamile, 1993). Semi-evergreen. Scape 23 in. (58 cm); flower 6.5 in. (16.5 cm). Early midseason. A wide-petaled clear medium pink self with a green throat. Very important hybridizing flower. Tetraploid. ('Love Goddess' × 'Crush on You') × 'Tetra Barbara Mitchell'. Award of Merit 2001. Honorable Mention 1998. *Photograph by Patrick Stamile.*

'Uptown Girl' (Patrick Stamile, 1993). Semi-evergreen. Scape 27 in. (69 cm); flower 5 in. (12.7 cm). Early midseason. A baby-ribbon pink self with a green throat. Tetraploid. 'Crush on You' × 'Peach Whisper'. Eugene S. Foster Award 2000. Honorable Mention 1998. *Photograph by Patrick Stamile.*

'Banned in Boston' (Doris Simpson, 1994). Dormant. Scape 26 in. (66 cm); flower 5 in. (12.7 cm). Midseason. A rose and cream-pink bitone with a green to light lemon-yellow throat. Diploid. 'Ruffled Ivory' × 'Dearest'. Honorable Mention 1998. *Photograph by Karen Newman.*

'Barbara Dittmer' (Mort Morss, 1994). Semi-evergreen. Scape 24 in. (61 cm); flower 3.75 in. (9.5 cm). Early. A coral orchid rose-pink with a gold edge and a magenta-rose eyezone above a yellow to bright green throat. Tetraploid. ('Shadow Dance' × 'Tetra Siloam Virginia Henson') × 'Angel's Smile'. Annie T. Giles Award 2003. Award of Merit 2006. Honorable Mention 2002. *Photograph by Patricia Bennett.*

'Chance Encounter' (Patrick Stamile, 1994). Evergreen. Scape 25 in. (63 cm); flower 6 in. (15 cm). Early midseason. A raspberry-rose blend with a gold edge above a green throat. Tetraploid. ((Seedling × 'Love Goddess') × 'Crush on You') × 'Tetra Barbara Mitchell'. L. Ernest Plouf Award 2000. Award of Merit 2001. Honorable Mention 1998. *Photograph by Patrick Stamile.*

'Ed Brown' (Jeff Salter, 1994). Semi-evergreen. Scape 28 in. (71 cm); flower 5.5 in. (14 cm). Early midseason. A clear baby-ribbon pink self with a gold edge above a green throat. Tetraploid. 'Something Wonderful' × 'Elizabeth's Dream'. Stout Silver Medal 2006. Award of Merit 2003. Honorable Mention 2000. *Photograph by Ted L. Petit and John P. Peat.*

'Splendid Touch' (Patrick Stamile, 1994). Evergreen. Scape 26 in. (66 cm); flower 5.75 in. (14.6 cm). Early midseason. A pink with a rose eye-zone above a green throat. Tetraploid. 'Silken Touch' × 'Tetra Barbara Mitchell'. Award of Merit 2002. Honorable Mention 1999. *Photograph by Patrick Stamile.*

'Allegheny Sunset' (Patrick Stamile, 1996). Dormant. Scape 20 in. (51 cm); flower 5.5 in. (14 cm). Midseason. A wide-petaled ruffled pink-rose blend with a green throat. Tetraploid. ('Ming Porcelain' × ('Pink Scintillation' × seedling)) × 'Seminole Wind'. *Photograph by Patrick Stamile.*

'Shimmering Elegance' (Patrick Stamile, 1994). Dormant. Scape 25 in. (63 cm); flower 6 in. (15 cm). Early midseason. A pink self with a green throat. Tetraploid. (Seedling × 'Silken Touch') × 'Seminole Wind'. L. Ernest Plouf Award 2002. Honorable Mention 2000. *Photograph by Patrick Stamile.*

'Effay Veronica' (Ted L. Petit, 1995). Dormant. Scape 21 in. (53 cm); flower 5.5 in. (14 cm). Early midseason. An extremely ruffled, wide-petaled pink self with a green throat. Tetraploid. 'Betty Warren Woods' × 'Shishedo'. *Photograph by Ted L. Petit.*

'At First Blush' (Jeff Salter, 1996). Semi-evergreen. Scape 24 in. (61 cm); flower 5.5 in. (14 cm). Early midseason. A cream to lavender-pink blend with a green throat. Tetraploid. 'Wedding Band' × seedling. Honorable Mention 2001. *Photograph by Francois Verhaert.*

'Better Than Ever' (Jeff Salter, 1996). Dormant. Scape 28 in. (71 cm); flower 4 in. (10 cm). Midseason. A coral-red blend with a gold edge above a green throat. Tetraploid. 'Wisest of Wizards' × 'Angel's Smile'. Honorable Mention 2004.

'Catalina' (Patrick Stamile, 1996). Dormant. Scape 22 in. (56 cm); flower 5 in. (12.7 cm). Early midseason. A light peach-pink blend with a green throat. Tetraploid. 'Crush on You' × 'Seminole Wind'. *Photograph by Patrick Stamile.*

'Classic Romance' (Jeff Salter, 1996). Semi-evergreen. Scape 30 in. (76 cm); flower 6 in. (15 cm). Midseason. A rose-pink blend with a green throat. Tetraploid. 'William Austin Norris' × 'Good Morning America'. *Photograph by Debbie and Duane Hurlbert.*

'Corinthian Pink' (Patrick Stamile, 1996). Dormant. Scape 26 in. (66 cm); flower 7.25 in. (18 cm). Early midseason. A pink with a rose-pink eyezone above a green throat. Tetraploid. ((Seedling × 'Love Goddess') × (seedling × 'Tetra Martha Adams')) × 'Seminole Wind'. Honorable Mention 2000. *Photograph by Patrick Stamile.*

'Desert Dreams' (Elizabeth H. Salter, 1996). Semi-evergreen. Scape 22 in. (56 cm); flower 3.5 in. (9 cm). Midseason. A dusty pink polychrome with a green throat. Tetraploid. Honorable Mention 2000.

'Edge of Heaven' (Jeff Salter, 1996). Semi-evergreen. Scape 28 in. (71 cm); flower 6.5 in. (16.5 cm). Midseason. A cream-pink self with a gold bubbly and knobby edge above a green throat. Tetraploid. Honorable Mention 2002. *Photograph by Sue Brown.*

'English Cameo' (Patrick Stamile, 1996). Dormant. Scape 26 in. (66 cm); flower 5.5 in. (14 cm). Early midseason. A wide-petaled nicely ruffled circular flower of a light cream-peach blend and a green heart. Tetraploid. ('Ming Porcelain' × ('Pink Scintillation' × seedling)) × 'Seminole Wind'. Honorable Mention 2004. *Photograph by Patrick Stamile.*

'Last Picture Show' (Patrick Stamile, 1996). Evergreen. Scape 26 in. (66 cm); flower 6 in. (15 cm). Late. A pink self with a green throat. Tetraploid. 'Peach Whisper' × 'Silken Touch'. Eugene S. Foster Award 2003. *Photograph by Patrick Stamile.*

'Moment to Treasure' (Jeff Salter, 1996). Semi-evergreen. Scape 26 in. (66 cm); flower 5.5 in. (14 cm). Early midseason. An extremely ruffled gold-edged soft coral-pink blend with a green throat. Tetraploid. *Photograph by John Benoot.*

'Patrician Splendor' (Patrick Stamile, 1996). Dormant. Scape 26 in. (66 cm); flower 6.25 in. (16 cm). Early midseason. A large wide-petaled cream-pink blend with a deep green throat. Tetraploid. (('Ming Porcelain' × 'Pink Scintillation') × seedling) × 'Seminole Wind'. *Photograph by Patrick Stamile.*

'Polynesian Love Song' (Jack B. Carpenter, 1996). Semi-evergreen. Scape 29 in. (74 cm); flower 5.5 in. (14 cm). Early midseason. A very ruffled peach self with a green throat. Tetraploid. Honorable Mention 2001. *Photograph by Tracy Heldt.*

'Rose Fever' (Patrick Stamile, 1996). Evergreen. Scape 25 in. (63 cm); flower 6 in. (15 cm). Early midseason. A large wide-petaled deep hot rose with a grass-green throat. Tetraploid. ('Crystalline Pink' × 'Only You') × 'Seminole Wind'. *Photograph by Patrick Stamile.*

'Spacecoast Ruffles' (John Kinnebrew, 1996). Evergreen. Scape 29 in. (74 cm); flower 6 in. (15 cm). Early midseason. A pink self with a green throat. Tetraploid. 'Elizabeth Salter' × seedling.

'Stolen Treasure' (Hazel Dougherty, 1996). Dormant. Scape 26 in. (66 cm); flower 6.5 in. (16.5 cm). Early midseason. A pink bitone with a cream border above a green throat. Diploid. 'Border Crossing' × seedling. Honorable Mention 2004. *Photograph by Beatrice Collins.*

'Timeless Romance' (Jeff Salter, 1996). Semi-evergreen. Scape 28 in. (71 cm); flower 5.5 in. (14 cm). Early midseason. A pink blend with a light cream-pink halo above a green throat. Tetraploid.

'Tomorrow's Glory' (Jeff Salter, 1996). Semi-evergreen. Scape 26 in. (66 cm); flower 5 in. (12.7 cm). Midseason. A lavender-pink blend with a yellow halo above a green throat. Tetraploid. 'Tomorrow's Dream' × seedling.

'Absolute Treasure' (Patrick Stamile, 1997). Evergreen. Scape 32 in. (81 cm); flower 7 in. (18 cm). Early midseason. An orchid rose self with a green throat. Tetraploid. 'Chance Encounter' × 'American Original'. Honorable Mention 2001. *Photograph by Patrick Stamile.*

'Big Sur' (Patrick Stamile, 1997). Semi-evergreen. Scape 30 in. (76 cm); flower 6.5 in. (16.5 cm). Early midseason. A rose self with a green throat. Tetraploid. 'Chance Encounter' × 'Seminole Wind'. Honorable Mention 2004. *Photograph by Patrick Stamile.*

'Tropical Experience' (Patrick Stamile, 1997). Evergreen. Scape 26 in. (66 cm); flower 7.25 in. (18 cm). Early. A peach and pink blend with a rose eyezone above a green throat. Tetraploid. 'Kathleen Salter' × 'Tetra Violet Explosion'. Honorable Mention 2003. *Photograph by Patrick Stamile.*

'After Awhile Crocodile' (Margo Reed, 1997). Semi-evergreen. Scape 28 in. (71 cm); flower 5.5 in. (14 cm). Late. A lightly ruffled light rose self with large white midribs above a lemon throat. Diploid. 'So Lovely' × 'Olallie Lois'. Eugene S. Foster Award 2005. Honorable Mention 2005. *Photograph by Debbie and Duane Hurlbert.*

'Dena Marie's Sister' (Jack B. Carpenter, 1997). Dormant. Scape 32 in. (81 cm); flower 6.5 in. (16.5 cm). Midseason late. A rose-pink self with a green throat. Diploid. Honorable Mention 2002. *Photograph by Debbie and Duane Hurlbert.*

'Frequent Comment' (John Rice, 1998). Evergreen. Scape 23 in. (58 cm); flower 5.5 in. (14 cm). Midseason. A rose-peach with a yellow eyezone and yellow ruffles above a green throat. Tetraploid. 'Ida's Magic' × 'Canton Harbor'. Honorable Mention 2003. *Photograph by Dorothie Hellman.*

'Bill Munson' (Ted L. Petit, 1998). Semi-evergreen. Scape 27 in. (69 cm); flower 5 in. (12.7 cm). Midseason. A pink self with a green throat. Tetraploid. (('Cherry Chapeau' × ('Betty Warren Woods' × 'Emerald Dawn')) × seedling). *Photograph by Ted L. Petit.*

'Helen Shooter' (John Shooter, 1998). Dormant. Scape 25 in. (63 cm); flower 7 in. (18 cm). Midseason. A light pink blend with a nicely ruffled edge above a light green throat. Diploid. ('Super Valentine' × 'Christy Smith') × 'Reaching'. Honorable Mention 2005. *Photograph by Debbie and Duane Hurlbert.*

'Rose Masterpiece' (Patrick Stamile, 1998). Dormant. Scape 24 in. (61 cm); flower 7 in. (18 cm). Extra early. A rose self with a green throat. Tetraploid. 'Seminole Wind' × 'Majestic Pink'. *Photograph by Patrick Stamile.*

'Fuchsia Kiss' (Patrick Stamile, 1998). Dormant. Scape 30 in. (76 cm); flower 6 in. (15 cm). Early midseason. A pink with a gold edge above a green throat. Tetraploid. 'Chance Encounter' × 'Shimmering Elegance'. *Photograph by Patrick Stamile.*

'Inherited Wealth' (Robert Carr, 1998). Evergreen. Scape 28 in. (71 cm); flower 5 in. (12.7 cm). Early. A pink blend with a heavy ruffled gold edge and an olive-green throat. Tetraploid. 'Victorian Collar' × 'America's Most Wanted'. Honorable Mention 2001. *Photograph by Robert Carr.*

'Rushing Delight' (Larry Grace, 1998). Evergreen. Scape 26 in. (66 cm); flower 5 in. (12.7 cm). Early midseason. A light rose-mauve with a touch of cinnamon, a thin halo of deeper rose-mauve and a yellow-gold edge above a yellow-gold throat. Tetraploid. 'Ida's Magic' × seedling. Honorable Mention 2003. *Photograph by Susan Okrasinski.*

'San Ignacio' (Patrick Stamile, 1998). Dormant. Scape 28 in. (71 cm); flower 5 in. (12.7 cm). Early midseason. A baby-ribbon pink with a green throat. Tetraploid. (('Enchanted Empress' × 'Pink Monday') × ('Custard Candy' × 'Eye Declare')) × 'American Original'. Honorable Mention 2005. *Photograph by Patrick Stamile.*

'Spacecoast Sensation' (John Kinnebrew, 1998). Semi-evergreen. Scape 18 in. (46 cm); flower 5.75 in. (14.6 cm). Early midseason. A pink self with a gold edge and a yellow throat. Tetraploid. 'John Kinnebrew' × 'Spacecoast Ruffles'.

'Spacecoast Starburst' (John Kinnebrew, 1998). Evergreen. Scape 25 in. (63 cm); flower 6 in. (15 cm). Early midseason. A pink-lavender blend with a yellow halo and a gold edge above a yellow throat. Tetraploid. 'Secret Splendor' × seedling. Award of Merit 2005. Honorable Mention 2002. *Photograph by Debbie and Duane Hurlbert.*

'Connie Burton' (Tom Wilson, 1999). Evergreen. Scape 24 in. (61 cm); flower 5.5 in. (14 cm). Early midseason. A coral-pink blend with a pink eyezone above a green throat. Diploid. *Photograph by Tom Wilson.*

'Spacecoast Sonata' (John Kinnebrew, 1998). Evergreen. Scape 30 in. (76 cm); flower 5.75 in. (14.6 cm). Early. A pink blend with a green throat. Tetraploid. 'Secret Splendor' × seedling. *Photograph by Sandi Jacques.*

'Treasure of Love' (Patrick Stamile, 1998). Dormant. Scape 26 in. (66 cm); flower 6.25 in. (16 cm). Midseason. A very clear rose-pink flower with wide ruffled petals and a green throat. Tetraploid. 'Raspberry Lustre' × 'Shimmering Elegance'. *Photograph by Patrick Stamile.*

'Darlington County' (Patrick Stamile, 1999). Dormant. Scape 24 in. (61 cm); flower 6 in. (15 cm). Early. A rose self with a green throat. Tetraploid. 'Rose Fever' × 'Shimmering Elegance'. *Photograph by Patrick Stamile.*

'Lori Goldston' (John Kinnebrew, 1999). Evergreen. Scape 25 in. (63 cm); flower 6.5 in. (16.5 cm). Early midseason. A heavily ruffled gold-edged lavender-pink with a lighter watermark and a green throat. Tetraploid. 'Untamed Glory' × seedling. Honorable Mention 2002. *Photograph by Francois Verhaert.*

'Spacecoast Cool Deal' (John Kinnebrew, 1999). Semi-evergreen. Scape 24 in. (61 cm); flower 6 in. (15 cm). Midseason. A lavender self with a yellow halo and gold edges above a yellow throat. Tetraploid. 'Wedding Band' × 'Ida's Magic'. *Photograph by Katie Cook.*

'Party Pinafore' (Wesley L. Kirby, 1999). Dormant. Scape 20 in. (51 cm); flower 5 in. (12.7 cm). Early midseason. A rose with baby-pink edges and a white to green throat. Diploid. Seedling × seedling. *Photograph by Francois Verhaert.*

'Southern Coral' (Patrick Stamile, 1999). Evergreen. Scape 30 in. (76 cm); flower 6 in. (15 cm). Early midseason. A coral with orange edges and a green throat. Tetraploid. ('Festive Art' × 'Rave On') × (('Late Again' × 'Admiral's Braid') × 'Chris Salter'). *Photograph by Patrick Stamile.*

'Spacecoast Fancy Dancer' (John Kinnebrew, 1999). Evergreen. Scape 31 in. (79 cm); flower 6 in. (15 cm). Early. A pink blend with gold edges and a green throat. Tetraploid. 'Spacecoast Starburst' × 'Something Wonderful'. Honorable Mention 2004. *Photograph by Francois Verhaert.*

'Spacecoast Peach Fringe' (John Kinnebrew, 1999). Semi-evergreen. Scape 24 in. (61 cm); flower 6 in. (15 cm). Early midseason. A peach-pink self with a peach-pink throat. Tetraploid. 'Betty Warren Woods' × seedling. Honorable Mention 2004.

'Taos' (Patrick Stamile, 1999). Dormant. Scape 6 in. (15.20 cm); flower 6 in. (15 cm). Early midseason. A pastel cream-pink blend with a gold edge and a green throat. Tetraploid. (('Ming Porcelain' × 'Crush on You') × seedling) × 'Shimmering Elegance'. Award of Merit 2007. Honorable Mention 2004. *Photograph by Patrick Stamile.*

'Age of Elegance' (Jeff Salter, 2000). Semi-evergreen. Scape 29 in. (74 cm); flower 6 in. (15 cm). Midseason. A lavender-rose blend with a large gold edge above a yellow to green throat. Tetraploid. 'David Kirchhoff' × unknown. *Photograph by Jeff Salter.*

'Edith Sliger' (Jeff Salter, 2000). Semi-evergreen. Scape 25 in. (63 cm); flower 5 in. (12.7 cm). Early midseason. A rosy pink-coral blend with a heavy gold edge above a green throat. Tetraploid. 'Ed Brown' × ('Classic Romance' × 'Timeless Romance'). Honorable Mention 2004. *Photograph by Francois Verhaert.*

'Victorian Lace' (Patrick Stamile, 1999). Evergreen. Scape 30 in. (76 cm); flower 6.75 in. (17 cm). Early midseason. A porcelain-pink with a gold braided edge and a green throat. Tetraploid. ('White Zone' × 'Alpine Snow') × 'Nordic Mist'. Honorable Mention 2005. *Photograph by Patrick Stamile.*

'Amanda's Intrigue' (Jeff Salter, 2000). Semi-evergreen. Scape 28 in. (71 cm); flower 5 in. (12.7 cm). Early midseason. A lavender-pink blend with large yellow edge above a yellow-green throat. Tetraploid. 'Moonlit Masquerade' × seedling. *Photograph by John Benoot.*

'Enchanting Esmerelda' (Jeff Salter, 2000). Semi-evergreen. Scape 26 in. (66 cm); flower 5.5 in. (14 cm). Early midseason. A bright intense rose-pink flower with a lighter watermark above a deep green throat. The petal edges are lightly ruffled with a lighter pink edge surrounded by a wire gold edge. Tetraploid. 'William Austin Norris' × 'Timeless Romance'. Honorable Mention 2003. *Photograph by Jeff Salter.*

'Icing on the Cake' (Jeff Salter, 2000). Semi-evergreen. Scape 30 in. (76 cm); flower 5.5 in. (14 cm). Early midseason. A pale pink with a lightly ruffled gold edge. Tetraploid. ('Moonlight Silence' × 'Moonlit Caress') × ('Chris Salter' × 'Arabian Magic'). Honorable Mention 2004. *Photograph by Karen Newman.*

Janet Benz' (John Benz, 2000). Dormant. Scape 28 in. (71 cm); flower 5.5 in. (14 cm). Midseason. A strawberry-rose with a darker rose eyezone above a green throat and serrated gold edge. Tetraploid. 'Radar Love' × 'Tetra Barbara Mitchell'. *Photograph by Francois Verhaert.*

'Moonlight Rhapsody' (Jeff Salter, 2000). Semi-evergreen. Scape 28 in. (71 cm); flower 5.5 in. (14 cm). Early midseason. A cream-pink blend with a ruffled gold edge above a dark green center. Tetraploid.

'Mount Herman Marvel' (Jack B. Carpenter, 2000). Evergreen. Scape 33 in. (84 cm); flower 7 in. (18 cm). Midseason. A lightly ruffled rose blend with a yellow to green throat. Tetraploid. 'Polynesian Love Song' × 'Tetra Dena Marie'.

'It's a Miracle' (Enman R. Joiner, 2000). Evergreen. Scape 28 in. (71 cm); flower 5 in. (12.7 cm). Early. A cloud-pink self above a green-yellow throat. Tetraploid. Seedling × seedling. Honorable Mention 2003. *Photograph by Francis Joiner.*

'Simply Glorious' (Jack B. Carpenter, 2000). Evergreen. Scape 22 in. (56 cm); flower 6 in. (15 cm). Early. A melon, peach, and pink blend above a green throat. Diploid. 'Gene Earl' × 'Calcasieu Rose'. *Photograph by Jack B. Carpenter.*

'Spacecoast Extreme Fashion' (John Kinnebrew, 2000). Semi-evergreen. Scape 21 in. (53 cm); flower 5.5 in. (14 cm). Early. A peach-pink blend with a tremendous, round flower form and perfect pie-crust gold ruffling. Tetraploid. 'Spacecoast Sweetness' × 'Spacecoast Starburst'. *Photograph by Francois Verhaert.*

'Touched by Magic' (Jeff Salter, 2000). Semi-evergreen. Scape 26 in. (66 cm); flower 5 in. (12.7 cm). Midseason. A coral-peach and rose blend with a heavy gold edge and round flat form. Tetraploid. 'Ida's Magic' × 'Wisest of Wizards'. *Photograph by Ted L. Petit and John P. Peat.*

'Carved in Stone' (Ted L. Petit, 2001). Semi-evergreen. Scape 20 in. (51 cm); flower 5.5 in. (14 cm). Midseason. A beautiful orchid to salmon-pink with heavily ruffled gold edges. The carving gives an added dimension to these flowers. Tetraploid. 'Kings and Vagabonds' × ('Romeo is Bleeding' × 'Romeo is Bleeding'). *Photograph by Ted L. Petit.*

'Belle Cook' (Malcolm Brooker, 2001). Semi-evergreen. Scape 24 in. (61 cm); flower 6 in. (15 cm). Midseason. A clear baby-ribbon pink, round, heavily ruffled gold-edged flower with a soft green throat. Tetraploid. 'Ed Brown' × 'Seminole Wind'. Honorable Mention 2005. *Photograph by Francois Verhaert.*

'Mandalay Bay Music' (Jeff Salter, 2001). Semi-evergreen. Scape 28 in. (71 cm); flower 6.5 in. (16.5 cm). Early midseason. A creamy white with hint of pink and a ruffled white to gold edge above a small lime-green throat. Tetraploid. Honorable Mention 2004. *Photograph by Debbie and Duane Hurlbert.*

'Ne Quitte Pas' (Ted L. Petit, 2001). Semi-evergreen. Scape 23 in. (58 cm); flower 5.5 in. (14 cm). Midseason. A pink with a gold edge. Tetraploid. 'Elusive Dream' × 'Ed Brown'. *Photograph by Ted L. Petit.*

'Finish With a Flourish' (Jeff Salter, 2002). Semi-evergreen. Scape 30 in. (76 cm); flower 5.5 in. (14 cm). Midseason. A light rose-pink bitone with copper-gold edge above a yellow-green throat. Tetraploid. *Photograph by Sue Brown.*

'Northern Fancy' (Patrick Stamile, 2002). Dormant. Scape 26 in. (66 cm); flower 5 in. (12.7 cm). Early midseason. A rose with a gold edge above a green throat. Tetraploid. 'Magic Amethyst' × (('Creative Edge' × 'Chris Salter') × 'Startle'). *Photograph by Patrick Stamile.*

'Berry Patch' (Jeff Salter, 2002). Semi-evergreen. Scape 26 in. (66 cm); flower 6 in. (15 cm). Midseason. A rose-pink blend with a large faint watermark and a bubbly wire gold edge above a green throat. Tetraploid. 'Ed Brown' × 'Timeless Romance'. Honorable Mention 2007. *Photograph by Debbie and Duane Hurlbert.*

'Fairest of Them' (Jeff Salter, 2002). Semi-evergreen. Scape 26 in. (66 cm); flower 6 in. (15 cm). Midseason. A bright pink with white ruffled edge above a yellow-green throat. Tetraploid. ('Ed Brown' × ('Admirals Braid' × ('Moonlit Caress' × seedling))).

'How Beautiful Heaven Must Be' (Jack B. Carpenter, 2002). Evergreen. Scape 26 in. (66 cm); flower 5.75 in. (14.6 cm). Early midseason. A very wide-petaled peach-pink with extremely ornate heavy gold ruffling that extends deep into the throat. Tetraploid. 'Ed Brown' × 'Larry Grace'. Honorable Mention 2005. *Photograph by Jack B. Carpenter.*

'Shores of Time' (Patrick Stamile, 2002). Dormant. Scape 26 in. (66 cm); flower 5.5 in. (14 cm). Early midseason. A rose with a heavy gold edge above a green throat. Tetraploid. ('Shimmering Elegance' × 'Ed Brown') × ('Red Fang' × 'Northern Glitter'). *Photograph by Patrick Stamile.*

'Spectral Elegance' (Patrick Stamile, 2002). Evergreen. Scape 23 in. (58 cm); flower 6.5 in. (16.5 cm). Early midseason. A pastel polychrome with a pink overlay above a green throat. Tetraploid. 'Ballerina on Ice' × 'Tetra Ruffled Masterpiece'. *Photograph by Patrick Stamile.*

'Cerise Masterpiece' (Patrick Stamile, 2003). Semi-evergreen. Scape 38 in. (96 cm); flower 7 in. (18 cm). Early midseason. A coral-peach with rose watermark and white edge above a chartreuse-green throat. Tetraploid. 'Chartered Course' × ('Musical Medley' × 'Seize the Night'). *Photograph by Patrick Stamile.*

'Racing With Destiny' (Ted L. Petit, 2003). Semi-evergreen. Scape 28 in. (71 cm); flower 6 in. (15 cm). Midseason. A pink with a gold watermark and a heavily ruffled gold edge above a green throat. Tetraploid. 'John Peat' × 'Ne Quitte Pas'. *Photograph by Ted L. Petit.*

'Symphony of Praise' (Tim Bell, 2003). Evergreen. Scape 27 in. (69 cm); flower 7 in. (18 cm). Midseason. A pink blend with a gold edge above a green throat. Tetraploid. 'Diamonds and Pearls' × 'Barbara Mitchell'. *Photograph by Tim Bell.*

'Roses and Gold' (Patrick Stamile, 2003). Evergreen. Scape 30 in. (76 cm); flower 6 in. (15 cm). Early midseason. A deep rose with a gold edge above a green throat. Tetraploid. ('Lake Effect' × 'Be Thine') × 'Song Writer'. *Photograph by Lanny Morry.*

'Let There Be Peace' (Jack B. Carpenter, 2004). Evergreen. Scape 36 in. (91 cm); flower 7 in. (18 cm). Early midseason. A soft baby pink self above a green throat. Tetraploid. 'Ed Brown' × 'Tetra Royal Pink Twist'. *Photograph by Jack B. Carpenter.*

'Worth It All' (Jack B. Carpenter, 2003). Evergreen. Scape 22 in. (56 cm); flower 6.5 in. (16.5 cm). Midseason. A pale pink self above a green throat. Tetraploid. ('All the Magic' × 'Tetra Red Step Ahead') × 'Tetra Royal Pink Twist'. *Photograph by Jack B. Carpenter.*

'Bill Robinson' (Frank Smith and Larry Grace, 2004). Semi-evergreen. Scape 20 in. (51 cm); flower 6.5 in. (16.5 cm). Early midseason. A pink with gold edge above a green throat. Tetraploid. 'Belle Cook' × seedling.

'Across the Universe' (Dan Trimmer, 2004). Evergreen. Scape 25 in. (63 cm); flower 6.5 in. (16.5 cm). Early midseason. An ivory-infused pink polychrome with heavy ruffled gold edge above a green throat. Tetraploid. 'London Calling' × seedling. *Photograph by Francois Verhaert.*

'Judy Farquhar' (Patrick Stamile, 2004). Evergreen. Scape 34 in. (86 cm); flower 7.5 in. (19 cm). Midseason. A pink with large heavily ruffled gold edge above a bright yellow to green throat. Tetraploid. ('Sangre de Cristo' × 'Fuchsia Kiss') × ((seedling × 'Big Blue') × 'Be Thine'). *Photograph by Francois Verhaert.*

'Our Friend Tom Wilson' (Jack B. Carpenter, 2004). Evergreen. Scape 26 in. (66 cm); flower 6 in. (15 cm). Early midseason. A lavender-pink self above a green throat. Diploid. 'Calcasieu Rose' × unknown. *Photograph by Jack B. Carpenter.*

'Sister of Praise' (Tim Bell, 2004). Dormant. Scape 22 in. (56 cm); flower 6 in. (15 cm). Midseason. A lavender-pink blend with a pale pink and cream edge above a green throat. Tetraploid. 'Diamonds and Pearls' × 'Tetra Barbara Mitchell'. Honorable Mention 2007. *Photograph by Tim Bell.*

'Aloha Hawaii' (Ted L. Petit, 2005). Semi-evergreen. Scape 30 in. (76 cm); flower 6.5 in. (16.5 cm). Evergreen. A large pink flower with extremely heavy substance and very ruffled gold edge above a green throat. Tetraploid. 'Reyna' × 'Tetra Champagne Elegance'. *Photograph by Ted L. Petit.*

'Carolyn Mann' (John Kinnebrew, 2005). Semi-evergreen. Scape 32 in. (81 cm); flower 6.5 in. (16.5 cm). Early midseason. A lavender-pink blend with a gold edge above yellow throat. Tetraploid. 'Anne McWilliams' × 'Jerry Nettles'. *Photograph by John Kinnebrew.*

'Spacecoast Tropical Passion' (John Kinnebrew, 2004). Semi-evergreen. Scape 22 in. (56 cm); flower 6 in. (15 cm). Midseason. An extremely ruffled peach-pink self above a yellow to green throat. Tetraploid. 'Jerry Nettles' × 'Lori Goldston'. Honorable Mention 2007. *Photograph by Francois Verhaert.*

'Barbie in Pink' (Ted L. Petit, 2005). Semi-evergreen. Scape 28 in. (71 cm); flower 8 in. (20 cm). Midseason. A pink with a gold edge above a green throat. Tetraploid. ('Ed Brown' × 'Tetra Dena Marie') × 'Kissed From Afar'. *Photograph by Ted L. Petit.*

'Carved Initials' (Ted L. Petit, 2005). Semi-evergreen. Scape 32 in. (81 cm); flower 6.5 in. (16.5 cm). Midseason. A coral self above a green throat. Tetraploid. 'Carved in Stone' × 'Bas Relief'. *Photograph by Ted L. Petit.*

'Eternally Grateful' (Ted L. Petit, 2005). Semi-evergreen. Scape 25 in. (63 cm); flower 6.5 in. (16.5 cm). Midseason. A pink with a gold edge above a green throat. Tetraploid. 'Expensive Taste' × 'J. T. Davis'. *Photograph by Ted L. Petit.*

'Florida Snow Angel' (Hugh Buntyn, 2005). Dormant. Scape 26 in. (66 cm); flower 5.5 in. (14 cm). Midseason. A pink bitone with brownish gold edge above a very green throat. Tetraploid. 'Bodacious Blush' × seedling. *Photograph by Francois Verhaert.*

'Sandra's Smile' (Paul Limmer, 2005). Dormant. Scape 34 in. (86 cm); flower 6 in. (15 cm). Midseason late. A lavender-pink with a yellow eyezone and gold edge above yellow throat. Tetraploid. ('Judge Judy' × seedling) × ('Ed Brown' × seedling). *Photograph by Paul Limmer.*

'Fame' (Frank Smith and Larry Grace, 2005). Dormant. Scape 26 in. (66 cm); flower 6 in. (15 cm). Early midseason. A dark rose with yellow watermark and edge above a green throat. Tetraploid. 'J. T. Davis' × 'Belle Cook'. *Photograph by Francois Verhaert.*

'Pauline Roderick' (Elvan Roderick, 2005). Semi-evergreen. Scape 30 in. (76 cm); flower 6 in. (15 cm). Midseason late. A pink with a ruffled gold edge above a bright green throat. Tetraploid. 'Debussy' × 'Darla Anita'. *Photograph by Elvan Roderick.*

'Smile Again' (Larry Grace and Frank Smith, 2005). Semi-evergreen. Scape 30 in. (76 cm); flower 6 in. (15 cm). Early midseason. A pink with a cream edge above a green throat. Tetraploid. 'Tetra Helena Louisa' × seedling.
Photograph by Frank Smith.

'Angels and Ecstacy' (John P. Peat, 2006). Semi-evergreen. Scape 24 in. (61 cm); flower 6 in. (15 cm). Early midseason. A soft pink flower with very heavy substance and a large tightly formed ruffled edges above a bright green throat. Tetraploid. 'Reyna' × ('Tetra Champagne Elegance' × 'Ed Brown'). *Photograph by John P. Peat.*

'Anita McMaster' (John P. Peat, 2006). Semi-evergreen. Scape 26 in. (66 cm); flower 5 in. (12.7 cm). Early midseason. A lavender-pink with a strong, tightly ruffled tangerine-orange rubber edge above a dark green center. Tetraploid. ('Sultry Smile' × 'Sultry Smile') × ('Eternity's Shadow' × ('Sultry Smile' × 'Sultry Smile')).
Photograph by John P. Peat.

'April Laquinta' (Ted L. Petit, 2006). Semi-evergreen. Scape 30 in. (76 cm); flower 8 in. (20 cm). Midseason. A extremely large clear pink with a heavily ruffled gold edge above a grass-green throat. Tetraploid. ('Glacier Bay' × 'Tetra Siloam Ralph Henry') × 'Belle Cook'. *Photograph by Ted L. Petit.*

'Bells and Whistles' (Ted L. Petit, 2006). Semi-evergreen. Scape 26 in. (66 cm); flower 6.5 in. (16.5 cm). Early midseason. A rose-pink deepening toward the petal edges. A nicely ruffled gold edge surrounds the flower above the grass-green throat. Tetraploid. ('Glacier Bay' × 'Tetra Siloam Ralph Henry') × 'Ed Brown'. *Photograph by Ted L. Petit.*

'Buddy Hudson' (Hugh Buntyn, 2006). Semi-evergreen. Scape 25 in. (63 cm); flower 5.5 in. (14 cm). Midseason. A light pink self with a heavy gold edge and green heart. Tetraploid. 'Ed Brown' × 'J. T. Davis'.

'Conquest Quay' (John P. Peat, 2006). Semi-evergreen. Scape 28 in. (71 cm); flower 6.5 in. (16.5 cm). Midseason. A super ruffled golden edge accents a wide-petaled pink above a dark pine-green throat. Tetraploid. 'Dreams of Heroes' × 'J. T. Davis'. *Photograph by John P. Peat.*

'Dance Among the Stars' (Ted L. Petit, 2006). Semi-evergreen. Scape 26 in. (66 cm); flower 6 in. (15 cm). Midseason. A wide-petaled round soft baby-ribbon pink with elegant ruffles above a deep, dark green throat. Tetraploid. ('Ed Brown' × 'Tetra Dena Marie') × ('Ed Brown' × 'Expensive Taste'). *Photograph by Ted L. Petit.*

'Forestlake Kimberli Jo Harding' (Fran Harding, 2006). Dormant. Scape 30 in. (76 cm); flower 5 in. (12.7 cm). Early midseason. A pale pink blend with a heavy yellow hooked and toothy ruffled edge above a green throat. Tetraploid. (('Forestlake Lacy Bloomers' × ('Forestlake Ragamuffin' × 'Light Years Away')) × 'Darla Anita'). *Photograph by Fran Harding.*

'Cool Confections' (Jeff Salter, 2006). Semi-evergreen. Scape 27 in. (69 cm); flower 6 in. (15 cm). Early midseason. A soft lavender-pink self with a strong gold bubbly edge and a light green throat below a yellow-gold watermark. Tetraploid. 'J. T. Davis' × 'Mandalay Bay Music'. *Photograph by Jeff Salter.*

'Elegant Expressions' (Jeff Salter, 2006). Semi-evergreen. Scape 27 in. (69 cm); flower 5.5 in. (14 cm). Early midseason. A bright lavender-pink with a heavy gold edge above a light green throat. Tetraploid. 'Sweet Tranquility' × (('Something Superb' × 'Foggy London Town') × ('Something Splendid' × 'Poets Reverie')). *Photograph by Jeff Salter.*

'George Washington' (Patrick Stamile, 2006). Evergreen. Scape 28 in. (71 cm); flower 6 in. (15 cm). Midseason. A nicely ruffled, wide-petaled pink with a gold edge above a green throat. Tetraploid. 'Shores of Time' × 'Walking in Beauty'. *Photograph by Patrick Stamile.*

'Heaven's Artwork' (Herbert Phelps, 2006). Semi-evergreen. Scape 24 in. (61 cm); flower 5.75 in. (14.6 cm). Early midseason. A soft coral-pink with heavy substance above a striking green throat. Tetraploid. (((J. T. Davis' × 'Tetra Ultimate Perfection') × 'Tetra Mountain Almond') × seedling). *Photograph by Herbert Phelps.*

'Pink Parakeet' (John P. Peat, 2006). Semi-evergreen. Scape 31 in. (79 cm); flower 7 in. (18 cm). Early midseason. A shrimp-pink flower with a huge chartreuse-green throat. Tetraploid. Seedling × ('Barbie in Pink' × 'Aloha Hawaii'). *Photograph by John P. Peat.*

'Promised Fulfilled' (Ted L. Petit, 2006). Semi-evergreen. Scape 26 in. (66 cm); flower 6 in. (15 cm). Midseason. A soft peach-pink flower with a heavily ruffled gold edge above a large, vibrant green throat. Tetraploid. ('Dreams of Heroes' × 'J. T. Davis') × ('J. T. Davis' × 'Tetra Neal Berry'). *Photograph by Ted L. Petit.*

'Lucky Kiss' (Frank Smith, 2006). Semi-evergreen. Scape 36 in. (91 cm); flower 6 in. (15 cm). Midseason. A coral flower with a contrasting chartreuse watermark and matching picotee edge above a large apple-green throat. Tetraploid. 'American Freedom' × 'Jacqueline Kennedy Onassis'. *Photograph by Frank Smith.*

'Princess Diana' (Frank Smith, 2006). Semi-evergreen. Scape 30 in. (76 cm); flower 5.5 in. (14 cm). Midseason. A baby-ribbon pink flower with a brilliant green throat and large bubbly cream-yellow edge. Tetraploid. 'Mandalay Bay Music' × seedling. *Photograph by Frank Smith.*

'Shamrock Blush' (Dan Trimmer, 2006). Evergreen. Scape 22 in. (56 cm); flower 6 in. (15 cm). Early. A heavily ruffled pink with a gold edge above a fluorescent green throat. Tetraploid. 'Ed Brown' × seedling. *Photograph by Dan Trimmer.*

'Simply Pink' (John P. Peat, 2006). Semi-evergreen. Scape 28 in. (71 cm); flower 6 in. (15 cm). Early midseason. A large very light clear pink with an extremely bright green throat. The wire gold serrated edge is tightly ruffled. Tetraploid. Seedling × seedling. *Photograph by John P. Peat.*

'Tranquil Horizon' (Ted L. Petit, 2006). Semi-evergreen. Scape 27 in. (69 cm); flower 7 in. (18 cm). Midseason. A large pink flower with extremely heavy, plastic-like substance. The form is impeccable, with wide, round petals, which are surrounded by a crimped ruffled gold edge above a large green throat. Tetraploid. 'Ed Brown' × 'Tetra Champagne Elegance'. *Photograph by Ted L. Petit.*

'Unbridled Spirit' (John Rice, 2006). Dormant. Scape 33 in. (84 cm); flower 5 in. (12.7 cm). Midseason late. A peach flower above a dark green throat, with large knobby teeth surrounding the petals. Tetraploid. 'Angelina Maria Lucas' × 'Forestlake Ragamuffin'. *Photograph by John Rice.*

'Time Can Not Erase' (Ted L. Petit, 2006). Semi-evergreen. Scape 24 in. (61 cm); flower 7 in. (18 cm). Midseason. A coral-pink with a heavy, ruffled gold edge. The large blooms have a big green throat at their center. Tetraploid. ('Belle Cook' × (('Ed Brown' × 'Tetra Dena Marie') × 'Expensive Taste')). *Photograph by Ted L. Petit.*

LAVENDER (LAVENDER TO PURPLE)

'Malaysian Monarch' (R. W. Munson Jr., 1986). Semi-evergreen. Scape 24 in. (61 cm); flower 6 in. (15 cm). Early midseason. A burgundy-purple self with large cream-white watermark above a green heart. Tetraploid. Award of Merit 1993. *Photograph by R. W. Munson, Jr.*

'Respighi' (R. W Munson Jr., 1986). Evergreen. Scape 20 in. (51 cm); flower 6 in. (15 cm). Early midseason. A wine-black with a chalky wine eyezone and a yellow-green throat. Tetraploid. ('Ethiopia' × 'Tetra Betty Barnes') × 'Royal Heiress'. Award of Merit 1996. Honorable Mention 1993. *Photograph by Karen Newman.*

'Court Magician' (R. W. Munson Jr., 1987). Evergreen. Scape 26 in. (66 cm); flower 5 in. (12.7 cm). Early midseason. A wide-petaled purple self with a chalky lilac eyezone and a yellow-green throat. Tetraploid. ('Asian Emperor' × 'Benchmark') × 'Royal Saracen'. Award of Merit 1994. *Photograph by R. W. Munson, Jr.*

'Ida's Magic' (Ida Munson, 1988). Evergreen. Scape 28 in. (71 cm); flower 6 in. (15 cm). Early midseason. A lavender with a lighter watermark, gold edge and a green throat. Extremely popular and important breeder. Tetraploid. ('Royal Saracen' × 'Enchanted Empress') × 'Ruffled Dude'. Stout Silver Medal 2001. Award of Merit 1999. Honorable Mention 1996. *Photograph by R. W. Munson, Jr.*

'Regal Finale' (Patrick Stamile, 1988). Dormant. Scape 26 in. (66 cm); flower 6 in. (15 cm). Late. A violet-purple self with a green throat. Diploid. 'Super Purple' × 'When I Dream'. Eugene S. Foster Award 1992. Honorable Mention 1992. *Photograph by Debbie and Duane Hurlbert.*

'Vino Di Notte' (David Kirchhoff, 1988). Evergreen. Scape 32 in. (81 cm); flower 5 in. (12.7 cm). Early. An imperial-purple self with a lime-green throat. Tetraploid. 'Zinfandel' × 'Midnight Magic'. Award of Merit 1995. *Photograph by David Kirchhoff.*

'Black Ambrosia' (Jeff Salter, 1991). Semi-evergreen. Scape 28 in. (71 cm); flower 5 in. (12.7 cm). Midseason. A black-purple self with a green throat. Tetraploid. Seedling × 'Quest for Excalibur'. Award of Merit 2003. Honorable Mention 1999. *Photograph by Ted L. Petit and John P. Peat.*

'Solomons Robes' (David L. Talbott, 1991). Evergreen. Scape 30 in. (76 cm); flower 6 in. (15 cm). Midseason. A royal-purple self with a jade-green throat. Diploid. 'Super Purple' × 'Princess Do Dat'. Award of Merit 1998. Honorable Mention 1995.

'David Kirchhoff' (Jeff Salter, 1992). Semi-evergreen. Scape 26 in. (66 cm); flower 5.5 in. (14 cm). Midseason late. A lavender blend with a green throat. Tetraploid. 'Tomorrow's Dream' × seedling. Award of Merit 2003. Honorable Mention 2000. *Photograph by Melanie Mason.*

'Shaka Zulu' (Steve Moldovan, 1992). Semi-evergreen. Scape 28 in. (71 cm); flower 6 in. (15 cm). Early midseason. A dark grape-purple with white edging and a pale watermark above a lemon-yellow cream-green throat. Tetraploid. 'Court Magician' × 'Mephistopheles'. Honorable Mention 1999. *Photograph by Steve Moldovan.*

'Chris Salter' (Jeff Salter, 1993). Semi-evergreen. Scape 26 in. (66 cm); flower 6 in. (15 cm). Midseason. A medium lavender self with a gold edge above a green throat. Tetraploid. Award of Merit 2000. Honorable Mention 1997. *Photograph by Ted L. Petit and John P. Peat.*

'Fortune's Dearest' (Mort Morss, 1994). Evergreen. Scape 25 in. (63 cm); flower 6 in. (15 cm). Early. A grape-purple with a white edge and a lighter grape-purple watermark above a chartreuse throat. Tetraploid. Award of Merit 2002. Honorable Mention 1999. *Photograph by David Kirchhoff.*

'Kings and Vagabonds' (Ted L. Petit, 1994). Evergreen. Scape 22 in. (56 cm); flower 6 in. (15 cm). Midseason. A gold-edged, heavily ruffled orchid cream-pink with a cream watermark above a green throat. Tetraploid. 'Desert Jewel' × 'Wrapped in Gold'. *Photograph by Ted L. Petit.*

'Tune the Harp' (Ra Hansen, 1994). Semi-evergreen. Scape 26 in. (66 cm); flower 6 in. (15 cm). Early midseason. A cream-lavender with light purple ruffles and a green throat. Diploid. Seedling × 'Sings the Blues'. R. W. Munson Jr. Award 2004. Award of Merit 2004. Honorable Mention 1999. *Photograph by Tracy Heldt.*

'Big Blue' (Patrick Stamile, 1995). Dormant. Scape 24 in. (61 cm); flower 6.5 in. (16.5 cm). Midseason. A wide-petaled lavender self with a green center. Tetraploid. 'White Zone' × 'Tetra Barbara Mitchell'. Honorable Mention 2000. *Photograph by Patrick Stamile.*

'Cameroon Night' (Dan Trimmer, 1996). Evergreen. Scape 36 in. (91 cm); flower 7.5 in. (19 cm). Early midseason. A dark purple self with lighter midribs above a green throat. Tetraploid. 'Cameroons Twister' × 'Tetra Peacock Maiden'. Honorable Mention 2001. *Photograph by Debbie and Duane Hurlbert.*

'Clothed in Glory' (Larry Grace, 1996). Evergreen. Scape 18 in. (46 cm); flower 7 in. (18 cm). Midseason. A lavender-mauve with a 0.5 in. (1.3 cm) to 0.6 in. (1.6 cm) gold knobby edge and a lavender halo above a large yellow to gold throat. Tetraploid. 'Collectors Choice' × 'Admiral's Braid'. Award of Merit 2004. Honorable Mention 2001. *Photograph by Larry Grace.*

'Cosmic Thunder' (Jeff Salter, 1996). Evergreen. Scape 24 in. (61 cm); flower 6 in. (15 cm). Early midseason. A red-purple blend with a creamy white-lavender halo above a green throat. Tetraploid. Honorable Mention 2002.

'Daughter of Magic' (Jeff Salter, 1996). Semi-evergreen. Scape 28 in. (71 cm); flower 6 in. (15 cm). Early midseason. A lavender-pink blend with a gold edge above a green throat. Tetraploid. 'Beguiled Again' × seedling.

'Divine Comedy' (Steve Moldovan, 1996). Semi-evergreen. Scape 31 in. (79 cm); flower 6 in. (15 cm). Midseason. A rose-purple with a yellow watermark above a lemon-yellow to green throat. Tetraploid. 'Ida's Magic' × 'Salem Witch'. Honorable Mention 2002. *Photograph by Steve Moldovan.*

'Dracula' (Mac Carter, 1995). Dormant. Scape 28 in. (71 cm); flower 6.5 in. (16.5 cm). Midseason. A black-purple with a white edge above a green throat. Tetraploid. (Seedling × 'Midnight Magic') × 'Cranberry Red'. *Photograph by Mac Carter.*

'Forbidden Desires' (Ted L. Petit, 1995). Semi-evergreen. Scape 19 in. (48 cm); flower 6 in. (15 cm). Midseason. A large dark grape to plum-purple with a lighter watermark, a green throat, and a heavy gold edge. Tetraploid. 'Louis the Sixteenth' × 'Arabian Magic'. Honorable Mention 2002. *Photograph by Ted L. Petit.*

'Ida's Braid' (Matthew Kaskel, 1996). Evergreen. Scape 23 in. (58 cm); flower 5 in. (12.7 cm). Midseason late. A lavender self with a yellow to green throat. Tetraploid. 'Ida's Magic' × 'Admiral's Braid'. Honorable Mention 2003. *Photograph by Matthew Kaskel.*

'Light Years Away' (Ted L. Petit, 1996). Dormant. Scape 21 in. (53 cm); flower 5.5 in. (14 cm). Midseason. An lavender to orchid self surrounded by a 0.5 in. (1.3 cm) dramatic gold edge with a green throat. Tetraploid. 'Eternity's Shadow' × 'Admiral's Braid'. Honorable Mention 2007. *Photograph by Ted L. Petit.*

'Hawaiian Nights' (Guy Pierce, 1996). Evergreen. Scape 26 in. (66 cm); flower 5.5 in. (14 cm). Extra early. A lightly ruffled dark purple with a black-purple eyezone above a green throat. Tetraploid. 'Silent Sentry' × 'Still Night'. *Photograph by Debbie and Duane Hurlbert.*

'Lake Effect' (Patrick Stamile, 1996). Dormant. Scape 23 in. (58 cm); flower 7.25 in. (18 cm). Midseason. A mauve-purple with a bluish gray-lavender eyezone above a green throat. Tetraploid. 'Druid's Chant' × 'Big Blue'. Honorable Mention 2003. *Photograph by Patrick Stamile.*

'Lord of Lightning' (Jeff Salter, 1996). Semi-evergreen. Scape 26 in. (66 cm); flower 6 in. (15 cm). Midseason. A purple self with a gold edge above a green throat. Tetraploid. Honorable Mention 2002. *Photograph by John Benoot.*

'Lord of Rings' (Steve Moldovan, 1996). Semi-evergreen. Scape 28 in. (71 cm); flower 5 in. (12.7 cm). Midseason. A medium purple blend with a cream-etched ink-violet band above a creamy lemon-yellow to green throat. Tetraploid. 'Court Magician' × 'Mountain Majesty'. Honorable Mention 2002. *Photograph by Steve Moldovan.*

'Prince Charming Returns' (Jeff Salter, 1996). Semi-evergreen. Scape 28 in. (71 cm); flower 4.5 in. (11.5 cm). Midseason. A red-grape self with a green throat. Tetraploid. 'Taken By Storm' × 'Midnight Rambler'. *Photograph by Ted L. Petit and John P. Peat.*

'Vatican City' (Steve Moldovan, 1996). Semi-evergreen. Scape 26 in. (66 cm); flower 6 in. (15 cm). Early midseason. A grape-purple blend with a lemon-cream to green throat. Tetraploid. 'Noble Lord' × 'Francis of Assisi'. Award of Merit 2007. Honorable Mention 2003. *Photograph by Karen Newman.*

'Magic Amethyst' (Patrick Stamile, 1996). Dormant. Scape 27 in. (69 cm); flower 5.5 in. (14 cm). Early midseason. An amethyst-lavender blend with a green throat. Tetraploid. 'Druid's Chant' × 'Big Blue'. Honorable Mention 2002. *Photograph by Patrick Stamile.*

'Sugar Pavilion' (Jeff Salter, 1996). Evergreen. Scape 24 in. (61 cm); flower 5.5 in. (14 cm). Midseason. A lavender-peach blend with a yellow eyezone above a yellow throat. Tetraploid. 'Untamed Glory' × ('Tomorrow's Dream' × seedling).

'Blueberry Frost' (Patrick Stamile, 1997). Evergreen. Scape 28 in. (71 cm); flower 5 in. (12.7 cm). Midseason. A slightly recurved and ruffled blue-purple blend and a green throat. Tetraploid. ('Winter Mint Candy' × 'Admiral's Braid') × 'Ida's Magic'. *Photograph by Patrick Stamile.*

'Orion Sky' (Matthew Kaskel, 1997). Evergreen. Scape 26 in. (66 cm); flower 5 in. (12.7 cm). Midseason. A purple with a lighter purple watermark. Tetraploid. ((Seedling × 'Wedding Band') × (seedling × 'Wedding Band')) × 'Sea of Love'.

'Art of Seduction' (Robert Carr, 1998). Evergreen. Scape 29 in. (74 cm); flower 6 in. (15 cm). Midseason. A royal-purple with a silver edge and a yellow-green throat. Tetraploid. ('Ruffled Dude' × ('Wedding Band' × 'Royal Heritage')) × 'Quality of Mercy'.

'Long John Silver' (Ra Hansen, 1998). Semi-evergreen. Scape 42 in. (107 cm); flower 6.5 in. (16.5 cm). Early midseason. A narrow-petaled silver-lavender self with a yellow throat. Diploid. 'Yabba Dabba Doo' × ('Cerulean Star' × seedling). Honorable Mention 2005. *Photograph by Rejean Millette.*

'Pagan Ritual' (Robert Carr, 1999). Evergreen. Scape 27 in. (69 cm); flower 5 in. (12.7 cm). Midseason. A rich smoky burgundy-purple flower, trimmed with a golden white bubbly edge that extends down into a green throat. Tetraploid. ((('Midnight Magic' × 'Decatur Curtain Call') × ('Midnight Magic' × 'Court Magician') × 'Rue Madelaine'))) × ('Arabian Magic' × 'Wedding Band'). Honorable Mention 2003. *Photograph by Francois Verhaert.*

'Lifting Me Higher' (Larry Grace, 1998). Evergreen. Scape 24 in. (61 cm); flower 6 in. (15 cm). Early midseason. A velvety burgundy magenta-rose with a wide gold edge and a green throat. Tetraploid. Seedling × 'Clothed In Glory'. Honorable Mention 2002. *Photograph by Larry Grace.*

'Darla Anita' (John Kinnebrew, 1999). Evergreen. Scape 30 in. (76 cm); flower 7 in. (18 cm). Early midseason. A lavender blend with very heavy ruffled gold edges and a green throat. Tetraploid. 'Ida's Magic' × 'Spacecoast Starburst'. Award of Merit 2006. Honorable Mention 2003. 2007 Extra Large Diameter Award. *Photograph by Francois Verhaert.*

'Scott Fox' (John P. Peat, 1999). Semi-evergreen. Scape 32 in. (81 cm); flower 5.5 in. (14 cm). Midseason. A dark purple with a black-purple eyezone and a wire white edge carrying tiny shark's teeth above a green throat. Tetraploid. 'Didgeridoo' × 'Maltese Falcon'. *Photograph by John P. Peat.*

'Forbidden Fantasy' (Jeff Salter, 2000). Semi-evergreen. Scape 29 in. (74 cm); flower 6 in. (15 cm). Midseason late. A clear dark purple with a silver to white bubbly edge and a lighter watermark above a deep green throat. Tetraploid.

'Todd Fox' (John P. Peat, 1999). Semi-evergreen. Scape 22 in. (56 cm); flower 5 in. (12.7 cm). Midseason. A royal-purple with a dark royal-purple eyezone above a green throat. Tetraploid. 'Didgeridoo' × 'Maltese Falcon'. *Photograph by John P. Peat.*

'Forces of Nature' (John P. Peat, 2000). Semi-evergreen. Scape 22 in. (56 cm); flower 6 in. (15 cm). Midseason. A dark purple flower with a bright gold crimped heavy bubbly edge and chalky watermark above a green throat. Tetraploid. ('Just Infatuation' × ('Banquet at Versailles' × 'Karla Kitamura')) × 'Clothed in Glory'. *Photograph by John P. Peat.*

'Jewel in a Crown' (Larry Grace, 2000). Evergreen. Scape 23 in. (58 cm); flower 6 in. (15 cm). Midseason. A pink-lavender blend. Tetraploid. 'Ida's Magic' × 'Clothed in Glory'. *Photograph by Larry Grace.*

'Cameroons Twister' (John Benz, 2000). Dormant. Scape 40 in. (101 cm); flower 7.5 in. (19 cm). Midseason late. A wine-purple with a large pale watermark above a lime-green throat. Tetraploid. 'Cameroons' × 'One Step Beyond'. *Photograph by Debbie and Duane Hurlbert.*

'Larger Than Life' (Jeff Salter, 2000). Semi-evergreen. Scape 28 in. (71 cm); flower 7 in. (18 cm). Midseason. A large rose-lavender with a huge gold edge above a deep green throat. Tetraploid. Seedling × 'David Kirchhoff'. Honorable Mention 2003.

'Spacecoast Surprise Purple' (John Kinnebrew, 2000). Semi-evergreen. Scape 24 in. (61 cm); flower 5 in. (12.7 cm). Early. A nicely ruffled purple with a white edge above a yellow to green throat. Tetraploid. 'Spacecoast Sweetness' × 'Desert Dreams'. *Photograph by John Benoot.*

'Storm of the Century' (Robert Carr, 2000). Evergreen. Scape 28 in. (71 cm); flower 5.75 in. (14.6 cm). Early midseason. A rich royal-purple with a bubbling gold edge above a dark green throat. Tetraploid. 'Ida's Magic' × 'Thunder and Lightning'. *Photograph by Francois Verhaert.*

'Electric Mist' (Jeff Salter, 2001). Semi-evergreen. Scape 28 in. (71 cm); flower 7 in. (18 cm). Midseason. A purple with yellow-green lighter eyezone above a green throat. Tetraploid. *Photograph by Susan Okrasinski.*

'Victorian Principles' (Jeff Salter, 2000). Semi-evergreen. Scape 26 in. (66 cm); flower 5.5 in. (14 cm). Early midseason. A bright lavender with a yellow watermark and a gold edge. Tetraploid. 'Untamed Glory' × seedling. Honorable Mention 2003. *Photograph by Ted L. Petit and John P. Peat.*

'Face of the Stars' (Ludlow Lambertson, 2001). Semi-evergreen. Scape 28 in. (71 cm); flower 5.5 in. (14 cm). Midseason. A round red-violet with a steely red-violet eye. Adorned in white teeth around the edges. Tetraploid. 'Morts Masterpiece' × seedling. *Photograph by Ludlow Lambertson.*

'John Peat' (Ted L. Petit, 2001). Semi-evergreen. Scape 22 in. (56 cm); flower 6 in. (15 cm). Midseason. A burgundy with a 0.5 in. (1.3 cm) heavy gold edge and a lighter watermark above a green throat. Very high bud count and super rebloomer. Tetraploid. ('Karla Kitamura' × 'Arabian Magic') × 'Clothed in Glory'. Honorable Mention 2004. *Photograph by Ted L. Petit.*

'Moving All Over' (Patrick Stamile, 2001). Dormant. Scape 30 in. (76 cm); flower 11 in. (28 cm). Extra early. A purple self above a deep green throat. Tetraploid. ('Star of India' × 'Tetra Green Widow') × ('Star of India' × 'Tetra Green Widow'). *Photograph by Patrick Stamile.*

'Premier Surprise' (Jeff Salter, 2001). Semi-evergreen. Scape 32 in. (81 cm); flower 5.5 in. (14 cm). Midseason. A purple self above a green throat. Tetraploid. *Photograph by Susan Okrasinski.*

'Spacecoast Easy Rider' (John Kinnebrew, 2001). Semi-evergreen. Scape 30 in. (76 cm); flower 5 in. (12.7 cm). Midseason late. A lavender with a yellow halo and edge above a green throat. Tetraploid. 'Arabian Magic' × 'Spacecoast Starburst'. *Photograph by Sue Brown.*

'Bella Sera' (Patrick Stamile, 2002). Evergreen. Scape 30 in. (76 cm); flower 6 in. (15 cm). Early midseason. A beautiful mauve-purple with a silver edge and lavender watermark above a green throat. Tetraploid. ('Bogalusa' × 'Seize the Night') × ('Big Sur' × 'One Step Beyond'). *Photograph by Patrick Stamile.*

'Collective Spirit' (Ted L. Petit, 2002). Semi-evergreen. Scape 24 in. (61 cm); flower 6 in. (15 cm). Midseason. A purple with a lighter watermark and a gold edge above a green throat. Tetraploid. 'Bloodfire' × 'John Peat'. *Photograph by Ted L. Petit.*

'Cosmic Sensation' (Jeff Salter, 2002). Semi-evergreen. Scape 32 in. (81 cm); flower 5.5 in. (14 cm). Midseason. A purple with white edge above a green throat. Tetraploid. *Photograph by Francois Verhaert.*

'Enticing Elegance' (Jeff Salter, 2002). Semi-evergreen. Scape 28 in. (71 cm); flower 6.5 in. (16.5 cm). Midseason. A lavender with heavy yellow-gold edge above a yellow-green throat. Tetraploid. 'David Kirchhoff' × ('Age of Elegance' × seedling).

'Essence of Royalty' (Jack B. Carpenter, 2002). Evergreen. Scape 26 in. (66 cm); flower 6 in. (15 cm). Midseason. A wide-petaled lavender-purple with deeper eyezone above an applique green throat. Tetraploid. 'Diamonds and Pearls' × 'Tetra Lavender Blue Baby'. *Photograph by John Benoot.*

'Lavender Heartthrob' (Patrick Stamile, 2002). Dormant. Scape 22 in. (56 cm); flower 7 in. (18 cm). Extra early. A wide and full clear lavender with a striking braided and ruffled gold edge above a green throat. Tetraploid. 'Magic Amethyst' × 'Debussy'. *Photograph by Patrick Stamile.*

'Mort Morss' (Jeff Salter, 2002). Semi-evergreen. Scape 27 in. (69 cm); flower 6 in. (15 cm). Midseason. A dark purple with a white toothy edge on both the sepals and petals. Tetraploid. 'Fortunes Dearest' × 'Forbidden Fantasy'. Honorable Mention 2005. *Photograph by Jeff Salter.*

'New Day Dawning' (Jack B. Carpenter, 2002). Evergreen. Scape 24 in. (61 cm); flower 4.5 in. (11.5 cm). Midseason. A medium purple with a nice watermark surrounded by a ruffled gold to white toothy edge above a green throat. Tetraploid. 'Magic Obsession' × 'Tetra Lavender Blue Baby'. *Photograph by John Benoot.*

'Popcorn Pete' (Ted L. Petit, 2002). Semi-evergreen. Scape 25 in. (63 cm); flower 6 in. (15 cm). Midseason. A dark plum-purple with a lighter watermark above a green throat. The petals are surrounded by a heavy bubbly gold edge which resembles an ornate sprinkling of white popcorn. Tetraploid. ('Arabian Magic' × 'Ice Wine') × 'Clothed in Glory'. *Photograph by Ted L. Petit.*

'Promised Day' (John P. Peat, 2002). Semi-evergreen. Scape 21 in. (53 cm); flower 7 in. (18 cm). Early midseason. A deep bright purple with a huge orange watermark above a small green throat. The edge is a tangerine-orange color with the substance of rubber. Tetraploid. ('Eternity Shadow' × ('Sultry Smile' × 'Sultry Smile')) × 'Forces of Nature'. *Photograph by John P. Peat.*

'Sea of Cortez' (Ted L. Petit, 2002). Semi-evergreen. Scape 23 in. (58 cm); flower 6 in. (15 cm). Midseason. A rich dark purple with a muted watermark eye and a heavy ruffled gold edge above a green throat. Tetraploid. ('Banquet at Versailles' × 'Arabian Magic') × 'Clothed in Glory'. *Photograph by Ted L. Petit.*

'Spacecoast Sharp Tooth' (John Kinnebrew, 2002). Evergreen. Scape 22 in. (56 cm); flower 5.5 in. (14 cm). Early. A rich purple surrounded with bright white shark's teeth above an apple-green throat. Tetraploid. 'Spacecoast Surprise Purple' × 'Fortunes Dearest'. Honorable Mention 2005.

'Summer Solstice' (Ted L. Petit, 2002). Semi-evergreen. Scape 24 in. (61 cm); flower 6.5 in. (16.5 cm). Midseason. A lavender with a gold edge above a green throat. Tetraploid. 'Clothed in Glory' × ('Arabian Magic' × 'Karla Kitamura'). *Photograph by Ted L. Petit.*

'Rock of Salvation' (Karol Emmerich, 2002). Semi-evergreen. Scape 18 in. (46 cm); flower 6.75 in. (17 cm). Midseason. A rose-violet with a cream halo and edge above an olive to lime-green throat. Tetraploid. 'Lifting Me Higher' × 'Shimmering Elegance'. *Photograph by Karol Emmerich.*

'Alexa Kathryn' (John Kinnebrew, 2003). Semi-evergreen. Scape 22 in. (56 cm); flower 6.25 in. (16 cm). Early midseason. A lavender with a chartreuse edge above a yellow to green throat. Tetraploid. 'Spacecoast Cool Deal' × 'Darla Anita'. *Photograph by John Kinnebrew.*

'Barbara Morton' (Ted L. Petit, 2003). Semi-evergreen. Scape 25 in. (63 cm); flower 6 in. (15 cm). Midseason. A clear lavender flower with a very heavy ruffled gold edge with a small charcoal eyezone above a green throat. Tetraploid. 'Eternity's Shadow' × 'Clothed in Glory'. *Photograph by Ted L. Petit.*

'Eva Lynn Cupchik' (Ted L. Petit, 2003). Semi-evergreen. Scape 27 in. (69 cm); flower 6 in. (15 cm). Midseason. A purple with lighter watermark and gold edge above a green throat. Tetraploid. 'Forbidden Desires' × 'Clothed in Glory'. *Photograph by Ted L. Petit.*

'Jay Farquhar' (Jack B. Carpenter, 2003). Evergreen. Scape 26 in. (66 cm); flower 6.5 in. (16.5 cm). Midseason. A purple with a white watermark eye and edge above a green throat. Tetraploid. 'Lifting me Higher' × ('Chris Salter' × 'Tetra Waxen Wonder'). Honorable Mention 2007. *Photograph by Debbie and Duane Hurlbert.*

'Café Mocha' (Ted L. Petit, 2003). Semi-evergreen. Scape 26 in. (66 cm); flower 6 in. (15 cm). Midseason. A purple and coffee blend with a lighter watermark and a gold edge above a green throat. Tetraploid. 'Promised Day' × 'John Peat'. *Photograph by Ted L. Petit.*

'Inca Puzzle' (Ted L. Petit, 2003). Semi-evergreen. Scape 28 in. (71 cm); flower 6 in. (15 cm). Midseason. A purple with a gold watermark and edge above a green throat. Tetraploid. 'Ancient Wisdom' × 'Regal Procession'. *Photograph by Ted L. Petit.*

'Leaving Me Breathless' (Ted L. Petit, 2003). Semi-evergreen. Scape 30 in. (76 cm); flower 6 in. (15 cm). Midseason. A purple with a chalk watermark and a gold edge above a green throat. Tetraploid. 'Eternity's Shadow' × 'John Peat'. *Photograph by Ted L. Petit.*

'Madonna Arsenault' (John P. Peat, 2003). Semi-evergreen. Scape 24 in. (61 cm); flower 7.5 in. (19 cm). Midseason late. A lavender-rose with an orange watermark and edge above a green throat. Tetraploid. (('Just Infatuation' × 'Banquet at Versailles') × 'John Peat') × ('Eternity's Shadow' × ('Sultry Smile' × seedling)). *Photograph by John P. Peat.*

'Spiny Sea Urchin' (Patrick Stamile, 2003). Semi-evergreen. Scape 27 in. (69 cm); flower 5.5 in. (14 cm). Early midseason. A lavender with a gold spiny edge above a green throat. Tetraploid. ('Shimmering Elegance' × 'Ed Brown') × 'Magic Lake'. Honorable Mention 2007. *Photograph by John Benoot.*

'Ana Maria Margetts' (John P. Peat, 2004). Semi-evergreen. Scape 22 in. (56 cm); flower 6 in. (15 cm). Early midseason. A purple with a light purple watermark and a gold edge above a green throat. Tetraploid. 'Forces of Nature' × ('Baby Jane Hudson' × 'Size Counts'). *Photograph by John P. Peat.*

'Sarah Goldstein' (Ted L. Petit, 2003). Semi-evergreen. Scape 27 in. (69 cm); flower 6 in. (15 cm). Midseason. A lavender with a gold edge above a green throat. Tetraploid. 'Barbara Morton' × 'Ancient Wisdom'. *Photograph by Ted L. Petit.*

'Ted Gardian' (John P. Peat, 2003). Dormant. Scape 16 in. (41 cm); flower 5.5 in. (14 cm). Midseason. A clear lavender flower with a heavy braided gold edge and a green throat. Tetraploid. 'Karl Petersen' × 'Light Years Away'. *Photograph by John P. Peat.*

'As Time Goes By' (Ted L. Petit, 2004). Semi-evergreen. Scape 28 in. (71 cm); flower 6 in. (15 cm). Midseason. A purple with lighter watermark and a gold edge above a green throat. Tetraploid. ('Banquet at Versailles' × 'Arabian Magic') × 'John Peat'. *Photograph by Ted L. Petit.*

'Beacon at Dusk' (Ted L. Petit, 2004). Semi-evergreen. Scape 24 in. (61 cm); flower 5.5 in. (14 cm). Midseason. A purple with lighter watermark and a gold edge above a green throat. Tetraploid. ('Bohemia After Dark' × ('Sultry Smile' × 'Forbidden Desires')) × ('Didgeridoo' × 'Clothed in Glory'). *Photograph by Ted L. Petit.*

'Emerald Starburst' (George Doorakian, 2004). Dormant. Scape 32 in. (81 cm); flower 5 in. (12.7 cm). Midseason. A green and raspberry above emerald-green throat. Diploid. Seedling × seedling. *Photograph by George Doorakian.*

'Heartbeat of Heaven' (Karol Emmerich, 2004). Semi-evergreen. Scape 32 in. (81 cm); flower 6.5 in. (16.5 cm). Midseason late. A pink-lavender with ivory-lavender halo etched in darker lavender edge trimmed gold above a yellow-green throat. Tetraploid. ('Fortune's Dearest' × 'Lifting Me Higher') × seedling. Honorable Mention 2007. *Photograph by Karol Emmerich.*

'Dr. Julius Charba' (Jack B. Carpenter, 2004). Evergreen. Scape 24 in. (61 cm); flower 5.5 in. (14 cm). Early midseason. A lavender with lavender-blue eyezone above a green throat. Tetraploid. Seedling × 'Mrs. John Cooper'. *Photograph by Jack B. Carpenter.*

'Royal Manor' (Ted L. Petit, 2004). Semi-evergreen. Scape 25 in. (63 cm); flower 6 in. (15 cm). Midseason. A rich purple with a heavy, ruffled gold edge and a lighter watermark above a dark green throat. Tetraploid. 'John Peat' × 'Bohemia After Dark'. *Photograph by Ted L. Petit.*

'Stirs the Soul' (Ted L. Petit, 2004). Semi-evergreen. Scape 22 in. (56 cm); flower 5.5 in. (14 cm). Midseason. A burgundy with a lighter watermark and a heavily ruffled gold edge above a green throat. Tetraploid. 'Promised Day' × 'Ted Gardian'. *Photograph by Ted L. Petit.*

'Born to Reign' (Karol Emmerich, 2005). Semi-evergreen. Scape 26 in. (66 cm); flower 6.5 in. (16.5 cm). Midseason. A cranberry-purple with rose-pink watermark and white-gold filigree edge above a yellow to green throat. Tetraploid. 'Lifting Me Higher' × 'Shaka Zulu'. *Photograph by Karol Emmerich.*

'Gold Miner's Daughter' (Ted L. Petit, 2005). Semi-evergreen. Scape 26 in. (66 cm); flower 6.5 in. (16.5 cm). Midseason. A lavender-pink with gold edge above a green throat. Tetraploid. ('John Peat' × 'Sarah Goldstein') × ('Darla Anita' × 'Promised Day'). *Photograph by Ted L. Petit.*

'All Things Regal' (Ted L. Petit, 2005). Semi-evergreen. Scape 23 in. (58 cm); flower 6 in. (15 cm). Midseason. A purple with a gold edge above a green throat. Tetraploid. ('Beacon at Dusk' × 'Popcorn Pete') × ('John Peat' × 'Leaving Me Breathless'). *Photograph by Ted L. Petit.*

'Gary Colby' (Ted L. Petit, 2005). Semi-evergreen. Scape 26 in. (66 cm); flower 8 in. (20 cm). Midseason. A rose with gold edge above a green throat. Tetraploid. 'John Peat' × 'Moment in the Sun'. *Photograph by Ted L. Petit.*

'Hebrew Maiden' (Tim Bell, 2005). Evergreen. Scape 25 in. (63 cm); flower 5.5 in. (14 cm). Midseason. A lavender-pink with a yellow edge above a yellow-green throat. Tetraploid. 'Ed Brown' × ('Druid's Chant' × 'Ida's Magic'). *Photograph by Tim Bell.*

'Heline Pressley' (John P. Peat, 2005). Semi-evergreen. Scape 26 in. (66 cm); flower 6.5 in. (16.5 cm). Early midseason. A deep purple with darker eye and gold picotee edge above a green throat. Tetraploid. 'Promised Day' × ('J. T. Davis' × 'Tetra Siloam Ralph Henry'). *Photograph by John P. Peat.*

'Lavender Perfection' (Ted L. Petit, 2005). Dormant. Scape 26 in. (66 cm); flower 6.5 in. (16.5 cm). Midseason. A bright lavender with a lighter watermark and a tightly ruffled gold edge above a green throat. Tetraploid. 'John Peat' × 'Moment in the Sun'. *Photograph by Ted L. Petit.*

'Moonlight Sail' (Patrick Stamile, 2005). Semi-evergreen. Scape 28 in. (71 cm); flower 6 in. (15 cm). Midseason. A purple with a slate lavender watermark and a ruffled gold edge above a green throat. Tetraploid. 'Bohemia After Dark' × (('Musical Medley' × 'Seize the Night') × 'Chartered Course').

'Rubber Ducky' (John P. Peat, 2005). Dormant. Scape 32 in. (81 cm); flower 6 in. (15 cm). Early midseason. A violet-lavender with a rubbery, tangerine-orange watermark and edge above a green throat. Tetraploid. ('Sultry Smile' × 'Sultry Smile') × 'Ted Gardian'. *Photograph by John P. Peat.*

'So Many Rivers' (Mort Morss, 2005). Semi-evergreen. Scape 26 in. (66 cm); flower 5 in. (12.7 cm). Early midseason. A violet with a blue-purple halo and a white brushed edge above a green throat. Tetraploid. Seedling × 'Tetra Lavender Blue Baby'. *Photograph by Mort Morss.*

'Spectacle of Wealth' (Ted L. Petit, 2005). Semi-evergreen. Scape 26 in. (66 cm); flower 6 in. (15 cm). Midseason. A lavender with a purple watermark above a green throat. Tetraploid. ('Sultry Smile' × 'Drowning in Desire') × 'John Peat'. *Photograph by Ted L. Petit.*

VANILLA LACE

'Vanilla Lace' (Kelly Mitchell, 2005). Dormant. Scape 20 in. (51 cm); flower 5 in. (12.7 cm). Early midseason. A lavender with a large cream edge above a green throat. Tetraploid. 'Key Lime Ice' × seedling. *Photograph by Kelly Mitchell.*

'Wonder of It All' (Robert Carr, 2005). Dormant. Scape 27 in. (69 cm); flower 5.75 in. (14.6 cm). Early. A very pale lavender with a yellow-gold edge above a green throat. Tetraploid. 'Mandalay Bay Music' × 'Wonders Never Cease'.

'China Clipper' (Dan Trimmer, 2006). Evergreem. Scape 26 in. (66 cm); flower 6.25 in. (16 cm). Early midseason. A nicely ruffled purple with a pale purple watermark and a wire white edge above a green throat. Tetraploid. 'Wild Cherry Round Up' × 'Doyle Pierce'. *Photograph by Dan Trimmer.*

'Clark Kent' (John P. Peat, 2006). Semi-evergreen. Scape 29 in. (74 cm); flower 8.5 in. (22 cm). Early midseason. A purple with a darker purple eyezone and wire purple picotee surrounded by white shark's teeth above a green throat. Tetraploid. 'Pirate's Ransom' × 'Fortune's Dearest'. *Photograph by John P. Peat.*

'Golden Diamond Dust' (John P. Peat, 2006). Semi-evergreen. Scape 28 in. (71 cm); flower 7 in. (18 cm). Midseason late. A dark burgundy flower with a strong 3/4 in. ruffled gold edge above a large yellow watermark and dark green center. Tetraploid. ('Eternity's Shadow' × ('Just Infatuation' × 'John Peat')) × (('Eternity's Shadow' × Eternity's Shadow') × 'Ferengi Gold'). *Photograph by John P. Peat.*

'Jennifer Trimmer' (Dan Trimmer, 2006). Evergreen. Scape 30 in. (76 cm); flower 6.75 in. (17 cm). Early midseason. A lavender-purple with a chalky white watermark and a gold edge above a bright green throat. Tetraploid. 'Bella Sera' × seedling. *Photograph by Dan Trimmer.*

'Leprechaun Prince' (Ted L. Petit, 2006). Semi-evergreen. Scape 31 in. (79 cm); flower 6 in. (15 cm). Midseason. A clear lavender-purple with a lighter watermark. The heavily ruffled petals are surrounded by a bubbly, crunchy gold to green edge above a deep green throat. Tetraploid. ('John Peat' × 'John Peat') × ('Leaving Me Breathless' × 'Gary Colby'). *Photograph by Ted L. Petit.*

'Orchid Electra' (Ted L. Petit, 2006). Semi-evergreen. Scape 25 in. (63 cm); flower 7 in. (18 cm). Midseason. An electric burgundy-wine flower with a lighter watermark with an orange cast above a green throat. Tetraploid. 'Leaving Me Breathless' × 'Regal Procession'. *Photograph by Ted L. Petit.*

'Serenity Bay' (Jeff Salter, 2006). Evergreen. Scape 26 in. (66 cm); flower 6 in. (15 cm). Midseason late. A pale lavender with a heavy ruffled gold edge above a vibrant green throat. Tetraploid. 'Jerry Nettles' × 'Mandalay Bay Music'. *Photograph by Jeff Salter.*

'Texas Feathered Fancy' (Jack B. Carpenter, 2006). Dormant. Scape 20 in. (51 cm); flower 5 in. (12.7 cm). Midseason. A lavender self with raised feathering above the green throat area. Diploid. 'Lavender Blue Baby' × unknown. *Photograph by Jack B. Carpenter.*

'Rachel Klee' (Ted L. Petit, 2006). Semi-evergreen. Scape 30 in. (76 cm); flower 7 in. (18 cm). Midseason. A deeply saturated, clear purple flower with ruffled gold edges above a dark green center. Tetraploid. 'Alexa Kathryn' × 'Collective Spirit'. *Photograph by Ted L. Petit.*

'Some Sweet Day' (Patrick Stamile, 2006). Evergreen. Scape 35 in. (89 cm); flower 6.25 in. (16 cm). Midseason. A lavender to rose with a chartreuse-green to gold edge above a green throat. Tetraploid. ('Arctic Lace' × 'Northern Glitter') × 'Walking on Beauty'. *Photograph by Patrick Stamile.*

'Time To Go' (John P. Peat, 2006). Dormant. Scape 30 in. (76 cm); flower 6 in. (15 cm). Early midseason. A lavender-pink with a huge tangerine-orange watermark and a very heavy, rubbery tangerine-orange edge above a green throat. Tetraploid. 'Sultry Smile' × 'Sultry Smile'. *Photograph by John P. Peat.*

RED (RED TO BLACK-RED)

'Big Apple' (Van M. Sellers, 1986). Evergreen. Scape 26 in. (66 cm); flower 5 in. (12.7 cm). Early midseason. A classic tailored cerise-red flower with a green throat. Diploid. 'When I Dream' × 'Super Purple'. Award of Merit 1992. *Photograph by John Eiseman.*

'Vintage Bordeaux' (David Kirchhoff, 1986). Evergreen. Scape 27 in. (69 cm); flower 5.75 in. (14.6 cm). Early. A dark cherry-red with a chartreuse throat. Tetraploid. 'Amadeus' × seedling. Award of Merit 1994. *Photograph by John Eiseman.*

'Siloam Paul Watts' (Pauline Henry, 1988). Dormant. Scape 18 in. (46 cm); flower 5 in. (12.7 cm). Midseason. A very bright wide-petaled ruffled red self with a green throat. Very highly regarded. Diploid. Award of Merit 1995. *Photograph by John Eiseman.*

'Superlative' (Lee E. Gates, 1986). Semi-evergreen. Scape 24 in. (61 cm); flower 6 in. (15 cm). Early. A dark red with a darker eyezone and a green throat. Tetraploid. Award of Merit 1996. Honorable Mention 1992. *Photograph by Karen Newman.*

'Bamboo Blackie' (Dalton Durio, 1988). Dormant. Scape 24 in. (61 cm); flower 5.5 in. (14 cm). Midseason. A deep reddish black self with a green-chartreuse throat. Tetraploid. ('Zorro' × 'Total Eclipse') × 'Spades'. Honorable Mention 1996. *Photograph by Ted L. Petit and John P. Peat.*

'Startle' (Eugene Belden, 1988). Dormant. Scape 26 in. (66 cm); flower 5 in. (12.7 cm). Midseason. A red bitone with a cream halo and a green throat. Very heavy gold edge. Tetraploid. 'Broadmore Red' × 'My Sunshine'. Honorable Mention 1999. *Photograph by John Benz.*

'Autumn Valentine' (David Kirchhoff, 1991). Evergreen. Scape 28 in. (71 cm); flower 6 in. (15 cm). Late. A cardinal-red spider self edged in gold with a yellow to chartreuse throat. Tetraploid. Seedling × 'Richard Connelly'. Eugene S. Foster Award 2006. *Photograph by Debbie and Duane Hurlbert.*

'Magic Carpet Ride' (David Kirchhoff, 1992). Evergreen. Scape 28 in. (71 cm); flower 6 in. (15 cm). Early midseason. A mandarin-red with a coral orange-red watermark above a yellow to yellow-green throat. Tetraploid. ('Bittersweet Holiday' × 'Regal Flame') × ('Study in Scarlet' × ('Grand Opera' × 'Amadeus')). Award of Merit 1999. Honorable Mention 1996.

'Velvet Beads' (Emily Olson, 1992). Dormant. Scape 28 in. (71 cm); flower 5 in. (12.7 cm). Early midseason. A flame-red self with a yellow to green throat. Tetraploid. ((Seedling × 'Midnight Magic') × (seedling × 'Dance Ballerina Dance')) × seedling. Honorable Mention 2000.

'Sultans Warrior' (Jeff Salter, 1991). Evergreen. Scape 23 in. (58 cm); flower 5 in. (12.7 cm). Midseason. A deep red self with a strong green center. Tetraploid. Seedling × 'Tetra Christmas'. *Photograph by John Eiseman.*

'Dragon King' (David Kirchhoff, 1992). Evergreen. Scape 22 in. (56 cm); flower 5.5 in. (14 cm). Early. A mandarin-red self with a vivid green throat. Tetraploid. 'Study in Scarlet' × 'Anastasia'. Award of Merit 2001. Honorable Mention 1997. *Photograph by Ted L. Petit and John P. Peat.*

'All American Chief' (Van M. Sellers, 1994). Dormant. Scape 32 in. (81 cm); flower 9 in. (23 cm). Early midseason. A red self with a yellow throat. 2006 Extra Large Diameter Award. Tetraploid. Award of Merit 2004. Honorable Mention 1999. *Photograph by Ted L. Petit and John P. Peat.*

'Francis of Assisi' (Steve Moldovan, 1994). Semi-evergreen. Scape 26 in. (66 cm); flower 6 in. (15 cm). Midseason. A burgundy-red to bright wine-red blend with a bold white picotee edge above a pale yellow to green throat. Tetraploid. ('Abba' × 'Shaka Zulu'). Award of Merit 2004. Honorable Mention 1999. *Photograph by Debbie and Duane Hurlbert.*

'Noble Warrior' (Jeff Salter, 1996). Semi-evergreen. Scape 28 in. (71 cm); flower 5.5 in. (14 cm). Early midseason. A nicely ruffled velvety red self with a yellow to green throat. Tetraploid. *Photograph by Francois Verhaert.*

'Romeo is Bleeding' (Ted L. Petit, 1996). Evergreen. Scape 23 in. (58 cm); flower 5.5 in. (14 cm). Midseason. A deep velvety highly ruffled red with a crunchy wire gold edge and a green throat. Tetraploid. 'Ida's Magic' × 'Midnight Magic'. Honorable Mention 2003. *Photograph by Ted L. Petit.*

'Hot Scheme' (Elizabeth H. Salter, 1997). Semi-evergreen. Scape 26 in. (66 cm); flower 3.5 in. (9 cm). Midseason. A red self with a gold edge and a gold to green throat. Honorable Mention 2007. Tetraploid.

'Drowning in Desire' (Ted L. Petit, 1996). Semi-evergreen. Scape 22 in. (56 cm); flower 5.5 in. (14 cm). Midseason. A rich fire-engine red with a lighter watermark, a green throat, and a crimped gold edge. Tetraploid. ('Midnight Magic' × 'Court Magician') × 'Ida's Magic'. *Photograph by Ted L. Petit.*

'Reason for Treason' (David Kirchhoff, 1996). Evergreen. Scape 32 in. (81 cm); flower 7 in. (18 cm). Midseason. A distinctive orange-red with a gold edge and a lighter watermark halo above a yellow to green throat. Tetraploid. ('White Tie Affair' × 'Enchanted Empress') × 'Perfect Pleasure'. Honorable Mention 2003. *Photograph by David Kirchhoff.*

'Langley Morning Glow' (Pam Erikson, 1997). Dormant. Scape 30 in. (76 cm); flower 5 in. (12.7 cm). Midseason. An orange-red self with a yellow throat. Diploid. *Photograph by Pam Erikson.*

'Passion District' (Robert Carr, 1997). Evergreen. Scape 28 in. (71 cm); flower 5.75 in. (14.6 cm). Midseason. A deep ruby-red with ruffles surrounded by a wire white edge with both an eye and a watermark above a green throat. Tetraploid. 'Midnight Magic' × 'Betty Warren Woods'. Honorable Mention 2001. *Photograph by Robert Carr.*

'Wish Fulfillment' (Patrick Stamile, 1997). Evergreen. Scape 28 in. (71 cm); flower 6.5 in. (16.5 cm). Midseason. A rose-red with a white edge above a green throat. Tetraploid. 'Ida's Magic' × 'Ebony Jewel'. *Photograph by Patrick Stamile.*

'Rocket Booster' (Victor Santa Lucia, 1997). Dormant. Scape 36 in. (91 cm); flower 7.5 in. (19 cm). Midseason. A red self with a yellow-green throat. Tetraploid. Honorable Mention 2002. *Photograph by Debbie and Duane Hurlbert.*

'Christmas Wishes' (Elizabeth H. Salter, 1998). Evergreen. Scape 24 in. (61 cm); flower 4 in. (10 cm). Midseason. A red self with a yellow to green throat. Tetraploid. (Seedling × 'Prince Red Bird') × ('Tetra Casey Boy' × seedling). Honorable Mention 2007. *Photograph by Debbie and Duane Hurlbert.*

'Mama's Cherry Pie' (Fay Shooter, 1998). Semi-evergreen. Scape 26 in. (66 cm); flower 6 in. (15 cm). Midseason. A cherry-red with a deeper red eyezone and a double edge of salmon-pink and white. Tetraploid. 'Whooperee' × 'Elizabeth Salter'. Honorable Mention 2004. *Photograph by Francois Verhaert.*

'Ransom Note' (Robert Carr, 1998). Evergreen. Scape 27 in. (69 cm); flower 5 in. (12.7 cm). Early midseason. A purple with a light purple watermark and a yellow-gold edge above a yellow-green throat. Tetraploid. 'Wedding Band' × 'Arabian Magic'. *Photograph by Robert Carr.*

'Out Back Red' (Jeff Salter, 1998). Semi-evergreen. Scape 28 in. (71 cm); flower 7 in. (18 cm). Midseason. A red self with a green throat. Tetraploid.

'Hearts of Fire' (Patrick Stamile, 1998). Evergreen. Scape 30 in. (76 cm); flower 6.25 in. (16 cm). Midseason. A red self with a green throat. Tetraploid. 'Ebony Jewel' × 'Aramis'. Honorable Mention 2002. *Photograph by Patrick Stamile.*

'Persian Ruby' (Dan Trimmer, 1998). Dormant. Scape 30 in. (76 cm); flower 8 in. (20 cm). Early midseason. A ruby-red self with a green throat. Tetraploid. 'Ruby Spider' × ('Nordic Night' × 'Tetra Regal Finale'). Honorable Mention 2005. *Photograph by Karen Newman.*

'Roses in Snow' (Dan Hansen, 1999). Semi-evergreen. Scape 24 in. (61 cm); flower 5 in. (12.7 cm). Early midseason. A red with ivory edges above an emerald-green throat. Tetraploid. 'Calgary Stampede' × 'Untamed Glory'. Award of Merit 2006. Honorable Mention 2003. *Photograph by Chuck Hubble.*

‘Spacecoast Cranberry Breeze’ (John Kinnebrew, 1999). Semi-evergreen. Scape 24 in. (61 cm); flower 5.5 in. (14 cm). Early midseason. A cranberry-red self with gold edges and a melon throat. Tetraploid. ‘Ida’s Magic’ × seedling. Honorable Mention 2002. *Photograph by Debbie and Duane Hurlbert.*

‘Pure Indulgence’ (Robert Carr, 2000). Evergreen. Scape 30 in. (76 cm); flower 5.5 in. (14 cm). Early. A rich deep red with a contrasting white picotee on its superbly ruffled edges. Tetraploid. (‘Ida’s Magic’ × (‘Harrod’s’ × ‘Study in Scarlet’)) × (‘Ida’s Magic’ × ‘Midnight Magic’). Honorable Mention 2003. *Photograph by Francois Verhaert.*

‘Samurai Warrior’ (Jeff Salter, 2000). Semi-evergreen. Scape 26 in. (66 cm); flower 5 in. (12.7 cm). Midseason. A red-burgundy self above a yellow and green throat. Tetraploid. ‘David Kirchhoff’ × unknown.

‘Spacecoast Hot Topic’ (John Kinnebrew, 2000). Evergreen. Scape 24 in. (61 cm); flower 4 in. (10 cm). Early midseason. A red self above a yellow to green throat. Tetraploid. Seedling × ‘Leonard Bernstein’. Honorable Mention 2003.

‘Cleopatra’s Jewel’ (Ted L. Petit, 2000). Semi-evergreen. Scape 30 in. (76 cm); flower 5.5 in. (14 cm). Early midseason. A red with a gold edge. Tetraploid. ‘Jack of Hearts’ × ‘Romeo is Bleeding’. *Photograph by Ted L. Petit.*

‘Jack of Hearts’ (Ted L. Petit, 2000). Semi-evergreen. Scape 22 in. (56 cm); flower 5.5 in. (14 cm). Midseason. An intense, saturated, velvety red with a lighter watermark. The petal edges are very ruffled and looped, carrying a crimped platinum to gold edge. Tetraploid. ‘Restless Warrior’ × ‘Drowning in Desire’. *Photograph by Ted L. Petit.*

'Eclipse of the Heart' (Ted L. Petit, 2001). Evergreen. Scape 25 in. (63 cm); flower 5.5 in. (14 cm). Midseason. A black-red with a rose watermark above a green throat. Tetraploid. 'Study in Scarlet' × 'Ida's Magic'. *Photograph by Ted L. Petit.*

'Mary Alice Stokes' (Dan Hansen, 2001). Semi-evergreen. Scape 25 in. (63 cm); flower 5 in. (12.7 cm). Early. A rosy red flower with a lightly ruffled pink and wire gold edge above a light green throat. Tetraploid. 'Roses in Snow' × unknown. *Photograph by Francois Verhaert.*

'Spacecoast Cranberry Kid' (John Kinnebrew, 2001). Semi-evergreen. Scape 24 in. (61 cm); flower 6 in. (15 cm). Early midseason. A clear, cranberry-red with a lighter inner halo, carrying wide, ruffled golden orange edges. Tetraploid. 'Spacecoast Cranberry Breeze' × 'Watermelon Wine'. Honorable Mention 2004.

'Spacecoast Raspberry Mist' (John Kinnebrew, 2001). Semi-evergreen. Scape 30 in. (76 cm); flower 5.5 in. (14 cm). Early midseason. A rose-red with a lighter halo and a gold edge above a green throat. Tetraploid. 'Arabian Magic' × 'Spacecoast Starburst'.

'Geneva Firetruck' (Dan Hansen, 2001). Semi-evergreen. Scape 30 in. (76 cm); flower 5.5 in. (14 cm). Early midseason. A red with yellow edge above green-yellow throat. Tetraploid. ('Calgary Stampede' × 'Alexandra') × 'Roses in Snow'. *Photograph by Sue Brown.*

'Scarlet Lace' (Patrick Stamile, 2001). Evergreen. Scape 27 in. (69 cm); flower 4.5 in. (11.5 cm). Early midseason. A red with a white bubbled and braided edge above a green heart with a yellow ringed throat. Tetraploid. ('Desperado Love' × 'Wish Fulfillment') × 'Edge of Eden'. *Photograph by Patrick Stamile.*

'Betty Ford' (David Kirchhoff, 2002). Semi-evergreen. Scape 30 in. (76 cm); flower 5.5 in. (14 cm). Extra early. A garnet-red with Chinese-red watermark halo above a yellow to green throat. Tetraploid. ('Leonard Bernstein' × 'Crimson Wind') × ('Torrid Tango × 'Forever Red'). Honorable Mention 2007. *Photograph by David Kirchhoff.*

'Carnival in Brazil' (Ted L. Petit, 2002). Semi-evergreen. Scape 25 in. (63 cm); flower 5 in. (12.7 cm). Midseason. A red with a lighter red watermark above a green throat. Tetraploid. 'Drowning in Desire' × ('Chinese Chariot' × 'Bloodfire'). *Photograph by Ted L. Petit.*

'Fire Down Below' (Ted L. Petit, 2002). Dormant. Scape 27 in. (69 cm); flower 6 in. (15 cm). Midseason. A deep, velvety blood-red with extremely wide petals. The petals have a heavy substance with a carved, textured surface and beautiful ruffling. Tetraploid. 'Richard Taylor' × 'Jack of Hearts'. *Photograph by Ted L. Petit.*

'Madly Red' (David Kirchhoff, 2002). Evergreen. Scape 18 in. (46 cm); flower 5 in. (12.7 cm). Extra early. A red with a gold edge and a yellow to green throat. Tetraploid. Seedling × seedling. *Photograph by Francois Verhaert.*

'Executive Decision' (Ted L. Petit, 2002). Semi-evergreen. Scape 23 in. (58 cm); flower 6 in. (15 cm). Midseason. A very bright fire-engine red with a wire gold edge. The center of the flower has a small lighter watermark surrounding a green heart. Tetraploid. ('Richard Taylor' × 'Jack of Hearts') × 'Drowning in Desire'. *Photograph by Ted L. Petit.*

'Jerry Nettles' (John Kinnebrew, 2002). Evergreen. Scape 28 in. (71 cm); flower 6 in. (15 cm). Early midseason. A lavender-purple, full, flat, and trimmed with magnificent, heavily ruffled, yellow-gold edges, which glows proudly from clear across the garden. Tetraploid. 'Spacecoast Starburst' × 'Ed Brown'. Honorable Mention 2005. *Photograph by John Kinnebrew.*

'Painting the Roses Red' (Jeff Salter, 2002). Semi-evergreen. Scape 26 in. (66 cm); flower 6 in. (15 cm). Midseason. A deep bright coral-peach with a gold edge that has large ruffles and tiny teeth. Tetraploid. 'Ed Brown' × 'Enchanting Esmeralda'. Honorable Mention 2007. *Photograph by Jeff Salter.*

'Passion in Paris' (Ted L. Petit, 2002). Semi-evergreen. Scape 24 in. (61 cm); flower 5.5 in. (14 cm). Early midseason. A rich, velvety dark red with a lighter watermark, which moves into a green throat. Tetraploid. 'Bloodfire' × 'Drowning in Desire'. *Photograph by Ted L. Petit.*

'Royal Renaissance' (Jeff Salter, 2002). Semi-evergreen. Scape 28 in. (71 cm); flower 5.5 in. (14 cm). Midseason. A rose-red with a heavy white edge. Tetraploid. Honorable Mention 2005. *Photograph by Jeff Salter.*

'Holiday Charmer' (Jeff Salter, 2003). Semi-evergreen. Scape 26 in. (66 cm); flower 6 in. (15 cm). Midseason. A rose-red with ivory-white ruffled edge above a green throat. Tetraploid.

'Spacecoast Royal Ransom' (John Kinnebrew, 2003). Evergreen. Scape 28 in. (71 cm); flower 6 in. (15 cm). Early. A cranberry-red with a lighter halo and a ruffled, golden yellow edge above a yellow to green throat. Tetraploid. 'Spacecoast Cranberry Kid' × 'Jerry Nettles'. *Photograph by John Kinnebrew.*

'Royal Hunter' (Jeff Salter, 2002). Semi-evergreen. Scape 28 in. (71 cm); flower 5.5 in. (14 cm). Early midseason. A rose-red with a paler watermark and eyezone above a yellow to green throat. Tetraploid. *Photograph by Francois Verhaert.*

'After the Fire' (Ted L. Petit, 2003). Semi-evergreen. Scape 27 in. (69 cm); flower 5.5 in. (14 cm). Midseason. A red with gold edge above a green throat. Tetraploid. 'Amber Storm' × (('Highland Lord' × 'Betty Warren Woods') × 'Fires of Fuji'). *Photograph by Ted L. Petit.*

'William Steen' (Ted L. Petit, 2003). Semi-evergreen. Scape 24 in. (61 cm); flower 5.5 in. (14 cm). Midseason. A velvety red with a gold edge above a green throat. Tetraploid. 'Bloodfire' × ('Romeo is Bleeding' × 'Romeo is Bleeding'). *Photograph by Ted L. Petit.*

'Cary Grant' (David Kirchhoff, 2004). Evergreen. Scape 30 in. (76 cm); flower 5.75 in. (14.6 cm). Midseason late. A clear raspberry-red with a lighter watermark halo and a gold edge above a yellow to lime-green throat. Tetraploid. 'Joan Derifield' × 'Betty Ford'. *Photograph by David Kirchhoff.*

'Fools Rush In' (Ted L. Petit, 2004). Semi-evergreen. Scape 22 in. (56 cm); flower 5.5 in. (14 cm). Midseason. A rose-red with a lighter watermark and a gold edge above a green throat. Tetraploid. ('Drowning in Desire' × 'William Steen') × ('Passion in Paris' × 'John Peat'). *Photograph by Ted L. Petit.*

'Bill Chapman' (David Kirchhoff, 2005). Evergreen. Scape 30 in. (76 cm); flower 6.5 in. (16.5 cm). Midseason. A ruffled blood-red self with wire white edge above a lime-green throat. Tetraploid. 'Cochineal Canvas' × 'Collard Dream'. *Photograph by David Kirchhoff.*

'Fabulous Fortune' (Robert Carr, 2005). Evergreen. Scape 30 in. (76 cm); flower 5 in. (12.7 cm). Midseason. A dark orange-red with pale yellow-orange halo and golden orange edge above yellow throat. Tetraploid. 'Pure Indulgence' × 'Candied Popcorn Perfection'.

'Christmas Beau' (Ted L. Petit, 2004). Semi-evergreen. Scape 24 in. (61 cm); flower 5.5 in. (14 cm). Midseason. A red self above a green throat. Tetraploid. ('Romeo is Bleeding' × 'Rainbow Gold') × 'Jack of Hearts'. *Photograph by Ted L. Petit.*

'Summer in New Orleans' (Ted L. Petit, 2004). Semi-evergreen. Scape 25 in. (63 cm); flower 6.5 in. (16.5 cm). Midseason. A rose with a lighter watermark and heavily ruffled wire gold edge above a green throat. Tetraploid. ('Pursuing Passion' × 'Bittersweet Symphony') × ('Racing with Destiny' × 'John Peat'). *Photograph by Ted L. Petit.*

'Born to Run' (Patrick Stamile, 2006). Evergreen. Scape 28 in. (71 cm); flower 6 in. (15 cm). Midseason. A nicely ruffled red with a gold edge carrying a slight watermark above a green throat. Tetraploid. 'Coronel Light' × 'Roses and Gold'. *Photograph by Patrick Stamile.*

'Nina Verhaert' (Gunda Abajian, 2005). Semi-evergreen. Scape 28 in. (71 cm); flower 6.5 in. (16.5 cm). Early midseason. A red with a light yellow shark's teeth edge above a green throat. Tetraploid. 'Fortune's Dearest' × 'Crocodile Smile'. *Photograph by Francois Verhaert.*

'Shirley Farmer' (John Benz, 2005). Dormant. Scape 24 in. (61 cm); flower 4.5 in. (11.5 cm). Midseason. A wide-petaled rose-red flower with a heavily ruffled gold edge. Tetraploid. 'Startle' × 'Angel's Smile'.

'Shirley's Romance' (John Benz, 2005). Dormant. Scape 24 in. (61 cm); flower 5.5 in. (14 cm). Midseason late. A burgundy-red with a gold edge above a green throat. Tetraploid.

'Peter Fernyhough' (David Kirchhoff, 2005). Semi-evergreen. Scape 36 in. (91 cm); flower 6 in. (15 cm). Extra early. A Cabernet-red self above a lemon to lime-green throat. Tetraploid. 'Barcelona Night' × 'Diana Grenfell'. *Photograph by David Kirchhoff.*

'Gilded Scarlet' (Frank Smith and Larry Grace, 2006). Semi-evergreen. Scape 30 in. (76 cm); flower 5.5 in. (14 cm). Early midseason. A red with gold edge above a green throat. Tetraploid. 'Front Porch Swing' × seedling. *Photograph by Lanny Morry.*

'I Wanna Piranha' (John Kinnebrew, 2006). Semi-evergreen. Scape 34 in. (86 cm); flower 6 in. (15 cm). Midseason. A coral-rose flower with a green throat and heavy shark's teeth edge on both the petals and the sepals. Tetraploid. ('Forestlake Ragamuffin' × 'Mort Morss') × 'Cosmic Sensation'. *Photograph by John Kinnebrew.*

'Kingdom of Hearts' (Jeff Salter, 2006). Semi-evergreen. Scape 24 in. (61 cm); flower 5.5 in. (14 cm). Midseason. A nicely ruffled pink-red with a lighter watermark and a gold edge above a green throat. Tetraploid. 'Heartfelt Secrets' × 'Holiday Charmer'.

'Red Corvette' (Ted L. Petit, 2006). Semi-evergreen. Scape 23 in. (58 cm); flower 5.5 in. (14 cm). Midseason. A vibrant electric red with a plush velvety texture above a deep green throat. Tetraploid. 'Christmas Beau' × 'Richard Taylor'. *Photograph by Ted L. Petit.*

'Wild at Heart' (Jeff Salter, 2006). Semi-evergreen. Scape 28 in. (71 cm); flower 6 in. (15 cm). Midseason. A dark red bitone with a large lighter watermark surrounded by a darker band above a bright green throat carrying a lightly ruffled gold edge. Tetraploid. ('Harmonious Simplicity' × 'Royal Renaissance') × ('Peppermint Pinwheel' × 'Painting the Roses Red'). *Photograph by Jeff Salter.*

'Much Ado About Magic' (Jeff Salter, 2006). Evergreen. Scape 24 in. (61 cm); flower 6 in. (15 cm). Early midseason. A bright clear rose-red flower with a large lighter watermark and lightly ruffled gold edge above a yellow to green throat. Tetraploid. 'Holiday Charmer' × 'Painting the Roses Red'. *Photograph by Jeff Salter.*

'Stumbling Stone' (Phil and Luella Korth, 2006). Dormant. Scape 35 in. (89 cm); flower 5.5 in. (14 cm). Early midseason. A rosy lavender with a gold edge and lighter-colored sepals above a green throat. Tetraploid. Seedling × 'Upon This Rock'. *Photograph by Phil and Luella Korth.*

BLACK

'Edge of Eden' (Ted L. Petit, 1994). Evergreen. Scape 20 in. (51 cm); flower 5.5 in. (14 cm). Midseason. A black-red self with gold edge and green throat. 'Midnight Magic' × ('Ida's Magic' x 'Queen's Cape'). *Photograph by Ted L. Petit.*

'Burning Embers' (Ted L. Petit, 1996). Semi-evergreen. Scape 23 in. (58 cm); flower 5.5 in. (14 cm). Midseason. A very dark black-red with a bubbly platinum to gold edge above a green throat. ('Court Magician' × 'Desert Jewel') x 'Edge of Eden'. *Photograph by Ted L. Petit.*

'Dakar' (Patrick Stamile, 1998). Evergreen. Scape 30 in. (76 cm); flower 5.25 in. (13 cm). Midseason. A black-purple-violet blend with a green throat. 'Ebony Jewel' × 'Tet. Crayola Violet'. *Photograph by Patrick Stamile.*

'Quote the Raven' (Ted L. Petit, 1995). Evergreen. Scape 25 in. (63 cm); flower 5.5 in. (14 cm). Midseason. A black-purple self with a green throat. ('Midnight Magic' × seedling) x 'Malaysian Monarch'. *Photograph by Ted L. Petit.*

'Ebony Jewel' (Patrick Stamile, 1997). Evergreen. Scape 27 in. (69 cm); flower 5 in. (12.7 cm). Midseason. A wide-petaled velvety black-red self with a chartreuse green throat. 'Darker Shade' × 'Forever Red'. *Photograph by Patrick Stamile.*

'Bohemia After Dark' (Ted L. Petit, 2000). Semi-evergreen. Scape 24 in. (61 cm); flower 5.5 in. (14 cm). Midseason. A very dark black-purple flower with a heavy gold edge, lighter watermark, and green throat. 'Sultry Smile' × 'Forbidden Desires'. *Photograph by Ted L. Petit.*

'Quest for Eden' (Ted L. Petit, 2001). Evergreen. Scape 20 in. (51 cm); flower 5 in. (12.7 cm). Midseason. A black self above a green throat. 'Edge of Eden' × ('Romeo is Bleeding' × seedling). *Photograph by Ted L. Petit.*

'Bourbon Street' (Ted L. Petit, 2003). Semi-evergreen. Scape 27 in. (69 cm); flower 5.5 in. (14 cm). Midseason. A black with a gold edge above green throat. 'Fire Down Below' x ('Romeo is Bleeding' x 'Jack of Hearts'). *Photograph by Ted L. Petit.*

'Larry's Obsession' (Ted L. Petit, 2005). Semi-evergreen. Scape 32 in. (81 cm); flower 6 in. (15 cm). Midseason. A black-purple with a white-toothed edge above green throat. 'John Peat' × 'Baby Jane Hudson'. *Photograph by Ted L. Petit.*

'Baby Jane Hudson' (Ted L. Petit, 2002). Semi-evergreen. Scape 26 in. (66 cm); flower 5.5 in. (14 cm). Midseason. A dark, velvety near black-purple with a pronounced bubbly gold to platinum edge. 'Edge of Eden' × seedling. *Photograph by Ted L. Petit.*

'Jane Mahan' (Ted L. Petit, 2004). Semi-evergreen. Scape 27 in. (69 cm); flower 6 in. (15 cm). Midseason. A black-purple with a gold edge above a green throat. ('Baby Jane Hudson' × 'Burning Embers') × ('Quest for Eden' × 'John Peat'). *Photograph by Ted L. Petit.*

Chapter Five

EYED AND EDGED DAYLILIES

The eyed daylilies developed from members of the species that had dark eyes in the flowers. Since then, hybridizers have made remarkable and dramatic changes in eyezone characteristics.

The size of the eye ranges from a very narrow band to more recent cultivars where the eye covers most of the petal surface. The shape of the eye has been altered, creating triangular or chevron-shaped as well as square eyes. Some eyes extend out on the midrib to reach the petal edge. Eye color has also been modified until many different eyezone colors now exist. In fact, the only blue color currently found in the daylily exists within the eyezone. The colors of the eye have also been intensified to make striking, saturated black as well as vivid blood-red eyes. Efforts to clarify the background color of the petal self have complemented the intensified colors of the eye, increasing the contrast within the flower.

The eyezone colors have also moved out along the petal edges to create a matching picotee. These picotee edges arose as a small wire of color extending from the eyezone as it touched the petal edge. Hybridizing efforts gradually pushed the eyezone color increasingly further around the petal edge, until it eventually formed an edge of dark contrasting color completely surrounding the flower petals.

While the vast majority of daylilies with picotee edges have eyes that match the picotee color, there are a few hybrids that exhibit a darker edge without an eye. While these picotee edges are currently not as dark, dramatic, or contrasting as those found on flowers with eyes, hybridizers are striving to create flowers with more dramatic contrasting picotee edges in flowers without a dark eyezone.

The width of the picotee edges has been increased, and more recently they have been surrounded by secondary edges of silver, gold, and white. This complexity has created a stunning and sometimes shocking effect in the modern hybrids. In some the eyes have become so large and the edges so wide that little petal self remains visible.

EYED DAYLILIES

'So Excited' (Ra Hansen, 1986). Evergreen. Scape 26 in. (66 cm); flower 5.5 in. (14 cm). Early midseason. A deep rose-pink recurved flower with a very large dark raspberry eyezone and lime throat. Diploid. Seedling × 'Ann Crochet'. Award of Merit 1993. *Photograph by Ra Hansen.*

'Always Afternoon' (Mort Morss, 1987). Semi-evergreen. Scape 22 in. (56 cm); flower 5.5 in. (14 cm). Early. A medium mauve edged in buff with a purple eyezone above a green throat. Tetraploid. ('Ring of Change' × 'Tiffany Palace') × 'Opus One'. Stout Silver Medal 1997. Don C. Stevens Award 1993. Award of Merit 1995. Honorable Mention 1992. *Photograph by Ted L. Petit and John P. Peat.*

'Charlie Pierce Memorial' (Charles F. Pierce, 1987). Semi-evergreen. Scape 24 in. (61 cm); flower 6 in. (15 cm). Early midseason. A lavender with a wine-purple eyezone and a green throat. Diploid. Award of Merit 1998. Honorable Mention 1995. *Photograph by Rejean Millette.*

'Pumpkin Kid' (Elsie Spalding, 1987). Evergreen. Scape 18 in. (46 cm); flower 5.5 in. (14 cm). Midseason. A dramatic burnt orange ruffled flower with a precise red band surrounding a shocking green throat. Diploid. Don C. Stevens Award 1992. Award of Merit 1992. *Photograph by John Eiseman.*

'Jedi Dot Pierce' (Dan Wedgeworth, 1988). Semi-evergreen. Scape 20 in. (51 cm); flower 6 in. (15 cm). Early midseason. A large rose-pink with slightly darker rose halo and a green throat. Diploid. Award of Merit 2001. Honorable Mention 1997. *Photograph by Ted L. Petit and John P. Peat.*

'Joe Marinello' (Patrick Stamile, 1989). Dormant. Scape 21 in. (53 cm); flower 5 in. (12.7 cm). Early. A cream-pink with a beautiful deep wine-purple eye above a green center. Tetraploid. 'Paper Butterfly' × 'Tetra Siloam Virginia Henson'. Award of Merit 1997. *Photograph by Patrick Stamile.*

'Tuscawilla Tigress' (Ra Hansen, 1988). Semi-evergreen. Scape 25 in. (63 cm); flower 7.25 in. (18 cm). Early midseason. A bright orange with a dark orange eyezone and a chartreuse throat. Tetraploid. 'Seductor' × 'Tetra Pat Mercer'. Award of Merit 1996. Honorable Mention 1992.

'Radiant Ruffles' (Edwin C. Brown, 1987). Semi-evergreen. Scape 24 in. (61 cm); flower 5 in. (12.7 cm). Midseason. A cream-ivory with a burgundy-red eyezone above yellow halo and a green throat. Diploid. 'Rosy Sunset' × 'Siloam Virginia Henson'. Award of Merit 1994. *Photograph by Ted L. Petit and John P. Peat.*

'Raspberry Candy' (Patrick Stamile, 1989). Dormant. Scape 26 in. (66 cm); flower 5 in. (12.7 cm). Early. A cream with a deep raspberry-red punctuated by cream midribs. Tetraploid. Seedling × 'Tetra Siloam Virginia Henson'. L. Ernest Plouf Award 1997. Award of Merit 1999. Honorable Mention 1996. *Photograph by Patrick Stamile.*

'Fooled Me' (Phil Reilly and Ann Hein, 1990). Dormant. Scape 24 in. (61 cm); flower 5.5 in. (14 cm). Early midseason. A golden yellow with a red edge and a deep red eyezone above a green throat. Tetraploid. Stout Silver Medal 2005. Award of Merit 2001. Honorable Mention 1998. *Photograph by Ted L. Petit and John P. Peat.*

'Wineberry Candy' (Patrick Stamile, 1990). Dormant. Scape 22 in. (56 cm); flower 5 in. (12.7 cm). Early midseason. A clear pink bloom with a red-purple eyezone and a green throat. Tetraploid. 'Tetra Siloam Virginia Henson' × 'Paper Butterfly'. L. Ernest Plouf Award 1998. Award of Merit 1997. Honorable Mention 1994. *Photograph by Patrick Stamile.*

'Pirate's Patch' (Jeff Salter, 1991). Evergreen. Scape 28 in. (71 cm); flower 6 in. (15 cm). Early midseason. An ivory-cream with a purple eyezone above a yellow to green throat. Tetraploid. 'Well of Souls' × 'Jungle Mask'. Don C. Stevens Award 1997. Award of Merit 1998. Honorable Mention 1995.

'Russian Easter' (David Kirchhoff, 1991). Evergreen. Scape 30 in. (76 cm); flower 6 in. (15 cm). Midseason. A yellow with mauve-rose edging and a mauve-rose eyezone above a green throat. Tetraploid. 'Scarlock' × 'Charles Johnston'. Award of Merit 1998. Honorable Mention 1995. *Photograph by John Eiseman.*

'Paige's Pinata' (Ra Hansen, 1990). Semi-evergreen. Scape 26 in. (66 cm); flower 6 in. (15 cm). Early midseason. A peach-pink flower with a very large bold fuchsia eye taking up most of the flower petals. Diploid. ('So Excited' × seedling) × 'Janice Brown'. Award of Merit 1997. *Photograph by Karen Newman.*

'Blue Moon Rising' (Elizabeth H. Salter, 1991). Semi-evergreen. Scape 24 in. (61 cm); flower 3 in. (7.6 cm). Midseason. A pale ivory-peach with blue-violet eyezone surround by thin rose-burgundy mascara band. Diploid. Honorable Mention 1997. *Photograph by John Benoot.*

'Daring Dilemma' (Jeff Salter, 1992). Semi-evergreen. Scape 24 in. (61 cm); flower 5 in. (12.7 cm). Midseason. A cream-tinted pink with a plum edge and eyezone above a green throat. Tetraploid. Award of Merit 2000. Honorable Mention 1997. *Photograph by Ted L. Petit and John P. Peat.*

'Creative Edge' (Patrick Stamile, 1993). Semi-evergreen. Scape 23 in. (58 cm); flower 6 in. (15 cm). Mid-season. A cream-lavender with a purple and gold picotee edge and a purple eyezone above a chartreuse throat. Tetraploid. ('Plum Candy' × 'Wintermint Candy') × 'Admiral's Braid'. Award of Merit 2001. Honorable Mention 1998. *Photograph by Patrick Stamile.*

'Mask of Time' (Jeff Salter, 1993). Semi-evergreen. Scape 26 in. (66 cm); flower 6 in. (15 cm). Midseason late. An orange-rose with a black-plum eyezone above a green throat. Tetraploid. Award of Merit 2000. Honorable Mention 1997. *Photograph by John Eiseman.*

'Moonlit Masquerade' (Jeff Salter, 1992). Semi-evergreen. Scape 26 in. (66 cm); flower 5.5 in. (14 cm). Early midseason. A cream with a dark purple eyezone and a very dark purple picotee above a green throat. Tetraploid. Stout Silver Medal 2004. Award of Merit 2002. Honorable Mention 1999. *Photograph by Ted L. Petit and John P. Peat.*

'Druid's Chant' (Patrick Stamile, 1993). Semi-evergreen. Scape 23 in. (58 cm); flower 6.5 in. (16.5 cm). Early midseason. A deep lavender with a purple eyezone above a green throat. Tetraploid. ('El Bandito' × 'Plum Candy') × 'Admiral's Braid'. Award of Merit 2002. Honorable Mention 1997. *Photograph by Patrick Stamile.*

'Ben Lee' (Ra Hansen, 1994). Semi-evergreen. Scape 20 in. (51 cm); flower 4 in. (10 cm). Midseason. A salmon-pink with a dark violet to lavender-blue eyezone above a bright green throat. Diploid. ('Misty Isle' × 'Surf') × seedling. Honorable Mention 1997. *Photograph by John Benoot.*

'Brookwood Ojo Grande' (Leo Sharp, 1994). Semi-evergreen. Scape 27 in. (69 cm); flower 6 in. (15 cm). Midseason. A gold with a red eyezone and a green throat. Diploid. Donn Fischer Memorial Cup 2005. Honorable Mention 2000.

'Cindy's Eye' (Jeff Salter, 1994). Semi-evergreen. Scape 30 in. (76 cm); flower 6 in. (15 cm). Midseason. An ivory-cream with a medium purple eyezone above a green throat. Tetraploid. Award of Merit 2002. Honorable Mention 1999. *Photograph by Ted L. Petit and John P. Peat.*

'Desperado Love' (Patrick Stamile, 1994). Semi-evergreen. Scape 26 in. (66 cm); flower 5 in. (12.7 cm). Midseason. A yellow with a plum-purple eyezone above a green throat. Tetraploid. 'El Desperado' × 'Pirate's Patch'. Award of Merit 2003. Honorable Mention 2000. *Photograph by Patrick Stamile.*

'Etched Eyes' (Matthew Kaskel, 1994). Evergreen. Scape 28 in. (71 cm); flower 5.5 in. (14 cm). Early. A cream-yellow with a raspberry eyezone. Tetraploid. ('Paper Butterfly' × ('Kate Carpenter' × seedling)) × 'Stairway to Heaven'. R. W. Munson Jr. Award 2002. Award of Merit 2003. Honorable Mention 1999. *Photograph by Sandi Jacques.*

'Wisest of Wizards' (Jeff Salter, 1994). Semi-evergreen. Scape 26 in. (66 cm); flower 5.5 in. (14 cm). Early midseason. An ivory-peach with gold-rose edge and pale rose eyezone. Tetraploid. Award of Merit 2003. Honorable Mention 2000. *Photograph by Ted L. Petit and John P. Peat.*

'Lipstick Traces' (Matthew Kaskel, 1994). Evergreen. Scape 22 in. (56 cm); flower 5 in. (12.7 cm). Early midseason. A yellow with a red eyezone above a yellow to green throat. Tetraploid. ((('Altarmira' × seedling) × 'Tetra Elsie Spalding') × 'Stairway to Heaven'). *Photograph by Matthew Kaskel.*

'All American Tiger' (Patrick Stamile, 1995). Evergreen. Scape 24 in. (61 cm); flower 5.5 in. (14 cm). Midseason. A deep burnt orange with a red eye and picotee edge above a green throat. Tetraploid. 'Tigger' × 'Pirate's Patch'. *Photograph by Patrick Stamile.*

'Canadian Border Patrol' (Jeff Salter, 1995). Semi-evergreen. Scape 28 in. (71 cm); flower 6 in. (15 cm). Early midseason. A cream with a purple edge and purple eyezone above a green throat. Tetraploid. Don C. Stevens Award 2000. Award of Merit 2001. Honorable Mention 1998.

'Langley Ruffled Ring' (Pam Erikson, 1995). Semi-evergreen. Scape 32 in. (81 cm); flower 5.5 in. (14 cm). Midseason. A cream with a pale pink eyezone above a gold to green throat. Diploid. 'Neal Berry' × seedling. *Photograph by Pam Erikson.*

'Alaqua' (Patrick Stamile, 1996). Evergreen. Scape 23 in. (58 cm); flower 5 in. (12.7 cm). Midseason. A yellow-cream with a burgundy eyezone above a green throat. Tetraploid. ('Dewberry Candy' × 'Pirate's Patch') × 'Creative Edge'. *Photograph by Patrick Stamile.*

'Wild Mustang' (Patrick Stamile, 1995). Dormant. Scape 23 in. (58 cm); flower 5.5 in. (14 cm). Midseason late. A cream-pink with a red eyezone above a green throat. Tetraploid. 'Cherry Pop' × ('Wineberry Candy' × 'Tetra Priscilla's Rainbow'). *Photograph by Beth Creveling.*

'All Fired Up' (Patrick Stamile, 1996). Evergreen. Scape 20 in. (51 cm); flower 6 in. (15 cm). Early. A peachy orange with a large red eye and picotee edge above a green throat. Tetraploid. ('Eye Declare' × ('Wineberry Candy' × 'Tetra Priscilla's Rainbow')) × 'Regal Braid'. Award of Merit 2005. Honorable Mention 2002. *Photograph by Patrick Stamile.*

'Baracuda Bay' (Jeff Salter, 1996). Semi-evergreen. Scape 26 in. (66 cm); flower 6 in. (15 cm). Midseason. A red to coral-rust with a darker eye and a prominent white toothed edge. Tetraploid. 'Mask of Time' × 'Mort's Masterpiece'. Honorable Mention 2001. *Photograph by Ted L. Petit and John P. Peat.*

'Angel Rodgers' (Tom Wilson, 1996). Dormant. Scape 25 in. (63 cm); flower 6 in. (15 cm). Midseason. A lavender with a dark lavender to purple eyezone above a green throat. Diploid. 'Jan Johnson' × 'Sambo Wilder'. Honorable Mention 2001. *Photograph by Francois Verhaert.*

'Awesome Blossom' (Jeff Salter, 1996). Evergreen. Scape 24 in. (61 cm); flower 5 in. (12.7 cm). Early midseason. An antique rose with raisin-plum eye and matching picotee edge. Tetraploid. Don C. Stevens Award 2004. Award of Merit 2004.

'Blue Eyed Butterfly' (Ludlow Lambertson, 1996). Semi-evergreen. Scape 24 in. (61 cm); flower 5.5 in. (14 cm). Early midseason. A near-white with a medium blue eyezone above a green throat. Tetraploid. 'Intricate Eyes' × 'Lonesome Dove'. *Photograph by Karen Newman.*

'Bubbling Edge' (Ted and Claudette Collins, 1996). Semi-evergreen. Scape 24 in. (61 cm); flower 5 in. (12.7 cm). Early midseason. A beige-pink with a light wine eyezone above a yellow to green throat. Tetraploid. 'Daring Dilemma' × 'Wedding Band'. Honorable Mention 2001. *Photograph by Karen Newman.*

'Cherokee Pass' (Elvan Roderick, 1996). Dormant. Scape 32 in. (81 cm); flower 5.5 in. (14 cm). Midseason late. A gold with red petal edges and a red eyezone above a green throat. Tetraploid. 'Council Fire' × 'Tigerling'. Eugene S. Foster Award 2004. Award of Merit 2005. Honorable Mention 2002. *Photograph by Elvan Roderick.*

'Forever in Time' (Jeff Salter, 1996). Semi-evergreen. Scape 30 in. (76 cm); flower 6 in. (15 cm). Midseason. A cream-ivory with a washed blue-violet eyezone above a green throat. Tetraploid. 'Winter Masquerade' × seedling. *Photograph by Leslie Mauck.*

'Golden Compass' (Jeff Salter, 1996). Evergreen. Scape 26 in. (66 cm); flower 6 in. (15 cm). Early midseason. A yellow with a purple-black eyezone above a green throat. Tetraploid. 'Moonlit Masquerade' × seedling. Honorable Mention 2007. *Photograph by Rejean Millette.*

'Eye on America' (Jeff Salter, 1996). Semi-evergreen. Scape 26 in. (66 cm); flower 5.5 in. (14 cm). Early midseason. A yellow-cream with a large dramatic black-plum eye with matching picotee and a green throat. Tetraploid. Honorable Mention 2002. *Photograph by Jeff Salter.*

'Good Old Boy' (Jeff Salter, 1996). Semi-evergreen. Scape 26 in. (66 cm); flower 5.5 in. (14 cm). Midseason. A golden yellow flower with a black-purple eyezone and matching picotee above a green throat. Tetraploid. *Photograph by Francois Verhaert.*

'Isle of Zanzibar' (Matthew Kaskel, 1996). Evergreen. Scape 28 in. (71 cm); flower 6 in. (15 cm). Early. A chrome-yellow with a purple eyezone above a green throat. Tetraploid. (Seedling × 'Pirate's Patch') × 'Tetra Elsie Spalding'. Honorable Mention 2003. *Photograph by Debbie and Duane Hurlbert.*

'Mardi Gras Ball' (Ted L. Petit, 1996). Semi-evergreen. Scape 23 in. (58 cm); flower 6 in. (15 cm). Midseason. A lavender with a purple eyezone and a double edge of purple and gold above a green throat. Tetraploid. ('Tetra Siloam Virginia Henson' × 'Ida's Magic') × 'Admiral's Braid'. Honorable Mention 2003. *Photograph by Ted L. Petit.*

'Momentum' (Emily Olson, 1996). Dormant. Scape 30 in. (76 cm); flower 6 in. (15 cm). Midseason. A lightly ruffled tawny rose bitone with a slightly darker eyezone above a green throat. Tetraploid. ((Seedling × 'Dance Ballerina Dance') × 'Heavenly Crown') × ((seedling × 'Dancing Shiva') × 'Red Fancy'). Honorable Mention 2002.

'Lavender Blue Baby' (Jack B. Carpenter, 1996). Dormant. Scape 28 in. (71 cm); flower 5.5 in. (14 cm). Early midseason. A lavender-blue with a lavender-blue eyezone above a green throat. Diploid. Stout Silver Medal 2007. L. Ernest Plouf Award 2003. Don C. Stevens Award 2007. Award of Merit 2004. Honorable Mention 2001. *Photograph by Jack B. Carpenter.*

'Mask of Eternity' (Jeff Salter, 1996). Evergreen. Scape 28 in. (71 cm); flower 6.5 in. (16.5 cm). Midseason. A cream with a purple eyezone. Tetraploid. 'Moonlit Masquerade' × seedling. Honorable Mention 2001. *Photograph by Leslie Mauck.*

'Montana Miss' (Elizabeth H. Salter, 1996). Semi-evergreen. Scape 28 in. (71 cm); flower 4.5 in. (11.5 cm). Midseason late. A rose with a red eyezone above a green throat. Diploid. Honorable Mention 1999. *Photograph by Andrea Weaver.*

'Monterrey Jack' (Dan Trimmer, 1996). Dormant. Scape 24 in. (61 cm); flower 5.5 in. (14 cm). Early. A cream-yellow with a wine-red eyezone above a green throat. Tetraploid. 'Tetra Siloam Gumdrop' × 'Tetra Wings of Chance'. Honorable Mention 2001. *Photograph by Dan Trimmer.*

'Strawberry Lace' (Jeff Salter, 1996). Semi-evergreen. Scape 28 in. (71 cm); flower 6 in. (15 cm). Early midseason. A pale ivory-cream with a bright rose eye and picotee below a gold edge with a small yellow-green throat. Tetraploid. 'Wisest of Wizards' × seedling. Honorable Mention 2002. *Photograph by Ted L. Petit and John P. Peat.*

'Cobalt Dawn' (Patrick Stamile, 1997). Evergreen. Scape 28 in. (71 cm); flower 5 in. (12.7 cm). Early midseason. A cream-white with a black-purple eye and edge above a green throat. Tetraploid. 'Awakening Dream' × ('Cherry Berry' × 'Royal Braid'). Honorable Mention 2003. *Photograph by Patrick Stamile.*

'Rainbow Candy' (Patrick Stamile, 1996). Dormant. Scape 28 in. (71 cm); flower 4.5 in. (11.5 cm). Early midseason. A cream with a purple, lavender, gray, and yellow eyezone above a green throat. Tetraploid. 'Blueberry Candy' × 'Tetra Little Print'. Honorable Mention 2007. *Photograph by Patrick Stamile.*

'Apple Pie Spice' (Enman R. Joiner, 1997). Evergreen. Scape 28 in. (71 cm); flower 3.5 in. (9 cm). Early midseason. An amber-yellow with a mauve-wine eyezone above a green throat. Tetraploid. *Photograph by Francis Joiner.*

'Eye Catching' (Patrick Stamile, 1997). Evergreen. Scape 23 in. (58 cm); flower 5 in. (12.7 cm). Early midseason. A cream-pink flower with a very large dramatic purple eye and matching wide picotee. Tetraploid. 'Festive Art' × ('Cherry Drop' × 'Royal Braid'). *Photograph by Patrick Stamile.*

'Islesworth' (Patrick Stamile, 1997). Evergreen. Scape 25 in. (63 cm); flower 5 in. (12.7 cm). Midseason. A cream with purple eyezone and edge above a green throat. Tetraploid. 'Creative Edge' × 'Pirate's Patch'. Honorable Mention 2003. *Photograph by Patrick Stamile.*

'Pumpkin Pie Spice' (Enman R. Joiner, 1997). Evergreen. Scape 26 in. (66 cm); flower 4.5 in. (11.5 cm). Early midseason. A buckskin with a mauve-wine eyezone above a green throat. Tetraploid. Honorable Mention 2001. *Photograph by Francis Joiner.*

'Sabine Baur' (Jeff Salter, 1997). Semi-evergreen. Scape 25 in. (63 cm); flower 6 in. (15 cm). Early midseason. An dramatic ivory-cream flower with bold black-purple eye and a bubbly edge of the same color. Tetraploid. 'Cindy's Eye' × 'Daring Deception'. Don C. Stevens Award 2002. Award of Merit 2005. Honorable Mention 2002. *Photograph by Ted L. Petit and John P. Peat.*

'Pamela Williams' (David Kirchhoff, 1997). Evergreen. Scape 28 in. (71 cm); flower 5 in. (12.7 cm). Early. An orange with a red eyezone and edge above a yellow-green throat. Tetraploid. (Seedling × ((seedling × 'Raging Tiger') × 'Russian Easter')). Honorable Mention 2001. *Photograph by John Benoot.*

'Rouge and Lace' (Matthew Kaskel, 1997). Evergreen. Scape 28 in. (71 cm); flower 5 in. (12.7 cm). Early midseason. A ruffled cream flower with a rouge-red eyezone. Tetraploid. (Seedling × 'Tetra Siloam Virginia Henson') × (seedling × (seedling × 'Wedding Band')). *Photograph by Matthew Kaskel.*

'Alice's Day Off' (Matthew Kaskel, 1998). Evergreen. Scape 27 in. (69 cm); flower 5.5 in. (14 cm). Early. A golden orange with a raisin-red eyezone above a gold to orange throat. Tetraploid. *Photograph by Debbie and Duane Hurlbert.*

'Bold Encounter' (Patrick Stamile, 1998). Evergreen. Scape 26 in. (66 cm); flower 5 in. (12.7 cm). Early midseason. An orchid cream with a plum-violet eyezone and picotee above a green throat. Tetraploid. ((('Wineberry Candy' × 'Royal Braid') × 'Creative Edge') × (('Tropical Snow' × 'Admiral's Braid') × 'Mort's Masterpiece')). Honorable Mention 2004. *Photograph by Patrick Stamile.*

'Brookwood Lee Causey' (Leo Sharp, 1998). Semi-evergreen. Scape 18 in. (46 cm); flower 5 in. (12.7 cm). Midseason. A gold with a very large red eyezone above a green throat. Diploid. 'Brookwood Ojo Grande' × seedling. Don C. Stevens Award 2003. Award of Merit 2005. Honorable Mention 2002. *Photograph by Francois Verhaert.*

'Calico Jack' (Dan Trimmer, 1998). Evergreen. Scape 28 in. (71 cm); flower 5.5 in. (14 cm). Early midseason. A yellow with a plum eyezone and a green throat. Tetraploid. 'Fooled Me' × 'Pirate's Patch'. Honorable Mention 2003.

'Cherrystone' (Patrick Stamile, 1998). Evergreen. Scape 27 in. (69 cm); flower 5 in. (12.7 cm). Early midseason. A pink with a cherry-red eyezone and edge above a green throat. Tetraploid. ('Raspberry Candy' × 'Pirate's Patch') × 'Creative Edge'. *Photograph by Patrick Stamile.*

'Classic Edge' (Patrick Stamile, 1998). Evergreen. Scape 26 in. (66 cm); flower 5.5 in. (14 cm). Early midseason. An orchid pink with a raspberry eyezone and a double edge of raspberry and orchid pink above a yellow throat. Tetraploid. 'Festive Art' × ('Cherry Berry' × 'Royal Braid'). Honorable Mention 2002. *Photograph by Patrick Stamile.*

'Destined to See' (Larry Grace, 1998). Evergreen. Scape 24 in. (61 cm); flower 6 in. (15 cm). Early midseason. A cream-yellow with a large lavender-patterned eyezone and a double edge of lavender and gold above a green throat. Tetraploid. Seedling × 'Create Your Dream'. Honorable Mention 2002. *Photograph by Sue Brown.*

'Edge of Paradise' (Patrick Stamile, 1998). Evergreen. Scape 26 in. (66 cm); flower 6 in. (15 cm). Midseason late. An orchid cream with a violet-plum eyezone and edge above a green throat. Tetraploid. 'El Desperado' × 'Creative Edge'. *Photograph by Patrick Stamile.*

'Martina Verhaert' (Mort Morss, 1998). Semi-evergreen. Scape 20 in. (51 cm); flower 5.75 in. (14.6 cm). Early midseason. A lavender with a violet-purple eyezone and picotee edge surrounded by a wire white edge above a yellow to green throat. Tetraploid. 'Forest Phantom' × 'Druid's Chant'. Honorable Mention 2003. *Photograph by Francois Verhaert.*

'Leona Esther' (Jack B. Carpenter, 1998). Dormant. Scape 30 in. (76 cm); flower 5 in. (12.7 cm). Midseason late. A lightly ruffled lavender-blue blend with a lavender-purple eyezone. Diploid. *Photograph by Francois Verhaert.*

'Mildred Mitchell' (Kelly Mitchell, 1998). Evergreen. Scape 26 in. (66 cm); flower 6.5 in. (16.5 cm). Early midseason. A lavender with a blue eyezone and edge above a green throat. Tetraploid. 'Emperor's Dragon' × 'Admiral's Braid'. Honorable Mention 2002.

'Moonstruck Madness' (Jeff Salter, 1998). Semi-evergreen. Scape 28 in. (71 cm); flower 5 in. (12.7 cm). Early midseason. A cream-white with a black eyezone and edge above a green throat. Tetraploid. 'Daring Deception' × seedling.

'Only Believe' (Larry Grace, 1998). Semi-evergreen. Scape 24 in. (61 cm); flower 7 in. (18 cm). Early midseason. A very large cream-pink with a burgundy-red eye and picotee with a wire gold edge. Tetraploid. 'Wedding Band' × 'Song Without Words'. Honorable Mention 2002. *Photograph by Larry Grace.*

'Piano Man' (Dan Trimmer, 1998). Evergreen. Scape 28 in. (71 cm); flower 4.5 in. (11.5 cm). Early midseason. A cream, near-white flower with a striking dark plum eyezone above a green throat. Tetraploid. 'Moonlit Masquerade' × 'Tetra Dragon's Eye'. Honorable Mention 2003. *Photograph by John Benoot.*

'Spacecoast Bold Scheme' (John Kinnebrew, 1998). Semi-evergreen. Scape 24 in. (61 cm); flower 4 in. (10 cm). Early midseason. A cream with a black-purple eyezone and picotee above a green throat. Tetraploid. ('Daring Dilemma' × 'Guiniver's Gift') × 'Daring Deception'. *Photograph by Tracy Heldt.*

'Spacecoast Double Edge' (John Kinnebrew, 1998). Semi-evergreen. Scape 24 in. (61 cm); flower 7 in. (18 cm). Early midseason. A lavender with a purple halo and purple picotee, edged in gold, above a green throat. Tetraploid. 'Something Wonderful' × 'Admiral's Braid'.

'Spacecoast Picotee Prince' (John Kinnebrew, 1998). Semi-evergreen. Scape 30 in. (76 cm); flower 6 in. (15 cm). Midseason. A lavender with a purple eyezone and picotee, edged in gold, above a yellow throat. Tetraploid. ('Wedding Band' × 'Something Wonderful') × 'Daring Deception'. *Photograph by John Benoot.*

'Prickled Petals' (Enman R. Joiner, 1998). Evergreen. Scape 24 in. (61 cm); flower 5 in. (12.7 cm). Midseason late. A seashell-pink with a smoky grape eyezone and edge above a green throat. Tetraploid. Seedling × 'Regal Braid'. Honorable Mention 2007. *Photograph by Francis Joiner.*

'Swashbuckler Bay Boy' (Jeff Salter, 1998). Semi-evergreen. Scape 29 in. (74 cm); flower 6 in. (15 cm). Midseason. A bright salmon-coral with large triangular deep black eye with bold black edge. Very dramatic. Tetraploid. ('Tetra Burning Desire' × seedling) × 'Mask of Time'. Honorable Mention 2007. *Photograph by Ted L. Petit and John P. Peat.*

'Trial By Fire' (Robert Carr, 1998). Evergreen. Scape 32 in. (81 cm); flower 5 in. (12.7 cm). Early midseason. An orange blend with a red-orange eyezone above a yellow-green throat. Tetraploid. ('Angelus Angel' × 'Midnight Magic') × 'America's Most Wanted'.

'Truly Angelic' (John Rice, 1998). Dormant. Scape 26 in. (66 cm); flower 5.5 in. (14 cm). Midseason. A mauve-rose with a lavender watermark, pink eyezone and a gold edge above a green throat. Tetraploid. 'Angel's Smile' × 'True Grit'. Honorable Mention 2003. *Photograph by John Benoot.*

'Unusual Revelations' (Enman R. Joiner, 1998). Evergreen. Scape 24 in. (61 cm); flower 6 in. (15 cm). Early midseason. A peach-amber self with a mauve-wine eyezone and edge above a medium green throat. Tetraploid. 'Barbara Kirby' × 'Regal Braid'. *Photograph by Francis Joiner.*

'Wolf Eyes' (Jeff Salter, 1998). Semi-evergreen. Scape 28 in. (71 cm); flower 5.5 in. (14 cm). Midseason. A cream-pink flesh with a purple eyezone and edge above a green throat. Tetraploid. ('Tetra Little Print' × seedling) × (seedling × 'Daring Dilemma'). *Photograph by Karen Newman.*

'Celebration of Angels' (Dan Trimmer, 1999). Evergreen. Scape 25 in. (63 cm); flower 5 in. (12.7 cm). Early. A cream with a black-purple eyezone above a green throat. Tetraploid. 'Moonlit Masquerade' × 'Tetra Dragon's Eye'. Award of Merit 2006. Honorable Mention 2002. *Photograph by Francois Verhaert.*

'Cherry Valentine' (Dan Trimmer, 1999). Evergreen. Scape 28 in. (71 cm); flower 4 in. (10 cm). Early. A bright pink with a crimson-red eyezone above a green throat. Tetraploid. ('Ruby Sentinel' × 'Tetra Enchanting Blessing') × 'Tetra Dragon's Eye'. Honorable Mention 2004. *Photograph by Dan Trimmer.*

'Cranberry Winter' (Dan Trimmer, 1999). Evergreen. Scape 20 in. (51 cm); flower 4.5 in. (11.5 cm). Early midseason. A cream-white with a dark red eyezone above a green throat. Tetraploid. ('Moonlit Masquerade' × ('Emperor's Dragon' × 'Tetra Elsie Spalding')) × 'Tetra Dragon's Eye'. *Photograph by Francois Verhaert.*

'Element of Surprise' (Robert Carr, 1999). Evergreen. Scape 28 in. (71 cm); flower 4.5 in. (11.5 cm). Early midseason. A salmon-coral with a dark coral eyezone above a yellow throat. Tetraploid. Unknown parent × 'Passion District'.

'I See You' (Larry Grace, 1999). Evergreen. Scape 20 in. (51 cm); flower 4.5 in. (11.5 cm). Early midseason. A cream-peach with a lavender-purple eyezone above a green throat. Tetraploid. Seedling × 'Regal Braid'.

'Jamaican Me Happy' (Dan Trimmer, 1999). Semi-evergreen. Scape 28 in. (71 cm); flower 5 in. (12.7 cm). Early midseason. A wide-petaled peach flower with a bold orange eyezone and pink edges above a green throat. Tetraploid. 'Raspberry Beret' × 'Tetra Ruffled Masterpiece'. *Photograph by Dan Trimmer.*

'Key to My Heart' (Robert Carr, 1999). Evergreen. Scape 25 in. (63 cm); flower 5 in. (12.7 cm). Early. A crimson with pale pink edges and a white picotee above a yellow to green throat. Tetraploid. 'Whooperee' × 'Avant Garde'. Honorable Mention 2002. *Photograph by Francois Verhaert.*

'Kisses Like Wine' (Dan Trimmer, 1999). Semi-evergreen. Scape 26 in. (66 cm); flower 5 in. (12.7 cm). Early. A yellow with a plum eyezone above a yellow to green throat. Tetraploid. 'Moonlit Masquerade' × 'Tetra Wings of Chance'. *Photograph by Francois Verhaert.*

'Malachite Prism' (George Doorakian, 1999). Semi-evergreen. Scape 36 in. (91 cm); flower 4.5 in. (11.5 cm). Midseason. A rose-pink flower with a large rose-purple chevron eye and an extremely pronounced green chevron throat. Diploid. 'Someplace Special' × seedling. Honorable Mention 2005. *Photograph by George Doorakian.*

'On To Something' (Larry Grace, 1999). Evergreen. Scape 38 in. (96 cm); flower 7 in. (18 cm). Early midseason. A lavender with a deep lavender eyezone above a green-chartreuse throat. Tetraploid. Seedling × 'Diane Joiner'. *Photograph by Susan Okrasinski.*

'Raspberry Beret' (Dan Trimmer, 1999). Evergreen. Scape 28 in. (71 cm); flower 6 in. (15 cm). Midseason. A gold-amber with a cranberry-red eyezone and thick ruffled picotee edges of the same color above a green throat. Tetraploid. 'Fooled Me' × 'Jungled Mask'. *Photograph by Susan Okrasinski.*

'Raspberry Winter' (Dan Trimmer, 1999). Dormant. Scape 28 in. (71 cm); flower 4 in. (10 cm). Early midseason. A clean pale pink with an unmistakable triangular red-etched complex eye above a dark green throat. Also carrying a double of red and gold. Tetraploid. 'Summer Blush' × 'Tetra Dragon's Eye'. Honorable Mention 2004. *Photograph by Francois Verhaert.*

'Tar and Feather' (Matthew Kaskel, 1999). Evergreen. Scape 26 in. (66 cm); flower 6.5 in. (16.5 cm). Midseason. A chrome-yellow with a black-purple eyezone above a lime-green throat. Tetraploid. Seedling × 'Isle of Zanzibar'. Award of Merit 2007. Honorable Mention 2002. *Photograph by Debbie and Duane Hurlbert.*

'Barbarian Princess' (Jeff Salter, 2000). Semi-evergreen. Scape 28 in. (71 cm); flower 6.5 in. (16.5 cm). Midseason. A lavender with purple-plum eye and plum edge above a green throat. Tetraploid. Honorable Mention 2007. *Photograph by John Benoot.*

'Steve Trimmer' (Dan Trimmer, 1999). Semi-evergreen. Scape 28 in. (71 cm); flower 5 in. (12.7 cm). Early midseason. A pale yellow with a plum eyezone and edge above a yellow to green throat. Tetraploid. 'Kisses Like Wine' × 'Calico Jack'. Honorable Mention 2004. *Photograph by Francois Verhaert.*

'Wild Horses' (Dan Trimmer, 1999). Evergreen. Scape 37 in. (94 cm); flower 7 in. (18 cm). Early. A cream-yellow with a black-purple halo above a yellow to green throat. Tetraploid. 'Moonlit Masquerade' × 'Tetra Cleopatra'. Award of Merit 2006. Honorable Mention 2002. *Photograph by Debbie and Duane Hurlbert.*

'Egyptian Queen' (Dan Trimmer, 2000). Evergreen. Scape 38 in. (96 cm); flower 7 in. (18 cm). Extra early. A narrow-petaled cream-peach flower with a striking purple eyezone on the petals and sepals. Tetraploid. 'Moonlit Masquerade' × 'Tetra Cleopatra'. *Photograph by Francois Verhaert.*

'Heat of the Moment' (Jeff Salter, 2000). Semi-evergreen. Scape 30 in. (76 cm); flower 6 in. (15 cm). Early midseason. A ruffled orange with a red eyezone and matching picotee edge above a yellow to green throat. Tetraploid. 'Winter Masquerade' × 'Sacred Drummer'. *Photograph by Francois Verhaert.*

'Fire and Fog' (Jeff Salter, 2000). Semi-evergreen. Scape 28 in. (71 cm); flower 6 in. (15 cm). Midseason. A light rose-red with dark red eye and yellow-gold edge above a yellow-green throat. Tetraploid. 'Chinese Chariot' × 'Sultans Warrior'.

'Hampshire Hoyden' (Elizabeth H. Salter, 2000). Semi-evergreen. Scape 26 in. (66 cm); flower 3.5 in. (9 cm). Midseason. A hot rose-pink blend with a darker rose pencil eyezone and a double edge of rose and gold above a green center. Tetraploid. 'Mayfair Season' × unknown. *Photograph by Debbie and Duane Hurlbert.*

'Julie Newmar' (Mort Morss, 2000). Evergreen. Scape 32 in. (81 cm); flower 7 in. (18 cm). Early. A pastel peach with a washed eye displaying a spider web configuration which is also displayed in a watermark design on the sepals. Tetraploid. (Seedling × 'Fortunes Dearest') × 'Gerda Brooker'. R. W. Munson Jr. Award 2006. Award of Merit 2007. Honorable Mention 2004. *Photograph by Mort Morss.*

'King of Masks' (Jeff Salter, 2000). Semi-evergreen. Scape 30 in. (76 cm); flower 6 in. (15 cm). Midseason. A cream-white with a plum-purple patterned eyezone and purple picotee edge above a yellow to green throat. Tetraploid. ('Moonlit Masquerade' × seedling) × unknown. *Photograph by Francois Verhaert.*

'Palace Garden Beauty' (Jack B. Carpenter, 2000). Evergreen. Scape 25 in. (63 cm); flower 5.5 in. (14 cm). Midseason. A lavender blend with a lavender watermark and lavender picotee edge. Tetraploid. Seedling × 'Tetra Lavender Blue Baby'. Honorable Mention 2004. *Photograph by John Benoot.*

'Lion of Judah' (Tim Bell, 2000). Evergreen. Scape 26 in. (66 cm); flower 5 in. (12.7 cm). Midseason. An apricot with a wine-colored eyezone and edge above an orange throat. Tetraploid. 'Canadian Border Patrol' × unknown. Honorable Mention 2003. *Photograph by Debbie and Duane Hurlbert.*

'Lunar Max' (Dan Trimmer, 2000). Evergreen. Scape 28 in. (71 cm); flower 6.5 in. (16.5 cm). Extra early. A pale gold-yellow with a plum eyezone above a green throat. Tetraploid. 'Etched Eyes' × 'Tetra Wings of Chance'. *Photograph by Debbie and Duane Hurlbert.*

'Paradise City' (Patrick Stamile, 2000). Evergreen. Scape 30 in. (76 cm); flower 5.5 in. (14 cm). Late. A cream-pink with a mauve-rose eyezone and picotee edge above a green throat. Tetraploid. 'Strawberry Fields Forever' × 'Lake Effect'. *Photograph by Patrick Stamile.*

'Parisian Adventure' (Jeff Salter, 2000). Semi-evergreen. Scape 30 in. (76 cm); flower 6 in. (15 cm). Midseason. A cream-melon with a raisin-plum eyezone with raisin picotee edge above a yellow to green throat. Tetraploid. 'Daring Deception' × seedling. *Photograph by Francois Verhaert.*

'Sweet Love of Heaven' (Larry Grace, 2000). Evergreen. Scape 21 in. (53 cm); flower 5.5 in. (14 cm). Midseason. A heavily ruffled satin-peach with a faint gray-purple eyezone and picotee. Tetraploid. Seedling × 'Shimmering Elegance'. Honorable Mention 2003.

'Touched by Grace' (Larry Grace, 2000). Evergreen. Scape 30 in. (76 cm); flower 5 in. (12.7 cm). Midseason. A peach-gold with a tangerine-orange eyezone above a green throat. Tetraploid. Seedling × 'Wisest of Wizards'. Honorable Mention 2007.

'Venetian Baroque' (Mort Morss, 2000). Evergreen. Scape 26 in. (66 cm); flower 5.75 in. (14.6 cm). Extra early. A pear-yellow with a wild berry and dark cherry eyezone and picotee edge above a yellow to green throat. Tetraploid. (Seedling × seedling) × seedling)) × (seedling × 'Frank Smith'). Honorable Mention 2003.

'Ageless Beauty' (Patrick Stamile, 2001). Evergreen. Scape 28 in. (71 cm); flower 5 in. (12.7 cm). Early. A pink flower with a red eye with a double red and gold ruffled edge above a green throat. Tetraploid. ('Strawberry Fields Forever' × 'Be Thine') × 'Strawberry Lace'. *Photograph by Patrick Stamile.*

'Spacecoast Gator Eye' (John Kinnebrew, 2000). Semi-evergreen. Scape 28 in. (71 cm); flower 6 in. (15 cm). Early midseason. A cream-lavender with a large dark purple eyezone and wide purple picotee surrounded by a gold edge. Tetraploid. 'Spacecoast Picotee Prince' × seedling. Honorable Mention 2003. *Photograph by John Benoot.*

'Adventures With Ra' (John P. Peat, 2001). Semi-evergreen. Scape 23 in. (58 cm); flower 5.5 in. (14 cm). Early midseason. A peach-pink flower with a burgundy-purple eyezone and picotee edge above a green throat. Tetraploid. ('Clothed in Glory' × 'Pirate's Ransom') × 'Mardi Gras Ball'. *Photograph by John P. Peat.*

'Champagne and Caviar' (John P. Peat, 2001). Dormant. Scape 22 in. (56 cm); flower 6 in. (15 cm). Midseason. A cream-peach with a grape-purple eyezone above a green throat. The thick rubbery purple picotee is surrounded by a gold edge. Tetraploid. ('Heady Wine' × 'Ida's Magic') × 'Mardi Gras Ball'. *Photograph by John P. Peat.*

'Francois Verhaert' (Patrick Stamile, 2001). Evergreen. Scape 24 in. (61 cm); flower 5.5 in. (14 cm). Early midseason. An orchid with a plum-violet eye and edge and chartreuse throat. The eye is almost black at times reaching out from the throat while the huge, deep, near-black violet-plum border reaches in from the edges leaving very little petal color left. Tetraploid. 'Bold Encounter' × 'Awesome Blossom'. Honorable Mention 2005. *Photograph by Patrick Stamile.*

'Hillbilly Heart' (Jeff Salter, 2001). Semi-evergreen. Scape 26 in. (66 cm); flower 5.5 in. (14 cm). Early midseason. A bright yellow with a large bold red eye and matching picotee ruffled edge. Tetraploid. 'Wisest of Wizards' × seedling. Honorable Mention 2004. *Photograph by Francois Verhaert.*

'Jamaican Music' (Dan Trimmer, 2001). Evergreen. Scape 37 in. (94 cm); flower 5 in. (12.7 cm). Early midseason. A cream-pink with a huge red eye and thick red ruffled picotee edge above a green throat. Tetraploid. 'Raspberry Beret' × 'Tetra Dragon's Eye'. Honorable Mention 2005.

'Just Kiss Me' (Robert Carr, 2001). Evergreen. Scape 26 in. (66 cm); flower 5.75 in. (14.6 cm). Early. A pale cream-pink with a red eye and edge above a yellow to green throat. Tetraploid. 'Mystical Rainbow' × 'America's Most Wanted'. *Photograph by Karen Newman.*

'Lee Pickles' (Jeff Salter, 2001). Semi-evergreen. Scape 28 in. (71 cm); flower 5.5 in. (14 cm). Early midseason. A cream-ivory with a soft bright rose eyezone and a double edge of ruffled rose and white-gold above a green center. Tetraploid. 'Wisest of Wizards' × 'Strawberry Lace'. Honorable Mention 2004. *Photograph by John Benoot.*

'Licorice Candy' (Patrick Stamile, 2001). Evergreen. Scape 24 in. (61 cm); flower 4 in. (10 cm). Early. A lovely cream-white flower with a dramatic violet-black eye and violet-black picotee above a green throat. Tetraploid. 'Creative Vision' × ('Panda Bear' × ('Border Bride' × 'Tetra Eye of Newt')). *Photograph by Patrick Stamile.*

'Night Shift' (John P. Peat, 2001). Semi-evergreen. Scape 19 in. (48 cm); flower 6 in. (15 cm). Midseason. A clear purple with a dark purple eyezone and near-black ruffled picotee edge above a striking green throat. Tetraploid. ('Karl Petersen' × 'Gail Fox') × 'Mardi Gras Ball'. *Photograph by John P. Peat.*

'Raise the Standard' (Larry Grace, 2001). Evergreen. Scape 22 in. (56 cm); flower 6 in. (15 cm). Early midseason. A rich cream with a darker eyezone and edge above a green heart throat. Tetraploid. 'Mardi Gras Ball' × 'Only Believe'. *Photograph by Susan Okrasinski.*

'Velvet Eyes' (Patrick Stamile, 2001). Semi-evergreen. Scape 30 in. (76 cm); flower 4.5 in. (11.5 cm). Early midseason. A red with a black eyezone above a green throat. Tetraploid. 'Mister Lucky' × 'Tetra Eye of Newt'. *Photograph by Patrick Stamile.*

'Open My Eyes' (Larry Grace, 2001). Evergreen. Scape 22 in. (56 cm); flower 5 in. (12.7 cm). Early. An golden orange with a dark purple eyezone and matching ruffled picotee edge above a green heart. Tetraploid. 'Awesome Blossom' × seedling. Honorable Mention 2007. *Photograph by Francois Verhaert.*

'Rapid Eye Movement' (Dan Trimmer, 2001). Evergreen. Scape 32 in. (81 cm); flower 6.75 in. (17 cm). Early midseason. A cream-yellow with a huge dark rose-burgundy eyezone and striking picotee of the same color above a yellow to green throat. Tetraploid. 'Canadian Border Patrol' × 'Tetra Indian Sky'. Honorable Mention 2005. *Photograph by Francois Verhaert.*

'Strawberry Lightening' (Ted L. Petit, 2001). Evergreen. Scape 23 in. (58 cm); flower 6 in. (15 cm). Midseason. A rose with a red eye and a red picotee surrounded by a ruffled gold edge above a green throat. Tetraploid. ('Misty Memories' × 'Splendid Touch') × 'Only Believe'. *Photograph by Ted L. Petit.*

'Blueberry Baroque' (Ted L. Petit, 2002). Semi-evergreen. Scape 26 in. (66 cm); flower 6 in. (15 cm). Midseason. A light peach flower with a dark purple eye and matching picotee edge surrounded by a dark gold edge. Tetraploid. 'Cosmic Dancer' × ('Tetra Exotic Echo' × 'Tetra Elsie Spalding'). *Photograph by Ted L. Petit.*

'Calling All Angels' (Dan Trimmer, 2002). Evergreen. Scape 21 in. (53 cm); flower 4 in. (10 cm). Early midseason. A dramatic huge cranberry-red eye and edge dominate the face of this bloom, often showing tiny gold teeth and a wire gold edge. Tetraploid. 'Rodeo Sweetheart' × 'Sabine Baur'. Honorable Mention 2007. *Photograph by Dan Trimmer.*

'Courting Trouble' (Jeff Salter, 2002). Semi-evergreen. Scape 28 in. (71 cm); flower 4.5 in. (11.5 cm). Early midseason. A coral-pink with black-purple eyezone above green to yellow throat. Tetraploid. *Photograph by Debbie and Duane Hurlbert.*

'Broaden Your Horizons' (John P. Peat, 2002). Semi-evergreen. Scape 19 in. (48 cm); flower 6 in. (15 cm). Early. A creamy pink flower with a bright dark red eye above a deep green throat. The 1/4 in. deep dark red bubbly edge is surrounded by a bubbly gold edge, often with large teeth randomly showing off. Tetraploid. 'Strawberry Fields Forever' × ('Pirate's Ransom' × 'Mardi Gras Ball'). *Photograph by John P. Peat.*

'Continental Holiday' (Jeff Salter, 2002). Semi-evergreen. Scape 28 in. (71 cm); flower 6 in. (15 cm). Early midseason. A pale cream with a hint of melon, a bright rose eyezone, and a heavily banded edge of rose and sparkling amber. Tetraploid. 'Lee Pickles' × ('Hillbilly Heart' × 'Barbarian Princess'). *Photograph by Francois Verhaert.*

'Delaware Doosy' (Jack B. Carpenter, 2002). Evergreen. Scape 24 in. (61 cm); flower 5.5 in. (14 cm). Midseason. A mulberry with deeper purple band and picotee edge above a yellow to green throat. Tetraploid. 'Festive Art' × 'Tetra Lavender Blue Baby'. *Photograph by John Benoot.*

'Eskimo Kisses' (Dan Trimmer, 2002). Evergreen. Scape 26 in. (66 cm); flower 4 in. (10 cm). Midseason. A creamy pale pink with a huge pink-red eye and edges above a green throat. Tetraploid. ('Emperors Dragon' × ('Tetra Elsie Spalding' × 'Raspberry Beret')) × 'Jenny Kissed Me'. *Photograph by Dan Trimmer.*

'Eyes on the Prize' (Karol Emmerich, 2002). Semi-evergreen. Scape 18 in. (46 cm); flower 5.5 in. (14 cm). Early midseason. A clear pink to a copper-pink flower with a dark velvety burgundy-black eyezone and picotee surrounded by a wire white edge above an olive-green heart. Tetraploid. 'Awesome Blossom' × seedling. *Photograph by Karol Emmerich.*

'Imperial Riddle' (John P. Peat, 2002). Semi-evergreen. Scape 24 in. (61 cm); flower 5.5 in. (14 cm). Early midseason. A cream, near-white flower with a large faint rose-red eyezone that bleeds out into the petals. The picotee edge is of the same color as the eye and is surrounded in gold with a rubber texture. Tetraploid. ('Restless Warrior' × ('Romeo is Bleeding' × 'Edge of Eden')) × ('Pirate's Ransom' × 'Didgeridoo'). *Photograph by John P. Peat.*

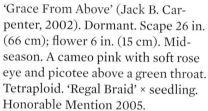

'Grace From Above' (Jack B. Carpenter, 2002). Dormant. Scape 26 in. (66 cm); flower 6 in. (15 cm). Midseason. A cameo pink with soft rose eye and picotee above a green throat. Tetraploid. 'Regal Braid' × seedling. Honorable Mention 2005.

'Exotic Treasure' (Jeff Salter, 2002). Semi-evergreen. Scape 28 in. (71 cm); flower 5 in. (12.7 cm). Early midseason. A pink-melon and flesh with a black-purple eyezone above a yellow to green throat. Tetraploid. *Photograph by Francois Verhaert.*

'Jane Trimmer' (Dan Trimmer, 2002). Evergreen. Scape 25 in. (63 cm); flower 5 in. (12.7 cm). Early midseason. A pale lavender bloom with a huge, bold black-purple eye and matching picotee edge on round full petals. Tetraploid. 'Gillian' × 'Sabine Baur'. Honorable Mention 2005. *Photograph by Dan Trimmer.*

'Just a Tease' (Jeff Salter, 2002). Semi-evergreen. Scape 25 in. (63 cm); flower 5 in. (12.7 cm). Early midseason. A cream with a lavender-rose eyezone and picotee edge above a green throat. Tetraploid. *Photograph by Francois Verhaert.*

'Lady Betty Fretz' (Ted L. Petit, 2002). Semi-evergreen. Scape 26 in. (66 cm); flower 6 in. (15 cm). Midseason. A cream flower with a large red eyezone and picotee surrounded by a heavy gold edge. Tetraploid. 'Only Believe' × 'Mardi Gras Ball'. *Photograph by Ted L. Petit.*

'Meet Joe Black' (Ted L. Petit, 2002). Semi-evergreen. Scape 26 in. (66 cm); flower 5.5 in. (14 cm). Early midseason. A clear peach to salmon-pink with a large, very dark, near-black eye, and a wide matching picotee above a deep green throat. Tetraploid. ('Mardi Gras Ball' × seedling) × 'Awesome Blossom'. Honorable Mention 2005. *Photograph by Ted L. Petit.*

'Midnight Dynamite' (Jack B. Carpenter, 2002). Evergreen. Scape 20 in. (51 cm); flower 4.5 in. (11.5 cm). Early. A dark purple with a near-black eyezone above a yellow to green throat. Diploid.

'Kansas Kitten' (Jack B. Carpenter, 2002). Dormant. Scape 22 in. (56 cm); flower 5 in. (12.7 cm). Midseason. A lavender-purple with a dark purple eyezone above a bright green throat. Diploid. 'Lavender Blue Baby' × 'Cranberry Eyed Picotee'. Honorable Mention 2005. *Photograph by Francois Verhaert.*

'Orange Electric' (Patrick Stamile, 2002). Evergreen. Scape 34 in. (86 cm); flower 5 in. (12.7 cm). Early midseason. An electric orange with red eye above a green throat. Tetraploid. 'Sungold Candy' × ('Panda Bear' × 'Awesome Blossom'). Honorable Mention 2007. *Photograph by Patrick Stamile.*

'Pat Garrity' (Patrick Stamile, 2002). Semi-evergreen. Scape 25 in. (63 cm); flower 5 in. (12.7 cm). Extra early. A bright gold with a ruby-red eyezone above a green throat. Tetraploid. 'Frank Smith' × 'Wyatt Earp'. *Photograph by Patrick Stamile.*

'Rock Solid' (Patrick Stamile, 2002). Dormant. Scape 27 in. (69 cm); flower 5 in. (12.7 cm). Early midseason. A cream with a plum-violet eyezone and edge above a green throat. Tetraploid. 'Inner Destiny' × 'Francois Verhaert'. *Photograph by Patrick Stamile.*

'Vivacious Pam' (John P. Peat, 2002). Semi-evergreen. Scape 25 in. (63 cm); flower 6.25 in. (16 cm). Early midseason. A pink with a brilliant red eye and picotee edge, red veins, heavy ruffling and a wire gold edge. Tetraploid. (('Kyoto Garden' × 'Creative Edge') × 'Mardi Gras Ball') × ('Pirate's Ransom' × 'Mardi Gras Ball'). *Photograph by John P. Peat.*

'Reyna' (John P. Peat, 2002). Semi-evergreen. Scape 25 in. (63 cm); flower 7.5 in. (19 cm). Early midseason. A very large cream flower with a faint pink to violet overcast, a darker creamy violet-pink eyezone surrounds bluish burgundy band bleeding in toward a green throat. Tetraploid. 'Big Blue' × 'Elusive Dream'. *Photograph by John P. Peat.*

'Time for Eternity' (Ted L. Petit, 2002). Semi-evergreen. Scape 26 in. (66 cm); flower 6 in. (15 cm). Midseason. Large, always showy, and consistently ornate with petal edges typically having a decorative ruffling, with "owl ears" folding and pleating. The petal self color is a cream to salmon-pink. Tetraploid. 'Opal Ring' × 'Living on the Edge'. *Photograph by Ted L. Petit.*

'Wild and Wonderful' (Patrick Stamile, 2002). Evergreen. Scape 36 in. (91 cm); flower 8.5 in. (22 cm). Early. A beige-pink with a large fern-green throat and a huge red chevron eye with sepals that twist and curl. Tetraploid. 'Waiting in the Wings' × ('Lavender Arrowhead' × 'Jabberwocky'). Honorable Mention 2007. *Photograph by Patrick Stamile.*

'Zahadoom' (Patrick Stamile, 2002). Dormant. Scape 28 in. (71 cm); flower 5.5 in. (14 cm). Early midseason. A light lavender with a bluish purple eyezone and matching picotee edge above a green throat. Tetraploid. 'Sabine Baur' × 'Tetra Lavender Blue Baby'. *Photograph by John Benoot.*

'Blackberries and Cream' (Dan Trimmer, 2003). Evergreen. Scape 26 in. (66 cm); flower 4.5 in. (11.5 cm). Early midseason. A cream-lavender with striking velvety black-purple eyezone above a bright green throat. Tetraploid. 'Celebration of Angels' × 'Tetra Dragon's Eye'. Honorable Mention 2007. *Photograph by Francois Verhaert.*

'Eye of the Matrix' (Ted L. Petit, 2002). Semi-evergreen. Scape 21 in. (53 cm); flower 6 in. (15 cm). Midseason late. A lavender with a purple eye and a gold edge above a green throat. Tetraploid. 'Didgeridoo' × 'Clothed in Glory'. *Photograph by Ted L. Petit.*

'Border Blessed' (Jack B. Carpenter, 2003). Dormant. Scape 22 in. (56 cm); flower 4.5 in. (11.5 cm). Early midseason. A peach with red eye and red-yellow edge above a green throat. Tetraploid. 'Grace from Above' × 'Cherokee Pass'. *Photograph by Jack B. Carpenter.*

'Bridey Greeson' (Frank Smith and Larry Grace, 2003). Semi-evergreen. Scape 26 in. (66 cm); flower 5.5 in. (14 cm). Early midseason. A rose-mauve with blue-violet watermark and blue-violet and yellow double edge above a green throat. Tetraploid. 'Tetra. Lavender Blue Baby' × 'Create Your Dream'. *Photograph by Debbie and Duane Hurlbert.*

'Dominic Brock-Cain' (John P. Peat, 2003). Semi-evergreen. Scape 20 in. (51 cm); flower 5.5 in. (14 cm). Early midseason. A cream-melon with red eye and gold-orange picotee edge above a green throat. Tetraploid. 'Adventures With Ra' × ('Mardi Gras Ball' × 'Gail Fox'). *Photograph by John P. Peat.*

'Lies and Lipstick' (John Kinnebrew, 2003). Semi-evergreen. Scape 25 in. (63 cm); flower 5.5 in. (14 cm). Early midseason. A pink with red eye and a reddish gold edge above a green throat. Tetraploid. 'Spacecoast Dragon Prince' × seedling. *Photograph by John Kinnebrew.*

'Queen's Coronation' (Ted L. Petit, 2003). Semi-evergreen. Scape 24 in. (61 cm); flower 6 in. (15 cm). Midseason. A pink with a red eyezone and picotee surrounded by a gold edge above a green throat. Tetraploid. 'Mardi Gras Ball' × 'Only Believe'. *Photograph by Ted L. Petit.*

'Edged in Red' (Jack B. Carpenter, 2003). Evergreen. Scape 24 in. (61 cm); flower 5 in. (12.7 cm). Early midseason. A cream with red eye above a green throat. Tetraploid. 'Senegal' × 'Grace from Above'.

'Red Eyed Fantasy' (Jack B. Carpenter, 2003). Evergreen. Scape 22 in. (56 cm); flower 5.5 in. (14 cm). Early midseason. A cream with a red eyezone above a green throat. Diploid. 'Carolina Cutie' × unknown. *Photograph by Francois Verhaert.*

'Sunday Sandals' (Frank Smith and Larry Grace, 2003). Semi-evergreen. Scape 22 in. (56 cm); flower 4 in. (10 cm). Midseason. An ivory with a violet eyezone and picotee edge above a green throat. Tetraploid. *Photograph by John Benoot.*

'Wild Cherry Round Up' (Dan Trimmer, 2003). Evergreen. Scape 24 in. (61 cm); flower 5 in. (12.7 cm). Early midseason. A ruffled shrimp-pink with a rouge-red eyezone and red wire picotee edge above a green throat. Tetraploid. 'Cherry Valentine' × 'Tetra Connie Burton'. Honorable Mention 2007. *Photograph by Francois Verhaert.*

'Come What May' (Ted L. Petit, 2004). Evergreen. Scape 28 in. (71 cm); flower 6 in. (15 cm). Midseason. A cream with rose eye and rose-gold edge above a green throat. Tetraploid. ('Mardi Gras Ball' × seedling) × 'Mardi Gras Ball'. *Photograph by Ted L. Petit.*

'Dancing With Julie' (Dan Trimmer, 2004). Evergreen. Scape 27 in. (69 cm); flower 5.75 in. (14.6 cm). Early midseason. A pink-lavender with dark pink eye above a green throat. Tetraploid. 'Sweeter Than Sugar' × 'Tetra Ruffled Masterpiece'. *Photograph by Francois Verhaert.*

'Terry Lyninger' (Jack B. Carpenter, 2003). Evergreen. Scape 24 in. (61 cm); flower 5.5 in. (14 cm). Early. A lightly ruffled gold flower with a brownish, burgundy-red eyezone above a green throat. Diploid. 'Brookwood Lee Causey' × 'Fantastic Voyage'. *Photograph by Francois Verhaert.*

'Doyle Pierce' (Frank Smith and Larry Grace, 2004). Semi-evergreen. Scape 34 in. (86 cm); flower 6 in. (15 cm). Early midseason. A lavender with bluish watermark and a bluish gold double edge above a green throat. Tetraploid. Seedling × 'Tetra Lavender Blue Baby'. Honorable Mention 2007. *Photograph by Francois Verhaert.*

'Gavin Petit' (Ted L. Petit, 2004). Semi-evergreen. Scape 27 in. (69 cm); flower 6.5 in. (16.5 cm). Midseason. A tangerine with black eye and edge above a green throat. Tetraploid. 'Awesome Blossom' × (seedling × 'Only Believe'). *Photograph by Ted L. Petit.*

'Jelly Maker' (John Shooter, 2004). Semi-evergreen. Scape 32 in. (81 cm); flower 6.5 in. (16.5 cm). Midseason. A creamy peach blend with a triangular raspberry-violet and cream-gold eye above an olive-green throat. Tetraploid. 'Grandpa Munster' × 'Tetra Siloam Ralph Henry'.

'Scott Bennett' (Mort Morss, 2004). Evergreen. Scape 28 in. (71 cm); flower 6.5 in. (16.5 cm). Early midseason. An apricot with a triple-banded eyezone of red, violet and purple above an apricot to green throat. Tetraploid. *Photograph by Francois Verhaert.*

'Elisa Dallas' (Dan Trimmer, 2004). Evergreen. Scape 25 in. (63 cm); flower 5 in. (12.7 cm). Early midseason. A pastel pink with red eyezone and matching ruffled picotee edge above a green throat. Tetraploid. ('Raspberry Beret' × 'Dan Mahoney') × 'Tetra. Connie Burton'. *Photograph by Francois Verhaert.*

'Woman at the Well' (Karol Emmerich, 2004). Semi-evergreen. Scape 22 in. (56 cm); flower 5 in. (12.7 cm). Midseason. An apricot flower with cranberry eyezone and picotee edge above a yellow to green throat. Tetraploid. 'Totally Tropical' × 'Wolf Eyes'. Honorable Mention 2007. *Photograph by Karol Emmerich.*

'Christmas Celebration' (Jack B. Carpenter, 2004). Evergreen. Scape 28 in. (71 cm); flower 6 in. (15 cm). Early midseason. A cranberry-red with a lighter eyezone above a green throat. Tetraploid. *Photograph by Jack B. Carpenter.*

'Shanghai Parasol' (Ted L. Petit, 2004). Semi-evergreen. Scape 24 in. (61 cm); flower 5.5 in. (14 cm). Midseason. A pink with a dark rose triangular eyezone and a 1/4 in. rose picotee surrounded by a wire gold edge above a green throat. Tetraploid. ('Lady Betty Fretz' × 'Strawberry Lightening') × ('Shadows of the Pyramid' × 'Vivacious Pam'). *Photograph by Ted L. Petit.*

'Ashwood Smokey Joe' (Richard Norris, 2005). Semi-evergreen. Scape 30 in. (76 cm); flower 5 in. (12.7 cm). Midseason. A purple with rose-purple eyezone and black-purple edge above a bright green throat. Tetraploid. ('Burning Inheritance' × 'Apache War Dance') × 'Tupac Amaru'.

'Bound for Glory' (Ted L. Petit, 2005). Semi-evergreen. Scape 24 in. (61 cm); flower 7 in. (18 cm). Midseason. A peach with charcoal eye and gold edge above a green throat. Tetraploid. 'Mardi Gras Ball' × 'Darla Anita'. *Photograph by Ted L. Petit.*

'Cerulean Warbler' (Ludlow Lambertson, 2005). Semi-evergreen. Scape 28 in. (71 cm); flower 5 in. (12.7 cm). Early midseason. A blue-lavender with gray-blue eye and edge with outer silver edge above a green throat. Tetraploid. Seedling × seedling. *Photograph by Ludlow Lambertson.*

'Elvin Archer' (Elizabeth H. Salter, 2005). Semi-evergreen. Scape 24 in. (61 cm); flower 3.5 in. (9 cm). Midseason. A light rose with red eye above a green throat. Diploid.

'Slap Me Sassy' (Ted L. Petit, 2004). Semi-evergreen. Scape 31 in. (79 cm); flower 6.5 in. (16.5 cm). Midseason. A lavender-rose with a black eyezone and picotee with a lightly ruffled wire gold edge above a yellow to green throat. Tetraploid. (('Awesome Blossom' × Kaskel seedling) × ('Swirling Spider' × 'Pirate's Ransom')) × ('Awesome Blossom' × 'Baracuda Bay'). *Photograph by Ted L. Petit.*

'Eyes Delight' (Ted L. Petit, 2005). Semi-evergreen. Scape 23 in. (58 cm); flower 6 in. (15 cm). Midseason. A lavender-pink with a purple eye and picotee surrounded by a gold edge above a green throat. Tetraploid. 'Mardi Gras Ball' × 'Darla Anita'. *Photograph by Ted L. Petit.*

'Fashion Police' (Dan Trimmer, 2005). Evergreen. Scape 34 in. (86 cm); flower 6.25 in. (16 cm). Midseason. A pale yellow with large mahogany-red eyezone and double edge of mahogany-red and gold above yellow-green throat. Tetraploid. 'Spice Hunter' × 'Calling All Angels'. *Photograph by John Benoot.*

'Jammin' With Jane' (John P. Peat, 2005). Semi-evergreen. Scape 30 in. (76 cm); flower 6.75 in. (17 cm). Midseason. A melon-cream with a purple-black eye and a wire gold edge above a green throat. Tetraploid. 'Awesome Blossom' × ('Firefly Nights' × 'Reyna'). *Photograph by John P. Peat.*

'Eyes Wide Shut' (Jeff Salter, 2005). Semi-evergreen. Scape 26 in. (66 cm); flower 5 in. (12.7 cm). Early midseason. A cream near-white with a wine-purple eyezone and knobby wine-purple picotee edge. Tetraploid. *Photograph by Jeff Salter.*

'Ledgewood's Pansy Eye' (Gunda Abajian, 2005). Semi-evergreen. Scape 29 in. (74 cm); flower 6.75 in. (17 cm). Early midseason. A light muted rose with a Concord-grape eyezone and wide picotee edge the same color as the eyezone outlined in cream above a green throat. Tetraploid. 'Sabine Baur' × seedling. *Photograph by Francois Verhaert.*

'Nocturnal Butterfly' (Ted L. Petit, 2005). Semi-evergreen. Scape 30 in. (76 cm); flower 6.5 in. (16.5 cm). Midseason. A burgundy with a purple eyezone and a wire gold edge above a green throat. Tetraploid. ('Bloodfire' × 'John Peat') × 'J. T. Davis'. *Photograph by Ted L. Petit.*

'Sailing at Dawn' (Ted L. Petit, 2005). Semi-evergreen. Scape 26 in. (66 cm); flower 6 in. (15 cm). Midseason. A plum with a grape eyezone and edge above a green throat. Tetraploid. 'Gavin Petit' × 'Doyle Pierce'. *Photograph by Ted L. Petit.*

'Saturday Night Fever' (Patrick Stamile, 2005). Evergreen. Scape 34 in. (86 cm); flower 9.5 in. (24 cm). Midseason. A yellow with a maroon eyezone above a green throat. Tetraploid. ('Inky Fingers' × 'Tetra Rainbow Spangles') × (seedling × 'Tetra Green Widow') × 'Webster's Pink Wonder')).

'Southwestern Memories' (Jeff Salter, 2005). Semi-evergreen. Scape 27 in. (69 cm); flower 7 in. (18 cm). Midseason. A yellow-cream with an orange-red washed eyezone and edge above a green throat. Tetraploid.

'Triple Cherries' (Ted L. Petit, 2005). Semi-evergreen. Scape 29 in. (74 cm); flower 5.5 in. (14 cm). Midseason. A peach-pink with a cherry-red eyezone and edge above a green throat. Tetraploid. ('Hampton Magic' × 'Cardassian Border') × 'Cherry Valentine'. *Photograph by Ted L. Petit.*

'Raspberries in Cream' (Patrick Stamile, 2005). Evergreen. Scape 27 in. (69 cm); flower 5 in. (12.7 cm). Early midseason. A cream near-white with a bold burgundy-purple eyezone and picotee edge above a striking green throat. Tetraploid. (('Mister Lucky' × 'Awesome Candy') × ('Panda Bear' × 'Awesome Candy')) × 'Ageless Beauty'. *Photograph by John Benoot.*

'Bread and Wine' (Tim Bell, 2005). Evergreen. Scape 29 in. (74 cm); flower 5.5 in. (14 cm). Midseason. A cream with grape eyezone and edge above a yellow to green throat. Tetraploid. 'Hem of His Garment' × 'Paradise City'. *Photograph by Tim Bell.*

'Key to Treasures' (Jack B. Carpenter, 2005). Evergreen. Scape 24 in. (61 cm); flower 6 in. (15 cm). Early midseason. A pink with a red eyezone and edge above a green throat. Tetraploid. Seedling × 'Tetra Flamboyant Dancer'. *Photograph by Jack B. Carpenter.*

'Henry Boykin' (James Townsend, 2005). Dormant. Scape 31 in. (79 cm); flower 7 in. (18 cm). Early midseason. A light peach with a purple eyezone and a purple ruffled yellow-gold double edge above a green throat. Tetraploid. 'Prince of Sharon' × 'Belle Cook'. Photograph by James Townsend.

'Circus Performer' (Ted L. Petit, 2005). Semi-evergreen. Scape 28 in. (71 cm); flower 6 in. (15 cm). Midseason. A peach-pink with a strong, black-purple eyezone and a black-red edge above a green throat. Tetraploid. 'Gavin Petit' × 'Tetra Dragon's Eye'. *Photograph by Ted L. Petit.*

'Reflection in Water' (Ted L. Petit, 2005). Semi-evergreen. Scape 22 in. (56 cm); flower 5.5 in. (14 cm). Midseason. A rose-lavender with a violet eyezone and ruffled picotee edge above a green throat. Tetraploid. ('Violet Reflections' × ('Mardi Gras Ball' × 'Rainbow Eyes')) × 'Tetra Lavender Blue Baby'. *Photograph by Ted L. Petit.*

'Nature's Poetry' (Ted L. Petit, 2005). Semi-evergreen. Scape 27 in. (69 cm); flower 7 in. (18 cm). Midseason. A peach with a purple-gold eyezone and picotee edge above a green throat. Tetraploid. 'Nothing Beautiful Lasts' × ('Mardi Gras Ball' × 'Adventures With Ra'). *Photograph by Ted L. Petit.*

'Voodoo Magic' (Larry Grace and Frank Smith, 2005). Semi-evergreen. Scape 32 in. (81 cm); flower 6 in. (15 cm). Early midseason. A golden yellow with a large dark black-purple eyezone and matching ruffled picotee. Tetraploid. 'Sabine Baur' × 'Hank Williams'. *Photograph by Frank Smith.*

'Adriana Margetts' (John P. Peat, 2006). Semi-evergreen. Scape 27 in. (69 cm); flower 7 in. (18 cm). Early midseason. A large tangerine-orange with a dark burgundy-purple eyezone and picotee edge surrounded by a serrated wire gold edge. Tetraploid. 'Vivacious Pam' × 'Gavin Petit'. *Photograph by John P. Peat.*

'Captain Picard' (John P. Peat, 2006). Semi-evergreen. Scape 24 in. (61 cm); flower 6.25 in. (16 cm). Midseason. A very bright cream-yellow flower overlaid with a chartreuse-green cast. The bright red eyezone and picotee is surrounded by a wire gold ruffled edge above a deep green center. Tetraploid. ('Douglas Lycette' × 'Mrs. John Cooper') × (('Oriental Opulence' × 'Clothed in Glory') × ('Reyna' × 'Mardi Gras Ball')). *Photograph by John P. Peat.*

'Linda Sierra' (John P. Peat, 2006). Dormant. Scape 27 in. (69 cm); flower 5 in. (12.7 cm). Early midseason. A cream-lavender flower with a striking sky-blue eyezone and picotee edge. Lightly ruffled with a fluorescent green throat. Tetraploid. ('Shadows of the Pyramids' × 'Clothed in Glory') × ('Rhapsody in Time' × Larry Grace seedling). *Photograph by John P. Peat.*

'Answering Angels' (Patrick Stamile, 2006). Evergreen. Scape 24 in. (61 cm); flower 5.5 in. (14 cm). Early midseason. A cream-yellow self with an extremely large plum eyezone that covers most of the petal self. Tetraploid. 'Calling All Angels' × 'Sue Brown'. *Photograph by Patrick Stamile.*

'Casa de Juan' (John P. Peat, 2006). Semi-evergreen. Scape 26 in. (66 cm); flower 7 in. (18 cm). Midseason. A pink with red veining and large red eyezone, sporting a 1/2 to 3/4 in. red picotee which is surrounded by a serrated white edge. Tetraploid. 'Lorikeet Springs' × ('Vivacious Pam' × 'Gavin Petit'). *Photograph by John P. Peat.*

'Queen's Circle' (Kelly Mitchell, 2006). Evergreen. Scape 26 in. (66 cm); flower 5 in. (12.7 cm). Early midseason. A red-violet with a black eyezone and black-silver edge above a yellow to green throat. Tetraploid. 'Awesome Blossom' × 'Tetra Lavender Blue Baby'. *Photograph by Kelly Mitchell.*

'Ruby Lipstick' (John Benz, 2006). Dormant. Scape 30 in. (76 cm); flower 6 in. (15 cm). Midseason. An lightly ruffled ivory-white flower with a bright red banded eyezone surrounding a large lime-green throat. Tetraploid. 'Monterry Jack' × 'Tetra Sophia Lips'.

'Sense of Wonder' (Dan Trimmer, 2006). Evergreen. Scape 24 in. (61 cm); flower 5.5 in. (14 cm). Early. An almond-pink with a red eyezone and a double red picotee edge surrounded in gold above a green throat. Tetraploid. 'Calling All Angels' × 'Tetra Connie Burton'. *Photograph by John Benoot.*

'Tony Thompson' (John P. Peat, 2006). Semi-evergreen. Scape 28 in. (71 cm); flower 8 in. (20 cm). Early midseason. A cream-pink with dark burgundy narrow chevron eyezone and picotee. A heavily ruffled gold edge accents the flower above a strong green throat. Tetraploid. 'Reyna' × 'Mardi Gras Ball'. *Photograph by Tony Thompson.*

'Parrot Tattoo' (John P. Peat, 2006). Semi-evergreen. Scape 24 in. (61 cm); flower 6 in. (15 cm). Midseason. A cream-pink flower with a candy-apple red eyezone and wide picotee edge surrounded in gold with tiny shark's teeth. Tetraploid. 'Vivacious Pam' × (Larry Grace seedling × 'Meet Joe Black').

'Sophia Armenis' (John P. Peat, 2006). Semi-evergreen. Scape 23 in. (58 cm); flower 5.5 in. (14 cm). Early. A cream-pink with a striking, candy-apple red chevron eyezone and picotee surrounded by a wine-white edge above a green throat. Tetraploid. 'Must Be Magic' × ('Didgeridoo' × 'Cherry Valentine'). *Photograph by John P. Peat.*

'Bumblebee Beautiful' (Jack B. Carpenter, 2006). Evergreen. Scape 28 in. (71 cm); flower 5 in. (12.7 cm). Early. An orange with a burgundy eyezone and edge above a green throat. Diploid. *Photograph by Jack B. Carpenter.*

'End of the Age' (Karol Emmerich, 2006). Dormant. Scape 32 in. (81 cm); flower 6 in. (15 cm). Midseason. A rusty, rose-apricot flower with a rusty burgundy eyezone and picotee edge surrounded by a second gold edge above a green throat. Tetraploid. 'Little Light of Mine' × 'Momentum'. *Photograph by Karol Emmerich.*

'Lake of Fire' (Karol Emmerich, 2006). Dormant. Scape 24 in. (61 cm); flower 7 in. (18 cm). Midseason. An apricot-peach with an orange-red eyezone and picotee edge surrounded by a second gold edge above a gold to green throat. Tetraploid. 'Light of the World' × ('Only Believe' × 'Eyes on the Prize'). *Photograph by Karol Emmerich.*

'Storm Shelter' (Karol Emmerich, 2006). Dormant. Scape 24 in. (61 cm); flower 5.5 in. (14 cm). Midseason. A light purplish-pink with a merlot eyezone and picotee edge trimmed in white. Tetraploid. ('Mask of Eternity' × 'Eyes on the Prize') × 'Tetra Dragon's Eye'. *Photograph by Karol Emmerich.*

'King of the Ages' (Karol Emmerich, 2006). Semi-evergreen. Scape 38 in. (96 cm); flower 6.5 in. (16.5 cm). Midseason. An ivory, pink, peach and apricot with white midribs, a burgundy eyezone, and picotee edge above a yellow to green throat. Tetraploid. 'Light of the World' × ('Only Believe' × 'Uppermost Edge'). *Photograph by Kyle Billadeau.*

'Moses in the Bulrushes' (Karol Emmerich, 2006). Semi-evergreen. Scape 20 in. (51 cm); flower 6 in. (15 cm). Midseason late. A peachy lavender-pink with a burgundy-violet feathered eyezone and picotee edge surrounded by a second gold above a yellow to green throat. Tetraploid. ('Only Believe' × 'Uppermost Edge') × ((Pirate's Lady' × seedling) × 'Mardi Gras Ball'). *Photograph by Karol Emmerich.*

'Turn up the Volume' (Jeff Corbett, 2006). Evergreen. Scape 26 in. (66 cm); flower 7 in. (18 cm). Early midseason. A large bloom with a large red-orange chevron eyezone and wide matching ruffled edge above a yellow to green throat. Tetraploid. 'Open My Eyes' × (('Lambada' × 'Admiral's Braid') × ('Born Too Late' × 'Wisest of Wizards')). *Photograph by Jeff Corbett.*

'Tambourine Man' (Ted L. Petit, 2006). Semi-evergreen. Scape 26 in. (66 cm); flower 6 in. (15 cm). Midseason. A deep, rich, burgundy-purple flower with a very dark purple eyezone and picotee edge surrounded by a wire gold edge above a lettuce-green throat. Tetraploid. 'Reyna' × 'Didgeridoo'. *Photograph by Ted L. Petit.*

'Passion and Style' (Ted L. Petit, 2006). Semi-evergreen. Scape 29 in. (74 cm); flower 7 in. (18 cm). Midseason. A lavender-rose base with a large purple eyezone and picotee surrounded by an orange-gold edge above a deep green throat. Tetraploid. ('Darla Anita' × 'John Peat') × ('Darla Anita' × 'John Peat'). *Photograph by Ted L. Petit.*

'Blues Clues' (John P. Peat, 2006). Semi-evergreen. Scape 21 in. (53 cm); flower 5.5 in. (14 cm). Midseason. A purple with a large bluish eyezone and bluish picotee edge surrounded by a wire gold edge above a green throat. Tetraploid. ('Ocean's Eleven' × 'Ne Quitte Pas') × 'Adventures With Ra'. *Photograph by John P. Peat.*

'Written on the Wind' (Ted L. Petit, 2006). Semi-evergreen. Scape 25 in. (63 cm); flower 6 in. (15 cm). Midseason. A dramatic rose-lavender flower with a dark purple eyezone and large picotee edge of dark purple above a green throat. Tetraploid. ('Gary Colby' × 'Meet Joe Black') × 'Jammin' With Jane'. *Photograph by Ted L. Petit.*

'Believe in Miracles' (Ted L. Petit, 2006). Semi-evergreen. Scape 28 in. (71 cm); flower 6 in. (15 cm). Midseason. A clear pink, big, bright, commanding flower with a deep rose-red eyezone and picotee surrounded by a wire gold edge above a deep green center. Tetraploid. 'Moment in the Sun' × 'Gavin Petit'. *Photograph by Ted L. Petit.*

'Bogart' (John P. Peat, 2006). Semi-evergreen. Scape 27 in. (69 cm); flower 5.5 in. (14 cm). Early midseason. A peach-pink overlaid in tangerine with a large triangular black-purple eyezone and picotee edge above a green center. Tetraploid. (('Storyville Child' × 'My Pirate Days') × 'Pirate's Ransom') × ('Meet Joe Black' × 'Gavin Petit'). *Photograph by John P. Peat.*

'Camaguay Cabaret' (John P. Peat, 2006). Semi-evergreen. Scape 24 in. (61 cm); flower 6 in. (15 cm). Midseason. A heavily ruffled flower with large looping ruffles, a bold burgundy-red eyezone and red picotee surrounded by a wire gold edge. Tetraploid. 'Lorikeet Springs' × ('Vivacious Pam' × 'Gavin Petit'). *Photograph by John P. Peat.*

'Irresistible Rainbow' (John P. Peat, 2006). Semi-evergreen. Scape 24 in. (61 cm); flower 5.5 in. (14 cm). Midseason. A cream near-white flower with a strong, heavily ruffled gold edge with a narrow purple eyezone and picotee of the same color above a green center. Tetraploid. 'Tony Thompson' × 'Lady Betty Fretz'. *Photograph by John P. Peat.*

'Unexpected Visitor' (John P. Peat, 2006). Semi-evergreen. Scape 18 in. (46 cm); flower 6 in. (15 cm). Early midseason. A wide-petaled, cream flower with a faint overlay of tangerine. A bold candy-apple red eyezone and picotee is surrounded by a wire gold edge above a dark green center. Tetraploid. 'Tony Thompson' × 'Vivacious Pam'. *Photograph by John P. Peat.*

'Ryan Pressley' (John P. Peat, 2006). Semi-evergreen. Scape 30 in. (76 cm); flower 5.5 in. (14 cm). Midseason late. A peach flower with a large dark purple eyezone and dark black-purple picotee above a green throat. Tetraploid. 'Gavin Petit' × 'Vivacious Pam'. *Photograph by John P. Peat.*

'Captured Time' (John P. Peat, 2006). Semi-evergreen. Scape 25 in. (63 cm); flower 6 in. (15 cm). Early midseason. A cream overlaid with a cantaloupe-orange and deep purple eyezone and picotee above a green throat. Tetraploid. ('Mardi Gras Ball' × Kaskel seedling) × (('Mardi Gras Ball' × 'John Peat') × 'Opal Ring'). *Photograph by John P. Peat.*

'Mango Delight' (John P. Peat, 2006). Semi-evergreen. Scape 18 in. (46 cm); flower 6.5 in. (16.5 cm). Early midseason. A super ruffled, gold-edged flower of creamy mango-sherbet with a burgundy-red eyezone and picotee above a green throat. Tetraploid. 'South Beach Sunset' × 'Tony Thompson'. *Photograph by John P. Peat.*

'Little Brandon' (John P. Peat, 2006). Semi-evergreen. Scape 28 in. (71 cm); flower 5 in. (12.7 cm). Early midseason. A cream-rose with a huge dark red eyezone and dark red ruffled picotee edge above a yellow to green throat. Tetraploid. 'Vivacious Pam' × ('Altered State' × 'Just One Look'). *Photograph by John P. Peat.*

'Tropical Shade' (Jeff Salter, 2006). Evergreen. Scape 27 in. (69 cm); flower 5.75 in. (14.6 cm). Midseason. A pale cream-pink and apricot with bright, intense rose eyezone and picotee edge above a small lime-green throat. Tetraploid. 'Tropical Cooler' × ('Continental Holiday' × 'Soho Style'). *Photograph by Jeff Salter.*

'Spacecoast Lipstick Kisses' (John Kinnebrew, 2006). Semi-evergreen. Scape 20 in. (51 cm); flower 5 in. (12.7 cm). Early midseason. A pastel pink flower with a red eyezone and wide matching picotee border. Tetraploid. 'Lies and Lipstick' × 'Renie's Delight'. *Photograph by John Kinnebrew.*

'Fool's Errand' (Jeff Salter, 2006). Semi-evergreen. Scape 28 in. (71 cm); flower 6.5 in. (16.5 cm). Midseason. A tangerine-cream self with a bold red eyezone and matching picotee above a dark green heart. Tetraploid. 'Footloose Fancy' × ('Red Cloud Mesa' × 'Southwestern Memories'). *Photograph by Jeff Salter.*

'Wizard at Large' (Jeff Salter, 2006). Evergreen. Scape 27 in. (69 cm); flower 7 in. (18 cm). Early midseason. A bright cream-yellow flower with a darker washed-red eyezone and double edge of red and yellow-gold. Tetraploid. 'Irresistible Charm' × 'Continental Holiday'. *Photograph by Jeff Salter.*

'Spacecoast Devil's Eye' (John Kinnebrew, 2006). Semi-evergreen. Scape 32 in. (81 cm); flower 5.5 in. (14 cm). Early midseason. A bright red flower with a velvety black eyezone above a green throat. Tetraploid. 'Spacecoast Shiner' × 'Velvet Eyes'. *Photograph by John Kinnebrew.*

‘The Reverend’ (Mort Morss, 2006). Evergreen. Scape 20 in. (51 cm); flower 7 in. (18 cm). Early. A cream flower with a large plum-purple eyezone and matching wide picotee edge surrounded by a toothy white edge. Tetraploid. *Photograph by Mort Morss.*

‘Ashton’s Giggles’ (Herbert Phelps, 2006). Semi-evergreen. Scape 26 in. (66 cm); flower 6 in. (15 cm). Early. A cream-tangerine with a huge dark purple eyezone and double edge of purple and gold. Tetraploid. (‘Destined to See’ × seedling) × ‘Awesome Blossom’. *Photograph by Herbert Phelps.*

‘Seagull’s Heaven’ (Frank Smith, 2006). Semi-evergreen. Scape 34 in. (86 cm); flower 6 in. (15 cm). Midseason. A saturated purple flower with a large silver-blue watermark and matching picotee edge. Tetraploid. ‘I Remember You’ × ‘Bella Sera’. *Photograph by Frank Smith.*

‘God Save the Queen’ (Mort Morss, 2006). Evergreen. Scape 30 in. (76 cm); flower 7 in. (18 cm). Early. A lavender with a large bluish purple eyezone and matching picotee surrounded by white shark’s teeth above a green throat. Tetraploid. (‘Moonfeather’ × ‘Martina Verhaert’) × ‘Scott Bennett’. *Photograph by Mort Morss.*

‘Black Eyed Bully’ (Keith Miner, 2006). Evergreen. Scape 30 in. (76 cm); flower 4.5 in. (11.5 cm). Early. A narrow-petaled lightly ruffled purple flower with a darker eyezone and variegated foliage. Tetraploid. ‘Velvet Eyes’ × ‘Meet Joe Black’. *Photograph by Keith Miner.*

‘Prissy Girl’ (Frank Smith, 2006). Semi-evergreen. Scape 28 in. (71 cm); flower 6 in. (15 cm). Midseason. A cream-pink with a distinct red eye and beautifully stitched red ruffling above a green throat. Tetraploid. ‘Hank Williams’ × ‘Tetra Connie Burton’. *Photograph by Frank Smith.*

'Goldenzelle' (Frank Smith, 2006). Semi-evergreen. Scape 32 in. (81 cm); flower 5 in. (12.7 cm). Midseason. An intense golden yellow flower with a deep cordovan-colored chevron-shaped eyezone and matching picotee. Tetraploid. 'Crazy Ivan' × 'Eye On America'. *Photograph by Frank Smith.*

'Carol Todd' (Dan Trimmer, 2006). Evergreen. Scape 30 in. (76 cm); flower 7 in. (18 cm). Early midseason. A large cream flower with a bold purple eyezone and a super ruffled double edge of gold and purple above a green throat. Tetraploid. ('Border Music' × 'Jane Trimmer') × 'Across the Universe'. *Photograph by Francois Verhaert.*

'Sea of Possibilities' (Ted L. Petit, 2006). Semi-evergreen. Scape 26 in. (66 cm); flower 7.5 in. (19 cm). Midseason. Dramatic flowers of dark purple with a black-purple eyezone and matching wide picotee surrounded by a serrated wire gold edge above a green throat. Tetraploid. ('Moment in the Sun' × 'Awesome Blossom') × 'Gavin Petit'. *Photograph by Ted L. Petit.*

'Aussie Delight' (Frank Smith, 2006). Semi-evergreen. Scape 28 in. (71 cm); flower 6 in. (15 cm). Midseason. A coral-burgundy with a velvety purple eyezone and matching picotee which is surrounded by a wire white to gold edge. Tetraploid. 'Doyle Pierce' × 'Hank Williams'. *Photograph by Frank Smith.*

'Orange City' (Dan Trimmer, 2006). Evergreen. Scape 29 in. (74 cm); flower 4.75 in. (12 cm). Early midseason. A bright orange with a screaming red eyezone above a yellow to green throat. Tetraploid. 'Lucky Dragon' × (seedling × 'Jane Trimmer'). *Photograph by Dan Trimmer.*

EDGED, NO-EYE DAYLILIES

'Beautiful Edgings' (Nita and Donald Copenhaver, 1989). Semi-evergreen. Scape 30 in. (76 cm); flower 7 in. (18 cm). Midseason. A triangular flower of cream with petals edged in rose with a green throat. Diploid. 'Best of Friends' × seedling. Award of Merit 2002. Honorable Mention 1999. *Photograph by Karen Newman.*

'Edged in Pink' (Patrick Stamile, 2006). Evergreen. Scape 38 in. (96 cm); flower 5.5 in. (14 cm). Midseason. A near-white with a rose-pink edge above a green throat. Tetraploid. ('Pink Intrigue' × 'Tetra Beautiful Edgings') × 'Tetra Forsyth Flaming Snow'. *Photograph by Patrick Stamile.*

'Coast to Coast' (Dan Trimmer, 2006). Semi-evergreen. Scape 21 in. (53 cm); flower 5.5 in. (13.97 cm). Midseason. A lavender-cream blend with a purple edge above a green throat. 'Pink Intrigue' × 'Tetra Seal of Approval'. *Photograph by Ted L. Petit.*

'Tipped in Rouge' (Patrick Stamile, 2006). Evergreen. Scape 30 in. (76 cm); flower 6 in. (15 cm). Midseason. A cream near-white with a rouge-red edge and red tips on the petals above a green throat. Tetraploid. ('Pink Intrigue' × 'Tetra Beautiful Edgings') × ('Picotee Dream' × 'Tetra Beauteau'). *Photograph by Patrick Stamile.*

'Willow Dean Smith' (John Rice, 2006). Evergreen. Scape 36 in. (91 cm); flower 6.5 in. (16.5 cm). Midseason late. A soft baby-ribbon pink with a darker pink edging above a yellow to green throat. Tetraploid. *Photograph by John Rice.*

'Romancing Summer' (Jeff Salter, 2006). Semi-evergreen. Scape 26 in. (66 cm); flower 5.5 in. (14 cm). Midseason. A blend of cream-yellow and orange with a darker rose picotee surrounded by a ruffled gold edge. Tetraploid. 'Delicate Details' × ('Egyptian Myth' × 'Citrus Sunrise'). *Photograph by Jeff Salter.*

Chapter Six

PATTERNED DAYLILIES

In addition to developing the solid eyes presented in the previous chapter, hybridizers have worked toward increasing the complexity of the flower by forming patterns within the eyezone or elsewhere in the flower. They have also altered other details of the flower to create fascinating patterns within the bloom. The patterns often change from day to day within a cultivar, so it is not always possible to see them. Many of the modern-patterned flowers also contain several types of patterns in the same flower, and new patterns are emerging each year. Since daylily lovers are often confused about what is meant by a patterned daylily, what follows is an explanation of some of the different types of patterns currently seen in daylilies.

'Ultraviolet Mood' (Patrick Stamile, 1997). Evergreen. Scape 26 in. (66 cm); flower 6 in. (15 cm). Midseason. A lavender with a yellow applique throat. Tetraploid. 'Driving Me Wild' × ('Heavenly Dragon' × 'Warrior Spirit'). *Photograph by Patrick Stamile.*

APPLIQUE THROATS

One of the early patterns seen in daylilies was a mother-of-pearl-like, iridescent, reflective pattern in the throat area. This first appeared in flowers such as Ida Munson's 'Chinese Temple Flower' (1988) and 'Pharaoh's Treasure' (1988). Bill Munson felt that the pattern in the throat looked as though it had been applied, and he used the term "applique throat" to describe these flowers. Further, the applique throat is generally surrounded by a darker halo or eye. At this point, most of these flowers are in the lavender or purple color range, and include 'Silent Sentry' (1992) by Jeff Salter and 'Ultraviolet Mood' (1997) by Pat Stamile. Although hybridizers have tried to take this pattern into other colors, we do not know of any successful attempts yet (imagine it on a red flower). More recent introductions include Jeff Salter's 'Lighter Than Air' (2002) and Elizabeth Salter's 'Korean Kite' (2005), while John Kinnebrew has introduced a number of striking applique patterns, including 'Catcher in the Eye' (2001), 'Spacecoast Sea Shells' (2003), and 'Spacecoast Behavior Pattern' (2006). John Peat's 'Rippled Oasis' (2005) has a patterned eye surrounding the applique throat, for even more complexity.

'Catcher in the Eye' (John Kinnebrew, 2001). Evergreen. Scape 30 in. (76 cm); flower 5 in. (12.7 cm). Early midseason. A lavender base color with a dark-purple eye and matching picotee edge enhanced by a patterned yellow applique throat. Tetraploid. Seedling × 'Daring Deception'. Honorable Mention 2004. *Photograph by John Benoot.*

'Lighter than Air' (Jeff Salter, 2002). Semi-evergreen. Scape 31 in. (79 cm); flower 6 in. (15 cm). Early midseason. A lavender with a lavender-plum eyezone above a yellow to green applique throat. Tetraploid. *Photograph by John Benoot.*

'Spacecoast Sea Shells' (John Kinnebrew, 2003). Evergreen. Scape 30 in. (76 cm); flower 5.5 in. (14 cm). Early midseason. A cream with a purple eyezone and edge above a yellow to cream applique throat. Tetraploid. 'Catcher in the Eye' × seedling. *Photograph by John Kinnebrew.*

'Korean Kite' (Elizabeth H. Salter, 2005). Semi-evergreen. Scape 26 in. (66 cm); flower 4.5 in. (11.5 cm). Midseason. A lavender with a deeper eyezone above a yellow-green throat. Tetraploid.

MASCARA EYES OR BANDS

A simple, solid eyezone does not create a pattern, even if it is in a new color range, such as blue. The eyezone must be more complex, and perhaps the simplest type of pattern is created by a circular thin "mascara" edge surrounding the eye. To the best of our knowledge, this term was also coined by Bill Munson with an obvious reference to women's makeup surrounding and enhancing the beauty of the eyes. One of the early examples of this pattern was 'Patchwork Puzzle' (1990) by Elizabeth Salter. More recently, examples include Grace Stamile's 'Blue Elf' (2006) and Elizabeth Salter's 'Nile Jewel' (2006), 'Heavens Rest' (2005), and 'Circle Upon Circle' (2005). The mascara eye, or dark band at the outside edge of the eye, often becomes part of more complex patterns. While the mascara band is often the same color (although usually darker), it can also be a different color, creating a dramatic contrasting effect.

'Spacecoast Behavior Pattern' (John Kinnebrew, 2006). Evergreen. Scape 32 in. (81 cm); flower 6 in. (15 cm). Early midseason. A light lavender flower with a purple-patterned eyezone and picotee above an arrow-shaped applique throat. Tetraploid. 'Spacecoast Sea Shells' × 'Lighter Than Air'. *Photograph by John Kinnebrew.*

'Rippled Oasis' (John P. Peat, 2006). Semi-evergreen. Scape 25 in. (63 cm); flower 5.5 in. (14 cm). Early midseason. A lavender-pink with a complex purple applique yellow eyezone and a purple edge above a green throat. Tetraploid. 'Meet Joe Black' × 'Catcher in the Eye'. *Photograph by John P. Peat.*

'Patchwork Puzzle' (Elizabeth H. Salter, 1990). Evergreen. Scape 18 in. (46 cm); flower 2.75 in. (7 cm). Early midseason. An cream-lemon with a washed lavender-purple eyezone banded in burgundy above a deep green throat. Diploid. Donn Fischer Memorial Cup 1995. *Photograph by John Eiseman.*

'Circle Upon Circle' (Elizabeth H. Salter, 2005). Evergreen. Scape 23 in. (58 cm); flower 4 in. (10 cm). Early midseason. A pink with cream-ivory pink eye above a yellow-green throat. Diploid. *Photograph by Elizabeth H. Salter.*

'Blue Elf' (Grace Stamile, 2006). Semi-evergreen. Scape 16 in. (41 cm); flower 3 in. (7.6 cm). Early midseason. A cream-pink diamond-dusted flower with a pale blue eyezone surrounded with fuchsia above a green throat. Diploid. Seedling × 'Little Secrets'. *Photograph by Patrick Stamile.*

'Nile Jewel' (Elizabeth H. Salter, 2006). Evergreen. Scape 22 in. (56 cm); flower 3.5 in. (9 cm). Midseason. A lavender with a very large blue-violet eyezone with darker burgundy mascara band above a green heart. Diploid. ('Way Out Yonder' × 'Out of the Blue') × (seedling × 'Heavenly Blue').

'Paper Butterfly' (Mort Morss, 1983). Semi-evergreen. Scape 24 in. (61 cm); flower 6 in. (15 cm). Early. A creamy peach-pink with a rosy violet blended veined eye bleeding out onto the petals. Tetraploid. (((Seedling × 'Chicago Two Bits') × 'Thais') × ('Silver Veil' × ('Knave' × 'Chicago Mist'))) × 'Chicago Mist'. Don C. Stevens Award 1987. Lenington All-American Award 1998. Award of Merit 1990. Honorable Mention 1987. *Photograph by Jay Tompkins.*

'Rainbow Candy' (Patrick Stamile, 1996). Dormant. Scape 28 in. (71 cm); flower 4.5 in. (11.5 cm). Early midseason. A cream with a grayish purple-lavender and yellow eyezone above a green throat. Tetraploid. 'Blueberry Candy' × 'Tetra Little Print'. *Photograph by Patrick Stamile.*

INWARD STREAKS

These flowers have a streaked veining moving inward from the edge of the eye toward the throat, or possibly outward toward the petal edges. This streaking is seen in flowers such as 'Paper Butterfly' (1983) by Mort Morss and 'Rainbow Candy' (1996) by Pat Stamile. Often, the streaking appears to begin at the outside edge of the eye, which can be set off by a dark mascara-type edge described previously. The color of the veining is generally the same as the mascara eye, and it often looks like the veins are painted along the top of the petal's natural veins. More recent examples include Elizabeth Salter's 'Tilting at Windmills' (2006) and 'Sorcery Rising' (2002); Ted Petit's 'Turn the Kaleidoscope' (2006), 'Entering Warp Speed' (2004), and 'Magical Passes' (2003); John Peat's 'Another Distraction' (2001) and 'Rippled Oasis' (2005); and Dan Trimmer's 'Jamaican Love' (2004).

'Another Distraction' (John P. Peat, 2001). Semi-evergreen. Scape 23 in. (58 cm); flower 5.75 in. (14.6 cm). Midseason. A near-white with a purple veined eyezone and edge above a green throat. Tetraploid. 'Sacred Drummer' × 'Mystical Rainbow'. *Photograph by John P. Peat.*

'Magical Passes' (Ted L. Petit, 2003). Semi-evergreen. Scape 24 in. (61 cm); flower 5 in. (12.7 cm). Midseason. A yellow with a burgundy-patterned eye above a green throat. Tetraploid. 'Shadows of the Pyramids' × 'Opal Ring'. *Photograph by Ted L. Petit.*

'Entering Warp Speed' (Ted L. Petit, 2004). Semi-evergreen. Scape 31 in. (79 cm); flower 6 in. (15 cm). Midseason. A yellow-gold with charcoal and burgundy-patterned eye. Tetraploid. 'Time in a Bottle' × ('Rainbow Eyes' × 'Opal Ring'). *Photograph by Ted L. Petit.*

'Turn the Kaleidoscope' (Ted L. Petit, 2006). Semi-evergreen. Scape 30 in. (76 cm); flower 5 in. (12.7 cm). Midseason. A light creamy flower with a patterned eyezone of a violet base and a burgundy to wine mascara edge. The lightly ruffled flowers often carry a matching wire picotee edge. Tetraploid. 'Sunday Sandals' × 'Gift of Mischief'. *Photograph by Ted L. Petit.*

CONCENTRIC CIRCLES OR BANDS

In some flowers, the eye breaks up into bands of alternating color that often form concentric circles (circles inside circles) moving out from the throat. These include flowers such as Pat Stamile's 'Mystical Rainbow' (1996) and 'Enchanted Rainbow' (1997), and Jeff Salter's 'Visual Intrigue' (2000) and 'Dark Mosaic' (1996). In the simplest forms of these patterns, it looks as though the eye has shattered into many pieces, typically alternating between dark and light shades. These flowers can be visually captivating, drawing the viewer in like the television series *The Twilight Zone*. More recent examples include Elizabeth Salter's 'Pocketful of Patterns' (2005), and Ted Petit's 'Time in a Bottle' (2001).

These concentric circles or banded eyes become more fascinating when the various rings are of a different color. Many of these flowers contain blue, violet, purple, red, and charcoal zones, such as Ted Petit's 'Through The Looking Glass' (2001), and Pat Stamile's 'Mississippi Blues' (2004), 'Fantasy Eyes' (2005), 'Screen Pattern', and 'Which Way' (2005).

The patterns can also be fascinating if the bands of color streak or become erratic in shape, such as Ted Petit's 'Infinity and Beyond' (2004), and Gerda Brooker's 'Victorian Garden Heavens Applause' (2006). Of course, some flowers have more complex patterns that include some combination of a dark mascara band, concentric layers and streaking, such as Ted Petit's 'Oceans Eleven' (2004), 'Queen of the Desert' (2004), and 'Aztec Headdress' (2003); Pat Stamile's 'Tricolor' (2006) and 'Static' (2006); Grace Stamile's 'Finding Blue' (2004); John Peat's 'Aurora Blues' (2006); and John Kinnebrew's 'Spacecoast Butterfly Effect' (2005) and 'Spacecoast Dragon Prince' (2002). Sometimes the concentric circles combine with inward streaks, or become non-circular, giving rise to dollops of color or arrowhead shapes, sometimes resembling birds in flight.

'Through the Looking Glass' (Ted L. Petit, 2001). Semi-evergreen. Scape 24 in. (61 cm); flower 6 in. (15 cm). Midseason. A salmon-pink self with a complex-patterned eye made up of many intricate layers above a deep green throat. Tetraploid. 'Opal Ring' × ('Forest Phantom' × 'Rainbow Eyes'). *Photograph by Ted L. Petit.*

'Time in a Bottle' (Ted L. Petit, 2001). Semi-evergreen. Scape 26 in. (66 cm); flower 6.5 in. (16.5 cm). Midseason. A yellow with a patterned eyezone above a green throat. Tetraploid. 'Etched Eyes' × ('Forest Phantom × 'Rainbow Eyes'). *Photograph by Ted L. Petit.*

'Finding Blue' (Grace Stamile, 2004). Semi-evergreen. Scape 20 in. (51 cm); flower 3 in. (7.6 cm). Early. A light cream-pink with grayish lavender-blue lined in fuchsia-patterned eye above a green throat. Diploid. ('Little Sensation' × ('Little Pleasure' × 'Little Fat Cat')) × ('Little Sensation' × ('Little Pleasure' × 'Little Fat Cat')). *Photograph by Patrick Stamile.*

'Infinity and Beyond' (Ted L. Petit, 2005). Semi-evergreen. Scape 28 in. (71 cm); flower 6 in. (15 cm). Midseason. A cream with a purple-patterned eyezone above a green throat. Tetraploid. 'Through the Looking Glass' × 'Rainbow Eyes'. *Photograph by Ted L. Petit.*

'Pocketful of Patterns' (Elizabeth H. Salter, 2005). Evergreen. Scape 28 in. (71 cm); flower 4 in. (10 cm). Early midseason. A lavender with a creamy ivory-washed violet eyezone above a yellow-green throat. Tetraploid.

'Screen Pattern' (Patrick Stamile, 2005). Dormant. Scape 26 in. (66 cm); flower 5.5 in. (14 cm). Midseason. A cream with a multicolored eyezone above a green throat. Tetraploid. 'Mysterious Eyes' × 'Tetra Crystal Blue Persuasion'. *Photograph by Patrick Stamile.*

'Aurora Blues' (John P. Peat, 2006). Semi-evergreen. Scape 21 in. (53 cm); flower 5.5 in. (14 cm). Semi-evergreen. A tangerine-peach flower with a triple eyezone of slate gray-blue, dark purple and burgundy above a green throat. Tetraploid. ('Ocean's Eleven' × 'Ne Quitte Pas') × 'Adventures With Ra'. *Photograph by John P. Peat.*

'Mississippi Blues' (Patrick Stamile, 2006). Evergreen. Scape 28 in. (71 cm); flower 5 in. (12.7 cm). Early midseason. A cream with a blue-violet eyezone surrounded by a band of purple above a green throat. Tetraploid. (('Sheer Water Blues' × 'Tetra Elfin Etching') × 'Delta Blues') × 'Tetra Seeing Blue'. *Photograph by John Benoot.*

'Static' (Patrick Stamile, 2006). Evergreen. Scape 30 in. (76 cm); flower 4.25 in. (11 cm). Midseason. An orchid with a broken deep navy multicolored triangular eyezone above a deep green throat. Tetraploid. 'Mysterious Eyes' × 'Bit of Blue'. *Photograph by Patrick Stamile.*

AVANT-GARDE PATTERNS

Other patterns are formed by different areas of light and shading in the flower outside of the eyezone area. The simplest form of this may be the result of lighter or darker-colored edges (such as 'Coast to Coast' (2006) by Dan Trimmer, or 'Banned in Boston' (1994) by Doris Simpson), which do not by themselves create a pattern. However, some flowers show an erratic distribution of light and dark across the flower, creating complex patterns. Elizabeth Salter's 'Elfin Illusion' (1995) is an excellent example of this. These flowers can have a lighter watermark on a darker petal self, or a dark eye on a light base. They typically have lighter borders on the petals, as in 'Fairy Firecracker' (1984) by Elizabeth Salter. Many of the tetraploid patterns of this type came from Steve Moldovan's 'Avant Garde' (1986) line, and have increasingly more complex patterns, such as those seen in Bob Carr's 'Altered State' (1997) and 'Aztec Priestess' (1997). More recent examples include John Peat's 'Erratic Behavior' (2002) and Elizabeth Salter's 'Spirited Style' (2005) and 'Chaotic Symmetry' (2003). The patterns in these flowers tend to change from day to day, such that flowers can at times appear quite formal, while on other days exotic patterns appear in the flower.

'Tricolor' (Patrick Stamile, 2006). Evergreen. Scape 25 in. (63 cm); flower 5.5 in. (14 cm). Early. An orchid cream with a multicolored complex eyezone above a green throat. Tetraploid. 'Mysterious Eyes' × 'Bit of Blue'. *Photograph by Patrick Stamile.*

'Elfin Illusion' (Elizabeth H. Salter, 1995). Semi-evergreen. Scape 22 in. (56 cm); flower 3.5 in. (9 cm). Midseason. A dark purple flower with a patterned lavender eyezone, lighter petal edges, and patterned sepals. Diploid. *Photograph by Ted L. Petit and John P. Peat.*

'Altered State' (Robert Carr, 1997). Evergreen. Scape 28 in. (71 cm); flower 5.5 in. (14 cm). Early midseason. A cherry-red with a darker red eyezone and a patterned pink border. Tetraploid. 'Whooperee' × 'Purely Exotic'. *Photograph by Ted L. Petit and John P. Peat.*

'Erratic Behavior' (John P. Peat, 2002). Dormant. Scape 26 in. (66 cm); flower 6.5 in. (16.5 cm). Early midseason. A light cream to pink flower with red veins and a huge chevron, candy-apple red eyezone that extends out almost to the tips of the petals with wide pink midribs shooting up the center of the eyezone. Tetraploid. ('Kabuki Ballet' × 'Street Urchin') × 'Altered State'. *Photograph by John P. Peat.*

'Lupita Vindaz' (John P. Peat, 2004). Dormant. Scape 20 in. (51 cm); flower 5 in. (12.7 cm). Early midseason. A pink with a red-patterned eyezone and sepals tipped in dark red above a green throat. Tetraploid. ('Avant Garde' × 'Altered State') × 'Just One Look'. *Photograph by John P. Peat.*

'Spirited Style' (Elizabeth H. Salter, 2005). Semi-evergreen. Scape 24 in. (61 cm); flower 3.5 in. (9 cm). Midseason. A lavender with a washed cream and violet eyezone above a green throat. Diploid.

WASHED EYEZONES

The "washed" eye patterns have a look all their own. The eyes are usually surrounded by a dark mascara line, and the inner eye has dark areas that tend to fade to lighter areas, taking on the washed look of an old pair of jeans. 'Little Print' (1992) is one of Elizabeth Salter's most famous washed eyes, along with her 'Enchanter's Spell' (1982) and newer 'Maze of Moonlight' (2001). More recently, Elizabeth has introduced 'Floating on Air' (2006).

'Enchanter's Spell' (Elizabeth H. Hudson, 1982). Semi-evergreen. Scape 18 in. (46 cm); flower 3 in. (7.6 cm). Midseason. An ivory self with a dark burgundy-purple washed eye bleeding out into the petals and sepals, and a lime-green throat. Diploid. Annie T. Giles Award 1991. Award of Merit 1992. *Photograph by John Eiseman.*

'Little Print' (Elizabeth H. Salter, 1992). Semi-evergreen. Scape 16 in. (41 cm); flower 2.75 in. (7 cm). Midseason. A light ivory-cream with a strongly washed eye of violet magenta that is edged in a deeper magenta. Diploid. 'Lady Jinx' × 'Enchanter's Spell'. Honorable Mention 2002. *Photograph by Ted L. Petit and John P. Peat.*

STIPPLING

There are patterns that are formed by stippling on the petals. These many dots of color create a plicata effect, which ranges from a speckled look to blotches of color. While speckled flowers are common in camellias, they are only now emerging in daylilies. While a simple, homogeneous stippling spread evenly across the flower surface may not create a pattern per se, the stippled dots can occur clumped together or spread apart in ways to create patterns. They are particularly interesting when the degree of stippling varies within the flower, creating eye patterns. Examples of this stippling include Ted Petit's 'Expanding Universe' (1998) and John Peat's 'Polka Dot Bikini' (2006). The most dramatic examples of this type of pattern occur when the stippling becomes extreme, erratic or creates stripes and freckled patterns, in flowers such as John Kinnebrew's 'Spacecoast Freaky Tiki' (2006), Mike Derrow's 'Pink Stripes' (2006), and Stan Holley's 'Sprinkled With Paprika' (2005).

'Spacecoast Freaky Tiki' (John Kinnebrew, 2006). Semi-evergreen. Scape 20 in. (51 cm); flower 3.5 in. (9 cm). Early midseason. A bright orange with red-stippled speckles above a green throat. Tetraploid. 'Spacecoast Tiny Inferno' × 'Raven's Rage'. *Photograph by John Kinnebrew.*

'Expanding Universe' (Ted L. Petit, 1998). Semi-evergreen. Scape 26 in. (66 cm); flower 5.5 in. (14 cm). Midseason. A cream with cinnamon stipples that form the eyezone as they cluster closer together. Tetraploid. ('Midnight Magic' × 'Shinto Etching') × ('Ida's Magic' × 'Wrapped in Gold'). *Photograph by Ted L. Petit.*

'Sprinkled with Paprika' (Stan Holley, 2005). Evergreen. Scape 18 in. (46 cm); flower 2 in. (5 cm) . Early midseason. A yellow with a hot red eyezone and red picotee edge covered in sprinkles or red above a green throat. Diploid. 'Cranberry Baby' × 'Dragon Circle'. *Photograph by Stan Holley.*

'Polka Dot Bikini' (John P. Peat, 2006). Semi-evergreen. Scape 22 in. (56 cm); flower 6 in. (15 cm). Early midseason. A cream-pink base color with a larger burgundy-purple eyezone made up of purple stipples above a green throat. Tetraploid. 'Gamma Quadrant' × seedling. *Photograph by John P. Peat.*

METALLIC EYES

One of the latest breaks are metallic eyes, which look as if aluminum foil has been glued on the petal and actually reflect the sunlight into your eyes. Examples include Ted Petit's 'Heavy Metal' (2001) and 'Lightening in a Bottle' (2006) as well as Pat Stamile's 'Metallic Butterfly' (2004) and John Peat's 'Spatial Anomalies' (2003). With each generation of seedlings, the eye is becoming larger and the shiny surface of the eye becomes more reflective. If this trend continues, as it appears to be, someday you may have to wear your sunglasses to view these beauties.

'Heavy Metal' (Ted L. Petit, 2001). Evergreen. Scape 27 in. (69 cm); flower 5.5 in. (14 cm). Midseason. A yellow with a complex-patterned metallic eyezone above a green throat. Tetraploid. ('Rings of Glory' × 'Chinese Cloisonne') × 'Opal Ring'. *Photograph by Ted L. Petit.*

'Spatial Anomalies' (John P. Peat, 2003). Semi-evergreen. Scape 27 in. (69 cm); flower 5.75 in. (14.6 cm). Early midseason. A cream with a silver eyezone and a purple-lavender picotee edge above a green throat. Tetraploid. Seedling × 'Heavy Metal'. *Photograph by John P. Peat.*

'Metallic Butterfly' (Patrick Stamile, 2004). Evergreen. Scape 23 in. (58 cm); flower 4.25 in. (11 cm). Early. A pink with orchid metallic silver rings above a green throat. Tetraploid. ('Huckleberry Candy' × 'Sheerwater Blues') × 'Tetra Mystic Mariner'. *Photograph by Patrick Stamile.*

'Lightening in a Bottle' (Ted L. Petit, 2006). Semi-evergreen. Scape 24 in. (61 cm); flower 5.5 in. (14 cm). Semi-evergreen. A copper-melon flower with a reflective, metallic, aluminum-foil eyezone surrounded by a band of burgundy above an apple-green throat. Tetraploid. 'Heavy Metal' × ('Through the Looking Glass' × ('Winter Palace' × 'Opal Ring')). *Photograph by Ted L. Petit.*

VEINING

One of the more unusual patterns forming in daylilies is a pattern formed by enhancing or darkening the natural veining in the flower, against a contrasting background. One of the most dramatic examples of this is John Shooter's 'Mapping Carolina' (1999). While simple veining may not create a pattern effect, the type of dramatic veining seen in 'Mapping Carolina' suggests that this may be an important new direction for pattern flowers. However, to date, it is impossible to tell where this trend may go.

RAINBOW EDGES AND MIDRIBS

Some of the latest breaks in the tetraploids have occurred when the multiple rings of color in the eye have moved out onto other parts of the petal. When the pattern moves out along the midrib, it creates a different look to the pattern, such as in 'In His Image' (2003) by Ted Petit.

Like picotee edges that match the eyezone moving out along the petal edges, the patterns within the eyezone area can also move out along the petal edges. These multiple-banded, multiple-colored picotees surround the petal edges, creating a rainbow effect. Flowers with multilayered and multicolored picotees are being produced, often surrounded by a heavy gold edge. Examples include Ted Petit's 'Wheel of Time' (2004) and 'Send Me a Rainbow' (2005). Hybridizers are working to increase these multicolored edges, resulting in wider edges and larger eyezones as well as layers of patterns that take up most of the petal surface.

'Mapping Carolina' (John Shooter, 1999). Dormant. Scape 26 in. (66 cm); flower 5 in. (12.7 cm). Midseason. A tan-purple bitone with purple veins and a silver-purple eyezone above a lemon-yellow to green throat. Diploid. Seedling × seedling. *Photograph by John Benoot.*

'Send Me a Rainbow' (Ted L. Petit, 2005). Semi-evergreen. Scape 29 in. (74 cm); flower 7 in. (18 cm). Midseason. A peach with a violet, purple, and gray eyezone and a gold edge above a green throat. Tetraploid. 'Through the Looking Glass' × ('Mardi Gras Ball' × 'Adventures With Ra'). *Photograph by Ted L. Petit.*

'Wheel of Time' (Ted L. Petit, 2005). Semi-evergreen. Scape 28 in. (71 cm); flower 5.5 in. (14 cm). Midseason. A peach with a purple-patterned eyezone and picotee edge above a green throat. Tetraploid. ('Higher than Love' × 'Time for Eternity') × ('Mardi Gras Ball' × 'Adventures With Ra'). *Photograph by Ted L. Petit.*

'Siloam David Kirchhoff' (Pauline Henry, 1986). Dormant. Scape 16 in. (41 cm); flower 3.5 in. (9 cm). Early midseason. An orchid pink with a cerise pencil and washed eyezone and a green throat. Diploid. Annie T. Giles Award 1995. Don C. Stevens Award 1996. Award of Merit 1993. Honorable Mention 1990. *Photograph by Ted L. Petit and John P. Peat.*

NARROW-FORMED PATTERNED DAYLILIES

For many years hybridizers have worked to create round daylilies with petals so wide that the sepals are hidden. But, for patterned daylilies, much of the charm is that the pattern is repeated on the sepals. Thus, the most striking effect is often observed in relatively narrow-petaled flowers, where the sepals are an important part of the overall flower image. Examples include the mimicking pattern on the sepals of Elizabeth Salter's 'True Blue Heart' (1993), 'Elfin Illusion' (1995), and her new 'Vivid Vision' (2001). So, ultimately, the patterns may play a very important role on more narrow flowers where the sepals are clearly visible, such as in spiders and unusual formed daylilies.

Each year, new, more exciting, and dramatic patterns are emerging. The patterns are becoming more complex, vivid, and metallic, are being overlaid on top of three-dimensional carving, and are expanding to cover most of the flower face.

'Witch Stitchery' (Mort Morss, 1986). Semi-evergreen. Scape 26 in. (66 cm); flower 5.5 in. (14 cm). Extra early. A cream-yellow self with a veined lavender eyezone edged in purple which bleeds out into the petal. Tetraploid. (Seedling × 'Chicago Two Bits') × 'Paper Butterfly'. Award of Merit 1997. *Photograph by John Eiseman.*

'Jason Salter' (Elizabeth H. Salter, 1987). Evergreen. Scape 18 in. (46 cm); flower 2.75 in. (7 cm). Early midseason. A deep yellow with a washed lavender-purple eyezone and picotee above a green throat. Diploid. 'Enchanter's Spell' × ('Enchanted Elf' × 'Cosmic Hummingbird'). Donn Fischer Memorial Cup 1993. Don C. Stevens Award 1994. Lenington All-American Award 2000. Award of Merit 1995. Honorable Mention 1992. *Photograph by Patrick Stamile.*

'Sings the Blues' (Ra Hansen, 1990). Semi-evergreen. Scape 26 in. (66 cm); flower 6 in. (15 cm). Midseason late. A medium lavender-rose with a variegated violet-blue and charcoal eyezone and emerald throat. Diploid. 'Surf' × 'Ruffled Ivory'. Honorable Mention 1994. *Photograph by Ra Hansen.*

'Blue Moon Rising' (Elizabeth H. Salter, 1991). Semi-evergreen. Scape 24 in. (61 cm); flower 3 in. (7.6 cm). Midseason. A pale ivory-peach with a blue-violet eyezone above a yellow to green throat. Diploid. *Photograph by John Eiseman.*

'Fancy Face' (Jack B. Carpenter, 1994). Evergreen. Scape 22 in. (56 cm); flower 5.5 in. (14 cm). Early midseason. A cream-gold with a dark mahogany multi-layered patterned eyezone above a green throat. Diploid. Honorable Mention 1999. *Photograph by John Benoot.*

'Crystal Blue Persuasion' (Elizabeth H. Salter, 1996). Evergreen. Scape 18 in. (46 cm); flower 2.75 in. (7 cm). Midseason. A pale lavender with a slate blue pencil edge and a magenta eyezone above a green throat. Diploid. Donn Fischer Memorial Cup 2006. Honorable Mention 2002. *Photograph by Elizabeth H. Salter.*

'Devil's Footprint' (Elizabeth H. Salter, 1992). Semi-evergreen. Scape 18 in. (46 cm); flower 8 in. (20 cm). Early midseason. A cream-yellow with a multiple-banded burgundy-purple to charcoal-gray eyezone layered above a green throat. Diploid. 'Alpine Mist' × 'Highland Mystic'. *Photograph by John Eiseman.*

'Gerda Brooker' (Mort Morss, 1995). Evergreen. Scape 30 in. (76 cm); flower 7 in. (18 cm). Early. A cream with red-violet edges and a triple eye of lavender-lilac above a yellow to green throat. Tetraploid. ((Seedling × 'Opus One') × ('Paper Butterfly' × 'Fantasy Finish')) × ((seedling × 'Opus One') × ('Paper Butterfly' × 'Fantasy Finish')). R. W. Munson Jr. Award 2005. Honorable Mention 2000. *Photograph by Elliot Turkiew.*

'Morrie Otte' (Elizabeth H. Salter, 1996). Semi-evergreen. Scape 18 in. (46 cm); flower 2.75 in. (7 cm). Midseason. A mauve with a silver-frost eyezone above a green throat. Diploid. Donn Fischer Memorial Cup 2002. Honorable Mention 2001. *Photograph by Ted L. Petit and John P. Peat.*

'Mystical Rainbow' (Patrick Stamile, 1996). Dormant. Scape 25 in. (63 cm); flower 5.5 in. (14 cm). Early midseason. A clear pink with multiple-banded rosy raspberry-charcoal and yellow eyezone above a green throat. Tetraploid. 'Exotic Candy' × 'Rainbow Eyes'. R. W. Munson Jr. Award 2003. Award of Merit 2004. Honorable Mention 2001. *Photograph by Patrick Stamile.*

'Bertie' (Elizabeth H. Salter, 1998). Semi-evergreen. Scape 24 in. (61 cm); flower 3.5 in. (9 cm). Early midseason. A pale lemon-cream with washed eye of pale violet-blue etched darker eye edge and a green throat. Tetraploid. 'Witches Wink' × 'Tetra Little Print'. Honorable Mention 2003. *Photograph by Ted L. Petit and John P. Peat.*

'George Jets On' (Rick Yost, 1999). Dormant. Scape 28 in. (71 cm); flower 3.75 in. (9.5 cm). Early midseason. A rose-cream bicolor with a yellow watermark surrounded by a cream-rose pencil-etched line above a yellow to green throat. Diploid. Seedling × seedling. Honorable Mention 2003. *Photograph by John Benoot.*

'Sacred Drummer' (Jeff Salter, 1996). Semi-evergreen. Scape 29 in. (74 cm); flower 6 in. (15 cm). Midseason. A pale pink with a blue-violet eyezone and a green throat. Tetraploid. *Photograph by Ted L. Petit and John P. Peat.*

'Faces of a Clown' (Jeff Salter, 1998). Semi-evergreen. Scape 26 in. (66 cm); flower 6 in. (15 cm). Early midseason. A bright gold-yellow with a washed magenta-violet patterned eye surrounding a green throat. Tetraploid. *Photograph by Ted L. Petit and John P. Peat.*

'Ornamental Focus' (Patrick Stamile, 1999). Evergreen. Scape 25 in. (63 cm); flower 7 in. (18 cm). Extra early. A cream-yellow with a burgundy-patterned eyezone, with bands of lavender and charcoal above a green throat. Tetraploid. (Seedling × ('Secret Splendor' × 'Druid's Chant')) × 'Great White'. *Photograph by Patrick Stamile.*

'Web of Intrigue' (Patrick Stamile, 1999). Evergreen. Scape 30 in. (76 cm); flower 6 in. (15 cm). Extra early. A pale orange with an etched pattern of lavender and purple above a green throat. R. W. Munson Jr. Award 2007. Award of Merit 2007. 2006 Early Season Bloom Award. Tetraploid. ('Moonlit Masquerade' × 'Magnificent Rainbow') × ('Etched Eyes' × 'Rainbow Eyes'). Honorable Mention 2003. *Photograph by Patrick Stamile.*

'Capture the Vision' (Larry Grace, 2000). Evergreen. Scape 22 in. (56 cm); flower 6 in. (15 cm). Early midseason. A cream with a multibanded lavender eye and picotee above a lime-green throat. Tetraploid. Seedling × 'Create Your Dream'.

'Visual Intrigue' (Jeff Salter, 2000). Semi-evergreen. Scape 29 in. (74 cm); flower 6 in. (15 cm). Early midseason. A pale ivory-cream with a complex blue-violet eyezone that appears on both the petals and the sepals. Tetraploid. Honorable Mention 2007. *Photograph by Francois Verhaert.*

'Blueberry Lemonade' (Ted L. Petit, 2002). Semi-evergreen. Scape 24 in. (61 cm); flower 5.5 in. (14 cm). Early midseason. A yellow with a charcoal-violet eyezone above a green throat. Tetraploid. ('Creative Edge' × 'Opal Ring') × 'Rhapsody in Time'. *Photograph by Ted L. Petit.*

'Texas Kaleidoscope' (Jack B. Carpenter, 2001). Evergreen. Scape 34 in. (86 cm); flower 6 in. (15 cm). Midseason. A mauve-pink with a striking patterned eyezone and a raspberry etching above a green throat. Diploid. Unknown parent × seedling. *Photograph by Jack B. Carpenter.*

'Blue Oasis' (Elizabeth H. Salter, 2002). Evergreen. Scape 20 in. (51 cm); flower 3.5 in. (9 cm). Early midseason. A pale cream-white flower with a large bold round washed eye of very intense blue-violet and surrounded by a darker purple band above a striking green throat. Diploid. 'Mystic Mariner' × 'In The Navy'. Honorable Mention 2005. *Photograph by Elizabeth H. Salter.*

'Reflections in Time' (Jeff Salter, 2002). Evergreen. Scape 30 in. (76 cm); flower 6 in. (15 cm). Midseason. A cream with washed-violet patterned eyezone and darker violet etching above a green throat. Tetraploid. 'Ancient Reflections' × 'Forever in Time'. *Photograph by Francois Verhaert.*

'In His Image' (Ted L. Petit, 2003). Semi-evergreen. Scape 25 in. (63 cm); flower 5.5 in. (14 cm). Midseason. A golden yellow with charcoal-patterned eye above a green throat. Tetraploid. 'Magical Passes' × 'Blueberry Lemonade'. *Photograph by Ted L. Petit.*

'Cedar Key' (Ted L. Petit, 2004). Semi-evergreen. Scape 29 in. (74 cm); flower 5.5 in. (14 cm). Midseason. A lavender with a violet-purple eyezone and picotee edge above a green throat. Tetraploid. 'Magical Passes' × ('Mardi Gras Ball' × 'Adventures With Ra'). *Photograph by Ted L. Petit.*

'Spacecoast Dragon Prince' (John Kinnebrew, 2002). Semi-evergreen. Scape 32 in. (81 cm); flower 5.5 in. (14 cm). Early midseason. A pink with a rose eyezone and matching rose picotee surrounded by a wire gold edge above a green throat. Tetraploid. 'Tetra Dragon's Eye' × 'Spacecoast Picotee Prince'. Honorable Mention 2005. *Photograph by John Benoot.*

'Basin Street Blues' (Ted L. Petit, 2004). Semi-evergreen. Scape 26 in. (66 cm); flower 6 in. (15 cm). Midseason. A plum with a blue-violet eye and picotee edge. Tetraploid. ('Violet Reflections' × 'Mrs. John Cooper') × ('Gilded Peacock' × 'Clothed in Glory'). *Photograph by Ted L. Petit.*

'Don Herrell' (John Rice, 2004). Semi-evergreen. Scape 21 in. (53 cm); flower 4.5 in. (11.5 cm). Midseason. A reddish mauve blend with violet-purple eye and violet and platinum edge above a green throat. Tetraploid. 'Angel's Braid' × 'Blueberry Sundae'. *Photograph by John Rice.*

'Lady Catherine Cuthill' (John P. Peat, 2004). Semi-evergreen. Scape 24 in. (61 cm); flower 5 in. (12.7 cm). Early midseason. A red with a darker eyezone and a lighter pink edge above a green throat. Tetraploid. ((('Avant Garde' × 'Altered State') × 'Strawberry Candy') × 'Lorikeet Springs'). *Photograph by John P. Peat.*

'Bird Talk' (Ludlow Lambertson, 2005). Semi-evergreen. Scape 24 in. (61 cm); flower 6.5 in. (16.5 cm). Early midseason. A creamy pastel with smoky slate blue eye and edge with gold border above a green throat. Tetraploid. (Seedling × 'Cretaceous Crunch') × 'Mildred Mitchell'. *Photograph by Ludlow Lambertson.*

'Blue Winged Warbler' (Ludlow Lambertson, 2005). Semi-evergreen. Scape 26 in. (66 cm); flower 5.5 in. (14 cm). Midseason. A creamy pastel with a dark blue eyezone and slight picotee edge above a green throat. Tetraploid. Seedling × seedling. *Photograph by Ludlow Lambertson.*

'Oceans Eleven' (Ted L. Petit, 2004). Semi-evergreen. Scape 20 in. (51 cm); flower 5 in. (12.7 cm). Midseason. A cream with a blue-violet eyezone above a green throat. Tetraploid. 'Magical Passes' × 'Tetra Dragon Dreams'. *Photograph by Ted L. Petit.*

'Blue Hippo' (Ludlow Lambertson, 2005). Semi-evergreen. Scape 26 in. (66 cm); flower 6 in. (15 cm). Early midseason. A cream with a large bluish eyezone and bluish picotee edge surrounded in gold above a green throat. Tetraploid. *Photograph by Ludlow Lambertson.*

'Little Peter Piper' (Grace Stamile, 2005). Semi-evergreen. Scape 20 in. (51 cm); flower 3 in. (7.6 cm). Midseason. A rose-purple with a darker eyezone and a lavender bordered edge above a green throat. Diploid. ('Little Sensation' × ('Little Pleasure' × 'Little Fat Cat')) × ((seedling × 'Little Angel Eyes') × ('Little Sensation' × seedling)). *Photograph by Patrick Stamile.*

'Monday Morning Blues' (Ted L. Petit, 2005). Semi-evergreen. Scape 26 in. (66 cm); flower 4.5 in. (11.5 cm). Midseason. A peach with a violet eyezone and a wire gold edge above a green throat. Tetraploid. 'Magical Passes' × 'Tetra Blue Moon Rising'. *Photograph by Ted L. Petit.*

'Violet Tranquility' (Ted L. Petit, 2005). Semi-evergreen. Scape 28 in. (71 cm); flower 5.5 in. (14 cm). Midseason. A lavender with blue-violet eyezone and a bluish picotee below a wire gold edge above a green throat. Tetraploid. 'Mrs. John Cooper' × 'Tetra Lavender Blue Baby'. *Photograph by Ted L. Petit.*

'Ancient Impact' (James Gossard, 2006). Semi-evergreen. Scape 30 in. (76 cm); flower 5 in. (12.7 cm). Midseason. A near-white self with a patterned blue, purple and maroon eyezone that also spills out on the sepals. Tetraploid. ('Forever in Time' × 'Isle of Dreams') × 'Creative Edge'.

'Beyond the Sea' (Ted L. Petit, 2006). Semi-evergreen. Scape 24 in. (61 cm); flower 5.5 in. (14 cm). Midseason. A soft lavender-violet, with a blue-violet eyezone surrounded by a darker purple mascara band above an applique to dark green throat. Tetraploid. ('Reyna' × 'Wheel of Time') × ('Cedar Key' × 'Sailing at Dawn'). *Photograph by Ted L. Petit.*

'Susie Tee' (Ted L. Petit, 2005). Semi-evergreen. Scape 24 in. (61 cm); flower 5 in. (12.7 cm). Midseason. A pink with a violet-blue eyezone and picotee edge above a green throat. Tetraploid. 'Violet Reflections' × 'Tetra Blue Moon Rising'. *Photograph by Ted L. Petit.*

'Bluegrass Music' (Larry Grace and Frank Smith, 2006). Semi-evergreen. Scape 28 in. (71 cm); flower 4.5 in. (11.5 cm). A cream flower with a large slate gray-blue and purple eyezone with a triple edge of purple, gray-blue and gold above a green throat. Tetraploid. 'Tetra Lavender Blue Baby' × ('Hank Williams' × 'Sunday Sandals'). *Photograph by Frank Smith.*

'Florida Scrub-Jay' (Ludlow Lambertson, 2006). Semi-evergreen. Scape 28 in. (71 cm); flower 6 in. (15 cm). Early midseason. An amber-pink with a blue- and gray-patterned eyezone and picotee edge above a green throat. Tetraploid. 'Bird Talk' × seedling. *Photograph by Ludlow Lambertson.*

'Ocean View' (Ted L. Petit, 2006). Semi-evergreen. Scape 30 in. (76 cm); flower 4.5 in. (11.5 cm). Midseason. A lavender self with a medium dark ocean blue eyezone and charcoal mascara picotee surrounded by a wire gold edge above a deep green throat. Tetraploid. 'Tetra Blue Moon Rising' × 'Rhapsody in Time'. *Photograph by Ted L. Petit.*

'Puddle Jumper' (John P. Peat, 2006). Semi-evergreen. Scape 23 in. (58 cm); flower 6.5 in. (16.5 cm). Early midseason. A peach flower with a very large multi-shaded red eyezone and a red picotee edge above a green throat. Tetraploid. 'Vivacious Pam' × ('Casa de Juan' × 'Sophia Armenis'). *Photograph by John P. Peat.*

'Ocean Blues' (John P. Peat, 2006). Semi-evergreen. Scape 32 in. (81 cm); flower 5.5 in. (14 cm). Midseason. A lavender flower with a triple-banded eyezone above a green throat. The eyezone is made up a darker slate gray-purple band surrounded by a larger grayish blue eyezone which is surrounded by a burgundy-purple band. Tetraploid. 'Mrs. John Cooper' × 'Oceans Eleven'. *Photograph by John P. Peat.*

'Patch of Blue' (Grace Stamile, 2006). Semi-evergeen. Scape 21 in. (53 cm); flower 3.5 in. (9 cm). Early midseason. An orchid magenta with blue-violet patterned eyezone edged in magenta above a green throat. Diploid. (('Little Sensation' × seedling) × (seedling × 'Little Angel Eyes')) × seedling. *Photograph by Patrick Stamile.*

'Smoky Eyes' (Patrick Stamile, 2006). Evergreen. Scape 25 in. (63 cm); flower 4.25 in. (11 cm). Early. A lavender with a multicolored complex eyezone and a dark purple wire picotee edge above a green throat. Tetraploid. 'Huckleberry Candy' × 'Tetra Ben Lee'. *Photograph by Patrick Stamile.*

'Exotic Pattern' (Jack B. Carpenter, 2007). Evergreen. Scape 30 in. (76 cm); flower 5.5 in. (14 cm). Midseason. A cream with a complex-banded purple eyezone on the petals and sepals above a lime-green to yellow throat. Diploid. 'Whole New Ball Game' × 'Texas Kaleidoscope'. *Photograph by Jack B. Carpenter.*

Chapter Seven

DOUBLES

Double daylilies are a passion for many gardeners and hybridizers. The extra petals and petaloids add a greater sense of fullness and depth to the flower, creating a beauty that has captured the imagination and hearts of flower lovers and breeders. Like double flowers of other genera, the large, double daylily flowers add a new dimension and gives a completely new look to the flower. As double daylilies have become more formal, they have increased in popularity, like double roses and camellias.

HISTORY OF DOUBLES

Double daylilies are by no means a new flower form. Plants of the *Hemerocallis* species found growing wild in China included *H. fulva* 'Kwanso' and *H. fulva* 'Flore Pleno', both doubles. Unfortunately, these flowers are triploids, which are sterile, and could not be used in creating modern hybrids.

The hybrid double daylily was created from single daylilies that sometimes had double tissue. These doubles, often only semi-double, began as narrow-petaled flowers without ruffling. As hybridizers worked on improving the doubles, the new flowers emerged with wider petals and ruffles, giving them a more finished look. Through generation after generation of double breeding, the blooms became more consistently and fully double. During the 1980s and 90s double tetraploid daylilies emerged, with heavier substance and clearer, brighter colors. Like tetraploid singles, initially there were no tetraploid doubles with which to work, which meant that the initial efforts to produce tetraploid doubles were arduous and slow. The pioneering efforts of hybridizers such as Betty Hudson, Patrick Stamile, David Kirchhoff, and Ted Petit slowly created breeding lines. More recently, hybridizers have brought the features of the modern single flower into the double lines, such as gold edging and heavily crimped ruffling. Hybridizers have also produced double daylilies in every color, as well as flowers with eyes, watermarks, and dramatically contrasting dark picotee edges.

FORM OF DOUBLES

To simply appreciate the exquisite beauty of double flowers it is not necessary to know the intricacies of their form. However, an even greater appreciation of double daylilies will result from understanding the way they are made. The double daylily is somewhat complex and ever changing, and it is worth a few extra minutes to study its nature.

An attempt at understanding and classifying double daylily forms is not new, and different individuals use different terms to describe daylily types. In 1945, in *Herbertia*, Arlow B. Stout published a description of the forms of doubling he observed along with suggested names for those forms. Some of his terms are still used more than 50 years later; however, no standard method of classifying doubles has yet been agreed upon. The following descriptions employ the most common terms in use among daylily hybridizers and enthusiasts.

Double daylilies are derived from single daylilies. The normal single daylily has three sepals, three petals, and six stamens (see the color illustration provided). The daylily is made of four whorls or layers: (1) sepals, (2) petals, (3) stamens, and (4) pistil, or carpel. The ideal way to form a double flower would be to add extra layers to the whorl of petals, creating multiple layers of petals. However, most double daylilies are formed by modifying the stamens.

Most double daylilies are created through the formation of petaloids. Though they look like extra petals, petaloids are stamens with extra tissue along their sides. Some flowers add tissue to only one side of the stamen–these petaloids are easy to recognize as modified stamens. Other flowers add tissue to both sides of the stamen–these resemble true petals, although the anther, or pollen sac, can generally be found on the petaloid. Sometimes, the anther becomes rudimentary or even non-existent, so that the petaloid looks like a perfectly normal petal. Because petaloids are formed from the stamen tissue and daylilies have only six stamens, six is the maximum number of petaloids that a daylily can have. If it has less than six petaloids, the remaining stamens will be normal,

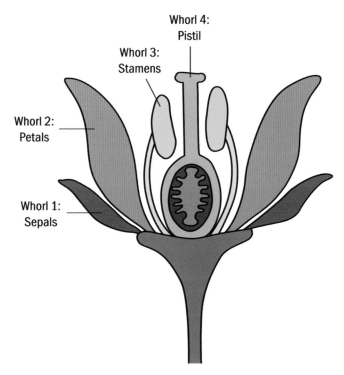

Whorl 4:
Pistil

Whorl 3:
Stamens

Whorl 2:
Petals

Whorl 1:
Sepals

Whorls of the daylily flower. *Watercolor by Richard Haynes*

and the flower will appear semi-double. Double flowers of most other genera contain extra layers of true petals, not simply modified stamens, and typically have many more than six extra petals. Therefore, most of the double daylilies currently sold are quite different from other double flowers.

Some double daylily flowers add tissue at the midrib of the petaloid. This midrib tissue usually projects upward and outward from the center of the petaloid, resembling the wings of a butterfly. The form of midrib tissue can vary. While some petaloids contain only a single wing, many petaloids have two wings of midrib tissue, and occasionally each individual wing can appear as two parallel layers of tissue. Midrib tissue gives the appearance of even more petals, giving the flower added fullness, particularly as this midrib tissue becomes large and ruffled.

Some "apparently single" daylilies, which contain only three true petals, also have extra tissue rising up from the midrib of the petals, similar to the extra tissue on petaloids. This formation has caused some disagreement as to whether these flowers should be classified as singles or doubles–currently they are referred to as "midrib doubles." Some people insist that these flowers are single because they have only three true petals. Others argue that if doubles can be produced by forming petaloid tissue from stamens, they can also be produced by forming petaloid tissue from petals. Midrib doubles, then, are flowers with only three true petals, with extra tissue generated from, or fused to, the midrib of those three true petals. This tissue is typically formed from the middle of the

Different forms of flower petaloids.
Photograph by Ted L. Petit and John P. Peat.

'Company of Swans' (Ted L. Petit, 1994). Evergreen. Scape 19 in. (48 cm); flower 5.5 in. (14 cm). Midseason. A light cream to ivory-white, with a green throat. The consistently double flowers are typically the formal hose-in-hose form as pictured, with the stamens intact. Tetraploid. 'Mykonos' × 'Champagne Chilling'. *Photograph by Ted L. Petit.*

'Unlock the Stars' (Ted L. Petit, 2006). Semi-evergreen. Scape 25 in. (63 cm); flower 6 in. (15 cm). Midseason. A soft lavender-pink with a gold edge above a green throat. Tetraploid. ('Susan Pritchard Petit' × 'John Peat') × 'Nature's Crown'. *Photograph by Ted L. Petit.*

petal at 45 to 90 degree angles, resembling two butterfly wings. The fact that midrib tissue can form on either the three regular petals of an otherwise single flower or on the midrib of petaloids indicates that this is an inherited characteristic in daylilies potentially separate and distinct from the production of extra petals or stamen-derived petaloids.

All of this is very different, however, from adding extra true petals. Flowers with extra true petals, called "supernumerary doubles," or sometimes "superdoubles," are rare in daylilies. Supernumerary doubles stack on additional layers of petals and retain their normal stamens. They typically have nine petals, six extra, along with all six stamens, as is shown in the image of Ted Petit's 'Richard Taylor Yates' (2006). We are not aware of any true extra-petaled supernumary doubles that have petaloids, although it is theoretically possible for a supernumerary double to have petaloids. Since these doubles have their stamens intact, they have the potential to turn their stamens into petaloids. Such flowers would then have nine petals plus six petaloids, for a magnificent total of 15 colored segments.

Unlike petaloids, which are limited to six, the possible number of extra true petals seems to be unlimited. Theoretically, many layers of petals could be stacked, one on top of the other, to produce a double daylily with the number of petals of a rose or camellia. The sterile *Hemerocallis fulva* var. *kwanso* and *H. fulva* 'Flore Pleno' are supernumerary daylilies with many columns of true petals. Although most daylily enthusiasts feel that these species plants lack much of the beauty of modern hybrids, they do have a form as yet not achieved among modern daylilies. However, after many decades of work, hybridizers are beginning to produce supernumerary double daylilies, leading the way in an area for further daylily breeding.

Double daylilies can also be categorized according to the form of the extra petals or petaloids. The two primary groups are the hose-in-hose types and the peony types. Hose-in-hose are flowers in which the petals or petaloids lie flat in layers, resembling the look of extra true petals, as may be seen in the photograph of 'Company of Swans'. This gives the flower an appearance similar to a camellia or fully opened rose. Any petaloids are usually full, not half petaloids, and there is usually no midrib tissue.

In other doubles, the petaloids stick up in the center of the flower, pointing outward like stamens. This form is referred to as peony, cockatoo, or petaloid doubling, as illustrated by Ted Petit's 'Unlock the Stars' (2006). The petaloids can be either half or full and may or may not have midrib tissue.

It is important not to think too rigidly about double daylily forms. The double form of a daylily can vary from day to day within an individual cultivar or even on a single plant, and new double forms are continuously emerging. Further, many cultivars that produce double flowers also produce single flowers, particularly early during the season. The degree of doubling appears to be temperature-dependent such that many of these cultivars produce single flowers in cool weather, but bear flowers that are more frequently double as the weather warms. With increased breeding, however, the modern double daylilies have become progressively more consistent in their doubling, and more shockingly beautiful.

'Richard Taylor Yates' (Ted L. Petit, 2006). Semi-evergreen. Scape 28 in. (71 cm); flower 6.5 in. (16.5 cm). Midseason. A hose-in-hose rose-pink with a lighter pink watermark, carrying a heavy popcorn-gold edge above a green throat. Tetraploid. (('Susan Pritchard Petit' × 'Formal Appearance') × 'Nature's Crown') × ('Unlock the Stars' × 'Inner Space'). *Photograph by Ted L. Petit.*

'Almost Indecent' (Lee E. Gates, 1986). Semi-evergreen. Scape 20 in. (51 cm); flower 6.5 in. (16.5 cm). Early. A lavender and cream blend double flower with a chalky chartreuse throat. Tetraploid. Ida Munson Award 1995. Award of Merit 1995. Honorable Mention 1991. *Photograph by Sue Brown.*

'Frances Joiner' (Enman R. Joiner, 1988). Dormant. Scape 24 in. (61 cm); flower 5.5 in. (14 cm). Midseason. One of the most popular doubles. A soft pink to rose blend. Diploid. Ida Munson Award 1993. Award of Merit 1995. *Photograph by Lynn Lewis.*

'Vanilla Fluff' (Enman R. Joiner, 1988). Dormant. Scape 34 in. (86 cm); flower 6 in. (15 cm). Midseason. A large ivory to cream self. Diploid. 'Ivory Cloud' × seedling. Ida Munson Award 1996. L. Ernest Plouf Award 1993. Award of Merit 1995. *Photograph by Ted L. Petit and John P. Peat.*

'Peach Magnolia' (Enman R. Joiner, 1986). Dormant. Scape 32 in. (81 cm); flower 5.5 in. (14 cm). Midseason late. A peach self with a green throat. Diploid. Ida Munson Award 2002. Award of Merit 1999. Honorable Mention 1995. *Photograph by Ted L. Petit and John P. Peat.*

'Scatterbrain' (Enman R. Joiner, 1988). Semi-evergreen. Scape 32 in. (81 cm); flower 6 in. (15 cm). Midseason. An extremely popular light peach-pink self with a light green throat. Diploid. 'Ivory Cloud' × seedling. Award of Merit 1996. *Photograph by Ted L. Petit and John P. Peat.*

'Bubbly' (Jan Joiner, 1989). Semi-evergreen. Scape 20 in. (51 cm); flower 3 in. (7.6 cm). Midseason. An apricot self with a green throat. Diploid. 'Champagne Bubbles' × 'Fairies Pinafore'. Donn Fischer Memorial Cup 2001. Honorable Mention 1993. *Photograph by Ted L. Petit and John P. Peat.*

'Almond Puff' (Patrick Stamile, 1990). Dormant. Scape 23 in. (58 cm); flower 6.5 in. (16.5 cm). Midseason. A beige-pink with ruffled petals above a green throat. Diploid. 'Salt Lake City' × 'Barbara Mitchell'. Ida Munson Award 1997. Award of Merit 1998. Honorable Mention 1995. *Photograph by Patrick Stamile.*

'Layers of Gold' (David Kirchhoff, 1990). Evergreen. Scape 24 in. (61 cm); flower 5 in. (12.7 cm). Early midseason. A medium gold self with a green throat. Tetraploid. Seedling × ((('Czarina' × 'Ed Kirchhoff') × 'Inez Ways') × ('Double Jackpot' × ('King Alfred' × seedling))). Ida Munson Award 1999. Award of Merit 1999. Honorable Mention 1994. *Photograph by Patrick Stamile.*

'Big Kiss' (Enman R. Joiner, 1991). Dormant. Scape 28 in. (71 cm); flower 5.5 in. (14 cm). Midseason. A light peach with a light rose eyezone above a light green throat. Diploid. 'Dublin Elaine' × 'Frances Joiner'. Award of Merit 2005. Honorable Mention 2002. *Photograph by Ted L. Petit and John P. Peat.*

'Siloam Olin Frazier' (Pauline Henry, 1990). Dormant. Scape 22 in. (56 cm); flower 5 in. (12.7 cm). Early. A ruffled hot rose-pink double with a lime-green throat. Diploid. Ida Munson Award 1997. Award of Merit 1997. *Photograph by Andrea Weaver.*

'Forty Second Street' (David Kirchhoff, 1991). Evergreen. Scape 24 in. (61 cm); flower 5 in. (12.7 cm). Midseason. A pastel pink with a bright rose eyezone above a yellow to green throat. Diploid. Ida Munson Award 1998. Award of Merit 1999. Honorable Mention 1996. *Photograph by David Kirchhoff.*

'Madge Cayse' (Enman R. Joiner, 1991). Dormant. Scape 24 in. (61 cm); flower 6 in. (15 cm). Midseason. A dark apricot self with a green throat. Diploid. 'Tangerine Twist' × 'Frances Joiner'. Award of Merit 1999. Honorable Mention 1994. *Photograph by Ted L. Petit and John P. Peat.*

'Roswitha' (Dan Trimmer, 1992). Dormant. Scape 14 in. (35.5 cm); flower 3.75 in. (9.5 cm). Early midseason. A peach with a purple eyezone above a green throat. Diploid. 'Exotic Echo' × 'Janice Brown'. Annie T. Giles Award 2005. Award of Merit 2003. Honorable Mention 1999. *Photograph by Ted L. Petit and John P. Peat.*

'Ruby Knight' (Jeff Salter, 1993). Semi-evergreen. Scape 25 in. (63 cm); flower 5.5 in. (14 cm). Early midseason. A velvety dark blood-red self. Tetraploid. *Photograph by John Eiseman.*

'Victoria's Secret' (Jeff Salter, 1991). Semi-evergreen. Scape 28 in. (71 cm); flower 5.5 in. (14 cm). Midseason late. A cream with a pink overlay, distinct gold edging, and a lime-green throat. Tetraploid. *Photograph by Ted L. Petit and John P. Peat.*

'Totally Awesome' (S. Glen Ward, 1993). Evergreen. Scape 28 in. (71 cm); flower 7 in. (18 cm). Early midseason. A rose-pink blend with a yellow-green throat. Diploid. 'Double Pink Treasure' × 'Brent Gabriel'. Ida Munson Award 2003. Honorable Mention 1997. *Photograph by John Eiseman.*

'Peggy Jeffcoat' (Jan Joiner, 1995). Dormant. Scape 18 in. (46 cm); flower 6.5 in. (16.5 cm). Midseason late. A cream-white hose-and-hose lightly ruffled double with a light green throat. Diploid. 'Jean Swann' × 'Rebecca Marie'. Ida Munson Award 2001. Award of Merit 2001. Honorable Mention 1998. *Photograph by Francis Joiner.*

'Angel Cups' (Jan Joiner, 1996). Dormant. Scape 30 in. (76 cm); flower 6 in. (15 cm). Midseason late. An ivory self with a yellow-green throat. Diploid. Honorable Mention 2000. *Photograph by Francis Joiner.*

'King Kahuna' (Clarence J. Crochet, 1994). Semi-evergreen. Scape 22 in. (56 cm); flower 6.5 in. (16.5 cm). Early midseason. A medium yellow self. Diploid. 'Olin Frazier' × 'Ellen Christine'. Ida Munson Award 2000. Award of Merit 2001. Honorable Mention 1998. *Photograph by Ted L. Petit and John P. Peat.*

'Amber Storm' (Ted L. Petit, 1996). Semi-evergreen. Scape 22 in. (56 cm); flower 5.5 in. (14 cm). Midseason. A red blend with a lighter edge above a green throat. Tetraploid. ('Highland Lord' × 'Ida's Magic') × 'Fires of Fuji'. *Photograph by Ted L. Petit.*

'Cardigan Bay' (Dan Trimmer, 1996). Evergreen. Scape 26 in. (66 cm); flower 5 in. (12.7 cm). Early midseason. A peach blend with a wine eyezone above a green throat. Tetraploid. 'Tetra Exotic Echo' × 'Tetra Yazoo Souffle'. *Photograph by Lynn Thor.*

'Frills and Fancies' (Jan Joiner, 1996). Evergreen. Scape 28 in. (71 cm); flower 5 in. (12.7 cm). Midseason late. A full double of a tigerlily-orange blend with a green throat. Diploid. *Photograph by Frances Joiner.*

'Two Part Harmony' (Matthew Kaskel, 1996). Evergreen. Scape 34 in. (86 cm); flower 4 in. (10 cm). Early. Straw-yellow with a wine-red eye-zone above a green throat. Tetraploid. ('One Fine Day' × (seedling × 'Ruby Sentinel')) × ('Fooled Me' × 'Tetra Janice Brown'). Award of Merit 2006. Honorable Mention 2003. *Photograph by Matthew Kaskel.*

'Anasazi' (Patrick Stamile, 1997). Evergreen. Scape 25 in. (63 cm); flower 6 in. (15 cm). Early midseason. A very deep clear pink self with a green throat. Full modern formed double. Tetraploid. (Seedling × 'Poetic Voice') × 'Shimmering Elegance'. *Photograph by Patrick Stamile.*

'Schnickel Fritz' (David Kirchhoff, 1996). Dormant. Scape 16 in. (41 cm); flower 5 in. (12.7 cm). Early midseason. A near-white self with a green throat. Diploid. 'Chardonnay' × ('Nagasaki' × 'Siloam Double Classic'). Ida Munson Award 2004. Award of Merit 2005. Honorable Mention 2000. *Photograph by David Kirchhoff.*

'Vision of Love' (Matthew Kaskel and Dan Trimmer, 1996). Evergreen. Scape 26 in. (66 cm); flower 6 in. (15 cm). Early. A rose self with a yellow-gold throat. Tetraploid. *Photograph by Debbie and Duane Hurlbert.*

'Denali' (Patrick Stamile, 1997). Evergreen. Scape 23 in. (58 cm); flower 8 in. (20 cm). Midseason late. A huge pink ruffled double with a green throat. Tetraploid. 'Victoria's Secret' × 'Big Blue'. Honorable Mention 2000. *Photograph by Patrick Stamile.*

'Night Embers' (Patrick Stamile, 1997). Semi-evergreen. Scape 30 in. (76 cm); flower 5 in. (12.7 cm). Midseason. A bing-cherry red with white edges and a green throat. Tetraploid. 'Double Phelan' × seedling. Ida Munson Award 2007. *Photograph by Patrick Stamile.*

'Piglet and Roo' (John P. Peat, 1998). Semi-evergreen. Scape 18 in. (46 cm); flower 3.5 in. (9 cm). Midseason. A small-flowered double peach-pink self. Tetraploid. 'Memories of Paris' × (('Wayne Johnson' × 'Renaissance Queen') × 'Merlot Rouge'). *Photograph by John P. Peat.*

'Ice Cream Dream' (Jan Joiner, 1999). Semi-evergreen. Scape 22 in. (56 cm); flower 7 in. (18 cm). Midseason. A pearl-blush self with a light green throat. Diploid. Seedling × seedling. Honorable Mention 2004. *Photograph by Francis Joiner.*

'Moses' Fire' (Enman R. Joiner, 1998). Dormant. Scape 22 in. (56 cm); flower 6 in. (15 cm). Midseason. A red self with a gold edge above a green throat. Tetraploid. Seedling × seedling. Award of Merit 2005. Honorable Mention 2001. *Photograph by Francis Joiner.*

'Gemini Jack' (Dan Trimmer, 1999). Semi-evergreen. Scape 25 in. (63 cm); flower 5 in. (12.7 cm). Early midseason. A lavender blend with a purple eyezone above a yellow to green throat, 95 percent double. Tetraploid. 'Cardigan Bay' × 'Tetra Janice Brown'. *Photograph by Francois Verhaert.*

'Jerry Pate Williams' (David Kirchhoff, 1999). Semi-evergreen. Scape 27 in. (69 cm); flower 5 in. (12.7 cm). Early. An intense peach with a pink-melon overlay and a faint rose-rouge watermark halo above an apricot throat, 100 percent double. Tetraploid. 'Most Happy Fellow' × (('Layers of Gold' × 'Cool Jazz') × ('Cool Jazz' × seedling)). Ida Munson Award 2005. Award of Merit 2006. Honorable Mention 2003. Early Season Bloom Award 2007. *Photograph by Francois Verhaert.*

'John Kirkland' (David Kirchhoff, 1999). Evergreen. Scape 28 in. (71 cm); flower 5.5 in. (14 cm). Early midseason. A salmon-pink with a peach-rose halo above a yellow to green throat , 98 percent double. Tetraploid. ('Pappy's Girl' × seedling) × (seedling × 'Tetra'. 'Siloam Double Classic'). Honorable Mention 2005. *Photograph by Lynn Thor.*

'Puccini' (Patrick Stamile, 1999). Evergreen. Scape 30 in. (76 cm); flower 7 in. (18 cm). Midseason. A cream-yellow blend with fluted ruffling above a green throat. Tetraploid. 'Clovette Adams' × 'John Kinnebrew'. *Photograph by Patrick Stamile.*

'Rose Corsage' (Patrick Stamile, 1999). Dormant. Scape 21 in. (53 cm); flower 5 in. (12.7 cm). Early midseason. A clear rose-pink double flower with ruffled edges and a green throat. Tetraploid. ((('Killer' × 'Forever Red') × 'Ricochet') × 'Tetra Siloam Double Classic'). *Photograph by Patrick Stamile.*

'Leader of the Pack' (John P. Peat, 1999). Semi-evergreen. Scape 23 in. (58 cm); flower 5 in. (12.7 cm). Midseason. A nine-petaled rose-red with a dark rose-red eyezone above a green throat, 100 percent double hose-and-hose. Tetraploid. 'Merlot Rouge' × ('Wayne Johnson' × 'Renaissance Queen'). *Photograph by John P. Peat.*

'Regal Puzzle' (Ted L. Petit, 1999). Dormant. Scape 24 in. (61 cm); flower 5 in. (12.7 cm). Midseason. A purple with a chalky purple watermark above a green throat. Tetraploid. ('Royal Saracen' × 'Highland Lord') × 'Impetuous Fire'. *Photograph by Ted L. Petit.*

'Second Millennium' (Ted L. Petit, 1999). Semi-evergreen. Scape 23 in. (58 cm); flower 6.5 in. (16.5 cm). Midseason. A large, striking, lipstick-red double flower with a very large lighter watermark and a green throat. Tetraploid. ('Grecian Sands' × (('Royal Saracen' × 'Highland Lord') × 'Impetuous Fire')). Honorable Mention 2007. *Photograph by Ted L. Petit.*

'Shadows Within' (Ted L. Petit, 1999). Semi-evergreen. Scape 25 in. (63 cm); flower 6 in. (15 cm). Midseason. A peach with a purple eyezone above a green throat. Tetraploid. (('Wayne Johnson' × 'Rosetta Stone') × ('Wayne Johnson' × 'Rosetta Stone')) × ('Tetra Exotic Echo' × 'Tetra Elsie Spalding'). *Photograph by Ted L. Petit.*

'All About Eve' (David Kirchhoff, 2000). Evergreen. Scape 26 in. (66 cm); flower 5 in. (12.7 cm). Early midseason. A peach-pink double with a rose halo watermark and tightly crimped ruffles. Tetraploid. Seedling. × 'Tetra Siloam Double Classic'. Honorable Mention 2003. *Photograph by David Kirchhoff.*

'Byron' (Patrick Stamile, 2000). Evergreen. Scape 26 in. (66 cm); flower 5 in. (12.7 cm). Midseason. An orange-mango blend with an olive-green throat. Blooms vary from hose-and-hose doubling to peony style but are never single. Tetraploid. 'Clovette Adams' × 'Denali'. *Photograph by Patrick Stamile.*

'Topguns Lola Scott' (Bob Scott, 1999). Dormant. Scape 25 in. (63 cm); flower 6 in. (15 cm). Midseason late. A yellow double with a red eyezone above a green throat. Diploid. Seedling × seedling. Ida Munson Award 2006. Award of Merit 2007. Honorable Mention 2004. *Photograph by Debbie and Duane Hurlbert.*

'Cardassian Border' (Ted L. Petit, 2000). Semi-evergreen. Scape 24 in. (61 cm); flower 5.5 in. (14 cm). Midseason. A cream with a purple eyezone above a green throat. Tetraploid. 'Champagne Supernova' × 'Cotillion Maiden'. *Photograph by Ted L. Petit.*

'Dark Wonder' (Patrick Stamile, 2000). Evergreen. Scape 27 in. (69 cm); flower 6 in. (15 cm). Midseason. A dark rich royal-purple double with a large silver watermark often showing off large white shark's teeth on the edges. Tetraploid. 'Plum Plume' × 'Denali'. *Photograph by Patrick Stamile.*

'Over the Top' (Patrick Stamile, 2000). Evergreen. Scape 28 in. (71 cm); flower 8 in. (20 cm). Midseason. A pink with a red eyezone. Tetraploid. ((('With This Ring' × 'Big Blue') × 'Lightning Strike') × 'Denali'). *Photograph by Patrick Stamile.*

'Cluster Muster' (Enman R. Joiner, 2001). Evergreen. Scape 24 in. (61 cm); flower 5 in. (12.7 cm). Midseason. A tiger-lily orange self above a green throat. Tetraploid. Seedling × 'Moses Fire'. Honorable Mention 2004. *Photograph by Francis Joiner.*

'Formal Appearance' (Ted L. Petit, 2000). Semi-evergreen. Scape 25 in. (63 cm); flower 5.5 in. (14 cm). Midseason. A pink self above a green throat. Tetraploid. 'Memories of Paris' × ('Wayne Johnson' × 'Betty Warren Woods'). *Photograph by Ted L. Petit.*

'Shirley Valentine' (Ted L. Petit, 2000). Semi-evergreen. Scape 24 in. (61 cm); flower 5.5 in. (14 cm). Midseason. A dark, rich, blood-red double with white edging on all segments. Tetraploid. 'Merlot Rouge' × ('Richard Taylor' × Munson seedling). *Photograph by Ted L. Petit.*

'Cosmic Dancer' (Ted L. Petit, 2001). Evergreen. Scape 23 in. (58 cm); flower 5.5 in. (14 cm). Midseason. A peach with a purple eyezone and picotee edge above a green throat. Tetraploid. ('Champagne Chilling' × 'Wedding Band') × 'Cardassian Border'. *Photograph by Ted L. Petit.*

'Kay Day' (David Kirchhoff, 2001). Evergreen. Scape 29 in. (74 cm); flower 6 in. (15 cm). Early. A medium coral-rose with a gold edge above a yellow to green throat. Tetraploid. 'Jerry Pate Williams' × 'Virginia Franklin Miller'. *Photograph by Francois Verhaert.*

'Susan Pritchard Petit' (Ted L. Petit, 2001). Semi-evergreen. Scape 20 in. (51 cm); flower 6 in. (15 cm). Midseason. A rich burgundy to rose-purple that slowly softens to a rose-pink as the season progresses. The petals and petaloids carry a pronounced gold edge. Tetraploid. ('Ambrosian Rhapsody' × 'Victoria's Secret') × 'John Kinnebrew'. Honorable Mention 2004. *Photograph by Ted L. Petit.*

'Double Image' (Patrick Stamile, 2002). Evergreen. Scape 29 in. (74 cm); flower 6 in. (15 cm). Early. A deep rose-pink blend with a darker rose-pink picotee above a green throat. Tetraploid. ('Clovette Adams' × 'Night Embers') × 'Puccini'. *Photograph by Patrick Stamile.*

'Outrageous Fortune' (Patrick Stamile, 2001). Evergreen. Scape 32 in. (81 cm); flower 6 in. (15 cm). Midseason. A rose-red with a knobby toothy gold edge, 90 percent double. Tetraploid. ('Dark Wonder' × (('Clovette Adams' × 'Lightning Strike') × 'Puccini')). *Photograph by Patrick Stamile.*

'Candyman Can' (Ted L. Petit, 2002). Semi-evergreen. Scape 34 in. (86 cm); flower 6.5 in. (16.5 cm). Midseason. A rose with a red eye and gold edge above a green throat. Tetraploid. ('Victoria's Secret' × 'Betty Warren Woods') × 'John Kinnebrew'. *Photograph by Ted L. Petit.*

'Doubly Delicious Dandy' (Jeff Salter, 2002). Evergreen. Scape 28 in. (71 cm); flower 6.5 in. (16.5 cm). Early midseason. A very large coral-pink, blended double with a darker halo eyezone. Tetraploid. 'John Kinnebrew' × seedling. *Photograph by Ted L. Petit and John P. Peat.*

'Flamenco Christmas' (Patrick Stamile, 2002). Evergreen. Scape 28 in. (71 cm); flower 6 in. (15 cm). Midseason. A red with a double white picotee edge above a green throat. Tetraploid. 'Keats' × 'Hearts of Fire'. *Photograph by Patrick Stamile.*

'Vanilla Sky' (Ted L. Petit, 2002). Semi-evergreen. Scape 23 in. (58 cm); flower 6 in. (15 cm). Midseason. A soft pink with darker pink and gold highlights and tightly crimped gold edges on consistently double blossoms. Tetraploid. 'Golden Mansions' × 'Senegal'. *Photograph by Ted L. Petit.*

'Micro Dots' (Jane Trimmer, 2003). Evergreen. Scape 28 in. (71 cm); flower 3 in. (7.6 cm). Early. A cantaloupe self above a green throat. Diploid. 'Penny Pinsley' × 'Tropical Delight'. *Photograph by Susan Okrasinski.*

'Separate Reality' (Ted L. Petit, 2002). Semi-evergreen. Scape 25 in. (63 cm); flower 5.5 in. (14 cm). Midseason. A consistently double, typically formal hose-in-hose peach-pink with a golden orange lightly ruffled edge. Tetraploid. 'Outer Fringes' × 'John Kinnebrew'. *Photograph by Ted L. Petit.*

'Fire Kissed' (Jan Joiner, 2003). Evergreen. Scape 20 in. (51 cm); flower 5.5 in. (14 cm). Midseason. A barn-red self above a green throat. Diploid. Seedling × seedling. *Photograph by Francis Joiner.*

'Nature's Crown' (Ted L. Petit, 2003). Semi-evergreen. Scape 24 in. (61 cm); flower 5.5 in. (14 cm). Midseason. A pink with a lighter watermark eyezone and a gold edge above a green throat. Tetraploid. (('Impetuous Fire' × 'Dripping With Gold') × 'Vision of Love') × ('Susan Pritchard Petit' × 'Clothed in Glory'). *Photograph by Ted L. Petit.*

'Torch Song Trilogy' (Ted L. Petit, 2003). Semi-evergreen. Scape 27 in. (69 cm); flower 6 in. (15 cm). Mid-season. A rose double with a lighter watermark and a gold edge above a green throat. Tetraploid. 'Shirley Valentine' × 'Susan Pritchard Petit'. *Photograph by Ted L. Petit.*

'Norma Desmond' (David Kirchhoff, 2004). Evergreen. Scape 30 in. (76 cm); flower 3.5 in. (9 cm). Midseason. A creamy lavender-orchid bitone with a white to gold-toothed edge above a yellow to chartreuse-green throat. Tetraploid. (('Plum Plume' × 'Manhattan Serenade') × (Seedling × 'Fortune's Dearest')) × 'John Kirkland'. *Photograph by David Kirchhoff.*

'Clark Gable' (David Kirchhoff, 2004). Evergreen. Scape 28 in. (71 cm); flower 6.5 in. (16.5 cm). Early midseason. A double flower of intense persimmon-orange self. Tetraploid. (('Big Peach Mama' × 'Tetra Siloam Double Classic') × seedling) × ('Margaret Tucker' × seedling). *Photograph by David Kirchhoff.*

'Signature Truffle' (David Kirchhoff, 2004). Evergreen. Scape 28 in. (71 cm); flower 6 in. (15 cm). Early midseason. A rosy coral-peach with a gold edge above a huge cloverleaf yellow to lime-green throat. Tetraploid. *Photograph by David Kirchhoff.*

'Exotic Etching' (Patrick Stamile, 2005). Dormant. Scape 19 in. (48 cm); flower 4.5 in. (11.5 cm). Midseason. A cream with a fuchsia-patterned eye-zone above a green throat. Tetraploid. 'Tetra Exotic Echo' × 'Valley Stream'. *Photograph by Patrick Stamile.*

'Gerrie Frankenberger' (Ted L. Petit, 2005). Semi-evergreen. Scape 22 in. (56 cm); flower 5.5 in. (14 cm). Midseason. A coral-rose with a burgundy eyezone and picotee edge above a green throat. Tetraploid. ('Wisest of Wizards' × 'Jenny Kissed Me') × 'Separate Reality'. *Photograph by Ted L. Petit.*

'Skeezix' (Patrick Stamile, 2005). Evergreen. Scape 38 in. (96 cm); flower 8.5 in. (22 cm). Early midseason. A pink self above a green throat. Tetraploid. ('Lavender Arrowhead' × 'Tetra Cerulean Star') × 'Linguini'. *Photograph by Patrick Stamile.*

'Trufflicious' (David Kirchhoff, 2005). Evergreen. Scape 27 in. (69 cm); flower 5.5 in. (14 cm). Early. A bright pastel cream-pink with a gold edge above a green throat. Tetraploid. ('John Kirkland' × seedling) × ('Seven Sisters' × ('Champagne Chilling' × seedling)). *Photograph by David Kirchhoff.*

'Glorious Autumn' (David Kirchhoff, 2005). Dormant. Scape 27 in. (69 cm); flower 5 in. (12.7 cm). Midseason. An orange double flower with red edge above a gold to green throat. Tetraploid. Seedling × 'Carrot Rouge Truffle'. *Photograph by David Kirchhoff.*

'Spacecoast Twice is Nice' (John Kinnebrew, 2005). Semi-evergreen. Scape 22 in. (56 cm); flower 5.5 in. (14 cm). Early midseason. A peach-pink double with wide ruffled petals and petaloids above a yellow throat. Tetraploid. 'Senegal' × seedling. *Photograph by John Kinnebrew.*

'Blonde Ambition' (Ted L. Petit, 2006). Semi-evergreen. Scape 24 in. (61 cm); flower 5 in. (12.7 cm). Midseason. A cream-orange sherbet flower with a dark red eyezone and picotee. An ornate, ruffled and fringed edge surrounds this often double flower. Tetraploid. 'Darla Anita' × ('Beacon at Dusk' × 'John Peat'). *Photograph by Ted L. Petit.*

'Ellen Laprise' (George Doorakian, 2006). Dormant. Scape 27 in. (69 cm); flower 6 in. (15 cm). Midseason. A yellow-pink blend self with a heavily ruffled gold edge and midrib cresting above a green throat. Tetraploid. *Photograph by George Doorakian.*

'Heart of Savannah' (Enman R. Joiner, 2006). Evergreen. Scape 28 in. (71 cm); flower 4 in. (10 cm). Midseason. A garnet-red double with lighter near-white picotee surrounded by a wire gold edge. Tetraploid. 'Savannah Fiesta' × seedling. *Photograph by Leslie Innel.*

'Little Maiden' (Grace Stamile, 2006). Semi-evergreen. Scape 18 in. (46 cm); flower 2.5 in. (6 cm). Early midseason. A rose-purple with a lighter white-pink edge above a green throat. Tetraploid. 'Little Show Stopper' × 'Cute as a Button'. *Photograph by Patrick Stamile.*

'Emily Gibson' (Ted L. Petit, 2006). Semi-evergreen. Scape 24 in. (61 cm); flower 6.5 in. (16.5 cm). Midseason. Large, very full, frilly, coral-pink double flowers carrying a ruffled bubbly gold edge. Tetraploid. ('Susan Pritchard Petit' × 'John Peat') × ('Unlock the Stars' × 'Denali'). *Photograph by Ted L. Petit.*

'Inner Space' (Ted L. Petit, 2006). Semi-evergreen. Scape 28 in. (71 cm); flower 6.5 in. (16.5 cm). Semi-evergreen. A peach with a burgundy-red eye and a wire gold edge above a green throat. Tetraploid. ('Cardassian Border' × 'Separate Reality') × ('Susan Pritchard Petit' × 'Shadows Within'). *Photograph by Ted L. Petit.*

'Mount Aetna' (Joyce Reinke, 2006). Dormant. Scape 28 in. (71 cm); flower 6 in. (15 cm). Midseason. A golden yellow double with a dark brown eyezone above a deep green throat. Diploid. 'Double Conch Shell' × 'Phenie Stephens'. *Photograph by Joyce Reinke.*

'Powder Puff Blush' (Jackie Pryor, 2006). Semi-evergreen. Scape 38 in. (96 cm); flower 6 in. (15 cm). Midseason. A pink-lavender with a darker edge above a yellow to green throat. Diploid. *Photograph by Jackie Pryor.*

'Torino' (Patrick Stamile, 2006). Evergreen. Scape 24 in. (61 cm); flower 5.5 in. (14 cm). Early midseason. A near-white self above a green throat. Tetraploid. 'Dream Runner' × 'Tetra Peggy Jeffcoat'. *Photograph by Patrick Stamile.*

'Una Semana Con Juan' (John P. Peat, 2006). Dormant. Scape 18 in. (46 cm); flower 5 in. (12.7 cm). Early midseason. A near-black dark purple with a velvety texture above a striking, vibrant green throat, 35 percent double. Tetraploid. (('Midnight Magic' × 'Spring Rite') × ('Midnight Magic' × 'Spring Rite')) × ('Trials of Life' × 'Susan Pritchard Petit'). *Photograph by John P. Peat.*

'Ruby Corsage' (Patrick Stamile, 2006). Semi-evergreen. Scape 22 in. (56 cm); flower 4.25 in. (11 cm). Midseason. A velvety ruby-red double self above a green throat. Tetraploid. ('Hearts of Fire' × seedling) × ('Hearts of Fire' × seedling). *Photograph by Patrick Stamile.*

'Turning Up the Heat' (Ted L. Petit, 2006). Semi-evergreen. Scape 22 in. (56 cm); flower 5 in. (12.7 cm). Midseason. A wide, saturated, dark purple picotee and eyezone on a melon-peach to orange double flower. Tetraploid. ('J. T. Davis' × 'Meet Joe Black') × 'Blueberry Baroque'. *Photograph by Ted L. Petit.*

'Truffle Mystic' (David Kirchhoff, 2007). Evergreen. Scape 30 in. (76 cm); flower 6 in. (15 cm). Early. A peach-pink double flower with a darker halo eyezone and a large orange to green throat. Tetraploid. ('Don't Look Back' × 'Jagged Edge') × seedling. *Photograph by David Kirchhoff.*

Chapter Eight

SPIDERS, VARIANTS, AND UNUSUAL FORMS

The daylily species first offered simple, narrow-petaled flowers with which hybridizers could work. When hybridizing efforts began in earnest in the 1940s, breeders concentrated their efforts on widening the petals to create a full-formed, round flower. Narrow-petaled flowers were definitely passé. This movement away from narrow-formed daylilies continued for more than 50 years with very few people expressing an interest in spiders. But styles change, and in the 1990s more people started working toward improving narrow-petaled daylilies. The modern spider has petals and sepals that are narrower and longer than the original species, creating flowers that look like real spiders. Again, hybridizers had to start from scratch in their attempts to produce tetraploid spiders. The result is a series of modern spiders that are graceful and elegant, complete with all the bells and whistles of the modern tetraploid. Spiders have become more interesting, getting larger and narrower, with new features such as ornate edges, teeth and tendrils, eyes and edges, patterns, and increased twisting and twirling.

With this increased interest in the spiders came increased scrutiny. Many flowers can have narrow petals, but are they narrow enough to be considered a spider? To clarify this issue, the American Hemerocallis Society wrote a definition for spiders and spider variants. Flowers that look like spiders, but are not quite narrow enough to actually be spiders, are called spider variants. They concluded that a true spider must have a petal length-to-width ratio of 5:1 or higher. A spider variant must have a petal length-to-width ratio of at least 4:1, up to but not including 5:1.

Another group of daylilies at first glance might appear to be spiders or variants, but they have wider petals than spiders, and the floral segments appear to have consistent "movement." These are grouped under the designation "unusual forms" and have gained a following of their own. In response to the new interest in unusual forms, the American Hemerocallis Society developed a definition for them as well. Unusual form daylilies fit into three categories: crispate, cascade, and spatulate. The crispate category was further subdivided into three types: pinching, twisting, and quilling. In flowers with crispate pinching, the floral segments have sharp folds giving a pinched or folded effect. Crispate flowers with twisting have floral segments with a corkscrew or pinwheel effect, while those with quilling have floral segments that turn upon themselves along their length to form a tubular shape. Cascading refers to those flowers with narrow floral segments that display a pronounced curling or cascading which revolves upon themselves like a wood shaving. Spatulate flowers have floral segments that are markedly wider at the end, like a kitchen spatula. Any daylily showing one or more of these characteristics (known as movement) in their flower segments is qualified to be an unusual form daylily as long as it does not meet the official definition of a spider or spider variant.

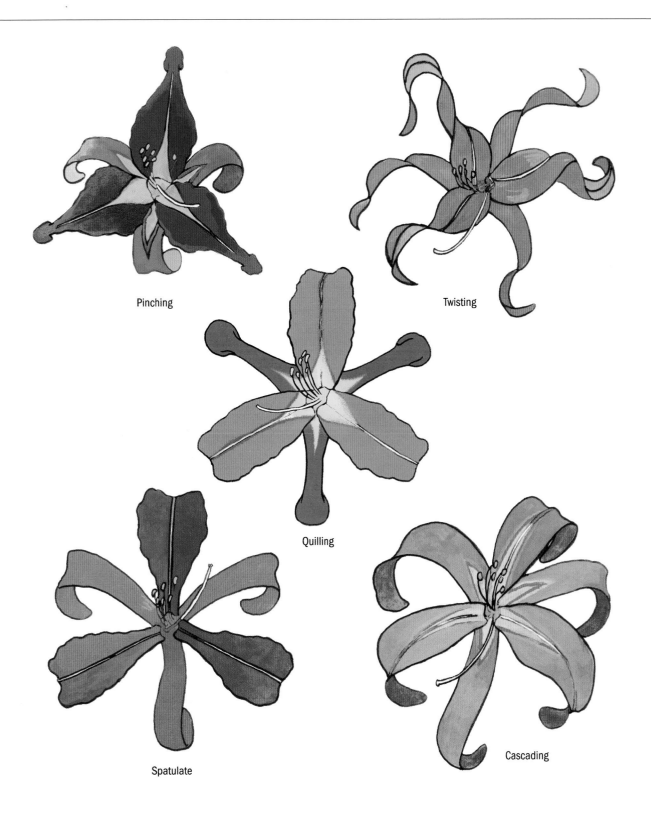

Pinching

Twisting

Quilling

Spatulate

Cascading

Types of unusual forms. *Watercolor by Richard Haynes*.

'Lacy Marionette' (Inez Tarrant, 1987). Evergreen. Scape 26 in. (66 cm); flower 7 in. (18 cm). Early mid-season. A bright yellow spider with a dark green throat. Diploid. 'Kindly Light' × seedling. Honorable Mention 1993. *Photograph by Mary Anne Leisen.*

'Lois Burns' (John Temple, 1986). Evergreen. Scape 30 in. (76 cm); flower 8.5 in. (22 cm). Early. A curled, bright yellow-green with a striking green throat. Diploid. Seedling × 'Green Widow'. *Photograph by Elliot Turkiew.*

'Spider Miracle' (W. B. Hendricks, 1986). Dormant. Scape 32 in. (81 cm); flower 8.5 in. (22 cm). Midseason. A yellow-green recurved self with a large strong green throat. Diploid. Lambert/Webster Award 2006. Award of Merit 1996. *Photograph by Ted L. Petit and John P. Peat.*

'Easy Ned' (Betty Brown, 1987). Evergreen. Scape 40 in. (101 cm); flower 6.5 in. (16.5 cm). Very late. A chartreuse self with a green throat. Diploid. 'Lady Fingers' × seedling. Eugene S. Foster Award 1998. Honorable Mention 1992. *Photograph by Mary Anne Leisen.*

'Wilson Spider' (William Oakes, 1987). Dormant. Scape 28 in. (71 cm); flower 7.5 in. (19 cm). Midseason. A purple bitone with a white eyezone and a chartreuse throat. Diploid. *Photograph by Mary Anne Leisen.*

'Holly Dancer' (Dorothy Warrell, 1988). Dormant. Scape 32 in. (81 cm); flower 7 in. (18 cm). Midseason. A brilliant red spider with a green throat. Diploid. ('Stoplight' × 'Monseigneur Garnet' × ('Stoplight' × 'Monseigneur'). Award of Merit 2007. *Photograph by Debbie and Duane Hurlbert.*

'Starman's Quest' (Clayton Burkey, 1989). Dormant. Scape 40 in. (101 cm); flower 7 in. (18 cm). Midseason. A violet-mauve semi-spider with a dark purple eyezone above a chartreuse to green throat. Diploid. 'Trahlyta' × 'Persian Pattern'. Award of Merit 2004. Honorable Mention 2001. *Photograph by Debbie and Duane Hurlbert.*

'Christmas Ribbon' (Patrick Stamile, 1991). Dormant. Scape 34 in. (86 cm); flower 8.5 in. (22 cm). Early. A deep Christmas-red self with a yellow throat. Tetraploid. 'Velvet Widow' × 'Tetra Open Hearth'. Honorable Mention 2004. *Photograph by Patrick Stamile.*

'Mountain Top Experience' (John Temple, 1988). Dormant. Scape 29 in. (74 cm); flower 6 in. (15 cm). Early. A green-yellow and rouge bicolor with a green throat. Diploid. 'Rainbow Spangles' × 'Lois Burns'. Honorable Mention 1991. *Photograph by Mary Anne Leisen.*

'Lavender Spider' (Eula Harris and Joyce Reinke, 1990). Dormant. Scape 32 in. (81 cm); flower 10 in. (25.5 cm). Early midseason. A light lavender spider with a darker halo, cream midribs, and a large yellow throat. Diploid. 'Kindly Light' × seedling. *Photograph by Ted L. Petit and John P. Peat.*

'Jan's Twister' (Jan Joiner, 1991). Evergreen. Scape 28 in. (71 cm); flower 11.5 in. (29 cm). Early midseason. A twisted cream-peach unusual form self with a green throat. Diploid. 'Jean Wise' × 'Kindly Light'. Lambert/Webster Award 2000. Lenington All-American Award 2003. Award of Merit 1997. Honorable Mention 1994. *Photograph by Francis Joiner.*

'Lola Branham' (Clayton Burkey, 1991). Dormant. Scape 38 in. (96 cm); flower 7.5 in. (19 cm). Midseason late. A lavender spider blend with a green throat. Diploid. 'Grapeade' × 'Lilting Lavender'. Lambert/Webster Award 2003. Honorable Mention 1999. *Photograph by Debbie and Duane Hurlbert.*

'Chevron Spider' (Ra Hansen, 1992). Evergreen. Scape 30 in. (76 cm); flower 10 in. (25.5 cm). Early midseason. A cream-peach spider variant with a burgundy-purple eyezone above a lime-green throat. Diploid. (Seedling × 'Spider Miracle') × seedling. Honorable Mention 1998. *Photograph by Rejean Millette.*

'Victorian Ribbons' (Bill and Joyce Reinke, 1993). Evergreen. Scape 40 in. (101 cm); flower 9 in. (23 cm). Midseason. A rose and yellow blend with a green throat. Diploid. *Photograph by Bill and Joyce Reinke.*

'Ruby Spider' (Patrick Stamile, 1991). Dormant. Scape 34 in. (86 cm); flower 9 in. (23 cm). Early. A ruby-red unusual formed self with a yellow throat. Tetraploid. 'Velvet Widow' × 'Tetra Open Hearth'. Lambert/Webster Award 2002. Award of Merit 2002. Honorable Mention 1999. *Photograph by Patrick Stamile.*

'De Colores' (John J. Temple, 1992). Evergreen. Scape 28 in. (71 cm); flower 8.5 in. (22 cm). Early. A rose, tan, and yellow 6.0:1 spider with a red-purple eyezone above a very green throat. Diploid. 'Mountain Top Experience' × 'Garden Portrait'. Honorable Mention 1999. *Photograph by Ted L. Petit and John P. Peat.*

'Yabba Dabba Doo' (Ra Hansen, 1993). Semi-evergreen. Scape 30 in. (76 cm); flower 10 in. (25.5 cm). Late. A medium purple spider variant self with a large chartreuse throat. Diploid. Eugene S. Foster Award 2007. Award of Merit 2000. Honorable Mention 1997. *Photograph by Debbie and Duane Hurlbert.*

'Marked by Lydia' (John Temple, 1994). Semi-evergreen. Scape 29 in. (74 cm); flower 8.5 in. (22 cm). Early. A medium yellow spider with a purple eyezone above a green throat. Diploid. 'Mountain Top Experience' × 'Garden Portrait'. Don C. Stevens Award 2005. Award of Merit 2003. Honorable Mention 1999. *Photograph by John Eiseman.*

'All American Windmill' (Clarence J. Crochet, 1995). Dormant. Scape 26 in. (66 cm); flower 7 in. (18 cm). Early midseason. A light orange polychrome with a dark orange eyezone. Diploid. 'Copper Windmill' × 'Yellow Angel'. Lambert/Webster Award 2004. Honorable Mention 1999. *Photograph by Ted L. Petit and John P. Peat.*

'Bradley Bernard' (Bill and Joyce Reinke, 1996). Semi-evergreen. Scape 38 in. (96 cm); flower 7 in. (18 cm). Midseason. A mauve brushed purple with a purple halo above a green throat. Diploid. 'Trahlyta' × seedling. Honorable Mention 2004. *Photograph by Bill and Joyce Reinke.*

'Lavender Handlebars' (Ned Roberts, 1994). Dormant. Scape 36 in. (91 cm); flower 8.5 in. (22 cm). Midseason. A lavender self with a yellow to green throat. Diploid. *Photograph by Curtis and Linda Sue Barnes.*

'Magic of Oz' (Heather Herrington, 1995). Dormant. Scape 37 in. (94 cm); flower 7 in. (18 cm). Midseason. A yellow-pink blend 4.0:1 spider/variant with a rose-pink eyezone above an intense green throat. Diploid. 'Green Widow' × (seedling × ('Wind Frills' × 'Rainbow Spangles')). Award of Merit 2003. Honorable Mention 1999. *Photograph by Duane Hulbert.*

'Crocodile Smile' (Dan Trimmer, 1996). Semi-evergreen. Scape 36 in. (91 cm); flower 8 in. (20 cm). Early midseason. A mulberry and ivory bicolor with a yellow to green throat. Tetraploid. 'Anastasia' × 'Tetra Spindazzle'. *Photograph by Dan Trimmer.*

'Pale Moon Windmill' (Clarence J. Crochet, 1996). Semi-evergreen. Scape 28 in. (71 cm); flower 6.5 in. (16.5 cm). Early. A cream blend with a light lavender halo above a dark green throat. Diploid. 'Enduring Love' × seedling. Honorable Mention 2000. *Photograph by Curtis and Linda Sue Barnes.*

'Curly Pink Ribbons' (Ra Hansen, 1996). Semi-evergreen. Scape 30 in. (76 cm); flower 6.5 in. (16.5 cm). Midseason. A medium pink with a wide yellow throat. Diploid. (Seedling × 'Cat's Cradle') × (seedling × 'Cat's Cradle'). Honorable Mention 2004. *Photograph by Chris Petersen.*

'Eggplant Escapade' (Margo Reed, 1996). Dormant. Scape 36 in. (91 cm); flower 6.5 in. (16.5 cm). Midseason. An eggplant-purple with a yellow throat. Diploid. 'Black Plush' × 'Trahlyta'. Honorable Mention 2003. *Photograph by Leslie Mauck.*

'Judge Roy Bean' (Bill and Joyce Reinke, 1996). Dormant. Scape 39 in. (99 cm); flower 9 in. (23 cm). Midseason late. A soft persimmon-gold self, 5.20:1 spider with creamy ribbing and a large light gold-green throat. Diploid. 'Persimmone' × 'Kindly Light'. Honorable Mention 2002. *Photograph by Bill and Joyce Reinke.*

'Planet Max' (Margo Reed, 1996). Semi-evergreen. Scape 42 in. (107 cm); flower 7 in. (18 cm). Early midseason. A dark purple self with a lemon-yellow throat. Diploid. Honorable Mention 2002. *Photograph by Margo Reed.*

'Shirley Temple Curls' (John Temple, 1996). Evergreen. Scape 24 in. (61 cm); flower 10 in. (25.5 cm). Early midseason. A light green with a burgundy eyezone and a deep green throat. Diploid. ('Lines of Splendor' × 'Garden Portrait') × ('Rainbow Spangles' × 'Lois Burns'). *Photograph by Ted L. Petit and John P. Peat.*

'Karen's Curls' (Bill and Joyce Reinke, 1997). Dormant. Scape 31 in. (79 cm); flower 7 in. (18 cm). Midseason. A lavender and cream bitone with a green throat. Diploid. 'Miss Jessie' × 'Rosy Lights'. Honorable Mention 2001. *Photograph by Debbie and Duane Hurlbert.*

'Let It Rip' (Jan Joiner, 1997). Evergreen. Scape 32 in. (81 cm); flower 10 in. (25.5 cm). Early midseason. A persimmon-orange blend with a green throat. Diploid. Honorable Mention 2000. *Photograph by Francis Joiner.*

'Curly Cinnamon Windmill' (Clarence J. Crochet, 1997). Dormant. Scape 28 in. (71 cm); flower 8.5 in. (22 cm). Early midseason. A yellow brushed cinnamon with a cinnamon chevron eye above a dark green throat. Diploid. 'Lacy Marionette' × 'Cat's Cradle'. Honorable Mention 2000. *Photograph by Debbie and Duane Hurlbert.*

'Laughing Giraffe' (Bob Schwarz, 1997). Dormant. Scape 36 in. (91 cm); flower 8 in. (20 cm). Midseason. A spidery bitone with orange-red toothy petals and lighter sepals. Tetraploid. Seedling × 'Tetra Spindazzle'. Honorable Mention 2003. *Photograph by Bob Schwarz.*

'Long Stocking' (Patrick Stamile, 1997). Evergreen. Scape 46 in. (117 cm); flower 9.5 in. (24 cm). Early midseason. A bright Christmas-red spider with a green throat. Tetraploid. 'Christmas Ribbon' × 'Swirling Spider'. *Photograph by Patrick Stamile.*

'Skinwalker' (Ned Roberts, 1997). Dormant. Scape 32 in. (81 cm); flower 8.5 in. (22 cm). Midseason. A lavender blend with a green throat. Diploid. Award of Merit 2005. Honorable Mention 2002. *Photograph by Julie Covington.*

'Do the Twist' (Ludlow Lambertson, 1998). Semi-evergreen. Scape 40 in. (101 cm); flower 7 in. (18 cm). Midseason. A medium pink-violet with a light orange-violet eyezone above a green throat. Tetraploid. 'Star of India' × ('Morticia' × seedling). *Photograph by Ludlow Lambertson.*

'Frilly Bliss' (Jan Joiner, 1998). Evergreen. Scape 34 in. (86 cm); flower 9 in. (23 cm). Midseason late. A powder-pink with a rose halo above a green throat. Diploid. Seedling × seedling. Lambert/Webster Award 2005. Honorable Mention 2002. *Photograph by Francis Joiner.*

'Brooklyn Twist' (Ludlow Lambertson, 1998). Semi-evergreen. Scape 28 in. (71 cm); flower 9 in. (23 cm). Midseason. A violet-red self with a green throat. Tetraploid. ('Christmas Ribbon' × 'Samar Star Fire') × (seedling × 'Alias Peter Parker'). *Photograph by Ludlow Lambertson.*

'Emmaus' (John J. Temple, 1998). Evergreen. Scape 28 in. (71 cm); flower 10 in. (25.5 cm). Early midseason. A yellow-green with a heavy maroon chevron eyezone above a green throat. Diploid. ('Mountain Top Experience' × 'Garden Portrait') × 'Wilson Spider'. Honorable Mention 2003. *Photograph by Elliot Turkiew.*

'On Silken Thread' (Ludlow Lambertson, 1998). Evergreen. Scape 36 in. (91 cm); flower 9 in. (23 cm). Midseason. A medium orange with a burnt orange eyezone and edge above a green throat. Tetraploid. (Seedling × seedling) × 'Tetra Spindazzle'. *Photograph by Ludlow Lambertson.*

'On the Web' (Ludlow Lambertson, 1998). Semi-evergreen. Scape 30 in. (76 cm); flower 7 in. (18 cm). Early midseason. A medium violet self with a green throat. Tetraploid. 'Alias Peter Parker' × seedling. *Photograph by Ludlow Lambertson.*

'Bark at Me' (Ned Roberts, 1999). Semi-evergreen. Scape 36 in. (91 cm); flower 7.5 in. (19 cm). Midseason. A red-purple with a purple eyezone above a yellow throat. Diploid. 'Lake Norman Spider' × 'Rainbow Spangles'. Honorable Mention 2003. *Photograph by Ned Roberts.*

'Grey Witch' (Margo Reed, 1999). Dormant. Scape 30 in. (76 cm); flower 6 in. (15 cm). Early midseason. A gray-lavender 4.22:1 spider/variant with a purple eyezone above a green throat. Diploid. 'Trahlyta' × unknown parent. Honorable Mention 2005. *Photograph by Margo Reed.*

'Wispy Rays' (Enman R. Joiner, 1998). Evergreen. Scape 36 in. (91 cm); flower 7.5 in. (19 cm). Midseason. A Pompeian-red with a ginger watermark above a yellow to green throat. Tetraploid. Seedling × 'Ruby Spider'. *Photograph by Francis Joiner.*

'Christmas Tidings' (Patrick Stamile, 1999). Evergreen. Scape 30 in. (76 cm); flower 8.5 in. (22 cm). Early. A red with a deep red eyezone above a green throat. Tetraploid. ('Swirling Spider' × 'Ruby Spider') × 'Long Stocking'. *Photograph by Patrick Stamile.*

'Jolly Red Giant' (Patrick Stamile, 1999). Evergreen. Scape 68 in. (173 cm); flower 8 in. (20 cm). Early. A red self with a chartreuse throat. Tetraploid. 'Star of India' × 'Long Stocking'. *Photograph by Patrick Stamile.*

'Lavender Arrowhead' (Patrick Stamile, 1999). Evergreen. Scape 36 in. (91 cm); flower 9 in. (23 cm). Early midseason. A lavender with a chartreuse watermark above a chartreuse-yellow applique throat. Tetraploid. 'Star of India' × ('Star of India' × 'Tetra Green Widow'). *Photograph by Patrick Stamile.*

'So Many Stars' (Matthew Kaskel, 1999). Evergreen. Scape 34 in. (86 cm); flower 6.5 in. (16.5 cm). Midseason late. A cream-purple with a purple eyezone above a chartreuse throat. Tetraploid. ((Seedling × 'Pirate's Patch') × (seedling × 'Pirate's Patch')) × 'Tetra Rainbow Spangles'. Honorable Mention 2007. *Photograph by Francois Verhaert.*

'Twisted Sister' (Bob Schwarz, 1999). Dormant. Scape 30 in. (76 cm); flower 8 in. (20 cm). Early. A pale rose above a green throat. Tetraploid. ('Mariska' × 'Heavenly Crown') × 'Tuxedo Junction'. *Photograph by Bob Schwarz.*

'Wind Beneath My Sails' (Ra Hansen, 1999). Semi-evergreen. Scape 48 in. (122 cm); flower 8 in. (20 cm). Early midseason. A dark red self, 4:33.1 spider/variant with an emerald-green throat. Diploid. 'Shimek September Morning' × seedling. Honorable Mention 2004.

'Royal Celebration' (Dan Trimmer, 1999). Evergreen. Scape 38 in. (96 cm); flower 12 in. (30.5 cm). Early midseason. A purple self with a green throat. Tetraploid. 'Cameroon Night' × 'Long Tall Sally'. Honorable Mention 2004. *Photograph by Francois Verhaert.*

'Spoons For Escargots' (John P. Peat, 1999). Semi-evergreen. Scape 28 in. (71 cm); flower 7 in. (18 cm). Midseason. A rose with darker veining and a large deep rose eye found on both the petals and sepals. The sepals are both quilled and spatulate. Tetraploid. (('Lin Wright' × 'Mardi Gras Ball') × 'Swirling Spider') × 'Misty Memories'. *Photograph by John P. Peat.*

'Cherokee Vision' (Joyce Reinke, 2000). Semi-evergreen. Scape 28 in. (71 cm); flower 7.5 in. (19 cm). Midseason. A gold with dark burgundy eye above light chartreuse throat. Diploid. 'Nashville Lights' × 'Chevron Spider'. *Photograph by Joyce Reinke.*

'Fantasy Frolic' (Jan Joiner, 2000). Evergreen. Scape 34 in. (86 cm); flower 10.5 in. (27 cm). Midseason. An apricot blend above a light green throat. Diploid. Seedling × seedling. *Photograph by Francis Joiner.*

'Happy Apache' (Dan Hansen, 2000). Semi-evergreen. Scape 24 in. (61 cm); flower 6.25 in. (16 cm). Early. A red with a wide lighter rustic-orange edge above a green throat. The sepals are spooned and twist and curl, a very unusual form. Tetraploid. 'Roses in Snow' × ('Calgary Stampede' × 'Untamed Glory'). Honorable Mention 2004.

'Heavenly Curls' (James Gossard, 2000). Dormant. Scape 24 in. (61 cm); flower 7 in. (18 cm). Midseason. A near-white self with a large green throat and petals that twist and curl. Diploid. 'Mormon Spider' × seedling. Honorable Mention 2005. *Photograph by Debbie and Duane Hurlbert.*

'Inky Fingers' (Patrick Stamile, 2000). Evergreen. Scape 36 in. (91 cm); flower 8 in. (20 cm). Early. A beautiful clear violet-purple with a huge deep Nile-green throat. Often the form is of crispate or a cascade. Tetraploid. ('Star of India' × 'Long Stocking') × ('Star of India' × 'Tetra Green Widow'). *Photograph by Patrick Stamile.*

'Jabberwocky' (Patrick Stamile, 2000). Evergreen. Scape 36 in. (91 cm); flower 8.5 in. (22 cm). Early. A red self above a grass-green throat. Tetraploid. ('Swirling Spider' × 'Ruby Spider') × ('Star of India' × 'Tetra Green Widow'). *Photograph by Patrick Stamile.*

'Lurch' (Patrick Stamile, 2000). Evergreen. Scape 30 in. (76 cm); flower 9.25 in. (23.5 cm). Early midseason. A cream with a lavender and purple-patterned eyezone above a green throat. Tetraploid. (('True Grit' × 'Admirals Braid') × (seedling × 'Song Without Words')) × 'Tetra Mountain Top Experience'. *Photograph by Patrick Stamile.*

'Octopus Hugs' (Patrick Stamile, 2000). Evergreen. Scape 38 in. (96 cm); flower 8 in. (20 cm). Early. A reddish orange bitone above a yellow throat. Tetraploid. ('Swirling Spider' × 'Ruby Spider') × 'Long Stocking'. *Photograph by Patrick Stamile.*

'Victorian Quills' (Joyce Reinke, 2000). Dormant. Scape 32 in. (81 cm); flower 8 in. (20 cm). Midseason. A creamy lavender-pink blend above a chartreuse extending to creamy ribbed throat. Diploid. 'Fellow' × 'Lilting Lavender'. *Photograph by Joyce Reinke.*

'Waiting in the Wings' (Patrick Stamile, 2000). Evergreen. Scape 32 in. (81 cm); flower 8 in. (20 cm). Early. A purple self above a green throat. Tetraploid. 'Inky Fingers' × seedling.

'Misty Twisty' (Ludlow Lambertson, 2000). Semi-evergreen. Scape 36 in. (91 cm); flower 7.5 in. (19 cm). Midseason. A light peach-pink with a lavender-pink eye above a green throat. Tetraploid. 'On the Web' × seedling. *Photograph by Ludlow Lambertson.*

'Purple People Eater' (Patrick Stamile, 2000). Evergreen. Scape 38 in. (96 cm); flower 9 in. (23 cm). Early. A black-purple bitone. Tetraploid. 'Star of India' × 'Red Suspenders'. *Photograph by Patrick Stamile.*

'Wings on High' (Patrick Stamile, 2000). Evergreen. Scape 42 in. (107 cm); flower 8 in. (20 cm). Early. An orchid self. Tetraploid. 'Star of India' × 'Tetra Mountain Top Experience'. *Photograph by Patrick Stamile.*

'Quasimodo' (Patrick Stamile, 2001). Evergreen. Scape 38 in. (96 cm); flower 9 in. (23 cm). Early. A red with a black-red eyezone above a green throat. Tetraploid. (('Star of India' × 'Long Stocking') × (seedling × 'Long Stocking')) × 'Moving All over'. *Photograph by Patrick Stamile.*

'Betty's Pick' (Ned Roberts, 2001). Semi-evergreen. Scape 38 in. (96 cm); flower 11 in. (28 cm). Early midseason. A pewter-flesh bicolor above a yellow-green throat. Diploid. Honorable Mention, 2007. *Photograph by Debbie and Duane Hurlbert.*

'Captain Nemo' (Bob Schwarz, 2001). Dormant. Scape 35 in. (89 cm); flower 5 in. (12.7 cm). Midseason late. A purple self above a green throat. Tetraploid. 'Bimini Twist' × 'Tetra Damsel in Distress'. *Photograph by Bob Schwarz.*

'Nathan Sommers' (Ned Roberts, 2001). Semi-evergreen. Scape 32 in. (81 cm); flower 8.5 in. (22 cm). Midseason. A raspberry-red self above a green throat. Diploid. *Photograph by Julie Covington.*

'Volusian Spider' (Dan Trimmer, 2001). Semi-evergreen. Scape 38 in. (96 cm); flower 7.5 in. (19 cm). Extra early. A peach with a dark purple eyezone above a green to yellow throat. Tetraploid. 'Moonlit Masquerade' × 'Tetra Cleopatra'. *Photograph by Karen Newman.*

'Alone With Maud' (Bob Schwarz, 2002). Dormant. Scape 35 in. (89 cm); flower 8 in. (20 cm). Midseason late. A champagne-pink blend above chartreuse throat. Tetraploid. ('Sea Urchin' × 'Lavender Light') × ('Tuxedo Junction' × 'Paper Butterfly').
Photograph by Bob Schwarz.

'Bi-Colored Bite' (Ludlow Lambertson, 2002). Semi-evergreen. Scape 32 in. (81 cm); flower 5 in. (12.7 cm). Early midseason. The petals are a rich, stippled, diamond-dusted deep rose with much deeper rose eye and the edge is surrounded with shark's teeth. Tetraploid. 'Stippled Stars' × 'Crocodile Smile'. *Photograph by Ludlow Lambertson.*

'Firefly Frenzy' (Jan Joiner, 2002). Evergreen. Scape 30 in. (76 cm); flower 8 in. (20 cm). Midseason. A lemon-drop self above a light green throat. Diploid. Seedling × seedling. Honorable Mention 2005. *Photograph by Francis Joiner.*

'Bali Watercolor' (Patrick Stamile, 2002). Evergreen. Scape 35 in. (89 cm); flower 9 in. (23 cm). Midseason. A lavender with a silver edge above a green throat. Tetraploid. 'Lavender Arrowhead' × 'Royal Celebration'.
Photograph by Patrick Stamile.

'Crescent Jump' (Patrick Stamile, 2002). Evergreen. Scape 36 in. (91 cm); flower 9.5 in. (24 cm). Early midseason. A lavender-pink bitone above a green throat. Tetraploid. ('Lavender Arrowhead' × ('Tetra Green Widow' × ('Tetra Cerulean Star')). *Photograph by Patrick Stamile.*

'Hang Six' (Patrick Stamile, 2002). Evergreen. Scape 43 in. (109 cm); flower 10.5 in. (27 cm). Early. A red self with a chartreuse-yellow throat. Tetraploid. 'Daniel Webster' × 'Web Browser'. *Photograph by Patrick Stamile.*

'Thin Man' (Dan Trimmer, 2002). Evergreen. Scape 42 in. (107 cm); flower 12 in. (30.5 cm). Midseason. A huge bright red with bold yellow midribs and yellow edges above a green throat. Tetraploid. (Seedling involving 'Swirling Spider' and 'Red Suspenders') × 'Long Tall Sally'. *Photograph by Dan Trimmer.*

'Velvet Ribbons' (Patrick Stamile, 2002). Evergreen. Scape 44 in. (112 cm); flower 11 in. (28 cm). Early midseason. A black-violet blend above a green throat. Tetraploid. ('Lavender Arrowhead' × 'Royal Celebration') × 'Skinny Marink'. *Photograph by Patrick Stamile.*

'Wild Child' (Jeff Salter, 2002). Semi-evergreen. Scape 24 in. (61 cm); flower 6 in. (15 cm). Midseason. A coral unusual formed flower. Tetraploid. ('Untamed Glory' × seedling) × ('Ed Brown' × 'Startle'). Honorable Mention 2005. *Photograph by Jeff Salter.*

'Dixie Rooster' (Ned Roberts, 2003). Semi-evergreen. Scape 35 in. (89 cm); flower 7.5 in. (19 cm). Midseason. A wine-purple self above a yellow-green throat. Diploid.

'Eight Miles High' (Ludlow Lambertson, 2003). Evergreen. Scape 30 in. (76 cm); flower 7.5 in. (19 cm). Midseason. A black-red with a darker black-red eyezone and a white shark's teeth edge above a green throat. Tetraploid. 'Way Cool' × (seedling × 'Way Cool'). *Photograph by Ludlow Lambertson.*

'French Twist' (Patrick Stamile, 2003). Evergreen. Scape 38 in. (96 cm); flower 9 in. (23 cm). Extra early. A red self above a green throat. Tetraploid. ('Christmas Tidings' × 'Web Browser') × 'Skinny Marink'.

'Gaboon Viper' (Brian Mahieu, 2003). Dormant. Scape 34 in. (86 cm); flower 6.5 in. (16.5 cm). Midseason late. A taupe with huge violet-etched band and darker violet-purple edge above lemon to chartreuse throat. Diploid. 'Trahlyta' × 'Spanish Fandango'.

'Laughing Skies' (Patrick Stamile, 2003). Evergreen. Scape 38 in. (96 cm); flower 10 in. (25.5 cm). Extra early. A lavender self above a green throat. Tetraploid. (((Seedling × seedling) × 'Inky Fingers') × ('Bluebird Sky' × ('Tetra Green Widow' × 'Tetra Cerulean Sky'))). *Photograph by Debbie and Duane Hurlbert.*

'Linguini' (Patrick Stamile, 2003). Evergreen. Scape 38 in. (96 cm); flower 10 in. (25.5 cm). Early midseason. A lavender self above a green throat. Tetraploid. ('Bluebird Sky' × ('Lavender Arrowhead' × 'Tetra Skinwalker')) × (('Star of India' × 'Long Stocking') × seedling).

'Sergeant Major' (Dan Trimmer, 2003). Semi-evergreen. Scape 44 in. (112 cm); flower 11 in. (28 cm). Early midseason. A red self above a green throat. Tetraploid. ((('Red Suspenders' × 'Long Tall Sally') × 'Swirling Spider') × 'Royal Celebration'). *Photograph by Alan Thor.*

'Billy Melo' (John P. Peat, 2004). Semi-evergreen. Scape 22 in. (56 cm); flower 8 in. (20 cm). Early midseason. A narrow-petaled burgundy-red with a dark purple-burgundy eyezone above a green throat. Tetraploid. ('Pirate's Ransom' × 'Swirling Spider') × ('Swirling Spider' × 'Spoons for Escargot'). *Photograph by John P. Peat.*

'Craig Green' (John P. Peat, 2004). Semi-evergreen. Scape 32 in. (81 cm); flower 9 in. (23 cm). Early midseason. A burgundy with deep burgundy eye and gold shark's teeth above a green throat. Tetraploid. ('Pirate's Ransom' × 'Swirling Spider') × 'Crocodile Smile'. *Photograph by John P. Peat.*

'Amber Curls' (Joyce Reinke, 2004). Semi-evergreen. Scape 30 in. (76 cm); flower 7 in. (18 cm). Early midseason. A tangerine-yellow with orange-red eye above green radiating to large golden yellow center throat. Diploid. 'English Vermilion' × 'Tomorrow's Song'. *Photograph by Joyce Reinke.*

'Blushing Octopus' (Patrick Stamile, 2004). Evergreen. Scape 39 in. (99 cm); flower 10.5 in. (27 cm). Extra early. A lavender-pink self above a green throat. Tetraploid. 'Runway Model' × ('Lavender Arrowhead' × 'Tetra Skinwalker'). *Photograph by Patrick Stamile.*

'Heavenly Mr. Twister' (James Gossard, 2004). Dormant. Scape 39 in. (99 cm); flower 8 in. (20 cm). Midseason. A pinkish red with darker eye above green-yellow throat. Diploid. 'Rings and Things' × 'Wildest Dreams'. *Photograph by Debbie and Duane Hurlbert.*

'Radioactive Curls' (James Gossard, 2004). Evergreen. Scape 30 in. (76 cm); flower 8.5 in. (22 cm). Midseason. A narrow-petaled maroon-red self above a huge green throat. The petals twist and curl, showing lots of motion. Diploid. 'Radiation Biohazard' × 'Rouge and Curls'. *Photograph by James Gossard.*

'Airy Delight' (Jan Joiner, 2005). Dormant. Scape 28 in. (71 cm); flower 9 in. (23 cm). Midseason. A crab-apple green sprinkled yellow bitone above a light green throat. Diploid. Seedling × seedling. *Photograph by Leslie Innel.*

'Erlo' (Bob Schwarz, 2005). Dormant. Scape 38 in. (96 cm); flower 7 in. (18 cm). Midseason late. A pumpkin self with a rouge halo. Tetraploid. Seedling × seedling. *Photograph by Bob Schwarz.*

'Lavender Stalactite' (James Gossard, 2005). Dormant. Scape 40 in. (101 cm); flower 7 in. (18 cm). Midseason. A lavender-rose with a slate blue eye and a lighter rose-lavender watermark above a green throat. Tetraploid. 'Orchid Majesty' × 'Lavender Handlebars'.

'Work With Me Annie' (Dan Bachman, 2004). Dormant. Scape 48 in. (122 cm); flower 6.25 in. (16 cm). Midseason. A violet-purple with thin white midribs above a chartreuse throat. Diploid. 'Stack the Deck' × 'Big Ross'. *Photograph by Dan Bachman.*

'Candy Cane Dreams' (Jim Murphy, 2005). Dormant. Scape 34 in. (86 cm); flower 6 in. (15 cm). Midseason. A red with yellow midrib and wide cream edge above yellow throat. Diploid. 'Unidentified Flying Object' × 'Murphy's Law'. *Photograph by Jim Murphy.*

'Military School' (Victor Santa Lucia, 2005). Dormant. Scape 30 in. (76 cm); flower 6 in. (15 cm). Midseason. A burgundy-purple with a chevron-patterned eye above a yellow to green throat. Diploid. 'Spanish Fandango' × seedling. *Photograph by Victor Santa Lucia.*

'Predatory Flamingo' (Margot Reed, 2005). Dormant. Scape 36 in. (91 cm); flower 7 in. (18 cm). Early midseason. A rose-pink self above a cream-yellow throat. Diploid. *Photograph by Margot Reed.*

'Wigglesworth' (Bob Schwarz, 2005). Dormant. Scape 36 in. (91 cm); flower 7 in. (18 cm). Midseason. A lavender self above a green throat. Tetraploid. 'Captain Nemo' × 'Twisted Sister'. *Photograph by Bob Schwarz.*

'Chief Leather Lips' (Sharon Fitzpatrick, 2005). Dormant. Scape 39 in. (99 cm); flower 10 in. (25.5 cm). Midseason. A dark purple self above a light green throat. Diploid. *Photograph by Sharon Fitzpatrick.*

'Scissorhands' (Clayton Burkey, 2005). Dormant. Scape 34 in. (86 cm); flower 7 in. (18 cm). Midseason late. A bright pink with a deep pinkish rose band above a tiny green heart throat. Diploid. 'Willie Belle' × 'Jurassic Spider'. *Photograph by Clayton Burkey.*

'Sharky's Revenge' (James Gossard, 2005). Dormant. Scape 28 in. (71 cm); flower 7.25 in. (18 cm). Midseason late. A yellow and red bitone with a darker red eyezone and a yellow shark's teeth edge above a green to yellow throat. Tetraploid. 'Green Fringe' × 'Startling Creation'.

'Dances With Giraffes' (Margo Reed, 2005). Dormant. Scape 60 in. (152 cm); flower 8 in. (20 cm). Midseason late. A gold-yellow with a rosy peach-blush eye above a green throat. Diploid. *Photograph by Margo Reed.*

'Flight of Orchids' (Margo Reed, 2005). Dormant. Scape 40 in. (101 cm); flower 6 in. (15 cm). Midseason. A lavender with a purple eyezone above a green throat. Diploid. *Photograph by Margo Reed.*

'Bed of Nails' (Ludlow Lambertson, 2006). Semi-evergreen. Scape 30 in. (76 cm); flower 6.5 in. (16.5 cm). Midseason. A large cream-amber self with a soft rose eyezone and matching picotee surrounded by a gold spikes, horns, and teeth. Tetraploid. 'Way Cool' seedling × 'Flying Saucer Blues'. *Photograph by Ludlow Lambertson.*

'Green Lines' (Jim Murphy, 2006). Dormant. Scape 40 in. (101 cm); flower 8 in. (20 cm). Midseason late. A clear yellow twisted crispate with a large green throat that radiates out on the petal in two distinct lines. Diploid. ('Sunny Sun' × 'Eggplant Escapade') × 'Magic of Oz'. *Photograph by Jim Murphy.*

'Heavenly Sudden Impact' (James Gossard, 2006). Semi-evergreen. Scape 35 in. (89 cm); flower 8.5 in. (22 cm). Midseason. A cream-pink with a huge dark maroon eyezone covering most of the flower. Diploid. 'Angelus Spangles' × 'Shirley Temple Curls'.

'Foxy Loxy' (Margo Reed, 2005). Dormant. Scape 56 in. (142 cm); flower 8 in. (20 cm). Midseason late. A gold-orange with a red chevron eyezone above a green throat. Diploid. 'Scarlett's Web' × seedling. *Photograph by Margo Reed.*

'Green Inferno' (James Gossard, 2006). Dormant. Scape 39 in. (99 cm); flower 7.5 in. (19 cm). Early midseason. A large neon-green and yellow spider with a very large dark to neon-green throat. Diploid. 'Royal Curls' × 'Great Red Dragon'. *Photograph by James Gossard.*

'Helmet Weichselbaum' (John P. Peat, 2006). Semi-evergreen. Scape 32 in. (81 cm); flower 11 in. (28 cm). Early midseason. A narrow-petaled burnt orange flower with a darker burnt orange eyezone. The edges carrying very large shark's teeth. Tetraploid. 'Fortune's Dearest' × ('Spoons for Escargot' × 'Craig Green'). *Photograph by John P. Peat.*

'Lightening Force' (James Gossard, 2006). Dormant. Scape 35 in. (89 cm); flower 7.5 in. (19 cm). Midseason. A large white unusual form crispate with a very large dark green throat. Diploid. 'Heavenly Angel Ice' × 'Heavenly Flight of Angels'. *Photograph by James Gossard.*

'Monocacy Summer Mist' (Margo Reed, 2006). Dormant. Scape 42 in. (107 cm); flower 7 in. (18 cm). Early midseason. A soft cream-yellow with a very large stippled rose eyezone above an intense green throat. Diploid. Seedling involving 'Lola Branham'. *Photograph by Margo Reed.*

'Pineapple Blast' (James Gossard, 2006). Evergreen. Scape 28 in. (71 cm); flower 7 in. (18 cm). Midseason. A cascade pink flower with a large dark red chevron eyezone above a striking green throat. Diploid. 'Oakes Love' × 'Malachite Prism'.

'Rosy Spangles' (Joyce Reinke, 2006). Dormant. Scape 42 in. (107 cm); flower 9 in. (23 cm). Midseason. A rosy pink spider with a silvery edge above a green radiating to cream-yellow throat. Diploid. 'Lee Reinke' × 'Chance'. *Photograph by Joyce Reinke.*

'Saber Tooth Tiger' (James Gossard, 2006). Dormant. Scape 32 in. (81 cm); flower 8.5 in. (22 cm). Midseason late. A yellow-orange bitone with a darker orange eyezone and yellow toothy edge above a yellow to green throat. Tetraploid. 'Forestlake Ragamuffin' × 'Tetra Spindazzle'. *Photograph by James Gossard.*

'Small World Twister' (Michael Miller, 2006). Dormant. Scape 42 in. (107 cm); flower 10 in. (25.5 cm). Midseason late. A pale lavender-pink with a large green throat. Diploid. 'Wilson Spider' × 'Long John Silver'. *Photograph by Michael Miller.*

'Stippled Starship' (Ludlow Lambertson, 2006). Semi-evergreen. Scape 29 in. (74 cm); flower 7 in. (18 cm). Midseason. A creamy pale rose flower with a stippled purple eyezone and picotee edge surrounded by huge white shark's teeth. Tetraploid. 'Stippled Stars' seedling × 'Jurassic Jaws'. *Photograph by Ludlow Lambertson.*

'Tahoe Snow Blizzard' (James Gossard, 2006). Evergreen. Scape 55 in. (140 cm); flower 9.5 in. (24 cm). Midseason. A near-white flower with a huge green throat and lightly ruffled petals and spooned sepals. Diploid. 'Heavenly Angel Ice' × 'Lavender Handlebars'.

‘Telltale Heart’ (George Doorakian, 2006). Dormant. Scape 38 in. (96 cm); flower 6.5 in. (16.5 cm). Midseason. A plum self with a large green throat and a very unusual distinctive purple-red eyezone. Diploid. *Photograph by George Doorakian.*

‘Time Stopper’ (James Gossard, 2006). Dormant. Scape 33 in. (84 cm); flower 7 in. (18 cm). Early midseason. An extra maroon-purple flower with a huge green throat extending way out on the petals surrounded by a darker purple eyezone. Diploid. ‘Heavenly Pink Butterfly’ × ‘Lavender Curls’. *Photograph by James Gossard.*

‘Winter Crown’ (Jeff Salter, 2006). Semi-evergreen. Scape 27 in. (69 cm); flower 6 in. (15 cm). Midseason. A pale ivory-cream flower with pinched and twisted petals and tiny teeth and serrations above a tiny green throat. Tetraploid. ‘Winter’s Angel’ × ((‘Waken to Winter’ × ‘Dreams of Destiny’) × (‘My Special Angel’ × ‘Moon Music’)). *Photograph by Jeff Salter.*

Chapter Nine

POLYTEPAL DAYLILIES

The typical single daylily has three sepals and three petals. The sepals and petals together are known as tepals. Polytepals, therefore, are flowers that contain more than the typical number of tepals. It would be easier to think of the flowers in their proper perspective if botanists had reversed the letters and referred to these flowers as "polypetaled," a term most people would easily understand. Most people first notice that these flowers have more than the typical three petals.

As explained in chapter 7, the daylily flower is composed of four whorls: (1) sepals, (2) petals, (3) stamens, and (4) the pistil, or carpel. Normally, each whorl has a characteristic number of 3 segments. Typically two stamens are associated with each petal, one attached to the center of the petal and the other attached to the edge, making six the usual number of stamens in the whorl. Every daylily has only one pistil, but upon close inspection you can see that it is divided into three parts. In short, the typical daylily is a three-part affair, with layers of flower parts all divisible by three.

The polytepal flower changes all this by increasing the basic number from three to four, five, or possibly even more. In cases in which the basic segments have been changed from three to four, each flower part exists in multiples of four.

This results in four sepals and four petals. Because there are four petals, each with its characteristic two stamens, the flower has eight stamens instead of the usual six. The pistil also contains four chambers. It is difficult to see that the pistil has four, rather than three, chambers, but the seed pod will show it more clearly. If you pollinate the pistil, allow a seed pod to form and mature, and you will clearly see that the seed pod has four seed chambers rather than the typical three.

While the most common polytepal daylilies have four rather than three components, the base number of segments does not appear to be limited. Four-petaled polytepal daylilies are most common, but several hybrids often produce five-petaled flowers. These also have five sepals, ten stamens, and a five-chambered pistil and seed pod. Evidence seems to indicate that the number of basic segments can be increased further, but we are not yet aware of any daylilies with more than five segments.

People often confuse polytepal daylilies with double daylilies because both contain more than the normal number of petals. Look again at the diagram of the daylily in chapter 7, and consider the concept of flower whorls or layers. Double daylilies increase the number of petals or petaloids either by adding extra whorls or layers of petals or by modifying stamens. Each whorl or layer of petals, however, still contains three petals. And the whorl of stamens still can only produce six petaloids. Polytepals, on the other hand, do something very different. First, no petaloid tissue is added to the stamens. Second, polytepals have only one layer of petals. Instead of adding layers, they change the number of petals within the single layer.

Polytepals are not universally loved. Many hybridizers see them as the ugly ducklings of daylilies. One daylily grower thought they were so ugly that whenever he saw a polytepal bloom he quickly picked it and threw it into the bushes before any garden visitor could see it. However, because hybridizers see "through" the flower into future generations, we see in the present polytepals the potential for great daylilies. Polytepals with four petals tend to look square, which has less of an aesthetic appeal for many people; however, we are in the infancy of this flower type. Most polytepals lack petal width and refinement, but such is typical of the early days of any breeding effort. With few exceptions, hybridizing efforts and breaks by serious hybridizers today occur at the tetraploid level. The first tetraploid polytepals have only recently become available, so breeding in this area should begin to quicken.

Many hybridizers hope to see polytepal flowers become more beautiful as modern daylily features are bred into them. One major goal is to breed five-petaled daylilies for the round and full look that five petals can impart. For example, the beautiful flowers of the hibiscus have five petals. Increasing petal width has also been a goal among normal single-daylily hybridizers in their work toward rounder flower form–five petals would instantly give an even rounder form to the flower. With additional petals, other features such as fancy edges become more dramatic. The possibilities for polytepal daylilies still can only be imagined: polytepal doubles would exponentially increase the number of flower petals and fullness of bloom, and polytepal spiders would have more hanging tendrils, looking more and more like spiders!

'Osterized' (Howard Hite and J. Davisson, 1999). Semi-evergreen. Scape 30 in. (76 cm); flower 10 in. (25.5 cm). Midseason. A yellow with white midribs above a green throat. Tetraploid. 'Yellow Mammoth' × 'Green Dolphin Street'. *Photograph by Leslie Mauck.*

'Starry Day' (Philip Adams and Evelyn Adams, 1991). Dormant. Scape 34 in. (86 cm); flower 5.5 in. (14 cm). Midseason. A clear yellow self with a vibrant green throat. Diploid. *Photograph by Bobby Baxter.*

'Tepaled Teddy' (Jack B. Carpenter, 1995). Dormant. Scape 26 in. (66 cm); flower 6.5 in. (16.5 cm). Midseason. A buff coral-peach blend with a bold mahogany-black eye and a yellow-green throat. Diploid. *Photograph by Bobby Baxter.*

'Chief Four Fingers' (Ned Roberts, 2002). Semi-evergreen. Scape 44 in. (112 cm); flower 6 in. (15 cm). Midseason. A dark red-purple with a black eye above a yellow to green throat. Diploid. *Photograph by Leslie Mauck.*

'The Moose Camped in a Tent on Tuesday' (Bobby Baxter, 2002). Evergreen. Scape 20 in. (51 cm); flower 3.75 in. (9.5 cm). Early. A softly ruffled yellow above a splashy green throat. Diploid. 'Guess Who' × seedling.

'Give Me Eight' (Bill and Joyce Reinke, 1993). Semi-evergreen. Scape 48 in. (122 cm); flower 8 in. (20 cm). Midseason late. A green-white self with a green throat. Diploid. 'Ice Carnival' × 'Old Mount Vernon'. Honorable Mention 1998. *Photograph by Bill and Joyce Reinke.*

'Four-Play' (Jeff Pansing, 1998). Semi-evergreen. Scape 24 in. (61 cm); flower 5.5 in. (14 cm). Early midseason. A deep cream-yellow with a very bright green throat' 90 percent polytepal. Diploid. 'Adjective' × 'Robert Quasdorf'. *Photograph by Ted L. Petit and John P. Peat.*

'Too Many Petals' (Bobby Baxter, 2002). Dormant. Scape 18 in. (46 cm); flower 4 in. (10 cm). Early. A cream with a purple eyezone above a chartreuse throat. Diploid. 'Forsyth Tepaled Double' × 'Dempsey Foursome'.

'Four Diamonds' (Ned Roberts, 2005). Semi-evergreen. Scape 28 in. (71 cm); flower 7 in. (18 cm). Early. A near-white blend above a green throat. Diploid. *Photograph by Ned Roberts.*

'Magical Indeed' (Ted L. Petit, 2005). Semi-evergreen. Scape 26 in. (66 cm); flower 6 in. (15 cm). Midseason. A cream self above a green throat. Tetraploid. 'Ben Adams' × ('Ferengi Gold' × 'Splendid Touch'). *Photograph by Ted L. Petit.*

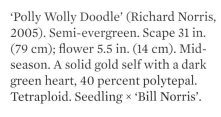

'Polly Wolly Doodle' (Richard Norris, 2005). Semi-evergreen. Scape 31 in. (79 cm); flower 5.5 in. (14 cm). Midseason. A solid gold self with a dark green heart, 40 percent polytepal. Tetraploid. Seedling × 'Bill Norris'.

'Delicate One' (Joyce Reinke, 2006). Dormant. Scape 38 in. (96 cm); flower 7 in. (18 cm). Midseason late. A sunny yellow with a pink-blush above a light green throat. The flowers also have a bright red triangular eye. Diploid. 'Green Widow' × 'Gadsden Pinwheel'. *Photograph by Joyce Reinke.*

'Hypnotized' (Ted L. Petit, 2006). Semi-evergreen. Scape 28 in. (71 cm); flower 8 in. (20 cm). Semi-evergreen. A copper with a purple eye above a green throat. Tetraploid. 'Baracuda Bay' × 'Tetra Open Hearth'. *Photograph by Ted L. Petit.*

'I Am Not a Mutant' (Bobby Baxter, 2006). Scape 23 in. (58 cm); flower 6 in. (15 cm). Midseason. A golden yellow self with a green throat, 100 percent polytepal. Diploid. 'Pancake Platypus' × 'I'm Different'.

'Release Your Inhibitions' (Bobby Baxter, 2006). Dormant. Scape 25 in. (63 cm); flower 6 in. (15 cm). Midseason. A pink crispate unusual form polytepal with a dark green throat. Diploid.

'Secret Agent Babe' (Bobby Baxter, 2006). Dormant. Scape 28 in. (71 cm); flower 7.5 in. (19 cm). Midseason. A yellow pinched crispate unusual form with a slight red eyezone, 75 percent polytepal. Diploid. 'Carolina Octopus' × 'Carolina Flying Poly Possum'.

'Zastrugi' (Dan Hansen, 2006). Semi-evergreen. Scape 25 in. (63 cm); flower 7.5 in. (19 cm). Midseason. A nicely ruffled slightly creped polytepal cream-yellow with a bright green throat. Diploid. 'Tuscawilla Snowdrift' × 'Richfield Earlene Garber'. *Photograph by Dan Hansen.*

'Ricochet Ruffles' (Chris Rogers, 2006). Evergreen. Scape 32 in. (81 cm); flower 6 in. (15 cm). Early. A pink self above yellow throat. Tetraploid. 'Hot Pink Fury' × 'Mount Herman Marvel'. *Photograph by Ted L. Petit.*

'Polar Wind' (Jack Kent, 2006). Scape 38 in. (96 cm); flower 7 in. (18 cm). Midseason late. A near-white five-petaled polytepal with a yellow to green throat. Tetraploid. *Photograph by Jack Kent.*

Chapter Ten

SMALL AND MINIATURE DAYLILIES

The small-flowered daylily has its own intrinsic appeal and dedicated following. The very small flowers create charming and delightful bouquets. They hold a special attraction, perhaps for the childlike, miniature world they seem to inhabit. The small-flowered daylily hybrids created by hybridizers are not simply smaller versions of large flowers, however. They have many characteristics that large-flower hybridizers wish to have in their lines.

By American Hemerocallis Society definition, miniature daylilies are flowers less than 3 in. (7.6 cm) across, and small flowers, or ponies, are those 3 to 4.5 in. (7.6 to 11.5 cm). Much of the work with small flowers has been carried out by the continuous efforts of hybridizers such as Elizabeth Salter, Pauline Henry, and Grace Stamile, who had to build an entire breeding line beginning from the large-flowered diploids. Each has left a personal stamp on the flowers she has created. Grace Stamile has created a series of small-flowered diploids and has moved on to creating a tetraploid line that includes eyed, edged, and even small-flowered doubles. More recently, she has worked with miniature tetraploids, which form her Broadway series. Before her death, Pauline Henry created the Siloam series of small-flowered daylilies, concentrating exclusively at the diploid level. Many of her flowers have interesting eyes or patterns. Elizabeth Salter started hybridizing small-flowered daylilies in the late 1960s when she was still in her late teens. She initially created complex eyes in diploids and moved toward boldly-colored eyes and blue eyes at the tetraploid level. Many patterns found in her miniatures are unique to her flowers, and other hybridizers are making intense efforts to bring these features into large-flowered tetraploids. Other hybridizers working with miniatures are striving for doubles, spiders, and other dramatic forms. Small daylilies are one focus that certainly continues to move at a rapid pace.

'Dragon's Orb' (Elizabeth H. Salter, 1986). Evergreen. Scape 20 in. (51 cm); flower 2.75 in. (7 cm). Midseason. A pale ivory-white self with a black eyezone and a chartreuse-lemon throat. Diploid. 'Corsican Bandit' × 'Dragon's Eye'. Donn Fischer Memorial Cup 1994. *Photograph by Curtis and Linda Sue Barnes.*

'Texas Sunlight' (Joyce Lewis, 1986). Dormant. Scape 28 in. (71 cm); flower 2.75 in. (7 cm). Midseason. A gold self. Diploid. Donn Fischer Memorial Cup 1990. Award of Merit 1990. Honorable Mention 1986. *Photograph by John Eiseman.*

'Strawberry Candy' (Patrick Stamile, 1989). Semi-evergreen. Scape 26 in. (66 cm); flower 4.5 in. (11.5 cm). Early midseason. A round recurved ruffled strawberry-pink blend with a rose-red eyezone and a golden green throat. Extremely popular cultivar. Tetraploid. 'Panache' × 'Tetra Siloam Virginia Henson'. Stout Silver Medal 1998. Annie T. Giles Award 1994. Don C. Stevens Award 1995. Award of Merit 1996. Honorable Mention 1993. *Photograph by Patrick Stamile.*

'Dark Avenger' (Elizabeth H. Salter, 1988). Semi-evergreen. Scape 18 in. (46 cm); flower 2.5 in. (6 cm). Midseason. A dark saturated red self with a yellow-green throat. Diploid. Donn Fischer Memorial Cup 1997. Award of Merit 1997. Honorable Mention 1993. *Photograph by Jay Tompkins.*

'Custard Candy' (Patrick Stamile, 1989). Dormant. Scape 24 in. (61 cm); flower 4.5 in. (11.5 cm). Early midseason. A round recurved cream-yellow with a bold maroon eye above a green throat. Tetraploid. (('Chicago Picotee Queen' × 'Byzantine Emperor') × 'Frandean') × 'Tetra Siloam Virginia Henson'. Stout Silver Medal 1999. Annie T. Giles Award 1996. Award of Merit 1996. Honorable Mention 1993. *Photograph by Patrick Stamile.*

'Tigerling' (Patrick Stamile, 1989). Dormant. Scape 25 in. (63 cm); flower 3.75 in. (9.5 cm). Midseason. A round brilliant light orange self with striking bright red eyezone and picotee, above a green throat. Tetraploid. 'Raging Tiger' × 'Tetra Siloam Virginia Henson'. Award of Merit 1997. *Photograph by Patrick Stamile.*

'Baby Blues' (Grace Stamile, 1990). Dormant. Scape 20 in. (51 cm); flower 2 in. (5 cm) . Midseason. A pale lavender with a washed gray-blue eyezone, edged with a fuchsia line, above a green throat. Diploid. ('Siloam Baby Talk' × 'Coming Out Party') × 'Siloam Tiny Tim'. Donn Fischer Memorial Cup 1999. Honorable Mention 1995. *Photograph by Patrick Stamile.*

'El Desperado' (Patrick Stamile, 1991). Dormant. Scape 28 in. (71 cm); flower 4.5 in. (11.5 cm). Late. A mustard-yellow with a wine-purple eyezone above a green throat. Tetraploid. 'El Bandito' × 'Blackberry Candy'. Don C. Stevens Award 2001. Award of Merit 2000. Honorable Mention 1997. *Photograph by Patrick Stamile.*

'Bibbity Bobbity Boo' (Elizabeth H. Salter, 1992). Semi-evergreen. Scape 18 in. (46 cm); flower 2.75 in. (7 cm). Early midseason. A lavender with a dark grape-purple eyezone above a green throat. Tetraploid. Seedling × 'Tetra Witch's Thimble'. Donn Fischer Memorial Cup 1998. Honorable Mention 1997. *Photograph by John Eisemen.*

'Indian Giver' (Elizabeth Ferguson, 1991). Semi-evergreen. Scape 20 in. (51 cm); flower 4.5 in. (11.5 cm). Early midseason. A purple with lavender edging and a medium purple watermark above a green throat. Diploid. Award of Merit 2000. Honorable Mention 1997. *Photograph by John Eiseman.*

'Blackberry Candy' (Patrick Stamile, 1992). Dormant. Scape 25 in. (63 cm); flower 4 in. (10 cm). Midseason. A wide-petaled nicely formed gold self with a strong near-black eye. Tetraploid. 'Raging Tiger' × 'Tetra Siloam Virginia Henson'. *Photograph by Patrick Stamile.*

'Dragon's Eye' (Elizabeth H. Salter, 1992). Semi-evergreen. Scape 24 in. (61 cm); flower 4 in. (10 cm). Midseason late. A famous rose-red eyezone on a clear pastel pink self, and a green throat. Diploid. 'Enchanters Spell' × 'Janice Brown'. Annie T. Giles Award 1997. Award of Merit 1998. Honorable Mention 1995. *Photograph by Ted L. Petit and John P. Peat.*

'In the Navy' (Elizabeth H. Salter, 1993). Semi-evergreen. Scape 18 in. (46 cm); flower 3 in. (7.6 cm). Midseason. A lavender to pink self with a dark navy-blue eye above a green throat. Very special. Diploid. Honorable Mention 2000. *Photograph by Ted L. Petit and John P. Peat.*

'Witches Wink' (Elizabeth H. Salter, 1993). Semi-evergreen. Scape 26 in. (66 cm); flower 3 in. (7.6 cm). Early midseason. A yellow with a plum eyezone above a green throat. Tetraploid. Seedling × 'Tetra Witch's Thimble'. Honorable Mention 1997. *Photograph by Ted L. Petit and John P. Peat.*

'Navajo Princess' (Ra Hansen, 1992). Semi-evergreen. Scape 24 in. (61 cm); flower 4.5 in. (11.5 cm). Midseason. A pale pink self with a large bold triangular rose eyezone above a deep triangular dark green throat. Very distinctive. Diploid. 'Futuristic Art' × 'Janice Brown'. Honorable Mention 1995. *Photograph by Ra Hansen.*

'Roses With Peaches' (David Kirchhoff, 1993). Semi-evergreen. Scape 22 in. (56 cm); flower 3.75 in. (9.5 cm). Extra early. A peach with a gold edge and a rose eyezone above a yellow throat. Tetraploid. ('Ming Porcelain' × ('Dunedrift' × 'Dance Ballerina Dance')) × 'Tetra Siloam Virginia Henson'. Annie T. Giles Award 2002. Honorable Mention 1997. *Photograph by Ted L. Petit and John P. Peat.*

'You Angel You' (Grace Stamile, 1993). Semi-evergreen. Scape 15 in. (38 cm); flower 2 in. (5 cm) . Midseason. A cream with a red eyezone above a green throat. Diploid. ('Cosmopolitan' × seedling) × 'Playful Pixie'. Donn Fischer Memorial Cup 2004. Honorable Mention 1998. *Photograph by Patrick Stamile.*

'Mary Ethel Anderson' (Elizabeth H. Salter, 1995). Semi-evergreen. Scape 18 in. (46 cm); flower 2.5 in. (6 cm). Midseason late. A cream with a dark red eyezone above a green center. Diploid. Donn Fischer Memorial Cup 2000. Award of Merit 2002. Honorable Mention 1999.

'Elegant Candy' (Patrick Stamile, 1995). Dormant. Scape 25 in. (63 cm); flower 4.5 in. (11.5 cm). Early mid-season. A wide-petaled nicely ruffled clear pink with a deep red band above a green heart. Tetraploid. 'Lady of Fortune' × 'Tetra Janice Brown'. L. Ernest Plouf Award 2001. Honorable Mention 1998. *Photograph by Patrick Stamile.*

'Breed Apart' (Elizabeth H. Salter, 1996). Semi-evergreen. Scape 26 in. (66 cm); flower 4.5 in. (11.5 cm). Midseason. An orange-coral blend with a green throat. Tetraploid. Honorable Mention 1999. *Photograph by Ted L. Petit and John P. Peat.*

'Dragon Heart' (Elizabeth H. Salter, 1996). Evergreen. Scape 28 in. (71 cm); flower 4 in. (10 cm). Midseason. Rose-pink with a bright red eyezone above a green throat. Diploid. 'Eye of Newt' × seedling. Honorable Mention 2003. *Photograph by Ted L. Petit and John P. Peat.*

'Beloved Deceiver' (Jeff Salter, 1996). Evergreen. Scape 24 in. (61 cm); flower 4.5 in. (11.5 cm). Midseason late. A round recurved soft pink with a large strong rose-red eye and a green throat. Tetraploid. *Photograph by Ted L. Petit and John P. Peat.*

'Her Majesty's Wizard' (Elizabeth H. Salter, 1996). Semi-evergreen. Scape 24 in. (61 cm); flower 4.5 in. (11.5 cm). Early midseason. A purple blend with a gold edge and a cream-purple halo above a green throat. Tetraploid. ('Elizabeth's Magic' × 'Tomorrow's Dream') × ('Elizabeth's Magic' × 'Tomorrow's Dream'). Honorable Mention 2001. *Photograph by Ted L. Petit and John P. Peat.*

'Tropical Delight' (Grace Stamile, 1996). Semi-evergreen. Scape 10 in. (25.5 cm) ; flower 2 in. (5 cm) . Early midseason. A rose-coral blend with a green throat. Diploid. 'Bubbly' × 'You Angel You'. Honorable Mention 2001. *Photograph by John Eiseman.*

'Broadway Nights' (Grace Stamile, 1997). Evergreen. Scape 22 in. (56 cm); flower 2.75 in. (7 cm). Early midseason. A deep purple with a black-purple eye and a green throat. Tetraploid. Seedling × 'Bibbity Bobbity Boo'. Honorable Mention 2003. *Photograph by Grace Stamile.*

'My Special Angel' (Elizabeth H. Salter, 1996). Semi-evergreen. Scape 26 in. (66 cm); flower 4.5 in. (11.5 cm). Early midseason. A bright cream flower with a heavy ruffled fringed edge and a green throat. Tetraploid. 'Regency Summer' × 'Angel's Smile'. Honorable Mention 2002. *Photograph by Ted L. Petit and John P. Peat.*

'Two To Tango' (Grace Stamile, 1996). Semi-evergreen. Scape 20 in. (51 cm); flower 3 in. (7.6 cm). Early midseason. A salmon-rose blend with a green throat. Diploid. 'Dragon's Eye' × 'You Angel You'. Honorable Mention 2003. *Photograph by Grace Stamile.*

'Little Wild Flower' (Grace Stamile, 1997). Semi-evergreen. Scape 13 in. (33 cm); flower 2 in. (5 cm) . Early midseason. A very cute miniature red to coral blend with a green throat. Diploid. 'Bubbly' × 'You Angel You'. Honorable Mention 2000. *Photograph by Patrick Stamile.*

'Strawberry Fields Forever' (Patrick Stamile, 1997). Evergreen. Scape 26 in. (66 cm); flower 4.5 in. (11.5 cm). Early midseason. A pink with a strawberry-rose eyezone and edge above a green throat. Tetraploid. 'Blueberry Candy' × 'Creative Edge'. Award of Merit 2004. Honorable Mention 2001. *Photograph by Patrick Stamile.*

'Huckleberry Candy' (Patrick Stamile, 1998). Dormant. Scape 20 in. (51 cm); flower 4.5 in. (11.5 cm). Early midseason. A cream with a blue eyezone above a green throat. Tetraploid. 'Exotic Candy' × 'Magnificent Rainbow'. Honorable Mention 2002. *Photograph by Patrick Stamile.*

'All In the Attitude' (Pam Erikson, 1999). Dormant. Scape 22 in. (56 cm); flower 3.5 in. (9 cm). Midseason. A deep pink with a maroon eyezone above a yellow to apple-green throat. Diploid. 'Dead Ringer' × 'Janice Brown'. *Photograph by Pam Erikson.*

'Little Red Dragon' (Dan Trimmer, 1999). Dormant. Scape 30 in. (76 cm); flower 3.75 in. (9.5 cm). Midseason. A dark pink with a crimson-red eyezone above a green throat. Tetraploid. ('Tetra Siloam Gumdrop' × 'Tetra Siloam Gumdrop') × 'Tetra Dragon's Eye'. Honorable Mention 2007.

'Bountiful Candy' (Patrick Stamile, 1998). Evergreen. Scape 26 in. (66 cm); flower 3.5 in. (9 cm). Early midseason. A cream with a raspberry-wine eyezone above a green throat. Tetraploid. 'Raspberry Candy' × 'Tetra Little Print'. *Photograph by Patrick Stamile.*

'Spacecoast Tiny Perfection' (John Kinnebrew, 1998). Semi-evergreen. Scape 18 in. (46 cm); flower 3 in. (7.6 cm). Early. A salmon-pink self with a gold edge above a green throat. Tetraploid. ('Little Mystic Moon' × (seedling × 'Elizabeth Salter')) × ('Little Mystic Moon' × (seedling × 'Elizabeth Salter')). Donn Fischer Memorial Cup 2003. Award of Merit 2005. Honorable Mention 2002. *Photograph by John Benoot.*

'Awesome Candy' (Patrick Stamile, 2000). Evergreen. Scape 25 in. (63 cm); flower 3.5 in. (9 cm). Early midseason. A cream-yellow with a dark complex, red eyezone and wire red picotee above a striking green throat. Tetraploid. 'Mister Lucky' × 'Beloved Deceiver'. Honorable Mention 2004. *Photograph by Patrick Stamile.*

'Sungold Candy' (Patrick Stamile, 2000). Evergreen. Scape 25 in. (63 cm); flower 3.5 in. (9 cm). Early midseason. A gold with a red eyezone. Tetraploid. 'Mister Lucky' × 'Beloved Deceiver'. Honorable Mention 2005. *Photograph by Patrick Stamile.*

'Magician's Apprentice' (Grace Stamile, 2002). Semi-evergreen. Scape 18 in. (46 cm); flower 2.75 in. (7 cm). Midseason. A purple with a white edge above a green throat. Diploid. ('Every Little Thing' × ('Little Sensation' × 'Tropical Delight')) × ('Little Sensation' × ('Little Pleasure' × 'Little Fat Cat')). *Photograph by Patrick Stamile.*

'Merry Moppet' (Elizabeth H. Salter, 2002). Semi-evergreen. Scape 27 in. (69 cm); flower 3.5 in. (9 cm). Early midseason. A golden yellow with a blood-red eyezone and picotee edge. Tetraploid. Honorable Mention 2005.

'Panther Eyes' (Patrick Stamile, 2000). Evergreen. Scape 25 in. (63 cm); flower 3.5 in. (9 cm). Early midseason. A luminescent yellow with a black eyezone and picotee above a green throat. Tetraploid. 'Mister Lucky' × ('Panda Bear' × ('Border Bride' × 'Tetra Eye of Newt')). Honorable Mention 2007. *Photograph by Patrick Stamile.*

'Green Treat' (Elizabeth H. Salter, 2002). Semi-evergreen. Scape 20 in. (51 cm); flower 3 in. (7.6 cm). Midseason. A lavender-purple with a green eye pattern above a green throat. Diploid. *Photograph by Elliot Turkiew.*

'Tour of Langley' (Pam Erikson, 2002). Dormant. Scape 20 in. (51 cm); flower 3 in. (7.6 cm). Midseason. An apricot-cream with a rose eyezone above a yellow throat. Diploid. 'Little Cupcake' × seedling. *Photograph by Pam Erikson.*

‘Lil’ Red Wagon’ (John Kinnebrew, 2003). Semi-evergreen. Scape 25 in. (63 cm); flower 8 in. (20 cm). Early. A red self above a green throat. Tetraploid. ‘Spacecoast Hot Topic’ × seedling. *Photograph by Francois Verhaert.*

‘Miniature Mime’ (Elizabeth H. Salter, 2003). Evergreen. Scape 18 in. (46 cm); flower 2 in. (5 cm) . Early midseason. An ivory with a red eye above a yellow to green throat. Diploid. ‘Mary Ethel Anderson’ × seedling.

‘Ledgewood’s Calico Blues’ (Gunda Abajian, 2005). Semi-evergreen. Scape 27 in. (69 cm); flower 3.75 in. (9.5 cm). Early. A light cream with a deep violet-blue patterned eyezone above a green throat. Tetraploid. ‘Crystal Blue Persuasion’ × ‘Wildest Dreams’. *Photograph by Francois Verhaert.*

‘Little Red Flirt’ (Grace Stamile, 2004). Semi-evergreen. Scape 16 in. (41 cm); flower 2.75 in. (7 cm). Early midseason. A red with a cream edge above a green throat. Diploid. (‘Little Wild Flower’ × ‘Cute as a Button’) × (‘Tropical Delight’ × (‘Arcadian Sprite’ × ‘All American Baby’)). *Photograph by Patrick Stamile.*

‘Little Damsel’ (Grace Stamile, 2005). Semi-evergreen. Scape 15 in. (38 cm); flower 2.5 in. (6 cm). Early midseason. A coral with a red pencil eyezone above a green throat. Diploid. ‘Little Wild Flower’ × seedling. *Photograph by Patrick Stamile.*

‘Spacecoast Small Talk’ (John Kinnebrew, 2005). Semi-evergreen. Scape 22 in. (56 cm); flower 3.75 in. (9.5 cm). Extra early. A yellow blend with a gold edge above a green throat. Tetraploid. ‘Spacecoast Perfect Angel’ × ‘Spacecoast Child Star’. *Photograph by John Benoot.*

'Winken Blinken and Nod' (Grace Stamile, 2005). Semi-evergreen. Scape 16 in. (41 cm); flower 2.5 in. (6 cm). Early midseason. An orchid with a purple-lavender eyezone edged in fuchsia above a green throat. Tetraploid. ('Little Sensation' × seedling) × seedling. *Photograph by Patrick Stamile.*

'Boogie Woogie Blues' (Grace Stamile, 2006). Semi-evergreen. Scape 24 in. (61 cm); flower 3 in. (7.6 cm). Midseason. A cream-pink with a blue eyezone edged in fuchsia above a green throat. The eye pattern is mimicked on the petaloids. Diploid. ('Little Sensation' × ('Arcadian Sprite' × 'Little Pleasure')) × 'Blue Alert'. *Photograph by Patrick Stamile.*

'Flames of Beauty' (Elizabeth H. Salter, 2006). Semi-evergreen. Scape 24 in. (61 cm); flower 3.5 in. (9 cm). Early. A bright burnt orange self with a darker ruffled edge and eyezone above a green center. Tetraploid. ('Hot Secret' × seedling) × John Kinnebrew seedling. *Photograph by Elizabeth H. Salter.*

'Black Fathom Depths' (Elizabeth H. Salter, 2006). Semi-evergreen. Scape 25 in. (63 cm); flower 3.5 in. (9 cm). Early midseason. A small maroon flower with a violet eyezone and burgundy halo above a bright green throat. Tetraploid. ('Wizards Heir' × ('Tetra Dragon Dreams' × 'Ed Brown')) × ('Her Majesty's Wizard' × ('Tetra Dragon Dreams' × seedling)). *Photograph by Elizabeth H. Salter.*

'Broadway Sparkler' (Grace Stamile, 2006). Dormant. Scape 16 in. (41 cm); flower 3.5 in. (9 cm). Early midseason. A rose-red with a bright candy-apple red eyezone above a green throat. Tetraploid. (Seedling × 'Tetra Siloam Tom Howard') × 'Broadway Dazzler'. *Photograph by Patrick Stamile.*

'Garden Greetings' (Elizabeth H. Salter, 2006). Semi-evergreen. Scape 23 in. (58 cm); flower 3.75 in. (9.5 cm). Early midseason. A rose-pink flower with a huge light pink watermark and a ruffled gold toothy edge above a large green throat. Tetraploid. 'Delightful Duchess' × 'Sanibel Sunset'. *Photograph by Elizabeth H. Salter.*

'Little Raven' (Grace Stamile, 2006). Semi-evergreen. Scape 16 in. (41 cm); flower 2.5 in. (6 cm). Early midseason. A deep black self with a lighter dark purple edge above a deep fluorescent green throat. Diploid. Seedling × ('Little Show Stopper' × 'Just My Size'). *Photograph by Patrick Stamile.*

'Merely Mystical' (Elizabeth H. Salter, 2006). Semi-evergreen. Scape 25 in. (63 cm); flower 4 in. (10 cm). Early midseason. A soft baby-ribbon pink with a pronounced toothy gold edge and deep green heart. Tetraploid. ('Waken to Winter' × 'Ed Brown') × ('Delightful Duchess' × 'Cosmic Courier'). *Photograph by Elizabeth H. Salter.*

'Mulberry Lane' (Elizabeth H. Salter, 2006). Semi-evergreen. Scape 26 in. (66 cm); flower 3.5 in. (9 cm). Early midseason. A clear pink flower with a large candy-apple red eyezone and wide matching picotee surrounded by a bubbly wire gold edge. Tetraploid. 'Merry Moppet' × (('Dixie Rhythm' × 'Renegade Ranger') × ('Footloose Fancy' × 'Tetra Dragon's Eye')). *Photograph by Elizabeth H. Salter.*

'Make Your Point' (Elizabeth H. Salter, 2006). Evergreen. Scape 19 in. (48 cm); flower 3 in. (7.6 cm). Midseason. A cranberry-cream self with a huge circular dark burgundy eyezone covering most of the flower surface, with a bright green heart. Diploid. ('Elvin Archer' × seedling) × ('Underwater Wonder' × seedling). *Photograph by Elizabeth H. Salter.*

'Plucky Pixie' (Elizabeth H. Salter, Seedling). Semi-evergreen. Scape 24 in. (61 cm); flower 3 in. (7.6 cm). Midseason. A cream with a striking bold round eyezone of burgundy-red above a green throat. Diploid. 'Summer Dragon' × ('Dragon's Eye' × unknown). *Photograph by Francois Verhaert.*

'Refuge Point' (Elizabeth H. Salter, 2006). Semi-evergreen. Scape 26 in. (66 cm); flower 2.75 in. (7 cm). A near-white self with a rose-red eyezone and matching wire picotee edge above a green throat. Tetraploid. ('Easy on the Eyes' × 'Footloose Fancy') × 'Mississippi Matchmaker'. *Photograph by Elizabeth H. Salter.*

'Spacecoast Shellcracker' (John Kinnebrew, 2006). Semi-evergreen. Scape 24 in. (61 cm); flower 3.5 in. (9 cm). Early midseason. A bright yellow flower with a brilliant red eyezone and picotee. Tetraploid. 'Madeline Nettles Eyes' × 'Awesome Candy'. *Photograph by John Kinnebrew.*

'Twilight Text' (Elizabeth H. Salter, 2006). Evergreen. Scape 18 in. (46 cm); flower 3.5 in. (9 cm). A pink flower with a patterned eyezone with shades of blue-violet surrounded by a burgundy band with a large green throat. Diploid. ('Cryptic Cipher' × 'Dream Spiral') × ('Blue Oasis' × 'Underwater Wonder'). *Photograph by Elizabeth H. Salter.*

'Rosabelle Van Valkenburgh' (Elizabeth H. Salter, 2006). Semi-evergreen. Scape 20 in. (51 cm); flower 3.5 in. (9 cm). Midseason. A burgundy-purple flower with a multibanded washed eyezone above a large green throat; the sepals display bright white edging. Diploid. ('Party Pinafore' × seedling) × ('Over the Line' × 'Spirited Style'). *Photograph by Elizabeth H. Salter.*

Chapter Eleven

HYBRIDIZING

One great joy of the daylily, and one of the major factors leading to its popularity, is that it is so easy to create your own new hybrids. Hybridizing allows for a wonderful expression of personal taste and a creative outlet for the spirit. Typically, each gardener develops a love for a particular flower over others because of favorite colors or forms, such as miniatures, spiders, or doubles. By breeding plants, you can create new plants that have enhanced or even new features tailored to your own personal liking. If you love miniatures but would like them even smaller, or would like some double miniatures, hybridizing is your chance to express those desires and create new, beautiful plants.

TECHNIQUES

The actual technique of hybridizing daylilies is quite simple; anyone can do it. Creating new hybrids that express your specific interests is easy with daylilies and one reason so many people have become captivated by daylilies. In fact, many daylily enthusiasts refer to hybridizing as an addiction, and refer to themselves as "hemaholics."

Simply stated, to create new daylily hybrids, simply take the pollen from one flower, spread it onto the pistil of another, harvest and plant the seeds, and within one or two years your newly created hybrids will bloom. Compare this to hybridizing orchids, for example, where the seeds must go to a laboratory to grow in test tubes, or camellias, which can take five to seven years to reach blooming size.

Hybridizing daylilies may not always be quite this simple, and does have its challenges, but there are also tricks that can make it easier. If the two parents of a particular desired cross do not bloom at the same time, you can collect pollen from the pollen parent when it is in bloom and store it for use when the pod parent blooms. Many hybridizers pick the flower they wish to use as a pollen parent and place the entire flower in the refrigerator. In the refrigerator, a daylily flower will remain relatively fresh for two or more days. As such, you can use one or more stamens each day. The flowers should be collected early in the day because exposure to midday heat causes a progressive loss in pollen viability and reduces the length of time that the flower will remain fresh in the refrigerator. If you have a limited amount of special pollen and would like to use it over a longer period of time, gently separate the anther with its attached pollen, from the stamen with a pair of tweezers, fingernail, or single-edged razor blade. The pollen can then be stored in the refrigerator for several months, or in the freezer for several years. Different hybridizers use a number of different storage containers for pollen, including simple packets made by folding aluminum foil, inexpensive plastic contact lens cases, match boxes, and other small plastic containers. Be sure to label the pollen, either directly on the container or on a piece of tape attached to the container.

Take care to keep the pollen dry, which may mean leaving the packet of pollen exposed in an air conditioned room for a few minutes before refrigerating it, or allowing the condensation to evaporate after removing it from the refrigerator or freezer. Pollen can be taken from the refrigerator many times and returned with little loss of viability as long as it is kept dry and away from the midday heat. Pollen can stay fresh for long periods of time and be used to make many, many crosses. When it is time to use the pollen, simply open the container and apply the pollen with an artist's brush or touch the stored anther to the pistil with a pair of tweezers (reverse tweezers are very helpful here, because they are normally clamped shut rather than open).

Unlike breeding the flowers of other genera, daylily breeders rarely bother to remove the stamens from flowers chosen to be the pod parent because the pistil of a daylily is such a long distance from the stamens. Early morning is the best time for pollinating daylilies; successful crosses become less and less likely as the day progresses. In general, diploids are more fertile than tetraploids and therefore can have a higher percentage of takes later in the day. Successful seed set is temperature dependent. Hot days are not good for pollination because few pods will set; any crossing should be made as early in the morning as possible, and preferably on plants in the shade. Cool, overcast days generally result in excellent seed set, even on crosses made late in the day. It is not necessary to cover the pollinated pistil to ensure that no unintended pollen reaches it, because the stigma is only receptive for a short period of time and the flower is open for only a single day.

Label the crosses as you make them, including the names of both parents. Many hybridizers use small white paper tags on strings, like those generally used for marking prices, which are readily available in most office supply stores. Be sure to use permanent markers or pencil so that the label will withstand the eight weeks of weather until the seeds are harvested. You may wish to use a record book as well, where more detailed information about the cross may be included. Methods of labeling, numbering, or otherwise recording crosses vary from person to person, and each breeder must find a system that works best for him or her. Some hybridizers use small pieces of color-coded telephone wire to mark their crosses. This is much quicker than recording each cross as it is made. Others use plastic "bread bag" sealers to slip on the base of the flower to mark their crosses.

A few days after pollination, the daylily flower will drop off. If pollination has been successful, a very small, green seed pod will be at the base of the former flower. If the cross did not take, no seed pod will form, which happens about half of the time even under the best conditions. The seed pod, once formed, will slowly enlarge and reach maturity within six to ten weeks, in midsummer to fall depending on the climate. When mature, the seed pod will turn brown and split open to reveal glossy black seeds. Keep a close watch on the seed pods as they mature, for once the pods crack open the seeds will easily scatter by wind and rain. If an untimely vacation or early frost means that you cannot harvest the seeds when they would normally mature outdoors, seed pods can be ripened indoors if they are already very near maturity. Simply break off the entire flower scape and place it in a vase of water.

Collect the seeds and store them in envelopes or sealable plastic bags labeled with the parentage. Refrigerate the seeds for a minimum of three weeks if they are to be planted without outdoor overwintering. Pure evergreen varieties will sprout without any chilling, but daylily seeds with dormancy in their background require refrigeration in order to sprout. Some research suggests that completely dried out seeds do not benefit from refrigeration; therefore, most hybridizers attempt to keep the seeds in a moist environment by placing a moist paper towel in the ziplock bag with the seeds. Ideally, the paper towel should not be soggy, as the seeds can rot if they get too wet. We have found it most convenient to squirt a solution of mild fungicide and water into the sealable plastic bags (using an old shampoo bottle) to keep the seeds moist and prevent rot during refrigeration. Any locally available fungicide usually works well.

Daylily seeds may be planted outside in the fall or spring, or started inside. Treat them as you would any other seeds. Sowing daylily seeds outdoors in the fall in cold climates runs the risk of killing some plants, and they also lose the benefit of the winter growing time. Most gardeners in cold climates start the seeds inside and overwinter seedlings in a greenhouse, sunny window, or under grow lights, often in the basement. In warmer climates, the seeds can be started outdoors in late summer to early fall, and they will grow all winter. Indoors or out, germination usually takes place within two weeks, although some seeds can be slow to germinate. Since daylily seeds do not sprout well, and can even be killed, in extreme heat, germination rates may be reduced by planting in full sun in the late summer in very hot climates, or by overheating the seeds during indoor sprouting. We have found that seed sprouting and survival is optimal at 75° to 80°F (or 23.9° to 26.7°C). When planting seedlings outdoors, they should be set about 4 to 5 in. (10 to 12.7 cm) apart in rows 1 to 1.5 ft. (30.5 to 45.7 cm) apart. Be sure to transfer the parentage information to the garden with the plants.

Once planted out, plants will flower in one to three years. In warm climates or in a greenhouse, if the seeds are planted in the early fall and the plants are fertilized heavily, they can bloom the following spring, within nine months.

GOALS

One critical question in any attempt to hybridize daylilies concerns ploidy—are the plants you want to cross diploids or tetraploids? This question is critical since diploids, those with the normal set of 22 chromosomes, will only cross with diploids, and tetraploids, those with 44 chromosomes, will only set seed with tetraploids. A diploid will not cross successfully with a tetraploid, no matter how hard you try to make seed.

How do you know whether your plants are diploid or tetraploid? Most nursery catalogs list a plant's ploidy, so look up the plant in the garden catalog from which you purchased it. If the plant is from a friend or some other source, look it up in a catalog from a major daylily garden (see Sources for Daylilies at the back of the book). The ultimate source is the American Hemerocallis Society Checklist. This series of books (or the CD or on-line version) lists all registered daylilies as well as their characteristics. An additional source of information is the yearly *Eureka Daylily Reference Guide* (see Additional Resources). It lists most daylilies in commerce and where to buy them and compares prices between the different sources. The more time-consuming way to check for ploidy is to cross the unknown plant with a plant that you know is a diploid or tetraploid. Plants of opposite ploidy may initially develop seed pods, but within a few weeks the pods will dry up and abort because no viable seeds are inside.

After establishing whether a plant is diploid or tetraploid, you can cross it with any other daylily of the same ploidy. You must then decide where you want to take the plant. You can cross almost any two flowers, but most crosses are designed to make improvements in different flower features. Daylilies are generally categorized based on the factors of flower size (large, small, or miniature), single or double, polytepal, spider, and so on. In order to "officially" fit into the categories, flowers have to meet the American Hemerocallis Society's designated criteria for that category, such as the petal length-to-width ratios for spiders. However, the flowers themselves often fall between official groups. For example, a flower may be very spidery looking, with long, narrow petals, but not actually reach the criterion for a spider as set forth by the American Hemerocallis Society. This plant may be very important for breeding, though.

When a flower falls within one group, do not hesitate to cross it with flowers from another group if it offers characteristics in the direction of your hybridizing goal. For example, the prominent and showy gold edge found on the newer tetraploid daylily hybrids originally appeared only on large-flowered, wide-petaled, single daylilies. Therefore, hybridizers interested in getting this petal edge on miniatures, spiders, or doubles had to breed them across categories. This route does, however, mean losing many desirable characteristics in the first generation, such as size, narrowness, or doubling, in order to ultimately achieve the goal of the gold edge. Though the categories listed above delineate most breeding (doubles to doubles, spiders to spiders, and so on) enthusiasts should not be afraid to cross flowers of different groups on the path toward a specific goal.

Pollinating a daylily. *Photograph by Ted L. Petit.*

A small, green newly forming seed pod can be seen at the base of the spent bloom. Also, notice the paper tag marking the pollen parent. *Photograph by Ted L. Petit.*

Green, maturing seed pods. *Photograph by Ted L. Petit.*

A brown, mature seed pod that has broken open, exposing the black seeds inside. *Photograph by Ted L. Petit.*

Chapter Twelve

CULTIVATION

Daylilies are among the most carefree plants in modern gardens. Compared to many other garden plants, their horticultural requirements are minimal, and they show good disease resistance. This carefree nature has been a major factor contributing to the popularity of the daylily.

CLIMATE

Daylilies will thrive in virtually any climate. As mentioned in chapter 1, while most daylilies do well across a large climatic range, certain varieties perform better in extreme climatic zones. For example, in very cold climates such as eastern Canada, dormant and cold-hardy evergreen daylilies perform better. In very hot climates such as the deep southern United States and northern Australia, evergreen varieties generally tend to perform better. Even in locations that receive only mild frosts, many dormant daylilies perform very well. Although most daylilies require some degree of winter chilling in order to survive or bloom, some varieties perform well even in frost-free climates.

PLANTING

Consider sunlight, soil, and water when planting daylilies. Daylilies prefer full sun, although they will grow happily in partial shade. The flowers benefit from midday to late-afternoon shade when the sun is at its hottest, particularly in hot, sunny climates and for dark-colored flowers, such as reds, purples, and blacks. These richly colored flowers often will scorch in full, hot sun. If grown in full shade, daylilies will usually survive but will produce fewer flowers or none at all, the scapes will be tall and lean toward the sun, and the foliage will be lanky.

Daylilies are not overly particular about soil conditions, although they do perform best in moist but well-drained soil. Prior to planting daylilies, loosen the soil as you would for any plant. Adding organic matter to your soil, such as manure, rotted leaves, compost, and so on, is always a benefit. Daylilies particularly like pine bark mulch, because it helps aerate the soil and improve drainage. Remember that any decaying organic matter requires nitrogen and will take it from the soil. Therefore, if you use un-composted organic matter, be sure to compensate by increasing the amount of nitrogen fertilizer. Prepare a hole large enough to accommodate the plant and form a mound at the bottom of the hole on which to set the plant. Place the plant and fill in the soil to the same height as before. The difference in the color of the leaves will indicate the level of the soil: the leaves will be white where they were below the soil. Although daylilies are tolerant of a wide range in soil pH, they prefer a slightly acidic soil. It is rare for daylilies not to flourish in the average garden because of an imbalance in soil pH; however, if plants fail to thrive, consider having the soil tested for pH by a local agricultural agent.

Daylilies need a lot of water but do not like to be in standing water. Although daylilies will survive in standing water far better than most other plants, do not plant them in areas where standing water is expected after heavy rains. Standing water strains the plant and decreases its disease resistance. During bloom season, daylilies especially need plenty of water to produce large, voluptuous blooms. Therefore, locate the plants where they can receive an adequate supply of water when needed. Although not required, mulch (including some organic matter) helps to retain water and keep the soil moist and cool.

To get the maximum enjoyment from your daylilies, they should be fertilized, particularly to enjoy the dramatic features of the newer hybrids. Any balanced fertilizer is adequate, such as 6–6–6 or 20–20–20 (nitrogen-phosphorus-potassium), and can usually be purchased in any local garden center. Generally, applications of fertilizer in the spring and prior to bloom time are sufficient to ensure good growth and healthy bloom. Some gardeners prefer to use time-release fertilizers to give a more continuous feeding, and supplement their fertilizers with minor elements, such as iron or magnesium. While daylilies will respond with bigger, more voluptuous blooms when given extra care (which may be particularly rewarding to see the full potential of the newer hybrids), this is not necessary.

DISEASES AND PESTS

Daylily rust is a yellow or orange powdery substance on the underside of the leaves that comes off when touched. Daylily rust is caused by the fungus *Puccinia hemerocallidis*. This disease does not occur in all countries, and first arrived in North America fairly recently. Because of its recent appearance, it is not well understood. Patrinias and daylilies are the only plants currently proven to be affected by this disease in its native lands. Patrinia (currently relatively uncommon in North American gardens) may, theoretically, enable daylily rust to overwinter in colder zones, although at this time there is no evidence to support this. While daylily rust can persist from year to year on daylilies alone in mild winter areas, it is killed during winter in cooler climates. Even if a plant becomes infected with rust, the rust will not overwinter in areas that receive prolonged freezing periods. In North America, rust cannot survive winters north of Georgia. Therefore, daylily rust is only a problem for southern gardeners.

There are tremendous differences between daylily cultivars in terms of their susceptibility to rust. While some gardeners in the southern United States have chosen to spray fungicides to control rust, many others have chosen to compost the most susceptible plants. Once these plants are gone, the remaining daylilies show relatively little damage from rust, with most of the damage occurring on the lower, senescent leaves. On relatively resistant plants, rust has little effect on the overall garden appearance of the plants. Also, some of the major daylily hybridizers are creating new daylily hybrids that are increasingly resistant to rust.

Rust appears to be worst during mild to warm rainy weather, with little evidence of it during extreme heat or cold. For those who insist on perfectly groomed gardens, with no trace of disease or damage, daylily rust can be controlled with fungicides. Check with your local extension service or equivalent for the latest control recommendations. During this period of culling highly susceptible cultivars and breeding more rust resistant ones, some gardeners have chosen to spray only occasionally during spring and fall, when the symptoms are worst. Other gardeners simply cull the most susceptible plants and ignore it on the rest.

Another disease problem found in daylilies is fungal or bacterial infection. This generally takes two forms: spring sickness or crown rot. Spring sickness most commonly occurs in colder climates in the spring when the plants are just beginning to come out of winter dormancy. The emerging leaves turn yellow and appear to die. If the yellow leaves are pulled from the plant, they have a very pungent rotten smell. Most plants suffering from spring sickness tend to recover on their own, although removing any dead tissue will aid new growth.

Crown rot develops almost exclusively during extremely hot and humid conditions. Therefore, this problem is most prevalent in climates closest to the equator during mid- to late summer. The plants begin to turn yellow, and an entire clump may die. If the leaves are pulled the entire plant typically will pull

A close-up of rust infected daylily leaves. The rust appears as orange to brown spots on the leaf. *Photograph by Ted L. Petit.*

A daylily plant infected with daylily rust. Note the orange and brown rust spots. *Photograph by Ted L. Petit.*

from the ground, accompanied by a strong smell of rot. Certain hybrids seem more susceptible to crown rot than others. Some daylily growers suggest using fungicides to treat rotting plants, but once the rot has appeared it is often too late to save the plant. Many daylily enthusiasts insist that any cultivar that appears to be susceptible to rot should not be treated but should be destroyed and culled from the garden, thus insuring that this genetic weakness is not passed on to any progeny through hybridization.

There is no general consensus as to whether crown rot or spring sickness is caused by a bacterial or fungal infection. However, most agree that fungus plays the major, if not total, part in summer crown rot. Because of this, most daylily gardeners do not divide their daylilies in the heat of summer; rather, they wait until the cool of autumn to cut their plants. If it is necessary to divide your daylilies in the summer, treatment with a contact and systemic fungicide greatly reduces the probability of rot. Another trick is to leave the plants out of the ground for one day to dry in the open air. This will allow any open wounds to dry and seal-over before being planted in the ground.

A number of insects can attack the daylily, although none cause serious problems for the average gardener. We have approximately 120,000 daylily

Thrip damage to flower blossom.
Photograph by Ted L. Petit and John P. Peat.

Thrip damage to flower buds. *Photograph by Ted L. Petit and John P. Peat.*

Enlarged, distorted and swollen flower buds showing damage from gall midge. *Photograph by Pam Erikson.*

plants. Such a large-scale monoculture generally leads to increased disease and insect vulnerability, but daylilies are so disease and pest resistant that we do not use any pesticides or other chemicals in the garden to combat these problems. However, under certain conditions some insects will attack the daylily.

Thrips typically thrive in cooler weather, making them a problem mainly in early spring. Thrips are very tiny insects, just barely visible to the naked eye, that resemble the top of an exclamation point (!). They do not kill the daylily, but they attack the developing scape and flower buds. The most common and irritating symptoms of thrip damage are flower buds that fail to develop, turn yellow, and fall off. If the damage is less extensive, the flowers will bloom, but they will be scarred and misshapen from the damage done to the bud. Most gardeners simply ignore this problem and wait for the weather to warm. Other gardeners use pesticides or organic means, such as introduced predators, to control thrips.

Spider mites and aphids are other insect pests that affect daylilies. Spider mites generally attack daylilies that are drought-stressed or grown in greenhouse conditions. They live on the underside of the leaf and create small webs similar to spider webs. Spider mites can be treated with insecticides, but often they can be easily controlled by frequent watering that includes spraying the leaves with water. Aphids, which are small white insects, are also sometimes found on daylily leaves, particularly in the spring. They do little harm and can generally be washed off with water from a garden hose.

Slugs and snails can also attack the daylily, most frequently in cooler wet climates. They chew on the sides of leaves, giving them a ragged edge. They tend to proliferate in wet garden areas, such as in mulch and dead leaves. Slug pellets can be used to control them if necessary. In most regions, simply removing the mulch or dead plant material is usually sufficient for their control.

In Europe and western Canada, the hemerocallis gall fly (or gall midge) has been reported to affect daylilies. The tiny white fly deposits its eggs in the newly forming daylily flower buds. The growing larvae feed on the developing flower bud, which becomes wider, distorted, discolored, and typically drops off before a flower is formed. The recommended treatment is to remove any distorted blooms and destroy them. In North America, the gall midge has been reported for a number of years now in British Columbia. At the time of this writing it has not yet become a major problem in Canada, nor has it spread to the United States.

Most daylily growers insist that the few insect and disease problems that affect daylilies are so minimal that no spraying or other treatment should be used. In fact, many are adamant that chemicals not be used on daylilies, insisting that the plants should be able to resist such maladies with little help other than routine care. They believe that any daylily not able to withstand insects and diseases without chemical intervention has no place in the garden.

PROPAGATION

Daylilies typically increase from one plant, or fan, into several during the average season, soon forming a clump. Early fall is the ideal time to divide daylily clumps, since it gives the newly planted fans a long time to become fully adjusted prior to the next spring's bloom time. Although the plants can be divided into single fans, the flowers often look better if left in small clumps of two to three fans. Large clumps left undivided for years generally produce blooms of inferior quality. Therefore, for optimal enjoyment of the plants, though it is not necessary it is best to divide daylily clumps periodically. It is difficult to suggest exactly how often to divide daylilies, because it depends on how quickly the daylilies divide, which in turn is dependent on the particular variety and where you live. Some daylilies, particularly diploids, will increase rapidly, while others, particularly tetraploids, may take many years to form large clumps. Daylilies generally multiply more rapidly in warmer climates, which also means more frequent dividing.

To divide a clump, first dig it up and remove as much soil as possible from the root mass. The dirt can be removed by spraying the roots with a garden hose. Removing the dirt allows a clearer view of the individual plants and their root masses. Often, plants in a clump will have separated their root systems naturally, allowing you to simply pry the plants apart. If the plants do not pull apart, use a knife to divide them. If the clump is cut into separate plants, make sure that each plant has some roots attached to it. Cutting the plant, however, makes it more susceptible to fungus infection on the open wounds, leading to rot. As mentioned above, it is best not to cut plants during the hot summer months; if forced to divide daylilies in the heat of summer, use a fungicide prior to planting.

Trim the leaves of newly divided plants back to approximately one-half to one-third their original length. Because the roots have been disturbed, the plants are less capable of supplying the leaves with water. Trimming the leaves allows the plant to survive while it reestablishes its root system. While dead or rotten roots can be removed, it is best to leave all live roots on the plant, and not to trim the roots, since the plant needs as much root system as possible to quickly re-establish.

Some daylilies develop proliferations, or small plants, on the flower scapes. Although they typically do not form roots, they can and often do so during prolonged rainy weather. Proliferations can be removed from the scape and treated like any other small plant or cutting. Induce the new plant to form new roots by placing it in a glass of water or treating it as you would a cutting. When the proliferations mature, they will be identical to the mother plant.

A clump of daylilies dug and ready to be divided. *Photograph by Ted L. Petit.*

Three fans being separated from the clump by being pulled apart by hand. *Photograph by Ted L. Petit.*

One fan being cut from the clump of three with a knife. *Photograph by Ted L. Petit.*

A single fan being separated from the clump after being cut. *Photograph by Ted L. Petit.*

A single daylily fan in a small hole in the ground, ready to be planted. *Photograph by Ted L. Petit.*

A single fan after being planted and marked for identification. *Photograph by Ted L. Petit.*

Chapter Thirteen

DAYLILIES
OF THE FUTURE

How can we predict the future, especially for something as complex and diverse as the daylily? A number of years usually elapse for each new hybrid daylily between its maiden bloom and being introduced into commerce. But by looking into the seedling fields of daylily hybridizers, we can catch a glimpse of what the future will hold, at least the near future. Although these plants may not be available for a few years, it is exciting to see the breaks and new features they exhibit. To show some of the newest hybridizing achievements, this book must picture flowers that are "still under number," those that have not yet been named; therefore, the plants in this chapter are grouped by hybridizer. Those who contributed photos to this chapter are listed in Sources for Daylilies and can be contacted directly about their flowers.

There is a long period of time between when a hybridizer first sees an exciting seedling and its eventual introduction into commerce. Initially the seedlings are selected and removed from the seedling field for further evaluation, which can span between three to six years depending on the climate and cultivar. This evaluation generally involves assessing overall plant characteristics (including dormancy, plant measurements, bud count, etc.), as well as the beauty and distinction of the flower. If the hybridizer is satisfied with both the plant and flowering habits, and feels that the daylily is worth introducing, he or she will eventually name the plant and register the name with the American Hemerocallis Society. Most of the daylilies pictured in this chapter are newly discovered seedlings, or seedlings still under evaluation by the hybridizers. These plants, therefore, have not yet been named, or fully evaluated, such that much of the information pertaining to the plant is currently not available. A few of the cultivars pictured are further along in this evaluation process; therefore, they have either already been named or more complete information has been supplied and is included.

These latest seedlings show many future trends in the daylily. Crosses between plants of differing hardiness are producing daylily plants much more tolerant of a wide climatic range. Flowers are becoming larger, with sturdier scapes, and flower substance is heavier and thicker, resulting in more weather-resistant blooms. Efforts to extend the bloom season continue to increase branching, bud count, and recurrent bloom. Carved and sculpted textures within the petal are adding a whole new dimension to the look of the flower. And the original push to widen the petals and make the daylily a round flower continues—many future cultivars are close to achieving this goal.

Flower colors are becoming clearer and more intense. The whites are whiter, and the reds and purples are more saturated and sun-fast. The elusive blue daylily appears to be on the horizon, developing out of the blue eyes. Eye patterns are larger, more dramatic and complicated, and available in a diverse range of colors. The latest styles mimic rainbows, butterfly wings, spider webs, and concentric circles. Stippled patterns are more pronounced and refined. Patterned daylilies generally are becoming more exotic and complex.

Picotee edges are becoming wider and more pronounced, including multiple colors or shades, often mimicking the pattern within the eye. These picotee edges are often surrounded by gold or lighter ornate edges. With the widening of the picotees and the expanding of the eyes, the petal self is progressively shrinking. The light edges are more complex, often involving gold, silver, yellow, orange, white, and more. These edges are often diamond-dusted, creating a sparkling and glittering effect in the sun. The ornate edges are becoming wider, too, and vary in texture from shark's teeth to hooks and horns, often combined with intense ruffling and crimping. In addition to gold or orange edges, we are now seeing chartreuse and green edges.

Spiders are growing narrower and larger, with ornate toothed and gold edges. Unusual forms are more diverse and consistent, often combining twisted and curled segments within one flower. Doubles are more fully double, with ornate gold and picotee edges and increased size and bud count. The relatively new midrib doubling is becoming very popular. Miniatures are even smaller, with double and tetraploid miniatures starting to appear.

The daylily is changing and evolving at an accelerating pace. Looking at the latest innovations makes the future possibilities seem endless. Clearly, in the years to come the daylily's beauty and popularity as a garden plant will be increasing around the world. Some flower forms, such as the tetraploid doubles, spiders, and miniatures, are in their infancy, as are polytepals and unusual form daylilies. It is exciting to think about what the future might bring to these flower types as well as others. If the trends outlined above continue, the singles will be round, ruffled, heavily substanced, and in every possible color, with ornate contrasting eyes, watermarks, and edges. The doubles will also share many of these features, while the spiders will probably become enormous and ornately decorated, and the five-petaled polytepal will likely become a reality. The future of the daylily appears to be limited only by the imagination of hybridizers everywhere, and the flower will surely continue to change as long as people can dream.

(Linda Agin, Seedling) A rose-red flower with patterned eyezone and white ruffled shark's teeth edge above a green center. *Photograph by Linda Agin.*

(Linda Agin, Seedling) A very wide-petaled deep dark red with a white wire edge above a green throat. *Photograph by Linda Agin.*

(Linda Agin, Seedling) A grape-purple with a lighter purple watermark and with a white shark's teeth edge on both the petals and sepals. *Photograph by Linda Agin.*

(Linda Agin, Seedling) A heavily ruffled wide-petaled baby-ribbon pink with a gold edge and a bright green throat. *Photograph by Linda Agin.*

(Linda Agin, Seedling) An extravagantly ruffled bright yellow flower with an apple-green throat. *Photograph by Linda Agin.*

(Linda Agin, Seedling) A heavily ruffled cream-yellow with a pink-blush above a green throat. *Photograph by Linda Agin.*

(Linda Agin, Seedling) A deep royal dark purple flower with a lighter grayish watermark and with an extremely toothy white edge. *Photograph by Linda Agin.*

(Linda Agin, Seedling) A cream with a narrow halo eyezone and picotee edge surrounded by a heavily ruffled gold edge. *Photograph by Linda Agin.*

(Linda Agin, Seedling) A dark purple with a large bluish eyezone and matching picotee surrounded by a wire white edge. *Photograph by Linda Agin.*

(Linda Agin, Seedling) A cream-pink flower with a triple edge of rose, pink, and gold, as well as a patterned eyezone above a green throat. *Photograph by Linda Agin.*

(Linda Agin, Seedling) A light lavender-rose self with a dark blue-violet eyezone and matching ruffled picotee edge surrounded by a wire gold edge. *Photograph by Linda Agin.*

(Linda Agin, Seedling) A tightly ruffled lavender with a slate gray-blue complex eyezone and matching picotee surrounded by white shark's teeth. *Photograph by Linda Agin.*

(Linda Agin, Seedling) A ruffled cream-lavender with a patterned gray-blue eyezone and matching picotee surrounded by a gold edge. *Photograph by Linda Agin.*

(Linda Agin, Seedling) A burgundy-purple flower with a wide gold edge and a wire bluish picotee and matching wire eyezone. *Photograph by Linda Agin.*

(Linda Agin, Seedling) A burgundy-rose flower with a lighter watermark, a green throat, and a white shark's teeth edge. *Photograph by Linda Agin.*

(Linda Agin, Seedling) An extremely wide-petaled very round pink flower with overlapping petals and a wide gold edge above a yellow to green throat. *Photograph by Linda Agin.*

(Linda Agin, Seedling) A cream-pink with a bright green throat and a heavily fringed gold edge. *Photograph by Linda Agin.*

(Linda Agin, Seedling) A wide-petaled grape-purple with a lighter bluish watermark eyezone and with a matching wire picotee surrounded by white shark's teeth. *Photograph by Linda Agin.*

(Linda Agin, Seedling) A cream with a peachy pink-blush with heavily ruffled, wide chartreuse-lemon edge and a matching lemon to green throat. *Photograph by Linda Agin.*

(Linda Agin, Seedling) A heavy substanced blue-pink self with a green throat and tightly crimped gold edges. *Photograph by Linda Agin.*

(Linda Agin, Seedling) A bright yellow to chartreuse flower with a deep green throat and matching ruffled deep green edge. *Photograph by Linda Agin.*

(Linda Agin, Seedling) A wide-petaled rose-purple self with a large light watermark, surrounded by ruffled pink and white edges above a green throat. *Photograph by Linda Agin.*

(Linda Agin, Seedling) A huge near-white purple watermark and surrounding light edge on a purple-rose self above a green throat. *Photograph by Linda Agin.*

(Linda Agin, Seedling) A large blue-violet eyezone and matching edge on a purple self with a green throat. *Photograph by Linda Agin.*

(Linda Agin, Seedling) A cream-pink flower with a green throat and a serrated, toothy chartreuse edge. *Photograph by Linda Agin.*

(Richard Aubin, Seedling) A lightly ruffled peach, orange-gold polychrome with a dark green edge and deep green heart. *Photograph by Richard Aubin.*

(Dan Bachman, Seedling) A red unusual formed flower with twisted and curled petals and sepals above a large yellow to green throat. *Photograph by Dan Bachman.*

(Richard Aubin, Seedling) A triangular formed peach-pink self with a darker rose eyezone and matching picotee surrounded by large gold shark's teeth. *Photograph by Richard Aubin.*

(Dan Bachman, Seedling) A black-red very narrow-petaled diploid with a large yellow-gold throat and lighter midribs. *Photograph by Dan Bachman.*

(Dan Bachman, Seedling) A very bright red unusual form with twisted and curled sepals and petals highlighted with lighter midribs. *Photograph by Dan Bachman.*

(Dan Bachman, Seedling) An orange-red with a large green throat displayed on the petals and sepals carrying a wire white edge. *Photograph by Dan Bachman.*

(Dan Bachman, Seedling) A black-red velvety narrow-petaled flower with a large yellow to green throat. *Photograph by Dan Bachman.*

(Tim Bell, Seedling) A lavender self with an applique throat surrounded by a dark purple-patterned eyezone with a matching lightly ruffled picotee edge. *Photograph by Tim Bell.*

(Dan Bachman, Seedling) An orange-red very narrow-petaled flower with a large yellow to green throat with twisted and curled sepals. *Photograph by Dan Bachman.*

(Dan Bachman, Seedling) A burgundy self with wide lighter midribs and ruffled, hooked, and knobby gold edge. *Photograph by Dan Bachman.*

(Tim Bell, Seedling) A large wide-petaled extravagantly formed lavender with a violet and purple edge and chevron halo surrounded by a heavily ruffled gold edge. *Photograph by Tim Bell.*

(Tim Bell, Seedling) A wide-petaled apricot self with a heavily ruffled, pleated edge. *Photograph by Tim Bell.*

(Tim Bell, Seedling) A wide-petaled lavender-purple with a lighter watermark and a ruffled gold edge. *Photograph by Tim Bell.*

(Tim Bell, Seedling) An apricot self with an intricately-patterned eyezone of burgundy-purple and a narrow matching picotee. *Photograph by Tim Bell.*

(Tim Bell, Seedling) A light lavender with a heavily ruffled gold edge and a darker picotee without an eyezone. *Photograph by Tim Bell.*

(Tim Bell, Seedling) A grape-purple with a large lighter watermark with a wire darker purple band and matching picotee surrounded by a ruffled gold edge. *Photograph by Tim Bell.*

(Tim Bell, Seedling) An apricot-peach self with dark green heart and a heavily ruffled gold edge. *Photograph by Tim Bell.*

(Tim Bell, Seedling) A large cream-white with a huge dark purple eyezone and thick matching picotee surrounded by a ruffled gold-white edge. *Photograph by Tim Bell.*

'MA × LMH' (Oliver Billingslea, Seedling) A deep royal-purple with a bluish cast with a light lavender watermark and matching picotee surrounded by a wire gold ruffled edge. *Photograph by Oliver Billingslea.*

'Specially For Sarah' (Oliver Billingslea, Seedling) A wide-petaled tangerine-orange with heavy ruffles with a dark green heart. *Photograph by Oliver Billingslea.*

(Tim Bell, Seedling) A salmon-pink with a large heavily ruffled gold edge with a green center. *Photograph by Tim Bell.*

'MMM × KLI-3' (Oliver Billingslea, Seedling) A thick substanced copper-orange with a heavily ruffled edge. *Photograph by Oliver Billingslea.*

'Stars and Angels' (Oliver Billingslea, Seedling) A heavily ruffled rose self with a wire white edge above a large chevron watermark and a tiny green center. *Photograph by Oliver Billingslea.*

(Josie Bomar, Seedling) A huge rose-pink with a heavily ruffled crimped edge above a green center. *Photograph by Josie Bomar.*

(Jack B. Carpenter, Seedling) A cream self with a very large complex-patterned eye of concentric dark purple and lighter bands and darker veins. *Photograph by Jack B. Carpenter.*

(Jeff Corbett, Seedling) A wide-petaled cream-peach with a very large, round candy-apple red eyezone and matching picotee above a green center. *Photograph by Jeff Corbett.*

(Jack B. Carpenter, Seedling) A wide-petaled cream-pink flower with a rose-red eyezone and matching very wide picotee surrounded by a huge ruffled gold edge. *Photograph by Jack B. Carpenter.*

(Jeff Corbett, Seedling) A pale cream-pink with a green throat and a beautifully ruffled gold edge. *Photograph by Jeff Corbett.*

(Jeff Corbett, Seedling) A bright burgundy-red double with a wire white edge. *Photograph by Jeff Corbett.*

(George Doorakian, Seedling) A narrow-petaled burgundy-red with a very large triangular yellow to green throat. *Photograph by George Doorakian.*

(George Doorakian, Seedling) A burgundy-red, narrow-petaled, twisted and curled unusual form with a large yellow to green throat. *Photograph by George Doorakian.*

(George Doorakian, Seedling) A royal-purple flower with a striking lightly ruffled white edge and a large triangular yellow to bright green throat. *Photograph by George Doorakian.*

(George Doorakian, Seedling) A dark purple with a very large yellow to dark green throat. *Photograph by George Doorakian.*

(George Doorakian, Seedling) A gray-blue flower with a large dark burgundy-purple eyezone above a yellow to green throat. *Photograph by George Doorakian.*

(George Doorakian, Seedling) A near-white flower with a triple-banded patterned eyezone of dark purple, gray-blue, and grape-purple. *Photograph by George Doorakian.*

(George Doorakian, Seedling) A narrow-petaled, lightly ruffled, unusual formed flower with a narrow, purple chevron-shaped eyezone above a bright green throat. *Photograph by George Doorakian.*

(George Doorakian, Seedling) A dark yellow-gold flower with a wide cream-white lightly ruffled edge above a dark green center. *Photograph by George Doorakian.*

(George Doorakian, Seedling) A lightly ruffled, grape-purple, narrow-petaled flower with a large striking yellow to green throat. *Photograph by George Doorakian.*

(George Doorakian, Seedling) A dark grape-purple with a large cream watermark, a wire white edge above a yellow to green throat. *Photograph by George Doorakian.*

(George Doorakian, Seedling) A lightly ruffled golden yellow flower with a very large dark green throat mimicked on both the petals and sepals. *Photograph by George Doorakian.*

(Karol Emmerich, Seedling) A large blue-violet eyezone and picotee with a burgundy halo on a purple flower above a green throat. *Photograph by Karol Emmerich.*

(George Doorakian, Seedling) A grape-purple flower with a darker purple eyezone and creamy yellow-patterned applique throat above a green center. *Photograph by George Doorakian.*

(George Doorakian, Seedling) A dark burgundy-purple flower with rolled back petals and a large yellow to green throat that appears to take up the whole flower face. *Photograph by George Doorakian.*

(Karol Emmerich, Seedling) A burgundy flower with a large-patterned violet eyezone on petals and sepals above a green throat. *Photograph by Karol Emmerich.*

(George Doorakian, Seedling) A lightly ruffled gray-burgundy flower with a dark burgundy-purple eyezone above a yellow to green throat. *Photograph by George Doorakian.*

(George Doorakian, Seedling) A golden yellow with a lighter, lightly ruffled, lemon-yellow edge above a large dark green throat. *Photograph by George Doorakian.*

(Karol Emmerich, Seedling) A large blue-violet eyezone and picotee on a burgundy flower. *Photograph by Karol Emmerich.*

(Karol Emmerich, Seedling) A large burgundy-purple flower with a faint bluish eyezone and matching picotee surrounded by a ruffled gold edge. *Photograph by Karol Emmerich.*

(Karol Emmerich, Seedling) A rich dark purple flower with a lighter watermark and very ruffled white-gold edge. *Photograph by Karol Emmerich.*

(Karol Emmerich, Seedling) A large burgundy-rose flower with a violet-blue eyezone and matching picotee surrounded by a heavily ruffled gold edge. *Photograph by Karol Emmerich.*

(Karol Emmerich, Seedling) A very round bright red flower with a lighter watermark and a heavily ruffled gold edge. *Photograph by Karol Emmerich.*

(Karol Emmerich, Seedling) A dark, rich purple flower with a lighter watermark, a green throat, and heavy white shark's teeth edge. *Photograph by Karol Emmerich.*

(Karol Emmerich, Seedling) A bright golden yellow, extremely heavily ruffled flower. *Photograph by Karol Emmerich.*

(Karol Emmerich, Seedling) A narrow formed, peach-pink flower with a darker-patterned eyezone on both petals and sepals. *Photograph by Karol Emmerich.*

(Karol Emmerich, Seedling) A mango-apricot flower with a blue-violet eyezone and picotee with a second gold edge. *Photograph by Karol Emmerich.*

(Karol Emmerich, Seedling) A dark burgundy-purple flower with a lighter watermark and a very wide white, fringed, toothy edge. *Photograph by Karol Emmerich.*

(Karol Emmerich, Seedling) An apricot with a large washed darker-patterned eyezone and matching washed picotee surrounded by a ruffled gold edge. *Photograph by Karol Emmerich.*

(Karol Emmerich, Seedling) A creamy salmon-pink flower with a huge burgundy-purple eyezone and edge covering most of the flower face. *Photograph by Karol Emmerich.*

(Karol Emmerich, Seedling) A very ruffled, heavy substanced purple flower with a large lighter watermark above a green throat. *Photograph by Karol Emmerich.*

(Karol Emmerich, Seedling) A clear rose-red flower with a large green throat and with a lighter watermark below a ruffled gold edge. *Photograph by Karol Emmerich.*

(Sharon Fitzpatrick, Seedling) An unusual formed pink with a large muted burgundy eyezone with twisted and curled sepals. *Photograph by Sharon Fitzpatrick.*

(Sharon Fitzpatrick, Seedling) A blush-pink with a large yellow to green throat with twisted and spooned petals and petaloids. *Photograph by Sharon Fitzpatrick.*

(James Gossard, Seedling) A narrow-formed burgundy flower with a darker eyezone and very toothy fringed edge. *Photograph by James Gossard.*

(Sharon Fitzpatrick, Seedling) A large baby-ribbon pink flower with a huge green throat. *Photograph by Sharon Fitzpatrick.*

(Sharon Fitzpatrick, Seedling) A grape-purple flower with a large yellow to green throat and a wire white edge. *Photograph by Sharon Fitzpatrick.*

(James Gossard, Seedling) A yellow narrow-formed flower with a multicolored patterned eyezone on the petals and sepals. *Photograph by James Gossard.*

(James Gossard, Seedling) A cream-mauve flower with a patterned eyezone of blue, charcoal, and burgundy above a green throat. *Photograph by James Gossard.*

(James Gossard, Seedling) A cream-mauve flower with a dark navy-blue eyezone surrounded by a burgundy band. *Photograph by James Gossard.*

(James Gossard, Seedling) A fire-engine red flower with a yellow to green throat and a gold, bubbly, and toothy edge. *Photograph by James Gossard.*

(James Gossard, Seedling) A dark burgundy flower with a multibanded patterned eyezone on the petals and sepals. *Photograph by James Gossard.*

(James Gossard, Seedling) A burgundy-rose double with very ruffled petals and petaloids. *Photograph by James Gossard.*

(James Gossard, Seedling) A dark burgundy-purple with a heavily fringed, toothy edge above a dark green throat. *Photograph by James Gossard.*

(Larry Grace, Seedling) A very heavy substanced peach self with a deep green throat and matching ruffled edge. *Photograph by Larry Grace.*

(James Gossard, Seedling) A dark purple flower with a green throat and a very toothy white edge on the petals and sepals. *Photograph by James Gossard.*

(James Gossard, Seedling) A near-black dark purple flower with a green throat and lighter, charcoal-brown edges. *Photograph by James Gossard.*

(James Gossard, Seedling) A dark yellow narrow-petaled double spider variant with a huge green throat. *Photograph by James Gossard.*

(James Gossard, Seedling) A cream-yellow with a complex-patterned burgundy-red eyezone above a green throat. *Photograph by James Gossard.*

(Larry Grace, Seedling) An extremely wide-petaled and sepaled round flower of rose-pink with a dark red eyezone and matching wire picotee edge. *Photograph by Larry Grace.*

(Larry Grace, Seedling) A soft melon-peach self with a nicely ruffled chartreuse edge above a green throat. *Photograph by Larry Grace.*

(Larry Grace, Seedling) A beautifully ruffled dark grape-purple flower with very heavy substance and a wire gold edge and a lighter watermark surrounding a green throat. *Photograph by Larry Grace.*

(Larry Grace, Seedling) A clear dark yellow to gold heavy substanced wide-petaled round flower with extremely wide sepals. *Photograph by Larry Grace.*

(Larry Grace, Seedling) A cream self with a dark purple eyezone and matching ruffled picotee edge above a large bold green throat. *Photograph by Larry Grace.*

(Larry Grace, Seedling) A rich dark velvety red self with a lighter watermark and a nicely ruffled wire gold edge above a dark green center. *Photograph by Larry Grace.*

(Larry Grace, Seedling) A peach-pink self with an extremely wide, heavily ruffled gold edge and a small green heart. *Photograph by Larry Grace.*

(Larry Grace, Seedling) A beautiful clear lavender self with a nicely ruffled gold edge and a golden watermark above a yellow to green throat. *Photograph by Larry Grace.*

(Larry Grace, Seedling) A beautifully formed round melon flower with heavy ruffled edges and extremely wide sepals. *Photograph by Larry Grace.*

(Larry Grace, Seedling) A nicely ruffled golden yellow self with a complex burgundy-purple eyezone. *Photograph by Larry Grace.*

(Larry Grace, Seedling) A near-black dark purple with an extremely pronounced gold and white shark's teeth edge above a green throat. *Photograph by Larry Grace.*

(Larry Grace, Seedling) A grape-purple self with a patterned eyezone surrounding a deep green throat. *Photograph by Larry Grace.*

(Larry Grace, Seedling) A tan-peach self with a violet-lavender eyezone and matching lightly ruffled picotee edge. *Photograph by Larry Grace.*

(Larry Grace, Seedling) A very heavy substanced melon-peach self with an extremely ruffled green edge above a deep dark green throat. *Photograph by Larry Grace.*

(Larry Grace, Seedling) A melon to mango self with a green- to purple-patterned eye on extremely heavy substanced, ruffled and pinched petals. *Photograph by Larry Grace.*

(Larry Grace, Seedling) A very large navy-blue patterned eyezone above a green throat, with wire violet picotee on a cream self. *Photograph by Larry Grace.*

(Larry Grace, Seedling) A huge near-black dark purple eyezone and wide matching picotee on a lavender-rose self and a green throat. *Photograph by Larry Grace.*

(Larry Grace, Seedling) A bright orange-gold flower with a lighter gold watermark and ruffled edges above a green throat. *Photograph by Larry Grace.*

(Larry Grace, Seedling) A melon to orange flower with a deep green throat and matching deep green ruffled edge. *Photograph by Larry Grace.*

(Larry Grace, Seedling) A very round, wide-petaled raspberry-red flower with a green heart and ruffled gold to chartreuse edges. *Photograph by Larry Grace.*

(Larry Grace, Seedling) A peach to melon-pink flower with a deep green heart, lighter watermark, and heavily ruffled chartreuse to green edge. *Photograph by Larry Grace.*

(Larry Grace, Seedling) A heavily substanced peach-mango self with a huge green throat and shadow lavender to silver eyezone. *Photograph by Larry Grace.*

(Larry Grace, Seedling) A deep purple self with a blue-violet eye and ruffled silver to white edges. *Photograph by Larry Grace.*

(Larry Grace, Seedling) A lightly patterned silver eyezone above a large deep green throat on a mango self. *Photograph by Larry Grace.*

(Larry Grace, Seedling) An unusual lavender to rose self with an orange watermark and matching picotee, surrounded by a heavily ruffled chartreuse edge. *Photograph by Larry Grace.*

(Larry Grace, Seedling) A heavy substanced melon-pink self with a deep green throat and matching green ruffled edges. *Photograph by Larry Grace.*

(Larry Grace, Seedling) A beautifully formed dark red with a gold filagree edge, a green throat and a very unusual patterned watermark extending far out on both sides of the petal midrib. *Photograph by Larry Grace.*

(Robert Grant-Downton, Seedling) An apricot self surrounded by a lacy, knobby, hooked edge of gold on the petals and sepals. *Photograph by Robert Grant-Downton.*

(Fran Harding, Seedling) A heavily hooked and knobby edge of gold on a soft melon-pink self above a tiny green center. *Photograph by Fran Harding.*

(Larry Grace, Seedling) A rich burgundy-purple with wide sepals, a deep green throat, lighter watermark, and golden chartreuse edge. *Photograph by Larry Grace.*

(Fran Harding, Seedling) A heavily ruffled cream-pink self with a tangerine to green throat. *Photograph by Fran Harding.*

(Fran Harding, Seedling) A peachy tangerine-pink with an extremely hooked and fringy edge above a tiny green heart. *Photograph by Fran Harding.*

(Stan and Bonnie Holley, Seedling) An ivory-cream flower with a striking burgundy-red eyezone and matching picotee above a green throat. *Photograph by Stan Holley.*

(Stan and Bonnie Holley, Seedling) An apricot-cream double with a heavy ruffled gold edge above a dark green center. *Photograph by Stan Holley.*

(Stan and Bonnie Holley, Seedling) A bright golden yellow flower with a green throat and very large looping ruffles. *Photograph by Stan Holley.*

(Stan and Bonnie Holley, Seedling) A burgundy-red double with shark's teeth on the petals and petaloids. *Photograph by Stan Holley.*

(Stan and Bonnie Holley, Seedling) A bright orange double with a large red eyezone and picotee on the petals and petaloids. *Photograph by Stan Holley.*

(Stan and Bonnie Holley, Seedling) A bright burgundy-red flower with extremely wide petals and a heavy gold edge above a green throat. *Photograph by Stan Holley.*

(Sandy Holmes, Seedling) An unusual formed dark purple with twisted and spooned sepals above a yellow to green throat. *Photograph by Michael Holmes.*

(Sandy Holmes, Seedling) An unusual formed rose-pink flower with a dark green throat below a lighter pink-rose watermark. *Photograph by Michael Holmes.*

(Sandy Holmes, Seedling) A narrow-petaled lavender self with a darker banded eyezone and a large yellow throat above a dark green center. *Photograph by Michael Holmes.*

(Sandy Holmes, Seedling) A dark purple self with a complex throat of green, yellow, and burgundy below a lighter watermark eyezone. *Photograph by Michael Holmes.*

(Sandy Holmes, Seedling) A burgundy-purple with a complex eyezone of dark purple to varying shades of purple above a dark green center. *Photograph by Michael Holmes.*

(Aaron Joiner, Seedling) A purple double with a ruffled gold edge on both the petals and sepals. *Photograph by Leslie Immel.*

(Enman R. Joiner, Seedling) A bright lavender with a violet-purple eyezone and matching picotee edge surrounded by a ruffled gold edge. *Photograph by Leslie Immel.*

(Enman R. Joiner, Seedling) A large rose-pink with a lightly ruffled gold edge sporting tiny shark's teeth. *Photograph by Leslie Immel.*

(Aaron Joiner, Seedling) A dark black-purple with a ruffled gold edge sporting tiny shark's teeth and knobs above a yellow throat. *Photograph by Leslie Immel.*

(Enman R. Joiner, Seedling) A rose-peach hose-and-hose double with narrow petals and a large bright tangerine-orange eyezone. *Photograph by Leslie Immel.*

(Jan Joiner, Seedling) A large burnt orange double with a darker eyezone and a lightly ruffled edge. *Photograph by Francis Joiner.*

(Aaron Joiner, Seedling) A bright peach-orange double with a large burgundy-red eyezone and a wire serrated gold edge. *Photograph by Leslie Immel.*

(Jan Joiner, Seedling) An unusual formed bright red double self with a wire white edge above an orange throat. *Photograph by Leslie Immel.*

(Jan Joiner, Seedling) A yellow double with a nicely ruffled edge above a green center. *Photograph by Leslie Immel.*

(Jan Joiner, Seedling) A lavender-purple with a heavy gold, knobby edge above a bright yellow to lime-green throat. *Photograph by Leslie Immel.*

(Jack Kent, Seedling) A cream five-petaled polytepal with a large purple eyezone and wire gold edge above a green throat. *Photograph by Jack Kent.*

'John Edward Kent' (Jack Kent, Seedling) A vibrant, bright, glowing orange flower with a dark burgundy eyezone and picotee above a green throat. *Photograph by Jack Kent.*

(John Kinnebrew, Seedling) A cream flower with a rich, dark black-purple eyezone and matching picotee surrounded by a gold edge. *Photograph by John Kinnebrew.*

(John Kinnebrew, Seedling) A bright yellow to gold with a near-black velvety eyezone and matching picotee above a green throat. *Photograph by John Kinnebrew.*

(John Kinnebrew, Seedling) A very bright golden yellow, wide-petaled, round flower with a striking green throat. *Photograph by John Kinnebrew.*

(John Kinnebrew, Seedling) A rose-burgundy flower with a lighter watermark, a green throat, and heavy, bubbly gold edge. *Photograph by John Kinnebrew.*

(John Kinnebrew, Seedling) A very dark black-red velvety flower with a green throat. *Photograph by John Kinnebrew.*

(John Kinnebrew, Seedling) A bright orange to gold flower with very deeply sculpted surface and with heavily ruffled petals. *Photograph by John Kinnebrew.*

(John Kinnebrew, Seedling) A large cream-orange double flower with a large violet-patterned eyezone on petals and petaloids. *Photograph by John Kinnebrew.*

(John Kinnebrew, Seedling) A lavender-pink flower with a green throat and a heavy gold edge. *Photograph by John Kinnebrew.*

(John Kinnebrew, Seedling) An apricot-peach flower with a large applique-patterned throat surrounded by a wide violet eyezone and picotee edge. *Photograph by John Kinnebrew.*

(John Kinnebrew, Seedling) A dark red flower with a lighter watermark and a heavy, ruffled, gold edge on wide petals. *Photograph by John Kinnebrew.*

(John Kinnebrew, Seedling) A bright, creamy, golden yellow flower with a very bright candy-apple red eyezone and picotee above a green throat. *Photograph by John Kinnebrew.*

(John Kinnebrew, Seedling) An orange-melon flower with a very large applique, palm-shaped throat beneath a radiating violet eyezone. *Photograph by John Kinnebrew.*

(John Kinnebrew, Seedling) An orange-gold flower with a radiating large applique-patterned throat surrounded by a burgundy eyezone. *Photograph by John Kinnebrew.*

(David Kirchhoff, Seedling) A wide-petaled, very ruffled dark coral-pink with a green heart. *Photograph by David Kirchhoff.*

(David Kirchhoff, Seedling) An orange-sherbet double flower with an extremely toothy fringed edge. *Photograph by David Kirchhoff.*

(John Kinnebrew, Seedling) A burnt orange flower with a large applique throat overlaying a deeply sculpted purple eyezone. *Photograph by John Kinnebrew.*

(David Kirchhoff, Seedling) A dark, deep red lightly ruffled self with a yellow to green throat. *Photograph by David Kirchhoff.*

(David Kirchhoff, Seedling) A wide-petaled bright red flower with a wire white edge above a dark green center. *Photograph by David Kirchhoff.*

(David Kirchhoff, Seedling) A lavender-pink double with a striking gold edge and a large lighter watermark above a green throat. *Photograph by David Kirchhoff.*

(David Kirchhoff, Seedling) A ruffled cream-white double flower with a slate grayish blue-patterned eyezone on the petals and petaloids above a green throat. *Photograph by David Kirchhoff.*

(David Kirchhoff, Seedling) A bright orange-gold flower with a deep green throat with cut petals forming large triangular center points. *Photograph by David Kirchhoff.*

(David Kirchhoff, Seedling) A ruffled red flower with a large triangular yellow to green throat. *Photograph by David Kirchhoff.*

(David Kirchhoff, Seedling) A grape-purple double flower with a white shark's teeth edge on the petals and petaloids. *Photograph by David Kirchhoff.*

(David Kirchhoff, Seedling) A soft lavender-pink double with a lighter watermark and a gold shark's teeth edge. *Photograph by David Kirchhoff.*

(David Kirchhoff, Seedling) A wide-petaled lavender-pink double with a wire gold lightly ruffled and serrated edge. *Photograph by David Kirchhoff.*

(Phil Korth, Seedling) A nicely ruffled wide-petaled red self with a slightly lighter watermark above a tiny green center. *Photograph by Phil Korth.*

(Phil Korth, Seedling) A beautifully ruffled burgundy-rose flower with a tightly crimped gold edge. *Photograph by Phil Korth.*

(David Kirchhoff, Seedling) A lightly ruffled rose-red double flower with a wire gold edge. *Photograph by David Kirchhoff.*

(Phil Korth, Seedling) A bright fire-engine red self with a darker eyezone and a gold ruffled edge sporting shark's teeth on both sepals and petals. *Photograph by Phil Korth.*

(Ludlow Lambertson, Seedling) A cream-tangerine self with a large violet-blue eyezone and picotee edge surrounded by a ruffled wire gold edge. *Photograph by Ludlow Lambertson.*

(Ludlow Lambertson, Seedling) A lavender-purple with violet-blue eyezone and picotee edge surrounded by gold shark's teeth. *Photograph by Ludlow Lambertson.*

(Ludlow Lambertson, Seedling) An unusual formed cream-peach with large chevron purple eyezone above a yellow to green throat. *Photograph by Ludlow Lambertson.*

(Ludlow Lambertson, Seedling) A cream-violet self with a violet-blue eyezone surrounded by a wire purple band and matching ruffled picotee edge surrounded in gold. *Photograph by Ludlow Lambertson.*

(Ludlow Lambertson, Seedling) A heavily ruffled light tangerine self with a violet-blue eyezone and ruffled picotee surrounded by an orange edge above an orange-yellow applique throat. *Photograph by Ludlow Lambertson.*

(Ludlow Lambertson, Seedling) A cream-white flower with a double eyezone of purple and violet-blue carrying out as a picotee edge surrounded in gold. *Photograph by Ludlow Lambertson.*

(Ludlow Lambertson, Seedling) A purple self with a violet-blue eyezone and matching ruffled picotee sporting bright white shark's teeth. *Photograph by Ludlow Lambertson.*

(Ludlow Lambertson, Seedling) A cream-peach self with a huge violet-purple eyezone and matching wide, ruffled picotee edge surrounded in gold. *Photograph by Ludlow Lambertson.*

(Ludlow Lambertson, Seedling) A burgundy-purple with a large violet-blue eyezone and matching picotee edge surrounded by a wire white edge. *Photograph by Ludlow Lambertson.*

(Tommy Maddox, Seedling) A wide-petaled cream-yellow with a purple eyezone and matching picotee surrounded by a ruffled gold edge above a green throat. *Photograph by Tommy Maddox.*

(Ludlow Lambertson, Seedling) A lavender flower with a violet-blue eyezone and matching wide picotee edge surrounded by a ruffled gold edge. *Photograph by Ludlow Lambertson.*

(Ludlow Lambertson, Seedling) A burgundy-rose with a large violet-blue eyezone and matching ruffled picotee above a bright green center. *Photograph by Ludlow Lambertson.*

(Tommy Maddox, Seedling) A creamy peach-pink flower with a burgundy eyezone and matching picotee edge surrounded by a nicely ruffled gold edge. *Photograph by Tommy Maddox.*

'Mr. Juggles' (Barry Matthie, Seedling) A large red spider variant with twisted and curled petals and sepals above a large orange to green throat. *Photograph by Barry Matthie.*

(Barry Matthie, Seedling) A large golden yellow spider with lightly ruffled edges on curled petals and sepals above a large green throat. *Photograph by Barry Matthie.*

(Barry Matthie, Seedling) A narrow-petaled purple bitone variant with a large green to yellow applique throat. *Photograph by Barry Matthie.*

(Barry Matthie, Seedling) A cream-yellow spider variant with nicely ruffled, twisted, curled, and spooned petals and sepals with a large green throat. *Photograph by Barry Matthie.*

(Barry Matthie, Seedling) A burnt orange variant with an orange-red eyezone above a yellow to green throat. *Photograph by Barry Matthie.*

(Barry Matthie, Seedling) A small-flowered cream-lavender with a purple eyezone and picotee surrounded in gold shark's teeth, 100 percent double. *Photograph by Barry Matthie.*

(Barry Matthie, Seedling) A narrow-petaled light burgundy spider variant with twisted and curled petals and sepals with a super large yellow to green throat. *Photograph by Barry Matthie.*

(Barry Matthie, Seedling) A cream-yellow flower with a giant chevron burgundy eyezone on the petals and sepals above a bright green throat. *Photograph by Barry Matthie.*

(Barry Matthie, Seedling) A large velvety burgundy narrow-petaled flower with a dark purple-black eyezone and matching wire picotee edge. *Photograph by Barry Matthie.*

(Barry Matthie, Seedling) A burgundy flower with a double eyezone of violet and purple and a matching picotee surrounded by a wire gold edge. *Photograph by Barry Matthie.*

(Barry Matthie, Seedling) A cream-yellow flower with a large black eyezone on the petals and sepals and matching picotee above a bright green throat. *Photograph by Barry Matthie.*

(Barry Matthie, Seedling) A narrow-petaled burgundy with a complex eyezone of four bands above a yellow to green throat. *Photograph by Barry Matthie.*

(Barry Matthie, Seedling) A bright orange with a large burgundy-purple eyezone with a matching picotee above a green throat. *Photograph by Barry Matthie.*

(Barry Matthie, Seedling) A narrow-petaled cream-rose with a large dark red chevron eyezone mimicked on the sepals above a bright green throat. *Photograph by Barry Matthie.*

(Michael Miller, Seedling) A wide-petaled pink flower with a nicely ruffled gold edge and a lighter watermark above a bright green throat. *Photograph by Michael Miller.*

(Barry Matthie, Seedling) A cream flower with a huge dark velvety purple eyezone that covers most of the petals above a green center. *Photograph by Barry Matthie.*

(Barry Matthie, Seedling) A tangerine-orange wide-petaled flower with a large burgundy eyezone and matching picotee with a lightly ruffled gold edge. *Photograph by Barry Matthie.*

(Michael Miller, Seedling) A wide-petaled peach self with carving on the petals and tightly crimped, serrated, gold shark's teeth edge. *Photograph by Michael Miller.*

(Michael Miller, Seedling) A large red spider variant with white midribs and lightly spooned sepals above a large yellow to green throat. *Photograph by Michael Miller.*

(Michael Miller, Seedling) A narrow-petaled white spider variant with twisted and curled petals and sepals above a large yellow to green throat. *Photograph by Michael Miller.*

(Michael Miller, Seedling) A purple variant with a large light cream-purple watermark above a yellow to green throat. *Photograph by Michael Miller.*

(Michael Miller, Seedling) A large light yellow lightly ruffled variant with twisted and curled petals and sepals above a bright green throat. *Photograph by Michael Miller.*

(Michael Miller, Seedling) A large narrow-petaled, lightly ruffled orange spider variant with twisted and often spooned sepals. *Photograph by Michael Miller.*

'Lavendar Hearthrob' × 'Leaving Me Breathless' (Keith Miner, Seedling) A dark grape-purple self with a nicely ruffled golden white edge with a lighter violet watermark. Honorable Mention 2007. *Photograph by Keith Miner.*

'Mandalay Bay Music' × 'See His Glory' (Keith Miner, Seedling) A wide-petaled cream-pink with a nicely ruffled gold to chartreuse edge above a bright green throat. *Photograph by Keith Miner.*

(Keith Miner, Seedling) A very wide-petaled peach-pink flower with heavy ruffles, slightly carved petals, and a gold edge. *Photograph by Keith Miner.*

(Mort Morss, Seedling) A wide-petaled grape-purple with a bluish eyezone and picotee edge above a green center. *Photograph by Mort Morss.*

'Raspberry Banana Cheesecake' × 'Open My Eyes' (Keith Miner, Seedling) A cream with a dark purple star-shaped chevron eyezone and matching picotee above a dark green center. *Photograph by Keith Miner.*

'Folkert Schellekens' (Mort Morss, Seedling) A lavender-rose self with a lavender eyezone surrounded by a darker band and matching double picotee edge surrounded in gold. *Photograph by John Benoot.*

(Mort Morss, Seedling) A rich dark purple with a slate blue eyezone and wire white edge above a bright green throat. *Photograph by Mort Morss.*

(Mort Morss, Seedling) A lavender with a blue eyezone and matching ruffled picotee edge above a green throat. *Photograph by Mort Morss.*

(Mort Morss, Seedling) A lavender-pink with a violet-patterned eye and deeply ruffled violet picotee edge surrounded in serrated white teeth. *Photograph by Mort Morss.*

(Mort Morss, Seedling) A cream-yellow with a burgundy eyezone and picotee edge surrounded by a ruffled gold edge above a green throat. *Photograph by Mort Morss.*

(Mort Morss, Seedling) A cream-lavender with a very complex-patterned eyezone above a green throat. *Photograph by Mort Morss.*

(Mort Morss, Seedling) A lavender-pink with a striking patterned eyezone of multiple bands and a purple picotee edge above a green throat. *Photograph by Mort Morss.*

(Jim Murphy, Seedling) A large golden yellow with lighter edges, twisted petals, and with sepals above a green center. *Photograph by Jim Murphy.*

(Jim Murphy, Seedling) A burnt orange with a very large eyezone that covers most of the petals and very little on the sepals. *Photograph by Jim Murphy.*

(Jim Murphy, Seedling) A rose-red lightly ruffled flower with white midribs above a yellow to green throat. *Photograph by Jim Murphy.*

(Jim Murphy, Seedling) A near-white with gently curved petals and sepals above a yellow throat. *Photograph by Jim Murphy.*

(Jim Murphy, Seedling) A golden yellow with a very large green throat carrying twisted and curled petals and sepals. *Photograph by Jim Murphy.*

(Jim Murphy, Seedling) A faint lavender bitone with a yellow watermark, lightly ruffled edges, and a green center. *Photograph by Jim Murphy.*

(Jim Murphy, Seedling) A velvety red with a wire white edge, white midribs, and a star-shaped watermark above a yellow to green throat. *Photograph by Jim Murphy.*

(Jim Murphy, Seedling) A large gold with curled petals and very long, spooned sepals above a green throat. *Photograph by Jim Murphy.*

(Jim Murphy, Seedling) A lightly ruffled, twisted, and curled burnt burgundy-red. *Photograph by Jim Murphy.*

(Jim Murphy, Seedling) A large burgundy-lavender with white midribs and twisted and curled petals and sepals. *Photograph by Jim Murphy.*

'Arrowhead' (John P. Peat, Seedling) An orange flower with a complex eyezone and an applique throat that forms patterns in the form of arrowheads. *Photograph by John P. Peat.*

(Jim Murphy, Seedling) A lavender-pink with a large burgundy eyezone above a yellow to green throat. *Photograph by Jim Murphy.*

'Appliqued' (John P. Peat, Seedling) A cream-peach flower with a patterned eyezone and throat. The applique cream-yellow is broken by darker midribs. *Photograph by John P. Peat.*

'Dark Eye Edge' (John P. Peat, Seedling) A large-flowered cream-peach with a large black-purple eyezone and matching wide black-purple picotee surrounded by a second gold edge. *Photograph by John P. Peat.*

'Forever Knights' (John P. Peat, Seedling) A near-black, dark purple with bright white shark's teeth above a lime-green throat. *Photograph by John P. Peat.*

'Moon Rainbow' (John P. Peat, Seedling) A burnt orange with a triple-banded complex eyezone of purple-red, gray-blue, and maroon. *Photograph by John P. Peat.*

'Red-Eyed' (John P. Peat, Seedling) A wide-petaled, creamy salmon-pink with a candy-apple red eyezone and matching ruffled, wide picotee edge. *Photograph by John P. Peat.*

'Knarly Red' (John P. Peat, Seedling) A bright red flower with a gnarly, toothy and fringed ruffled gold edge. *Photograph by John P. Peat.*

'Prince John' (John P. Peat, Seedling) A deep velvety red heavy substanced flower with a heavily ruffled gold edge. *Photograph by John P. Peat.*

'Tony Thompson' Seedling (John P. Peat, Seedling) A wide-petaled, soft cream-sherbet with a bright cherry-red eyezone and matching picotee edge. *Photograph by John P. Peat.*

'Toothy Red' (John P. Peat, Seedling) A bright red flower with a ruffled white shark's teeth edge. *Photograph by John P. Peat.*

'Tropical Snowflake' (John P. Peat, Seedling) A cream, near-white flower with a strong chartreuse and gold tightly ruffled edge. *Photograph by John P. Peat.*

'White Blue Eye' (John P. Peat, Seedling) A near-white with a fluorescent blue-purple eyezone and matching wire picotee edge above a fluorescent green throat. *Photograph by John P. Peat.*

'Toothy Red Eye' (John P. Peat, Seedling) A peach with a dark red eyezone and matching picotee surrounded by gold shark's teeth. *Photograph by John P. Peat.*

'Velvet-Red' (John P. Peat, Seedling) A bright cherry-red flower with a velvety texture and a looped edge surrounded by a wire white edge. *Photograph by John P. Peat.*

'White Blue Eye 2' (John P. Peat, Seedling) A near-white flower with a navy to sky-blue eyezone above a screaming green throat. *Photograph by John P. Peat.*

(John P. Peat, Seedling) A cream with a peach overlay and a heavy gold ruffled edge above a dark lime-green throat. *Photograph by John P. Peat.*

(John P. Peat, Seedling) A cream with a large dark purple eyezone and a complex throat of varying shades of purple and raised tissue forming bumps. *Photograph by John P. Peat.*

(John P. Peat, Seedling) A wide-petaled, burnt orange flower with a dark black-purple eyezone and matching picotee edge. *Photograph by John P. Peat.*

(John P. Peat, Seedling) A multibanded, complex-eyed cream flower. The eyezone consists of shades of purple, gray, blue, and burgundy. *Photograph by John P. Peat.*

(John P. Peat, Seedling) A light lavender with nicely ruffled gold edge and a large yellow watermark above a dark green center. *Photograph by John P. Peat.*

(John P. Peat, Seedling) A grape-purple with a near-black eyezone and matching picotee edge above a small yellow to green center. *Photograph by John P. Peat.*

(John P. Peat, Seedling) A heavy substanced peach-pink with a nicely ruffled edge and a deep dark green throat. *Photograph by John P. Peat.*

(John P. Peat, Seedling) A light pink heavy substanced flower with tightly ruffled chartreuse and gold edge above a lime-green center. *Photograph by John P. Peat.*

(John P. Peat, Seedling) A large near-white with a nicely ruffled gold edge and a fluorescent lime-green throat. *Photograph by John P. Peat.*

(John P. Peat, Seedling) A cream-rose with a large burgundy-red eyezone and a wide burgundy-red ruffled picotee edge. *Photograph by John P. Peat.*

(John P. Peat, Seedling) A light orange to cream flower with a double edge of gold and burgundy-red and a matching burgundy-red eyezone. *Photograph by John P. Peat.*

(John P. Peat, Seedling) A burgundy-red with a large yellow watermark above a dark green center and a nicely ruffled gold edge. *Photograph by John P. Peat.*

(John P. Peat, Seedling) A cream with a pink overlay and a large red eye-zone with red veining and a double edge of gold and deep red. *Photograph by John P. Peat.*

(John P. Peat, Seedling) A large tangerine-orange unusual form with lightly ruffled petals and sepals. *Photograph by John P. Peat.*

(John P. Peat, Seedling) A deep red double with a toothy, fringed edge of gold. *Photograph by John P. Peat.*

(John P. Peat, Seedling) A very large shrimp-red double flower weighing approximately 0.25 pound (113.4 grams). *Photograph by John P. Peat.*

(John P. Peat, Seedling) A burgundy-purple unusual form with a darker purple eyezone and shark's teeth edge of white. *Photograph by John P. Peat.*

(John P. Peat, Seedling) A burgundy-purple velvety flower with wide petals and ruffled, sometimes looped gold edge. *Photograph by John P. Peat.*

(John P. Peat, Seedling) A fire-engine red with a wire gold edge on the petals and sepals. *Photograph by John P. Peat.*

(John P. Peat, Seedling) A nicely ruffled coral-pink with a large yellow to fluorescent lime-green throat and a wire gold edge. *Photograph by John P. Peat.*

(John P. Peat, Seedling) A heavily ruffled and looped golden yellow with heavy substance and a deep, dark green throat. *Photograph by John P. Peat.*

(John P. Peat, Seedling) A cream with a gold overlay and a large burgundy-purple eyezone and matching wide ruffled picotee edge. *Photograph by John P. Peat.*

(John P. Peat, Seedling) A cream-peach with a very large black-purple eyezone and wide matching picotee surrounded by a ruffled chartreuse and gold edge. *Photograph by John P. Peat.*

(John P. Peat, Seedling) A burnt orange flower with a near-black eyezone and matching picotee edge. *Photograph by John P. Peat.*

(John P. Peat, Seedling) A very wide-petaled tangerine-orange with heavy ruffles and loops and a darker red eyezone and wire picotee edge. *Photograph by John P. Peat.*

(John P. Peat, Seedling) A cream with large purple eyezone and quadruple edge of purple, gray-white, and purple surrounded by a further wire white edge. *Photograph by John P. Peat.*

(John P. Peat, Seedling) A cream-orange with a bright fire-engine red chevron eyezone and a heavily ruffled red picotee edge surrounded by a wire gold trim. *Photograph by John P. Peat.*

(John P. Peat, Seedling) A bright velvety yellow with a chartreuse overlay, a nicely ruffled edge, and a striking lime-green throat. *Photograph by John P. Peat.*

(John P. Peat, Seedling) A large, beautifully ruffled cream to golden yellow with chartreuse coloring on gold edges. *Photograph by John P. Peat.*

(Ted L. Petit, Seedling) A large lavender with a green throat, large watermark, and heavily ruffled gold to chartreuse edge. *Photograph by Ted L. Petit.*

(Ted L. Petit, Seedling) A peach to melon self with a large patterned washed eyezone, a green throat and picotee edge surrounded by a ruffled gold edge. *Photograph by Ted L. Petit.*

(Ted L. Petit, Seedling) A lavender-rose self with a large green throat and patterned eyezone with several layers of matching patterned picotees surrounded by a gold edge. *Photograph by Ted L. Petit.*

(Ted L. Petit, Seedling) A very heavy substanced coral-pink self with a green heart and heavily ruffled gold edge. *Photograph by Ted L. Petit.*

(Ted L. Petit, Seedling) A cream-white double with a large rose watermark and wide matching picotee edge. *Photograph by Ted L. Petit.*

(Ted L. Petit, Seedling) A very large lavender flower with a broad dramatic purple eye and matching picotee, surrounded by a wide, ruffled gold edge. *Photograph by Ted L. Petit.*

(Ted L. Petit, Seedling) A pale lavender self with a blue-violet eyezone and matching wide blue-violet picotee edge. *Photograph by Ted L. Petit.*

(Ted L. Petit, Seedling) A clear lavender self with a green throat and ruffled green edge. *Photograph by Ted L. Petit.*

(Ted L. Petit, Seedling) A cream-peach self with a deep green throat and a patterned eye with a matching patterned multiple edge surrounded by a green throat. *Photograph by Ted L. Petit.*

(Ted L. Petit, Seedling) A very dramatic purple chevron eye and matching wide picotee on a peach to orange self. *Photograph by Ted L. Petit.*

(Ted L. Petit, Seedling) A burgundy-rose double with a heavy, wide gold edge on the petals and petaloids. *Photograph by Ted L. Petit.*

(Ted L. Petit, Seedling) A mauve-lavender with a green throat and a very wide, heavily ruffled gold edge. *Photograph by Ted L. Petit.*

(Ted L. Petit, Seedling) An extremely ruffled, wide-petaled cream flower with a green throat. *Photograph by Ted L. Petit.*

(Ted L. Petit, Seedling) A blue-patterned eyezone and matching picotee above a green throat on a lavender self. *Photograph by Ted L. Petit.*

(Ted L. Petit, Seedling) An extremely wide gold to chartreuse ruffled edge taking up most of the petal surface, on a lavender-rose self with a large watermark and a green throat. *Photograph by Ted L. Petit.*

(Ted L. Petit, Seedling) A deep vibrant red self above a green throat, with very wide petals surrounded by a gold edge. *Photograph by Ted L. Petit.*

(Ted L. Petit, Seedling) A wide-petaled burgundy-rose flower with a heavily ruffled gold edge and watermark above a green throat. *Photograph by Ted L. Petit.*

(Ted L. Petit, Seedling) A very large, dramatic, dark purple eyezone and matching picotee on a lavender-cream self above a green throat. *Photograph by Ted L. Petit.*

(Ted L. Petit, Seedling) A very large rose-red flower with a green throat, large watermark, and wide, heavily ruffled gold edge. *Photograph by Ted L. Petit.*

(Ted L. Petit, Seedling) A light yellow to gold flower with a deep green throat and wide, heavily ruffled chartreuse to green edges. *Photograph by Ted L. Petit.*

(Ted L. Petit, Seedling) A light lavender-pink self with a large blue eyezone surrounded by a rose mascara eye above a green throat. *Photograph by Ted L. Petit.*

(Ted L. Petit, Seedling) A lavender-rose double with an extremely large dark purple eyezone and matching wide picotee on the petals and petaloids. *Photograph by Ted L. Petit.*

(Ted L. Petit, Seedling) An electric red self above a green throat with a ruffled gold edge. *Photograph by Ted L. Petit.*

(Ted L. Petit, Seedling) An extremely heavy substanced, very flat, round cream-yellow flower with a green throat and very tightly crimped petal edges. *Photograph by Ted L. Petit.*

(Ted L. Petit, Seedling) A dark black-red to black-purple flower with a huge, dramatic, wide gold ruffled edge above a green throat. *Photograph by Ted L. Petit.*

(Ted L. Petit, Seedling) A yellow to gold flower with an extremely wide ruffled edge taking up most of the petal surface. *Photograph by Ted L. Petit.*

(Ted L. Petit, Seedling) A very wide-petaled gold flower with a heavy substance and wide ruffles above a green throat. *Photograph by Ted L. Petit.*

(Ted L. Petit, Seedling) A round soft pink flower with a deep green throat and matching green ruffled edge. *Photograph by Ted L. Petit.*

(Ted L. Petit, Seedling) A vibrant, electric red self with a ruffled gold edge above a green throat. *Photograph by Ted L. Petit.*

(Ted L. Petit, Seedling) A deep red self with a large watermark above a green throat and a heavily ruffled gold edge. *Photograph by Ted L. Petit.*

(Ted L. Petit, Seedling) A vibrant orange-red flower with a lighter watermark, a green throat, and ruffled gold edge. *Photograph by Ted L. Petit.*

(Ted L. Petit, Seedling) A burgundy-purple self with a heavily ruffled, wide gold edge and lighter watermark above a green throat. *Photograph by Ted L. Petit.*

(Ted L. Petit, Seedling) A clear lavender-violet self with a blue-violet eye surrounded by a violet halo, and wide matching picotee edges, surrounded by a gold edge. *Photograph by Ted L. Petit.*

(Ted L. Petit, Seedling) A dormant, black-red to black-purple self with a heavily ruffled gold edge and lighter watermark above a pinched green throat. *Photograph by Ted L. Petit.*

(Ted L. Petit, Seedling) A heavy substanced deep red self with a lighter watermark, a green throat, and ruffled gold edges. *Photograph by Ted L. Petit.*

(Ted L. Petit, Seedling) A medium red self with a huge lighter watermark taking up most of the petal surface, above a green throat, surrounded by a ruffled gold edge. *Photograph by Ted L. Petit.*

(Ted L. Petit, Seedling) A soft pink flower with extremely wide sepals, ruffled gold edge, and a green throat. *Photograph by Ted L. Petit.*

(Ted L. Petit, Seedling) A patterned blue eyezone above a green throat on a lavender-rose self with a violet picotee. *Photograph by Ted L. Petit.*

(Ted L. Petit, Seedling) An extremely large light lavender flower with a huge chartreuse watermark and matching wide chartreuse to gold edge. *Photograph by Ted L. Petit.*

(Ted L. Petit, Seedling) A dark lavender flower with a green throat, large watermark, and wide, ruffled gold edge. *Photograph by Ted L. Petit.*

(Ted L. Petit, Seedling) A very wide-petaled, deep velvety dark red self with heavily ruffled gold edges above a green throat. *Photograph by Ted L. Petit.*

(Ted L. Petit, Seedling) A light cream to melon self with a ghostly violet eye and matching picotee, surrounded by a ruffled gold edge. *Photograph by Ted L. Petit.*

(Ted L. Petit, Seedling) A melon double hose-in-hose flower with a dark purple eyezone and matching picotee on the petals and petaloids. *Photograph by Ted L. Petit.*

(Ted L. Petit, Seedling) A cream to light flesh self with an extremely complex-patterned eyezone of lavender and charcoal, surrounded by a lavender picotee above a green throat. *Photograph by Ted L. Petit.*

(Herbert Phelps, Seedling) A velvety grape-purple with a bright fluorescent green throat below a darker eyezone carrying a ruffled wire white edge. *Photograph by Herbert Phelps.*

(Herbert Phelps, Seedling) A wide-petaled, heavy substanced pink with a wide ruffled edge above a dark green center. *Photograph by Herbert Phelps.*

(Ted L. Petit, Seedling) A bright raspberry-red flower with a green throat, lighter watermark, and ruffled gold edge. *Photograph by Ted L. Petit.*

(Herbert Phelps, Seedling) A bright orange-red with a darker eyezone, a ruffled wire gold edge above a bright green throat. *Photograph by Herbert Phelps.*

(Herbert Phelps, Seedling) A cream-peach with a dark purple eyezone and matching picotee surrounded by gold shark's teeth above a green center. *Photograph by Herbert Phelps.*

(Herbert Phelps, Seedling) A rose-red with a lighter watermark eyezone and a ruffled edge sporting white to gold shark's teeth. *Photograph by Herbert Phelps.*

(Herbert Phelps, Seedling) A cream with a large rose-purple eyezone and matching picotee surrounded by a wire gold edge above a green throat. *Photograph by Herbert Phelps.*

(Herbert Phelps, Seedling) A cream-yellow with a large bright candy-apple red eyezone and matching ruffled picotee edge above a green center. *Photograph by Herbert Phelps.*

(Herbert Phelps, Seedling) A wide-petaled lavender-pink with a nicely ruffled wire gold edge above a bright green throat. *Photograph by Herbert Phelps.*

(Herbert Phelps, Seedling) A heavily ruffled light pink with a wide gold to chartreuse edge above a large bright green throat. *Photograph by Herbert Phelps.*

(Herbert Phelps, Seedling) A wide-petaled lavender-pink with a darker banded eyezone and a lightly ruffled gold edge above a yellow to green throat. *Photograph by Herbert Phelps.*

(Herbert Phelps, Seedling) A heavy substanced wide-petaled pink with nicely ruffled gold edge above a bright green center. *Photograph by Herbert Phelps.*

(Leon Payne, Seedling) A burnt pink with a darker eyezone on a large flower with heavy gold ruffled edges. *Photograph by Leon Payne.*

(Leon Payne, Seedling) A bright near-white with a striking red eyezone and a large yellow to green throat with spooned sepals. *Photograph by Leon Payne.*

(Herbert Phelps, Seedling) A cream-pink, narrow-petaled self with darker veining and a darker eyezone above a yellow to green throat. *Photograph by Herbert Phelps.*

(Leon Payne, Seedling) A large heavy substanced, super ruffled burnt orange flower with a carved yellow to dark green throat. *Photograph by Lean Payne*

(Leon Payne, Seedling) A cream-pink sporting a large dark red chevron eyezone and carrying twisted and curled petals. *Photograph by Leon Payne.*

'America's Most Wanted' × 'Empire Returns' (Lee Pickles, Seedling) A nicely ruffled wide-petaled waxy gold flower with carving down into a green throat. *Photograph by Lee Pickles.*

'Steve Trimmer' × 'Candied Popcorn Perfection' (Lee Pickles, Seedling) A cream with a large purple eyezone and matching picotee edge surrounded by a wire gold edge. *Photograph by Lee Pickles.*

(Lee Pickles, Seedling) A creamy tan-orange with a circular burgundy eyezone and matching picotee with nicely ruffled wire gold edge. *Photograph by Lee Pickles.*

'Mandalay Bay Music' × 'Wonders Never Cease' (Lee Pickles, Seedling) A wide-petaled soft pink with a nicely ruffled gold edge above a yellow to green throat. *Photograph by Lee Pickles.*

(Lee Pickles, Seedling) A tangerine-orange with nicely carved petals and beautifully ruffled edge above a very dark green center. *Photograph by Lee Pickles.*

(Lee Pickles, Seedling) A lavender-purple with a darker banded eyezone and picotee surrounded by a nicely ruffled gold edge. *Photograph by Lee Pickles.*

(Lee Pickles, Seedling) A wide-petaled cream-pink with a banded darker eyezone and very heavy ruffled gold edge above a dark green center. *Photograph by Lee Pickles.*

(Jackie Pryor, Seedling) A narrow-petaled variant of copper-rose with darker veins and a large star-shaped yellow to green throat. *Photograph by Jackie Pryor.*

(Jeff Pryor, Seedling) A cream with a large rose-red eyezone and matching picotee surrounded by a wire gold edge. *Photograph by Jeff Pryor.*

(Jackie Pryor, Seedling) A grape-purple with a violet-blue eyezone and a nicely ruffled edge with a wire white edge. *Photograph by Jackie Pryor.*

(Jeff Pryor, Seedling) A lavender with a darker eyezone and a nicely ruffled wire white edge. *Photograph by Jeff Pryor.*

'Now and Forever' × 'J. T. Davis #4' (Carroll Quarry, Seedling) A cream-lavender with a darker picotee, no eyezone and tightly ruffled gold to chartreuse edge above a bright green throat. *Photograph by Carroll Quarry.*

('Secret Splendor' × 'Big Blue') × ('Darla Anita' × 'Clothed in Glory') (Carroll Quarry, Seedling) A wide-petaled lavender-pink with a nicely ruffled gold edge above a yellow to dark green center. *Photograph by Carroll Quarry.*

(Margo Reed, Seedling) A lightly ruffled light lavender with a darker banded eyezone above a yellow throat. *Photograph by Margo Reed.*

(Margo Reed, Seedling) A lavender, very narrow-petaled flower with a burgundy chevron eyezone above a yellow to green throat. *Photograph by Margo Reed.*

(Margo Reed, Seedling) A lightly ruffled velvety red unusual form with twisted and spooned sepals and petals above a yellow to green throat. *Photograph by Margo Reed.*

(Margo Reed, Seedling) A narrow-petaled cream flower with very large burgundy-red eyezone that is mimicked on the sepals. *Photograph by Margo Reed.*

(Margo Reed, Seedling) An orange-red unusual form with twisted sepals and veined petals above a yellow throat. *Photograph by Margo Reed.*

(Margo Reed, Seedling) A cream near-white narrow-petaled lightly ruffled and pinched flower with a yellow throat. *Photograph by Margo Reed.*

(Margo Reed, Seedling) A lightly ruffled burnt orange with a darker burgundy eyezone above a large yellow to green throat. *Photograph by Margo Reed.*

(Margo Reed, Seedling) A light burgundy-red flower with twisted and curled petals and sepals above a yellow to green throat. *Photograph by Margo Reed.*

(Margo Reed, Seedling) A cream flower with twisted and curled petals and sepals above a large yellow throat. *Photograph by Margo Reed.*

(Margo Reed, Seedling) A pussy-willow purple flower with spooned sepals and twisted, lightly ruffled petals. *Photograph by Margo Reed.*

(Margo Reed, Seedling) A burnt orange-red with a darker eyezone and twisted and curled lightly ruffled petals and sepals. *Photograph by Margo Reed.*

(Margo Reed, Seedling) A bright fire-engine red with a wire gold edge and lighter midribs above a large yellow to green throat. *Photograph by Margo Reed.*

(Joyce Reinke, Seedling) A rose-pink veined flower with a darker red eyezone and white midribs above a yellow to green throat. *Photograph by Joyce Reinke.*

(Joyce Reinke, Seedling) A near-white spider with spooned sepals and petals above a large yellow to green throat. *Photograph by Joyce Reinke.*

'Apache' (Phil Reilly, Seedling) A cream with a dark purple-black eyezone extending out on the midribs forming a star shape, with a matching picotee surrounded by a wire gold edge. *Photograph by Phil Reilly.*

(Joyce Reinke, Seedling) A rose-red with a faint lighter watermark and a darker banded eyezone with lighter pink-white lightly ruffled edges. *Photograph by Joyce Reinke.*

(Joyce Reinke, Seedling) A narrow-petaled lavender with a star-shaped dark purple eyezone with light midribs. *Photograph by Joyce Reinke.*

(Joyce Reinke, Seedling) A narrow-petaled lavender-rose with a large rose eyezone surrounded by a darker band of dark rose-red above a large yellow to dark green throat. *Photograph by Joyce Reinke.*

(John Rice, Seedling) A rose-pink with a heavily ruffled orange-gold edge above a bright yellow to green center. *Photograph by John Rice.*

'Small Strawberry Kid' (Ned Roberts, Seedling) A pink unusual form with a strawberry eyezone and spooned sepals above a large green throat. *Photograph by Ned Roberts.*

(Joyce Reinke, Seedling) A coral-peach bitone with darker rose-pink sepals and a star-shaped burgundy-red eyezone above a yellow to green throat. *Photograph by Joyce Reinke.*

'Ned's Yellow Eye' (Ned Roberts, Seedling) A lightly ruffled cream-yellow with a rose eyezone above a green throat and twisted and spooned sepals. *Photograph by Ned Roberts.*

(Ned Roberts, Seedling) A strawberry-red unusual form with curled and spooned sepals and petals above a yellow to green throat. *Photograph by Ned Roberts.*

(Ned Roberts, Seedling) A lavender-purple unusual form with spooned and curled petals and sepals. *Photograph by Ned Roberts.*

(Alex Salter, Seedling) A narrow-formed burgundy flower with an extremely complex, rippled patterned eyezone on both petals and sepals. *Photograph by Alex Salter.*

(Elizabeth H. Salter, Seedling) A small mauve-pink flower with a banded bluish eyezone surrounded by a burgundy halo. *Photograph by Elizabeth H. Salter.*

(Alex Salter, Seedling) A narrow-formed peach flower with a large burgundy eyezone on petals and sepals. *Photograph by Alex Salter.*

(Alex Salter, Seedling) A deep purple, narrow-formed flower with a large green throat and an arrowhead-patterned eyezone. *Photograph by Alex Salter.*

(Elizabeth H. Salter, Seedling) A brightly-patterned eyezone with a wide burgundy halo above a green throat on a small pink flower. *Photograph by Elizabeth H. Salter.*

(Elizabeth H. Salter, Seedling) A multibanded charcoal-violet and burgundy eyezone on a small flesh-colored flower. *Photograph by Elizabeth H. Salter.*

(Elizabeth H. Salter, Seedling) A small bright rose flower with a pale bluish eyezone surrounded by a wire burgundy band above a fluorescent green throat. *Photograph by Elizabeth H. Salter.*

(Elizabeth H. Salter, Seedling) A deep navy-blue eyezone surrounded by a burgundy halo on a salmon-pink small flower. *Photograph by Elizabeth H. Salter.*

(Elizabeth H. Salter, Seedling) A very large pale blue eyezone with a burgundy halo on a salmon-colored small flower. *Photograph by Elizabeth H. Salter.*

(Elizabeth H. Salter, Seedling) A washed charcoal and violet-gray-patterned eyezone on petals and sepals of a narrow-formed small burgundy flower. *Photograph by Elizabeth H. Salter.*

(Elizabeth H. Salter, Seedling) A small cream flower with a bright red eyezone and wide picotee above a green throat surrounded by a serrated wire gold edge. *Photograph by Elizabeth H. Salter.*

(Elizabeth H. Salter, Seedling) A small cream-yellow flower with a patterned burgundy eyezone and picotee above a green throat. *Photograph by Elizabeth H. Salter.*

(Elizabeth H. Salter, Seedling) A small apricot flower with a complex, multicolored eyezone on petals and sepals above a green heart. *Photograph by Elizabeth H. Salter.*

(Elizabeth H. Salter, Seedling) A multibanded patterned eyezone above a green throat on a peachy mauve-pink small flower. *Photograph by Elizabeth H. Salter.*

(Elizabeth H. Salter, Seedling) A small burnt orange flower with a multibanded patterned eyezone above a green throat. *Photograph by Elizabeth H. Salter.*

(Elizabeth H. Salter, Seedling) A small peach-pink flower with a complex-patterned eyezone above a green throat. *Photograph by Elizabeth H. Salter.*

(Elizabeth H. Salter, Seedling) A creamy, golden yellow small flower with flaring patterned eyezone above a green throat. *Photograph by Elizabeth H. Salter.*

(Elizabeth H. Salter, Seedling) A very ornately fringed and toothy small mauve-pink flower with a lighter halo above a green heart. *Photograph by Elizabeth H. Salter.*

(Jeff Salter, Seedling) An extremely saturated candy-apple red with a lighter watermark above a lime-green throat. *Photograph by Jeff Salter.*

(Jeff Salter, Seedling) A velvety red with lighter watermark above a green throat surrounded by a ruffled gold edge. *Photograph by Jeff Salter.*

(Elizabeth H. Salter, Seedling) A small mauve-pink flower with a large pink eyezone surrounded by a burgundy-red halo. *Photograph by Elizabeth H. Salter.*

(Jeff Salter, Seedling) A lemon-gold flower with a dark purple shattered-pattern eyezone and wire picotee above a green throat. *Photograph by Jeff Salter.*

(Jeff Salter, Seedling) A candy-apple red with a triangular pink watermark above a green throat surrounded by a heavily ruffled gold edge. *Photograph by Jeff Salter.*

(Jeff Salter, Seedling) A large fire-engine red with a green throat and bubbly gold edge. *Photograph by Jeff Salter.*

(Jeff Salter, Seedling) A burgundy-red flower with a lighter watermark above a green throat surrounded by a heavily ruffled white-gold edge. *Photograph by Jeff Salter.*

(Jeff Salter, Seedling) A large dark burgundy flower with extremely wide gold edge and matching large gold watermark above a green heart. *Photograph by Jeff Salter.*

(Jeff Salter, Seedling) A wide-petaled, heavily ruffled red with near-white edge above a green heart. *Photograph by Jeff Salter.*

(Jeff Salter, Seedling) A very wide golden white edge on a burgundy-red flower with a lighter watermark and a green throat. *Photograph by Jeff Salter.*

(Jeff Salter, Seedling) An extremely ruffled, gold- and wide-edged coral-pink flower with a green heart. *Photograph by Jeff Salter.*

(Jeff Salter, Seedling) A very round rose-pink with a large green throat and fringed gold edge. *Photograph by Jeff Salter.*

(Jeff Salter, Seedling) A near-white flower with a large, round, dark red eyezone and matching picotee above a fluorescent green throat. *Photograph by Jeff Salter.*

(Jeff Salter, Seedling) An orchid-pink with a burgundy eyezone and half picotee surrounded by an extremely ruffled gold edge. *Photograph by Jeff Salter.*

(Jeff Salter, Seedling) A cream-yellow with an intense blood eyezone and matching picotee above a star-shaped green throat. *Photograph by Jeff Salter.*

(Jeff Salter, Seedling) A cream-white flower with a huge burgundy-purple eyezone and wide picotee edge above a green center. *Photograph by Jeff Salter.*

(Jeff Salter, Seedling) A narrow-formed flower with a large bright burgundy-patterned eyezone and picotee on both the petals and the sepals. *Photograph by Jeff Salter.*

(Jeff Salter, Seedling) A wide-petaled cream flower with a striking rose eyezone and picotee surrounded by a second ruffled gold edge above a green throat. *Photograph by Jeff Salter.*

(Jeff Salter, Seedling) A extremely toothy-edged pink flower with a large purple eyezone and edge above a green throat. *Photograph by Jeff Salter.*

'Million Dollar Legs' (Bob Schwarz, Seedling) An orange-red spatulate, unusual formed, with sepals that are quilled and hooked. *Photograph by Bob Schwarz.*

(Jeff Salter, Seedling) A peach self with a huge orange-red eyezone and wide picotee that takes up most of the flower face. *Photograph by Jeff Salter.*

(Jeff Salter, Seedling) A heavily fringed, toothy-edged white flower with a large red-burgundy eyezone and matching picotee above a green throat. *Photograph by Jeff Salter.*

(Bob Scott, Seedling) A narrow-petaled peach-pink double with lightly ruffled edges above a yellow to green throat. *Photograph by Bob Scott.*

(Bob Scott, Seedling) A narrow-petaled yellow double flower with a large burgundy-purple eyezone and matching picotee. *Photograph by Bob Scott.*

(Frank Smith, Seedling) A cream-pink with a heavily ruffled chartreuse edge and a green throat. *Photograph by Frank Smith.*

(Frank Smith, Seedling) A wide-petaled soft pink with a heavily ruffled gold edge and a dark green center. *Photograph by Frank Smith.*

(Bob Scott, Seedling) A ruffled rose with narrow petals and a darker rose eye above a yellow to green throat. *Photograph by Bob Scott.*

(Frank Smith, Seedling) A wide-petaled cream-pink with heavy golden chartreuse ruffled edges above a lime-green throat. *Photograph by Frank Smith.*

(Frank Smith, Seedling) A very flat, recurved, ruffled orange self with a green throat. *Photograph by Frank Smith.*

(Frank Smith, Seedling) A large mauve-purple with a violet-purple eyezone and picotee edge surrounded in ruffled gold. *Photograph by Frank Smith.*

(Frank Smith, Seedling) A large rose self with a wide, heavily ruffled gold edge. *Photograph by Frank Smith.*

(Frank Smith, Seedling) A cream-pink with a ruffled gold edge, a green throat and very wide sepals. *Photograph by Frank Smith.*

(Frank Smith, Seedling) A cream flower with a large near-black patterned eyezone on the petals and sepals. *Photograph by Frank Smith.*

(Frank Smith, Seedling) A rose-pink with a wide dark burgundy-red picotee on petals and sepals with a wire gold edge. *Photograph by Frank Smith.*

(Frank Smith, Seedling) A bright burnt orange self with nicely ruffled petals and a green heart. *Photograph by Frank Smith.*

(Frank Smith, Seedling) A wide-petaled bright coral-orange with heavy ruffles and a deep green heart. *Photograph by Frank Smith.*

(Frank Smith, Seedling) A medium purple self with a blue-violet watermark and matching picotee surrounded by a gold edge. *Photograph by Frank Smith.*

(Frank Smith, Seedling) A grape-purple self with a lighter watermark and matching picotee and ruffled gold edge. *Photograph by Frank Smith.*

(Frank Smith, Seedling) A light purple self with a blue-violet eyezone and matching ruffled picotee. *Photograph by Frank Smith.*

(Frank Smith, Seedling) A cream self with a large burgundy-red eyezone and matching lightly ruffled picotee. *Photograph by Frank Smith.*

(Frank Smith, Seedling) A cream self with a very large dark velvety burgundy eyezone and wide matching heavily ruffled picotee. *Photograph by Frank Smith.*

(Frank Smith, Seedling) A near-black dark purple eyezone and wide matching picotee on a violet-cream flower. *Photograph by Frank Smith.*

(Frank Smith, Seedling) A cream-pink flower with a cherry-red eyezone and matching picotee and ruffled gold edge. *Photograph by Frank Smith.*

(Frank Smith, Seedling) A cream with a very large near-black eyezone and matching picotee surrounded by a ruffled wire gold edge. *Photograph by Frank Smith.*

(Frank Smith, Seedling) A large near-black eyezone and matching wide picotee on a cream-rose self. *Photograph by Frank Smith.*

(Frank Smith, Seedling) A very dark velvety burgundy eyezone and matching picotee on a cream-pink self. *Photograph by Frank Smith.*

(Frank Smith, Seedling) A lightly ruffled near-white with a blue-violet eyezone above a striking green throat. *Photograph by Frank Smith.*

(Grace Stamile, Seedling) A diamond-dusted cream-orange mini with a large chevron, velvety red eyezone and matching wire picotee edge. *Photograph by Patrick Stamile.*

(Grace Stamile, Seedling) A cream with greenish aqua-blue complex eyezone surrounded by a burgundy-purple band above a lime-green throat. *Photograph by Patrick Stamile.*

(Grace Stamile, Seedling) A rose-pink mini with a large burgundy-red eyezone and darker veining above a deep green center. *Photograph by Patrick Stamile.*

(Grace Stamile, Seedling) A rose mini with a Caribbean-blue eyezone surrounded by a burgundy-purple band above a green throat. *Photograph by Patrick Stamile.*

(Grace Stamile, Seedling) A tiny dark grape-purple with a darker complex eye of black and grape-purple above a green throat. *Photograph by Patrick Stamile.*

(Grace Stamile, Seedling) A grape-purple small flower with darker veining and a complex eyezone of purple, gray and blue-purple often showing purple arrowheads. *Photograph by Patrick Stamile.*

(Grace Stamile, Seedling) A small rose bitone with a complex eyezone of white, gray, and rose above a grass-green throat. *Photograph by Patrick Stamile.*

(Grace Stamile, Seedling) A rose pom-pom self with a lighter, wide pink edge, and darker veining with lavender midribs. *Photograph by Patrick Stamile.*

(Grace Stamile, Seedling) A small lavender-rose with a complex eye of violet, gray, blue, and purple above a cream-green throat. *Photograph by Patrick Stamile.*

(Grace Stamile, Seedling) A small popcorn double of rose with lighter ruffled edges of pink to near-white. *Photograph by Patrick Stamile.*

'Orange Grove' (Patrick Stamile, Seedling) A bright orange with a very bright reddish orange eyezone and wide picotee edge. *Photograph by Patrick Stamile.*

'Shamrock Dew' (Patrick Stamile, Seedling) A wide-petaled golden yellow flower with a heavily ruffled chartreuse edge. *Photograph by Patrick Stamile.*

(Patrick Stamile, Seedling) A cream-yellow with a dark purple complex eyezone of bands of slate gray-blue, purple, and burgundy. *Photograph by Patrick Stamile.*

(Patrick Stamile, Seedling) A cream double with a complex eye of blues, purple and slate gray with matching picotee edge. *Photograph by Patrick Stamile.*

(Patrick Stamile, Seedling) A cream-lavender with a complex eyezone showing triangular shapes that are often mimicked on the sepals. *Photograph by Patrick Stamile.*

(Patrick Stamile, Seedling) A cream with a lavender overlay and a complex eyezone of purple streaked with cream bands and a purple picotee. *Photograph by Patrick Stamile.*

(Patrick Stamile, Seedling) A cream with a complex, washed eyezone of varying shades of blue and a purple band above a striking green throat. *Photograph by Patrick Stamile.*

(Patrick Stamile, Seedling) A cream near-white with a dark navy-blue eyezone of different shades and a burgundy-purple band. *Photograph by Patrick Stamile.*

(Patrick Stamile, Seedling) A ruffled rose with a huge cream watermark that gives the illusion of an edge with no eye above a green throat. *Photograph by Patrick Stamile.*

(Patrick Stamile, Seedling) A tangerine-orange with a huge purple eyezone and matching wide picotee taking up most of the flower face. *Photograph by Patrick Stamile.*

(Patrick Stamile, Seedling) A lavender with a striking dark complex Caribbean-blue eyezone with a purple band and matching picotee edge. *Photograph by Patrick Stamile.*

(Patrick Stamile, Seedling) A cream with ruffled purple edges and no eyezone above a deep green throat. *Photograph by Patrick Stamile.*

(Patrick Stamile, Seedling) A fire-engine red with a heavy gold ruffled edge above a yellow to green heart. *Photograph by Patrick Stamile.*

(Patrick Stamile, Seedling) A rose velvety red with a lighter watermark and a ruffled gold edge and a deep green center. *Photograph by Patrick Stamile.*

(Patrick Stamile, Seedling) A lavender-pink with a dark green throat and a nicely ruffled gold edge surrounded by a chartreuse edge. *Photograph by Patrick Stamile.*

(Patrick Stamile, Seedling) A lavender-pink with a lighter watermark and a ruffled gold edge above a green center. *Photograph by Patrick Stamile.*

(Patrick Stamile, Seedling) A cream with a pink overlay and an extremely ruffled gold edge with chartreuse highlights above a deep green center. *Photograph by Patrick Stamile.*

(Patrick Stamile, Seedling) A cream-yellow with an extremely large burgundy-purple eyezone and picotee edge surrounded by a wide toothy gold edge. *Photograph by Patrick Stamile.*

(Patrick Stamile, Seedling) A rose-pink with very wide petals and sepals and beautifully ruffled gold edge also showing off some sculpting near the throat. *Photograph by Patrick Stamile.*

(Patrick Stamile, Seedling) A bright velvety red with wide petals, a lighter watermark eyezone and a gold ruffled edge above a green throat. *Photograph by Patrick Stamile.*

(Patrick Stamile, Seedling) A wide-petaled rose-pink with a heavily ruffled gold to chartreuse edge above a yellow to green throat. *Photograph by Patrick Stamile.*

(Patrick Stamile, Seedling) A rose with an extremely large burgundy-red eyezone and matching picotee above a small green heart. *Photograph by Patrick Stamile.*

(Patrick Stamile, Seedling) A bright lavender with a lighter pink water-mark, and a nicely ruffled gold to chartreuse edge above a green center. *Photograph by Patrick Stamile.*

(Patrick Stamile, Seedling) A clear burgundy with a heavily ruffled gold edge sporting hooks and knobs above a green throat. *Photograph by Patrick Stamile.*

(Patrick Stamile, Seedling) A cream with an orange overlay and large striking burgundy eyezone broken up by the lighter midribs and a matching burgundy picotee edge. *Photograph by Patrick Stamile.*

(Patrick Stamile, Seedling) A lightly ruffled lavender with a large dark purple chevron eyezone and wire purple picotee edge. *Photograph by Patrick Stamile.*

(Patrick Stamile, Seedling) A lavender self with a dark purple eyezone and matching wide dark purple-black picotee edge. *Photograph by Patrick Stamile.*

(Patrick Stamile, Seedling) A peach-pink with a double eyezone of grape-purple and blue which is mimicked around the edges below the ruffled gold edge. *Photograph by Patrick Stamile.*

(Patrick Stamile, Seedling) A wide-petaled burgundy-red with a large ruffled gold edge above a yellow to green throat. *Photograph by Patrick Stamile.*

(Patrick Stamile, Seedling) A heavily ruffled burgundy-red with a lighter watermark and a wide gold edge. *Photograph by Patrick Stamile.*

(Patrick Stamile, Seedling) A golden orange flower with a large applique yellow to green throat surrounded by a red eyezone and picotee edge. *Photograph by Patrick Stamile.*

(Patrick Stamile, Seedling) A cream near-white flower with a purple-blue eyezone surrounding a yellow to green applique throat also carrying a purple-blue picotee edge. *Photograph by Patrick Stamile.*

(Patrick Stamile, Seedling) A cream-pink with a large applique throat and a deep burgundy-purple eyezone and matching picotee edge. *Photograph by Patrick Stamile.*

(Patrick Stamile, Seedling) A cream with a star-shaped chevron dark purple eyezone split by wide white midribs and a picotee edge of black-purple. *Photograph by Patrick Stamile.*

(Patrick Stamile, Seedling) A golden orange flower with a large matching applique throat surrounded by a burgundy-red eyezone and picotee edge. *Photograph by Patrick Stamile.*

(Patrick Stamile, Seedling) A lavender with a triple edge of grape-purple, blue, and gold and an eyezone of bluish tones and a wire band of grape-purple. *Photograph by Patrick Stamile.*

(Doug Stirling, Seedling) A wide-petaled tangerine-pink with a pink overlay surrounded by a heavily ruffled darker orange edge. *Photograph by Doug Stirling.*

(Doug Stirling, Seedling) A cream-peach unusual form with nicely ruffled and knobby edges. *Photograph by Doug Stirling.*

(Dan Trimmer, Seedling) A soft pink with heavily ruffled and looped edges of gold and a darker eyezone above a lime-green throat. *Photograph by Dan Trimmer.*

(Dan Trimmer, Seedling) A baby-ribbon pink with wide petals and tightly ruffled gold edge above a large green throat. *Photograph by Dan Trimmer.*

(Doug Stirling, Seedling) A copper-rose with a large burgundy eyezone surrounding a very large yellow to green throat. *Photograph by Doug Stirling.*

(Dan Trimmer, Seedling) A grape-purple with a striking blue eyezone and matching picotee surrounded in a wire gold edge. *Photograph by Dan Trimmer.*

(Dan Trimmer, Seedling) A lavender-pink with a heavily ruffled gold edge above a green throat. *Photograph by Dan Trimmer.*

(Dan Trimmer, Seedling) A very wide-petaled lavender with darker veins, a darker violet-blue eyezone and a very ruffled wire gold edge. *Photograph by Dan Trimmer.*

(Dan Trimmer, Seedling) A wide baby-ribbon pink with a chartreuse throat and matching gold to chartreuse ruffled edge. *Photograph by Dan Trimmer.*

(Dan Trimmer, Seedling) A cream near-white with blue-gray eyezone surrounded by a purple band with a matching ruffled picotee edge which is highlighted in gold. *Photograph by Dan Trimmer.*

(Dan Trimmer, Seedling) A cream-orange with a pronounced purple eyezone and matching wide, ruffled picotee with gold highlights. *Photograph by Dan Trimmer.*

(Dan Trimmer, Seedling) A pink with very wide petals, a large rose eyezone, and matching heavily ruffled picotee above a yellow to green throat. *Photograph by Dan Trimmer.*

(Dan Trimmer, Seedling) A heavy substanced, wide-petaled pink with an extremely heavy ruffled gold edge above a green center. *Photograph by Dan Trimmer.*

(Dan Trimmer, Seedling) A rose-burgundy with large velvety black-purple eyezone and wide matching ruffled picotee. *Photograph by Dan Trimmer.*

(Dan Trimmer, Seedling) A lavender with a large yellow throat above a green heart and heavily ruffled wide gold edge. *Photograph by Dan Trimmer.*

(Dan Trimmer, Seedling) A bright lavender-pink with wide ruffled petals and darker banded eyezone above a bright green throat. *Photograph by Dan Trimmer.*

(Dan Trimmer, Seedling) A cream-white with a large dark black-purple eyezone with matching wide ruffled picotee edge. *Photograph by Dan Trimmer.*

(Dan Trimmer, Seedling) A rose-pink ruffled double with a tangerine-orange edge. *Photograph by Dan Trimmer.*

(Dan Trimmer, Seedling) A cream double with a large purple eyezone and matching ruffled picotee edge above a bright green throat. *Photograph by Dan Trimmer.*

(Dan Trimmer, Seedling) A bright orange with very heavy wide ruffles and pleated edges. *Photograph by Dan Trimmer.*

(Jane Trimmer, Seedling) A lightly ruffled lavender with a complex eyezone of purple, slate gray-blue, and burgundy-purple above a lime-green throat. *Photograph by Jane Trimmer.*

(Jane Trimmer, Seedling) A narrow-petaled violet-pink with a large lavender-blue eyezone with a darker lavender band above a very large yellow to green throat. *Photograph by Jane Trimmer.*

(Jane Trimmer, Seedling) A cream near-white with a large purple, veined eyezone with a darker purple band and a wire purple picotee above a yellow to green throat. *Photograph by Jane Trimmer.*

(Jane Trimmer, Seedling) A lightly ruffled, pinched-petaled pink with a faint watermark surrounded by a band of purple. *Photograph by Jane Trimmer.*

(Jane Trimmer, Seedling) A lightly ruffled grape-purple with veins of darker purple and a complex eyezone of varying shades of purple. *Photograph by Jane Trimmer.*

'Beyond the Moon' (Francois Verhaert, Seedling) A wide-petaled golden yellow flower with a large chevron-shaped dark purple eyezone and matching picotee edge. *Photograph by Francois Verhaert.*

'On the Seventh Day' (Francois Verhaert, Seedling) A nicely ruffled, thick substanced, light tangerine-peach with a burgundy eyezone above a dark green center. *Photograph by Francois Verhaert.*

(Francois Verhaert, Seedling) A wide-petaled, nicely ruffled near-white with a faint pink overlay above a lime-green throat. *Photograph by Francois Verhaert.*

'One Day In Your Life' (Francois Verhaert, Seedling) A cream with a lightly ruffled edge and a darker eyezone and matching wire picotee. *Photograph by Francois Verhaert.*

(Francois Verhaert, Seedling) A wide-petaled light peach-pink with a purple eyezone and matching picotee edge above an applique throat. *Photograph by Francois Verhaert.*

(Scott Yewchuk, Seedling) A large purple spider variant with twisted and curled petals and sepals, white midribs, and a large yellow to green throat. *Photograph by Scott Yewchuk.*

DAYLILY SOCIETIES

The best place to begin enjoying daylilies is to join a daylily society, of which there are several. The American Hemerocallis Society (AHS) is the largest, and is also the international society responsible for registering daylilies. It costs U.S. $25.00 a year, which includes a subscription to *The Daylily Journal*. This journal, published four times per year, is a thick publication on glossy paper with many full-color pictures of daylilies and articles about daylily gardening. To join, send your check, payable to the American Hemerocallis Society, to:

Pat Mercer, AHS Executive Secretary
Department WWW, P.O. Box 10
Dexter, GA 31019
U.S.A.
(912) 875-4110
E-mail: gmercer@nlamerica.com

The official A.H.S. Home Page may be viewed at: http://www.daylilies.org/

In addition to the A.H.S., there are societies located in other countries around the world, including the following:

Canadian Hemerocallis Society
16 Douville Court
Toronto, Ontario M5A 4E7
Canada
(416)362-1682
http://www.distinctly.on.ca/chs/

British Hemerocallis & Hosta Society Membership Secretary
Chapelmere, Rodley,
Westbury-on-Severn, Glos. GL14 1QZ
U.K.
http://www.hostahem.org.uk/
The Australian Daylily Society

Joan B. Campbell
P.O. Box 134
Woodridge, Qld. 4114
Australia
http://www.australiandaylily.com/

Hemerocallis Europa
Elke Brettschneider, General Secretary and Treasurer
Schlomerweg 22
41352 Korschenbroich
Germany
http://www.hemerocallis-europa.org/

Fachgruppe Hemerocallis
Gellschaft der Staudenfreunde
Norbert Graue,
Stockflethweg 208
22417 Hamburg
Germany
http://gds-hem-fachgruppe.homepage.t-online.de/

VIDEO ON HYBRIDIZING

Much of the information concerning the actual techniques of hybridizing daylilies is contained in a very helpful and informative, step-by-step beautiful color video. This video, titled "We're In the Hayfield Now Daylily Gardens Video" is available for $19.95 plus taxes and shipping.

Henry Lorrain
We're In the Hayfield Now
4704 Pollard Rd.
Orono, Ontario L0B 1M0
Canada
(905) 983-5097
http://www.hayfield.ca/

BUYER'S GUIDE

Eureka Daylily Reference Guide, published annually, is an excellent source of information about where to find daylilies. It is a printed price-comparison of thousands of daylily cultivars, with many photographs, as well as the addresses of the nurseries where you can purchase these cultivars. The *Guide* is available for $32.95 plus shipping and handling, and $19.95 plus shipping and handling for a 2-set CD supplement.

Ken Gregory
Eureka Daylily Reference Guide
416 Webb Cove Rd,
Asheville, NC 28804
(828) 236-2222

DAYLILY DISPLAY GARDENS

There are hundreds of AHS–recognized display gardens located across North America. A complete current list can be found in each spring issue of *The Daylily Journal*, published by the A.H.S. Most of the gardens listed in Sources for Daylilies can also be visited during the bloom season to view the daylilies.

DAYLILY MEETINGS

There are hundreds of daylily meetings held year-round not only by the A.H.S. and its 15 regions, but by many local clubs. Here we highlight the most popular with the largest number of speakers.

Canadian-American Daylily
Symposium
(annual; last weekend in March)
Niagara Falls, Ontario
16 Douville Court
Toronto, ON M5A 4E7
(416) 362-1682
http://www.distinctly.on.ca/can_am/

The Lake Tahoe International Daylily
Conference
Lake Tahoe, California
(bi-annual conference in September/
October)
Nancy Bailey, Registrar
P.O. Box 1276
Middletown, CA 95461-1276
http://www.tahoedaylilyconference.org/index.asp

The American Hemerocallis Society
National Meeting
http://www.daylilies.org/AHSconv.html

The American Hemerocallis Society
Regional Meetings
http://www.daylilies.org/AHSconv.html

Sources for Daylilies

Most daylilies found in large gardening centers are very old hybrids or unnamed varieties. Newer named varieties can be found from the sources listed below. When first introduced from the top hybridizers, daylilies can be quite expensive, often in the $100 to $200 price range. However, the price quickly drops as the plants multiply and become more readily available. Many excellent daylilies are available in the $10 range, as well as every price in between. The sources below range from expensive new introductions to inexpensive, tried-and-true daylilies. Many of these suppliers have catalogs with color pictures.

UNITED STATES

Linda Agin
511 Bumblebee Court
Prattville, AL 36067
(334) 361-0139

Art Gallery Gardens
Ludlow and Rachel Lambertson
203 Oakapple Trail
Lake Helen, FL 32744
(386) 228-3010
http://www.artgallerygardens.com/

Bell's Daylily Garden
Tim and Linda Bell
1305 Griffin Rd.
Sycamore, GA 31790
(229) 256-1234
http://www.bellsdaylilygarden.com/

John Benz
12195 6th Avenue
Cincinnati, OH 45249-1143
(513) 489-1281
http://www.benzgardens.com/

Browns Ferry Gardens
Charles Douglas
13515 Browns Ferry Rd.
Georgetown, SC 29440
(843) 546-3559
http://www.brownsferrygardens.
com/

California Daylilies
Keith Miner
195-2 Geraldson Road
Newcastle, CA 95658
(916) 599-4616
http://www.picturetrail.com/perennialist

Carolina Daylilies
Tom Bruce
645 Barr Rd.
Lexington, SC 29072-2369
(803) 356-4733
http://www.carolinadaylilies.com/

Chattanooga Daylily Gardens
Lee Pickles
1736 Eagle Dr.
Hixson, TN 37343-2533
(423) 842-4630
http://www.chattanoogadaylilies.
com/

Christie's Daylilies
Christie & Ronnie Dixon
6131 Lanes Bridge Road
Jesup, GA 31545
(912) 586-2273
http://www.dixondelights.com/

Crochet Daylily Garden
Beth Crochet
P.O. Box 425
Prairieville, LA 70769
(225) 673-8491
http://www.eatel.net/
~crochetgarden/

Daylily World
David Kichhoff & Mort Morss
1301 Gilberts Creek Road
Lawrenceburg, KY 40342
(407) 416-9119
http://www.daylilyworld.com/

Floyd Cove Nursery
Patrick & Grace Stamile
Box 4001
Enterprise, FL 32725
(386) 232-7379
http://www.distinctly.on.ca/stamile/

Forestlake Gardens
Frances Harding
306 Birchside Circle
Lake of the Woods,
Locust Grove, VA 22508
(540) 972-2890
http://www.forestlakedaylily.com/

Frank Smith Daylilies
Frank Smith
2815 W. Ponkan Road
Apopka, FL 32712
(407) 886-4134
http://www.franksmithdaylilies.com/

Gold Coast Daylilies
Stan & Bonnie Holley
3775 Clover Valley Road
Rocklin, CA 95677
(916) 624-4409
http://www.goldcoastdaylilies.com/

Graceland Gardens
Larry Grace
12860 West US 84
Newton, AL 36352
(334) 692-5903

Greywood Farm
Darlyn Wilkinson
85 River Road
Topsfield, MA 01983-2110
Fax: 978-887-8625
http://www.greywoodfarm.com/

Happy Moose Daylily Gardens
Bobby Baxter
P.O. Box 558
Rolesville, NC 27571
(919) 569-2173
http://www.happymoosegardens.com

Heavenly Gardens
James Gossard
1069 Amity Road
Galloway, OH 43119
(614) 853-0522
http://www.daylilynet.com/

Iron Gate Gardens
Van Sellers & Victor Santa Lucia
2271 County Line Rd,
Kings Mountain, NC 28086
(704) 435-6178
http://www.irongategardens.com/

Jeff and Jackie's Daylilies
Jeff & Jackie Pryor
179 Smith Road
Clinton, TN 37716
(865) 435-4989
http://www.daylilybiz.com/

Joiner Gardens
Royce and Jan Joiner and Family
P.O. Box 16842
Savannah, GA 31416
(912) 355-3101
http://www.joinergardens.com/

Kinnebrew Daylily Garden
John Kinnebrew, Jr.
Box 224, 6044 Palm St.,
Scottsmoor, FL 32775-0224
(321) 267-7985
http://www.kinnebrewdaylilygarden.com/

Ladybug Daylilies
Dan Hansen
1852 S.R. 46
Geneva, FL 32732-7248
(407) 349-2688
http://www.ladybugdaylilies.com/

Ledgewood Gardens
Tony and Gunda Abajian
1180 Citation Dr.,
Deland, FL 32724
(386) 740-8786
http://www.ledgewoodgardens.com/

Le Petit Jardin
Ted L. Petit
P.O. Box 55
McIntosh, FL 32664
(352) 591-3227
http://www.distinctly.on.ca/petit/
http://www.petitdaylilies.com

Lily Farm
Jack Carpenter
7725 HWY 7 West
Center, TX 75935
(936) 598-7556
http://www.lilyfarm.com/

Majestic Nursery & Gardens
2100 N. Preble County Line Road
West Alexandria, OH 45381
(937) 833-5100
http://www.majesticnurseryandgardens.com/

Marietta Gardens
John, Faye & Elizabeth Shooter
P.O. Box 70
Marietta, NC 28362
(910) 628-9466
http://www.mariettagardens.com/

Nor'East Daylilies
Mary Collier Fisher
P.O. Box 215
Nutting Lake, MA 01864
(617) 525-1007
http://www.daylily.net/gardens/noreastdaylilies/

Oakes Daylilies
William and Stewart Oakes
P.O. Box 268, 8204 Monday Road
Corryton, TN 37721
(800) 532-9545
http://www.oakesdaylilies.com/

Old Whispering Hills
Pat Sayers
19 Greenhill Lane
Huntington, NY 11743
(631) 261-5400
http://www.patsayers.com/

Pinecliffe Daylily Gardens
Don and Kathy Smith
6745 Foster Road
Philpot, KY 42366
(800) 329-5459
http://www.daylily-discounters.com/

Rainbow Acres
Kelly Mitchell
Box 2191
North Highlands, CA 95660
(916) 331-3732
http://www.rainbowacres.net/

Rainbow Daylily Garden
Bob & Mimi Schwarz
8 Lilla Lane
East Hampton, NY 11937
(631) 324-0787
http://www.daylily.net/bobandmimi/

Ridaught Daylily Farm
Jerome & Reba Ridaught
12309 NW 112th Ave.
Alachua, FL 32615
(386) 462-3740
http://www.ridaught.com

Rollingwood Gardens
Jeff & Elizabeth Salter
3912 S.W. 170th St.
Archer, FL 32618
(352) 536-3975
http://www.rollingwoodgarden.com

Roycroft Daylily Nursery
Bob Roycroft
942 Whitehall Avenue
Georgetown, SC 29440
(843) 527-1533
http://www.roycroftdaylilies.com/

Bob Scott Nursery
Bob Scott
10116 W. Wilshire
Yukon, OK 73099
(888) 721-2022
http://www.bobscottnursery.com/

Singing Oakes Garden
Jim & Peggy Jeffcoat
1019 Abell Road
Blythewood, SC 29016
(803) 786-1351
http://www.singingoakesgarden.com/

Small World Gardens
Larry, Paulette & Michael Miller
16204 Mistora Rd.
Chester, VA 23831
(804) 520-0807
http://www.distinctly.on.ca/small-worldgardens/

Springwood Gardens
Karol Emmerich
7302 Claredon Drive
Edina, MN 55439-1722
(952) 941-9280
http://www.springwoodgardens.com/

Stephen's Lane Gardens
Bill & Joyce Reinke
3223 Gum Flat Road
Bells, TN 38006
(731) 663-3744
http://www.daylily.net/gardens/stephenslane.htm

The Garden On Cedar Hill Road
Sharon & Bob Fitzpatrick
3050 Cedar Hill Road
Canal Winchester, OH 43110
(614) 837-2283
http://www.home.att.net/~hemnut/wsb/html/view.cgi-home.html-.html

Thoroughbred Daylilies
John & Annette Rice
6615 Briar Hill Road
Paris, KY 40361
(859) 435-0000
http://www.thoroughbreddaylilies.com

Tom's Daylilies
Tom Maddox
16001 Abilene Street
Biloxi, MS 39532
(228) 239-0357
http://www.tomsdaylilies.com/

Tranquil Lake Nursery, Inc.
Philip Boucher and Warren Leach
45 River Street
Rehoboth, MA 02769-1395
(508) 252-4002
http://www.tranquil-lake.com/

Water Mill Gardens
Dan & Jane Trimmer
1280 Enterprise-Osteen Road
Enterprise, FL 32725-9401
(386) 574-2789
http://www.trimmerdaylily.com/

Wonderland of Daylilies
Herbert & Gale Phelps
620 Harmony Trail
Magnolia, KY 42757
(270) 528-5325
http://www.wonderlandofdaylilies.com/

Woodhenge Gardens
Jim Murphy & Margo Reed
3191 Plank Rd.
North Garden, VA 22959
(434) 979-3999
http://www.daylily.net/piedmontperennials/

CANADA

Bonibrae Daylilies
Barry Matthie
RR#1, 497 Matthie Rd.,
Bloomfield, ON K0K 1G0
(613) 393-2864
http://www.fairyscapedaylilies.com/bonibrae.htm

Cross Border Daylilies
John Peat
16 Douville Court
Toronto, ON M5A 4E7
(416) 362-1682
http://www.distinctly.on.ca/peat/

Erikson's Daylily Gardens
Pam Erikson
24642 51st Avenue
Langley, BC V2Z 1H9
(604) 856-5758
http://www.plantlovers.com/erikson/

Floral And Hardy Gardens
Betty Fretz
R.R. #3, 6728 Sideroad 18
Moorefield, Ontario N0G 2K0
(519) 638-3937
http://www.floralandhardy.ca/

Gardens Plus
Dawn Tack
136 County Road # 4 (Donwood)
Peterborough, ON K9L 1V6
(705) 742-5918
http://www.gardensplus.ca/

Pleasant Valley Gardens
Joel Thomas Polston and Doug Sterling
7465 W. Third St.
Dayton, OH 45427
(937) 835-5231
http://www.pleasantvalleygardens.net/

Rejean Millette
62-7th Avenue
St-Ambroise De Kildare, QC J0K ICO
(450) 756-4893
http://www.daylily.ca/

The Potting Shed
Jack Kent
#44 Haldimand Rd. 17
Dunnville, Ontario
N1A 2W4
(905) 701-8921
http://www.pottingshed.org/

We're in the Hayfield Now Daylily Gardens
Henry Lorrain
4704 Pollard Rd., R.R. 1
Orono, ON L0B 1MO
(888) 818-7234
http://www.hayfield.ca/

AUSTRALIA

Daylilies By Clare (mail order only)
Mrs. E. C. Bewsher
12 Brook Road
Glenbrook, NSW 2773
02-47-395336
http://www.home.exetel.com.au/bewsher/

Daylilies by the Lake
Joan and Neville Charman
702 Pacific Highway
Belmont South
Lake Macquarie, NSW
http://www.users.on.net/~lotsahems/

Daylily Display Centre
4042 Bundaberg Road
Gin Gin QLD 4671
07 4157 4353
http://www.daylily.com.au/

Meads Daylily Gardens
Debbie & Neale Mead
264 Learoyd Rd.,
Acacia Ridge, Qld 4110
07 3273 8559
http://www.daylilygardens.com.au/

Mountain View Daylily Nursery
Scott Alexander
P.O. Box 458, Policeman's Spur Road
Maleny, Qld 4552
07 5494 2346

EUROPE

Apple Court
Hordle Lane
Hordle, Lymington,
Hampshire SO41 0HU
United Kingdom
+44 (0)1590 642130
http://www.applecourt.com/

Casa Rocca Daylilies
Marc King-Lamone
Via Santa Caterina 6
14030 Rocca D'Arazzo
Italy
http://www.casarocca.com/

Eurocallis
Francois Verhaert
Fatimalaan 14
B-2243 Pulle (Zandhoven)
Belgium
0(032)496 166 366

Govaerts, Cor
Broechemsesteenweg 330
B-2560 Nijlen
Belgium
32-34-81-78

Huys Benoot
John Benoot
Lieveberm 4 - 8340 Damme
050 50 13 13
http://www.users.pandora.be/gardens/

To find more daylily gardens online, visit: http://www.abacom.com/chacha/garden.htm. This website, created by Charlotte Chamitoff of Quebec, Canada, is consistently being updated with the correct links to garden sites from around the world.

Bibliography

American Hemerocallis Society. 1957. *Hemerocallis Check List 1893 to July 1, 1957.*

———. 1983. *Hemerocallis Check List July 1, 1973 to December 1, 1983.*

———. 1989. *Hemerocallis Check List January 1, 1984 to December 31, 1988.*

———. 1990. *Hemerocallis Check List July 1, 1957 to July 1, 1973.* Reprint.

———. 1994. *Hemerocallis Check List 1989–1993.*

———. 1999. *Hemerocallis Check List 1994–1998.*

———. 2006. *Hemerocallis Check List 1890–2006.*

Barnes, L. S. 2004. "The Daylily Species." In *The Daylily: A Guide for Gardeners,* John P. Peat and Ted L. Petit. Portland, Oregon: Timber Press. 10–20.

Dahlgren, Clifford, and Yeo Dahlgren. 1985. *The Families of the Monocotyledons.* Berlin/New York: Springer Verlag.

Eddison, S. 1992. *A Passion for Daylilies: The Flowers and the People.* New York: Henry Holt.

Erhardt, W. l992. *Hemerocallis: Daylilies.* Portland, Oregon: Timber Press.

Gatlin, F. 1995. *Daylilies–A Fifty-Year Affair: A Story of a Society and Its Flower.* Edgerton, Missouri: American Hemerocallis Society.

Grenfell, D. 1998. *The Gardener's Guide to Growing Daylilies.* Portland, Oregon: Timber Press.

Hu, Shiu-Ying. 1968. "An Early History of Daylily." *American Horticulture Magazine* 47(2): 51–85.

Munson, Jr. R. W. 1989. *Hemerocallis: The Daylily.* Portland, Oregon: Timber Press.

Peat, John P. and Ted L. Petit, 2004. *The Daylily: A Guide for Gardeners.* Portland, Oregon: Timber Press

Petit, Ted L. and John P. Peat, 2000. *The Color Encyclopedia of Daylilies.* Portland, Oregon: Timber Press.